T0321218

Developing Knowledge Societies for Distinct Country Contexts

Nuno Vasco Lopes
University of Minho, Portugal

Rehema Baguma
Makerere University, Uganda

A volume in the Advances in
Knowledge Acquisition, Transfer,
and Management (AKATM) Book
Series

Published in the United States of America by
    IGI Global
    Information Science Reference (an imprint of IGI Global)
    701 E. Chocolate Avenue
    Hershey PA, USA 17033
    Tel: 717-533-8845
    Fax: 717-533-8661
    E-mail: cust@igi-global.com
    Web site: http://www.igi-global.com

Library of Congress Cataloging-in-Publication Data

Library of Congress Cataloging-in-Publication Data

Names: Lopes, Nuno Vasco, 1976- editor. | Baguma, Rehema, 1976- editor.
Title: Developing knowledge societies for distinct country contexts / Nuno
    Vasco Lopes and Rehema Baguma, editors.
Description: Hershey, PA : Information Science Reference, [2019]
Identifiers: LCCN 2018057674| ISBN 9781522588733 (hardcover) | ISBN
    9781522588740 (ebook) | ISBN 9781522591122 (softcover)
Subjects: LCSH: Information literacy. | Knowledge management.
Classification: LCC ZA3075 .D478 2019 | DDC 028.7--dc23 LC record available at https://lccn.loc.
gov/2018057674

This book is published in the IGI Global book series Advances in Knowledge Acquisition, Transfer,
and Management (AKATM) (ISSN: 2326-7607; eISSN: 2326-7615)

British Cataloguing in Publication Data
A Cataloguing in Publication record for this book is available from the British Library.

All work contributed to this book is new, previously-unpublished material.
The views expressed in this book are those of the authors, but not necessarily of the publisher.

For electronic access to this publication, please contact: eresources@igi-global.com.

Advances in Knowledge Acquisition, Transfer, and Management (AKATM) Book Series

ISSN:2326-7607
EISSN:2326-7615

Editor-in-Chief: Murray E. Jennex, San Diego State University, USA

MISSION

Organizations and businesses continue to utilize knowledge management practices in order to streamline processes and procedures. The emergence of web technologies has provided new methods of information usage and knowledge sharing.

The **Advances in Knowledge Acquisition, Transfer, and Management (AKATM) Book Series** brings together research on emerging technologies and their effect on information systems as well as the knowledge society. **AKATM** will provide researchers, students, practitioners, and industry leaders with research highlights surrounding the knowledge management discipline, including technology support issues and knowledge representation.

COVERAGE

- Cognitive Theories
- Cultural Impacts
- Information and Communication Systems
- Knowledge Acquisition and Transfer Processes
- Knowledge Management Strategy
- Knowledge Sharing
- Organizational Learning
- Organizational Memory
- Small and Medium Enterprises
- Virtual Communities

IGI Global is currently accepting manuscripts for publication within this series. To submit a proposal for a volume in this series, please contact our Acquisition Editors at Acquisitions@igi-global.com or visit: http://www.igi-global.com/publish/.

Titles in this Series

For a list of additional titles in this series, please visit:
http://www.igi-global.com/book-series/advances-knowledge-acquisition-transfer-manage-
ment/37159

Practice-Based and Practice-Led Research for Dissertation Development
Robin Throne (Independent Researcher, USA)
Information Science Reference • © 2021 • 288pp • H/C (ISBN: 9781799866640) • US
$185.00

Optimizing Data and New Methods for Efficient Knowledge Discovery and Information
Resources Management Emerging Research and Opportunities
Susan Swayze (The George Washington University, USA)
Information Science Reference • © 2020 • 198pp • H/C (ISBN: 9781799822356) • US
$155.00

Intellectual Property Rights and the Protection of Traditional Knowledge
Nisha Dhanraj Dewani (Guru Gobind Singh Indraprastha University, India) and Amulya
Gurtu (Austin E. Cofrin School of Business, University of Wisconsin-Green Bay, USA)
Information Science Reference • © 2020 • 296pp • H/C (ISBN: 9781799818359) • US
$195.00

Knowledge Management Practices in the Public Sector
Vasileios Ismyrlis (Hellenic Statistical Authority, Greece) Theodore Tarnanidis (University
of Macedonia, Greece) and Efstratios Moschidis (University of Macedonia, Greece)
Information Science Reference • © 2020 • 263pp • H/C (ISBN: 9781799819400) • US
$195.00

Current Issues and Trends in Knowledge Management, Discovery, and Transfer
Murray Eugene Jennex (San Diego State University, USA)
Information Science Reference • © 2020 • 450pp • H/C (ISBN: 9781799821892) • US
$185.00

701 East Chocolate Avenue, Hershey, PA 17033, USA
Tel: 717-533-8845 x100 • Fax: 717-533-8661
E-Mail: cust@igi-global.com • www.igi-global.com

Table of Contents

Detailed Table of Contents

Chapter 1

This chapter illuminates the significance of researcher-practitioner engagement in knowledge production and the impact it has on socioeconomic development. Knowledge production and sharing have a significant impact on the transformation of society. It highlights the importance of knowledge co-production through engaged scholarship research that achieves the twin goals of rigor and relevance. Engaged scholarship research creates a more pleasant relationship between scholars, non-academic practitioners and communities in creation of knowledge. This research approach however, is rarely applied in many research institutions and universities. Engaged scholarship research approach is therefore preferred because it empowers local communities to participate and contribute in making decisions that affect their lives. The chapter concludes by reiterating collaboration and stakeholder involvement that generate knowledge based on practical experiences and which are mutually beneficial and relevant in solving society problems.

Chapter 2

The chapter attempts to do a comprehensive literature review on knowledge societies describing its main concepts, dimensions, aspects, and actors/players. In addition to the literature review, it proposes a framework to build knowledge societies. The framework presents seven dimensions, which have been extracted from the literature where each dimension is characterized by several aspects collected from the literature. The framework can be used by decision makers around the world as a useful tool for building robust knowledge societies in different context-specific environments.

Rehema Baguma, Makerere University, Uganda
Susana Finquelievich, University of Buenos Aires, Argentina

Generating and developing knowledge societies is a key element for sustainable development as defined in the 2030 Agenda for Sustainable Development Goals adopted by the United Nations in 2015. Based on a limited natural resource base, Rwanda chose to take an approach to development that differs from that of its neighbours by making ICTs the cornerstone of its development. With this focus, government of Rwanda (GoR) took a Pro-ICT led public policy that has led to several public reforms such as but not limited to liberalization of the telecom sector, enactment of laws to govern electronic messages, signatures, transactions, data protection, cyber-security and ICT usage, development of relevant infrastructure and establishment of key institutions such as the Rwanda Utilities and Regulatory Agency (RURA) and Rwanda Information Society Authority (RISA). These reforms have in turn led to a fast-growing ICT sector in Rwanda compared to that of the neighbours. To-date, Rwanda is one of the fastest growing African countries in ICT. In 2015, Rwanda emerged as the third best ICT country in Sub-Saharan Africa behind South Africa and Seychelles. In 2016, it moved one position up and emerged 2nd behind Seychelles. The fast-growing ICT sector has stimulated entrepreneurial creativity and growth across the economy. This chapter examines the best practices that Rwanda has applied in her journey to a knowledge society that could possibly help other countries in the region pursuing the same objective. The chapter also briefly reviews challenges and gaps in Rwanda's journey to a knowledge society and suggests recommendations for further improvement.

Ekta Sinha, University of Mumbai, India

In 2015, world leaders gathered at the United Nations (UN) to adopt 17 Sustainable Development Goals to achieve several extraordinary things by 2030. Among these 17 goals of sustainable development, 'Quality Education' has been recognized as the fourth most important thing in order to transform our world. Obtaining a quality education is the foundation to improving people's lives and sustainable development. India, which is now one of the fastest growing economies of the world, is continuously thriving to transform and facilitate quality education for all, irrespective of the gender, caste, and socio-economic status to leverage county's demographic dividend. Such initiatives have been helpful in creating and sustaining a knowledge society and economy where people learn and build their capabilities to add value through knowledge development, improvement, and innovation. The efforts taken by India to improve the creation, storage, and dissemination of knowledge have helped her to build human capital and face the challenges of dynamic and ambiguous environment. This chapter discusses critical activities contributing to the desired change, highlights prevailing structural and socio-economic issues, and in the course of the analysis identifies some critical areas for improvement.

Chapter 5

Continuing knowledge, skills, and practice update through continuing education, which then becomes the lever of society and the recipe for a successful future. This chapter aims to initiate a discussion about the concepts of knowledge societies, globalization, and their perceptions and impact on knowledge management in relation to the Brazilian educational reality. From a theoretical-methodological perspective, continuing education is considered as a key element that can sustain knowledge management and foster knowledge societies. This question is the reason why this intensity of the offer of continuing education nowadays becomes pertinent, as well as to look at how the knowledge societies have seduced people to consume more and more knowledge. The conclusions raise the question of how societies of knowledge have become a contemporary imperative, justified by the acceleration of time in different spaces and driven by globalization. As knowledge management has contributed to this movement, it is necessary for professionals to be more flexible and resourceful, as well as about what can happen to the individuals who cannot keep up with the demands of the market and become disposable in society.

Chapter 6

This chapter explores how the knowledge societies are being developed in different local, national, regional, and international societies and more in particular how the women and girls in Kanungu are developing their knowledge within the clans. The methodology followed to generate a set of questions: What are clans? and Does belonging to a clan group have an individual or group impact on their identity (as Bakiga/Banyankole/Bahororo/Bairu/Bahima) Ugandans? Why are women in Kanungu district organizing in paternal clans? How new is the trend? What is its origin? Are there women, girls who do not identify with clans? What are the basic socio-economic challenges confronting the girls and women of Kanungu? Has local government and development partners tried to deal with the challenges of women? With what results? Is organizing in Clan Groups matriarchy? Is it empowerment or cementing submissiveness? Is it increasing women work load? What is its effect on men-masculinity? In order to understand how the clan groups' learn, a feminist qualitative ethnographic approach was used. Women's personal stories were collected through focus group discussions and interviews to explore their experiences on the prospects and challenges of clan group activities. A sample of five women and five men randomly picked was used. Therefore, this chapter aims to stimulate sharing knowledge and learning about women's lives in rural areas; document women's narratives; show the economic development trends in Uganda; promote self-actualization, self-awareness, and pride among women as equal citizens of Uganda; and motivate reading and learning and contribute to creation of rural libraries.

Chapter 7

Showkat Ahmad Wani, DLIS, University of Kashmir, India

The chapter demonstrates the concept of information, knowledge, and the knowledge society. Stress was given to highlight the information and knowledge needs of artisans, problems faced by them, and how they can achieve socio-economic development in a knowledge society. The particular ascent was given to highlight the perceptions and beliefs of willow-works artisans of district Ganderbal, India. The sample of 100 artisans was surveyed and it was founded that majority of them are between the age group of 20-40 years; 63% among them are educated (ranging from 5th–PG above), and there are both genders which practice willow-works, but the majority of them are males. Their tenet is that knowledge can change their standard of living, if there are provisions in knowledge society for creating and disseminating the new knowledge among these artisans pertinent to technology, scientific cultivation of raw materials, marketing, availability of new markets, and potential exploitation by entrepreneurs.

Chapter 8

Innocent Chirisa, University of Zimbabwe, Zimbabwe
Gift Mhlanga, University of Zimbabwe, Zimbabwe
Abraham Rajab Matamanda, University of the Free State, South Africa
Roselin Ncube, Women's University in Africa, Zimbabwe

This chapter intends to have answer the questions: How did Ian Smith structure his government and economy and survive sanctions for sixteen years (1965-1979) and become innovative? Why, under almost similar conditions, did Robert Mugabe fail to bring the economy do its toes? In cases, what was the role of knowledge societies and what role did they play to bridge the gap between society and them towards meaningful development? The study uses desktop review as the basis of getting data and information useful in building this theoretical case study of Zimbabwe in the period 1965 to 2018. The robustness of an economy under a stringent economic environment is a function of its ability to tap and harness the prowess of its knowledge societies. It is recommended that strong links between the private, public, and knowledge sectors are required and this must happen in an environment with trust, transparency, accountability, rule of law, and commitment translating into a powerful connubio for transformation.

Chapter 9
Influence of Information Systems and Technology on Hospitality Business
Performance in Albania 206
Lerida Shkrepa, Epoka University, Albania
Alba Demneri Kruja, Epoka University, Albania

The transition from a closed economy to an open, market economy created new opportunities for the development of tourism in Albania. Tourism is known as one of the industries with the largest use of information technology (IT), but for various reasons, application of information systems (IS) in Albanian hotels is lower compared to other countries in Balkan region and other countries in Europe. Many processes and operations are handled in old and traditional ways. Most of the entrepreneurs do not know the benefit of using IS in the daily processes of the hotels. However, the demand of hospitality services dictates the need of using contemporary IS to gain competitive advantage and to survive in the market. IS and technology impacts competitiveness, management of information flow, and the decision-making process. They have influenced performance of the hotel sector through changing the nature of tourism services and the target market. This chapter aims to establish the extent of usage of these systems in the overall performance of the hotels in Tirana, the capital of Albania.

Preface

Knowledge societies understand how the world works, have awareness of the facts, are familiar with the processes, and have the capacity and appropriate skills to rapidly adapt to the environment changes to live a better life. There is not a magic formula to create knowledge societies. Each country has its own culture, institutions, organization, and ancestral knowledge. Although at the outset we know the role of our institutions in society, we miss to know how they should work together to achieve the well-being of their citizens as common goal. Each institution as its own role in contributing to that common goal. Academia and schools produce knowledge, companies and industry produce goods and services and government regulates and supervises the interaction between all these key players. This ecosystem composed of academia, industry, government, and citizens should interplay together in virtuous circles capable of ensuring sustainable economic, social, and environmental sustainability for the generations that come.

The rising question here is how we can put these key players working together at a fast pace to achieve the common goal. The technology is an enabler tool and a catalyzer, capable of connecting the entire ecosystem and introduce intelligence into our processes and systems accelerating in this way the knowledge acquisition. However, technology per se is not enough we are still discovering the right mechanisms to work collaboratively and cooperatively towards common goals putting aside our own interests.

This book sheds light on how developing countries mainly in Africa are operationalizing the knowledge societies. The knowledge is being built on top of the existing knowledge, culture, and wisdom of native people without massive disruptions to their beliefs and traditions. The government is aware of the challenge of preserving their identity and wisdom accumulated during centuries or even millenniums by your ancestors.

This book gives a unique overview of what is being done in Africa on knowledge societies with delicious details about their culture and traditions.

Nuno Vasco Lopes

ACKNOWLEDGMENT

A special thanks to my children Bárbara, Gonçalo e Mariana for their patience during my absences and for their love and support.

Chapter 1

Knowledge Co-Production and Sustainable Socio-Economic Development:
An Engaged Scholarly Approach

Robert Tweheyo
Kyambogo University, Kampala, Uganda

ABSTRACT

This chapter illuminates the significance of researcher-practitioner engagement in knowledge production and the impact it has on socioeconomic development. Knowledge production and sharing have a significant impact on the transformation of society. It highlights the importance of knowledge co-production through engaged scholarship research that achieves the twin goals of rigor and relevance. Engaged scholarship research creates a more pleasant relationship between scholars, non-academic practitioners and communities in creation of knowledge. This research approach however, is rarely applied in many research institutions and universities. Engaged scholarship research approach is therefore preferred because it empowers local communities to participate and contribute in making decisions that affect their lives. The chapter concludes by reiterating collaboration and stakeholder involvement that generate knowledge based on practical experiences and which are mutually beneficial and relevant in solving society problems.

DOI: 10.4018/978-1-5225-8873-3.ch001

INTRODUCTION

Societies world over, have rested on knowledge production, and knowledge has always played an important role in prosperity and social well-being of people. Barge and Zalabak (2008) argue that knowledge production has been at the center of growth and development of society since time immemorial. Knowledge production is the process of generating knowledge that is evidenced based from the real world rather than merely reflecting on the scientist views (Tweheyo, 2018). In Africa, people are constantly struggling to maintain their rights, their heritage/traditions and their facts, in a system still dominated by western views. The work of Barge and Zalabak (2008) reveals that knowledge creation helps people to understand, make sense of, and apply the information available to solve problems. Empirical data reveals that some countries (especially Scandinavian and western European countries, have moved toward becoming knowledge-driven societies and surpassed African countries in development (World Bank 1998; United Nations 2005). This is due to the fact that African countries still believe and depend on foreign knowledge other than trusting their own indigenous knowledge.

BACKGROUND

The Concept of Knowledge

Knowledge is a concept that has been debated with regard to who possess it and how it is used and also with regard to issues of evidence, authority and expertise of the owner (Holland et al, 2010; Lloyd et al, 2005). Knowledge may be regarded as a public good: one person's use of a particular piece of knowledge does not preclude the use of that same knowledge by others, and when a piece of knowledge is already in the public domain, it is difficult for its creator to prevent others from using it. As Abdelrahman and Papamichil (2016) put it, knowledge is so important but cannot be effective unless it is shared, utilized and integrated in any given organizational culture. In reality, knowledge, cannot be easily acquired and applied individually. It has to be shared with others. Bock et al (2005), refer to knowledge sharing as a voluntary process of transferring and disseminating knowledge from one person to another or group of persons in an organization.

Tacit Knowledge and Explicit Knowledge

Knowledge is broadly categorized as tacit and explicit. Tacit knowledge is a mix of mounted experience, values, contextual information and expert insights that provides an individual with a framework for evaluating and incorporating new experiences and information (United Nations (UN), 2005). It is acquired through one's own experience or reflections on the experiences of others. It is intangible, without boundaries and dynamic. It is highly personal and hard to formalize, making it difficult to communicate or share with others. Subjective insights, intuitions and feelings are all in the category of tacit knowledge. Tacit knowledge can easily be communicated in group discussions.

Explicit knowledge refers to "justified belief" that is codified in a formal and systemic language. It can be stored, retrieved and transmitted with relative ease and through various means, including modern Information Communication Technology (UNESCO, 2012). While explicit knowledge can be easily transferred across time and space, tacit knowledge, which is in people's minds, can be accessed on a first-person basis, and it takes time to develop. Effective creation and application of knowledge depends on the broader context; cultural institutions and governance Mugadas et al, 2016). Knowledge must be integrated into effective systems of research institutions, innovation-driven enterprises, universities, and other establishments. Because knowledge is considered as one of the key factors of production and is expensive to create, rich countries have broadened the protection of intellectual property rights (especially patents) and thus, have increased the amount of knowledge that is secured and monopolized (Mugadas et al 2016). Such actions contribute to an unequal distribution of knowledge across and within countries, a situation that has led to knowledge gap between the rich and poor countries. This justifies the need for knowledge co-production among local institutions and communities.

What is a Knowledge Society?

Knowledge society refers to a society in which the creation, dissemination, utilization of information and knowledge constitute the most important factor of production. In such a society, knowledge possessions (also known as intellectual capital) are the most powerful source of wealth, in addition to land, labor, and physical or financial capital (UNESCO, 2013; Weerakoon et al, 2020). To different people, the term "knowledge society" has several meanings (Melnikas (2010). First, it is used by social scientists to describe and analyze the transformation towards the so-called postindustrial society (UNESCO, 2016). Second, it is used to refer to a normative vision that people or corporations desire to realize. Third, it is used as a symbol, rather than a clear-cut concept, under which various subject matters are studied. Apparently, the difference among these three practices is imprecise. In this section, the author is using the term knowledge society to refer to a strategy of engaged scholarship that should be followed in producing and sharing knowledge (Tweheyo, 2018; Tweheyo & Baguma, 2018).

Although the term knowledge society is frequently evoked, it is rarely defined and explored in a systematic way. However, the key features of a knowledge society are outlined by Dobrin and Popa (2007) as follows: (1) a society in which production, transmission, and application of knowledge is dominant; (2) a society in which the price of most commodities is determined by the knowledge needed for their development and sale rather than by the raw material and physical labor that is needed to produce them; (3) a society in which a large portion of the population is educated; (4) a society in which a vast majority of the population have access to information and communication technologies; (5) a society in which a large portion of the labor force is knowledgeable and experienced to perform their jobs well; (6) a society in which both individuals and the state invest heavily in education, research and development; and (7) a society that is required to innovate continually for members' well-being.

Knowledge is the critical engine of socio-economic development. A knowledge society emerges whenever members of different professional groups and corporations who formerly kept information and knowledge specific to themselves start to share such information and knowledge with other social and professional groups and corporations (Abdelrahman and Papamichail, 2016). Furthermore, a knowledge society develops when there is increase in number of people and members of social groups who partake in the knowledge-making processes are recognized as experts and producers of valid knowledge. The establishment of systems of knowledge sharing (informal societies, scholars, and universities) portrays a growing numbers of members of a society participating in knowledge production (Wong, 2010). However, facilitating knowledge transfer and exchange is almost invariably accompanied by fierce discussions about access, control and regulation of its distribution. However, these issues result from the tension between production and distribution of knowledge, and between confidentiality, trust and the interests of the public domain that are inherent to a global knowledge society.

In principle, knowledge sharing is a prerequisite for socioeconomic development (Nissen et al, 2014). Knowledge can add value to society's well-being and progress by enhancing their livelihoods and contributing to social, cultural, political and economic development (UNESCO, 2012).The diverse forms of knowledge that are deeply rooted in the population and its relationship with the environment as well as in cultural cohesion, have allowed many of these communities to maintain a sustainable use and management of natural resources. Their knowledge help to protect the environment and to enhance their resilience; their ability to observe, adapt and mitigate the effects of climate change. They are able to face new and complex circumstances that have often severely impacted on their way of living (UNESCO, 2016). Negative consequences, such as brain drain (the emigration of one country's highly educated people to other countries offering better economic

4

and social opportunity), is likely to be expected. There is no clear-cut threshold from which societies become knowledge societies. It is more about processes (knowledge production, learning, innovation, and creativity) than about fulfilling static objectives (UNESCO, 2016).

Indicators used to evaluate the development of knowledge society (such as educational attainment, investment in research and development, and Internet access) show that the knowledge gap has been widening (Dattakumar et al, 2016). This is partly because knowledge produces further knowledge and this in turn increases the level of knowledgeable society and hence increased productivity. It is rather risky for a country or company to rely largely on unskilled labor and natural resource–based goods. Countries, companies, and people who do not invest sufficiently in education and new technologies for acquisition and dissemination of knowledge will find it increasingly difficult to catch up with those that invest in knowledge acquisition. It is important to note that, investment in education and new technologies is not enough; rather, it is necessary to create appropriate conditions to foster innovation, creativity, and cooperation through engaged research (Van de Ven, 2007).

The present day knowledge society debates agree on one fundamental characteristic that, a knowledge society depends upon large-scale collection and distribution of information on the basis of which knowledge is produced and multiplied and this process happens at a global level (Melnikas, 2010). Furthermore, a knowledge society generates, processes, shares and makes knowledge available to all members of the society.

INFORMATION COMMUNICATION TECHNOLOGY (ICT), KNOWLEDGE SHARING AND SOCIO-ECONOMIC DEVELOPMENT

Knowledge sharing is essential for sustainable development and provides part of the solutions to the global challenges. Nissen et al (2014) argue that knowledge sharing is much needed to integrate different disciplines, ideas and views of the institution's members into sustainable development plans. Sustainable development denotes conservation of the ecosystem and natural resources from depletion while promoting sustainable food security. Fostering sustainable development requires involvement of people and their varying perspectives. ICT enables and empowers individuals' to share knowledge and thus contributing to Sustainable Development Goals (SDGs). Access to information and knowledge is, however, far from reality in some contexts (Mugadas et al, 2016). Many people are still excluded from the benefits of the information revolution because of existing challenges in access to affordable ICTs as well as a lack of appropriate policies and skills Tweheyo, 2018).

In order to realize the potential of broadband in accelerating social and economic progress of countries, there is still an urgent need to bridge the gap between the richest and poorest countries and to address disparities of human capacities in developing countries as well as within countries. Overcoming these challenges will help humanity to reap full value from the opportunities of knowledge sharing. The emergence of the Information Society has raised many hopes in the 21st century. Engaged scholarship with information communication technology present a new knowledge–based society and knowledge economy for sustainable development (Melnikas, 2010; Weerakoon et al, 2020).

Socio-economic development is the process in the transformation of a society. Socio-economic development is measured with indicators, such as GDP, life expectancy, literacy levels and employment opportunities. Changes in less-tangible factors are also considered, such as personal dignity, freedom of association, personal safety and freedom from fear of physical harm, and the extent of participation in civil society programs. The concept of sustainable development emerged as a new paradigm during the last 2 decades. The definition most frequently referred to is the one provided by the World Commission on Environment and Development (WCED), characterizing the concept as "development that meets the needs of the present without compromising the ability of future generations to meet their own needs" (WCED, 1987, p.43). In 1992, at the Earth Summit in Rio Brazil, more than 178 countries adopted a plan of action to build a global partnership for sustainable development to improve human lives and protect the environment. In 2000, Millennium Development Goals (MDGs) were adopted by UN member states to protect the environment and reduce extreme poverty by 2015. This was later followed by the 2030 agenda with 17 Sustainable Development Goals (SDGs) in 2015 which has helped to put sustainable development on the international and local policy agenda, making the concept a vision so impossible to ignore that all kinds of interest groups are actively battling for hegemony regarding its realization.

Knowledge Co-Production and Sustainable Development

Co-production of knowledge between academic and non-academic communities is a prerequisite for research that aims more at sustainable development paths (Pohl et al, 2010). Sustainable development requires production of knowledge that strikes a balance between scientific and other forms of knowledge. Throughout history, progress in human societies has come about as a result of improved understanding of the world and acquisition of knowledge of the environment. This is essential in giving them ability to identify new ways of working and doing daily activities. The knowledge upon which such new understanding is based is derived from informal or organized discussions and observation; where organized observation is more commonly referred to as research (UNESCO, 2012). Acquisition of new knowledge is a fundamental driver of societal development. Knowledge is a source of power and has been an integral component of societal thinking, and has demonstrated itself in the establishment and support of universities and research institutions.

Knowledge, in itself, however, can only empower, and thus is not a sufficient factor for ensuring society progress, as it cannot dictate the choices that societies make. The way knowledge is used to identify societal goals and make choices that societies make is intricately linked with the values that a society holds. Human values, in turn, are largely derived from the culture of which the society is a part (UNESCO, 2016). Sustainable development and knowledge –based society require adequate theoretical approaches. Creation and development of knowledge-based society and knowledge economy are perceived as one of the most important priorities of a modern society and its life style development as well as socio-economic, political, science and technological progress (Melnikas, 2010).

While knowledge remains a prerequisite for society transformation, there is increasing awareness that the challenges facing humanity today, differ from those of the past, and that new types of knowledge are needed to support the continued development of a global society which now exceeds seven billion individuals and which is likely to grow to nine or ten billion by the middle of this century (Wong, 2010). Human societies have always and will always be dependent on the earth's natural resources for their economic growth, development, and well-being. The earth's resources are however, limited and numerous studies indicate that human activities are altering global processes including the ecosystem (UNESCO, 2012). Human-caused climate change and environmental degradation are the best known examples of this, but there are many others. It is important to note that we are living in a period where human activities have become a dominant force impacting on the function of the earth as well.

Under the influence of similar theories and concepts, knowledge has been de-naturalized and unpacked. Knowledge is generated from networks involving such different actors as researchers (academics), practitioners and community based associations. The networks in which these people operate are multidimensional and irregular in nature and they emerge on different measures; from very local and place-bound to global level. Moreover, they comprise different types of practices, which in turn are grounded on different types of instruments and other absolute mobiles involved. However, it also puts us in a position of recognizing possibilities for managing the interaction between human activities and the environment. This knowledge makes human beings the first creatures with the power to actually control the trajectory of the relationship with nature (UN, 2015). Sustainable development within this framework requires that human demand for resources respects the needs of the future generation and the earth's capacity to supply these resources

(Melnikas, 2010). It also requires the establishment of mechanisms for sharing critical resources within a global population where all have a right to development (Shelat and Mbuya, 2018).

The International Alliance of Research Universities (IARU), recognizes that traditional university disciplines must work together in innovative ways to generate new knowledge needed for society to respond to these new challenges. This is instrumental both in bringing disciplines together to address potential solutions to the challenges of climate change and also, in generating media and public interest in the results of climate change research (IARU, 2016). It is important to focus on what is the state of the planet and its people and what ought to be done to positively change the state of the planet and its people (UNESCO, 2013). Given what is already known, it is important to focus on collective efforts and the will of political leadership to choose those pathways that lead towards those common goals of living well and living sustainably.

As humanity is likely to face formidable challenges as a result of climate change, mechanisms for ensuring combined efforts in generating mutually benefiting knowledge are needed. This issue reiterates the challenges already being faced in achieving sustainable development, but also the uplifting message that knowledge is power, and that engaged scholarship research has the potential of helping humanity to identify sustainable societal trajectories and, thus, giving humanity the power to control its future. It is important that knowledge societies embrace and adopt engaged scholarship research paradigm (Melnikas, 2010).

Sustainable development should conserve the ecosystem and the natural resources from depletion while creating new products/services for future business sustainability. Fostering sustainable development requires involvement of different stakeholders as well as change of practices and beliefs. The foundation of knowledge generation and management, is based on intellectual capital to achieve organizational society's goals. Knowledge generation and sharing act as the catalyst for transformational change to achieve SDGs (Abdelrahman et al 2016). This calls for engaged scholarship that embraces inclusive decision-making and engages the community as knowers rather than mere study subjects (Van de Ven 2007), as a competitive advantage over basic and close-minded research that does not interact and learn with stakeholders. This justifies the need for focusing on the best practices that come as a result of interacting with people and putting their views into consideration which provide a very good foundation for sustainable development.

ENGAGED SCHOLARSHIP RESEARCH APPROACH AND KNOWLEDGE PRODUCTION

Engaged scholarship research is described as "a participative form of research for obtaining the advice and perspectives of key stakeholders (academic researchers, communities and non-academic practitioners) to understand and solve a complex social problem" (Van de Ven, 2007). Engaged scholarship is a new way of bridging the gap between the university and civil society (Beaulieu et al, 2018). Engaged scholarship research approach solves problems associated with technological innovations and globalization due to its focus on knowledge-driven society. This approach is designed to work across the theory–practice boundary and, through a pluralistic methodology, to advance knowledge by leveraging multiple perspectives. Engaged Scholarship is considered to be a research strategy that consists of four fundamental activities: Problem Formulation, Theory Building, Research Design and Problem-Solving (See figure 1: Diamond model adopted from Van de Ven, 2007).

Figure 1. Engaged scholarship Diamond Model (adopted from Van de Ven, 2007)

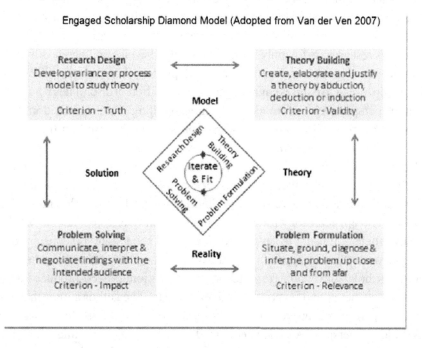

Engaged scholarship enhances and maintains networking and collaborative partnerships. According to Van de Ven (2007), engaged scholarship research has a number of facets: a form of collaborative inquiry between academics and practitioners that leverage their different perspectives to learn about a problem domain and generate useful knowledge for solving it; a relationship involving mutual respect and collaboration to produce a learning community and an identity of how scholars view their relationships with their communities and their subject matter. Collaboration has become essential and an emerging alternative to traditional scientific approach where problems under study are presented in new and innovative ways and solutions are legitimized (Beaulieu et al, 2018). According to Oates (2006), a combination of paradigms is possible if research being undertaken is not representative of one paradigm and the choice is well justified. Denzin & Lincoln (2003), highlight how different kinds of knowledge may be derived through observing a phenomenon from different philosophical perspectives. Accordingly, developing a philosophical position requires a researcher to make logical assumptions concerning the nature of society and science as different philosophical positions yielding different results (Costello & Donellan, 2012; Mirembe, 2015).

Engaged scholarship research approach philosophy adopts constructivism and pragmatic epistemological stance with a critical realist ontological position (Van de Ven, 2007; Van de Ven, 2010). It combines different philosophical approaches and allows researchers to apply multiple models, theories and perspectives that are constructed and identified during the research process (Van de Ven, 2007). Engaged scholarship research requires engaging others from different disciplines who contribute different perspectives and models for understanding the problem domain being examined (Van de Ven, 2007). It is an approach that is based on the assumption that practical knowledge (knowledge of how to do things) in a professional domain is derived at least in part from research (knowledge from science). Quite often, is usually translating and diffusing research knowledge into practice. Knowledge of theory and practice are two distinct phenomena; each one reflecting a different ontology and epistemology for addressing different questions (Van de Ven, 2007).

Nevertheless, it is not to say that knowledge of theory and practice are different and each one stands in opposition of the other rather, they complement each other. Engaged scholarship enables researchers and practitioners to co-produce knowledge that advance theory and practice in a given domain. The author argues that engaged scholarship research approach is appropriate because of its focus on different stakeholders' perspectives and specialized knowledge, overcoming the difficulties associated with individual researcher's views (Knol, 2013). Engaged scholarship is collaborative and dialogical research between academics, practitioners and the affected community (Van de Ven, 2007; Costello & Donellan, 2012). Engaged scholarship is a social science research approach that involves "others" outside academia who may have expertise, wisdom, insights and lived experiences regarding a given phenomenon (Holland et al, 2010; Van de Ven, 2007)).

There has been a growing concern in higher education regarding the relevance and social impact of research for nonacademic communities in the public sphere. Engaged scholarship research has emerged as a response to this concern. Scholars endeavor to produce theory and research that enable individuals, groups and communities to respond better to significant social problems (Barreno et al, 2013; Barge & Shockley-Zalabak, 2008)). Engaged scholarship is an approach towards inquiry that (a) focuses on significant ethical, social and civic problems; (b) involves crafting reflexive research practices that enable collaboration between academic and non-academic communities; (c) co-creates and produces knowledge through a collaborative research process between academics and nonacademic (Barge, 2016). Therefore, engaged scholarship emerges as a result of concerns about academic research becoming less relevant in solving social problems and the widening gap between theoretical knowledge and practice (Costello & Donnellan, 2012; Van de Ven, 2007). Engaged scholarship expands the capabilities of scholars to study complex problems and create the kind of knowledge that advances both science and practice (Van de Ven, 2007).

Multi-stakeholder engagement is essential and a unique approach in addressing issues affecting grass root societies. The key to empowering people for sustainable development and peace is enhancing inclusive education that reaches out to all members of society, education that takes into consideration the knowledge of local people, and education that provides genuine lifelong learning opportunities for all societal members (UNESCO, 2012).

In the context of the constant expansion of Internet and the potential use of the emerging information communication technologies (ICTs), there is need to facilitate interaction of community members and to generate and acquire knowledge of ICT. It is important to promote inclusive knowledge production by encouraging freedom of expression for members to easily participate freely (UNESCO, 2012).

Indigenous Knowledge Societies

Indigenous knowledge and traditional practices are fundamental in building pathways for advancing innovative strategies for sustainable development. It is what local people know and do and what they have known and done for generations. It denotes thoughts and beliefs existing among the local communities to which they attach value in sustaining their livelihoods. Indigenous knowledge is integral to cultural practices and encompasses language, systems and organization of a given community. It further involves resource use practices, social interactions, ritual and spiritual development. These unique ways of knowing are important facets for the world's cultural diversity, and in providing a foundation for comprehensive knowledge societies (Dattakumar et al, 2016). The diverse forms of knowledge, deeply rooted in peoples' relationship with their environment as well as cultural groups, have allowed many of these communities to maintain sustainable use and management of natural resources. This is further helping communities to protect their environment and to enhance their resilience; their ability to observe, adapt and mitigate climate change-related problems. Nevertheless, many indigenous communities face new and complex circumstances that have often severely impacted their way of living (UN, 2005). Whereas scientific knowledge is a key factor in the innovation process, indigenous knowledge systems form pathways to sustainable development which are respectful of the environment (Mansell, et al, 2013). Knowledge is recognized as a common or public good that needs to be shared universally. Therefore, knowledge societies ought to ensure full respect for cultural diversity, and that every culture has got the right to create and disseminate their work/knowledge in the language they very well understand.

Global ICT connectivity and affordability is experiencing positive trends, although a section of the world's population still lacks access to Internet. Accessibility to internet remains an important challenge especially in sub Saharan countries like Uganda. Engaged scholarship offers shared space for knowledge creation and sharing that reflects on views of different groups and this in turn has the following benefits:

(1) Self-organization of people/groups with own intention, direction and mission. Participants in the group must get involved in knowledge discussions and cannot be mere onlookers. A good group needs to be multidisciplinary, needs to have a caring and loving chair, as well as intention and direction.

(2) An open forum that allows divergent views and all-encompassing, i.e. developing a sense of openness to the views of others.

(3) Transcending the habitual patterns of time, space and self. A group leader lets participants share time and space that transcend their own limited perspectives or boundaries.

(4) Multi-discipline and multi-viewpoint dialogues. A good group enables essential dialogues that allow participants to view themselves as needing one another. The quality of the conversations a group creates is one of the most important measures of the quality of knowledge created.

(5) Equal access to the center and maximum capacity with minimum conflict. Every participant in a good group is at the same distance from the center. However, the center is not a fixed point. In a group anyone has the potential to be a center and the center can change as the context evolves. The centers sphere is constantly moving and everyone in the group has equal opportunity of being at the center.

Collaborative Decision-Making and Knowledge Production

Collaboration has been considered a way to address the challenges of the 2st century, fostering the necessary innovation, growth and productivity for parties involved. A number of studies reveal that collaboration can be strongly influenced by knowledge sharing (Beaulieu et al, 2018). Collaboration promotes relationship and high level of knowledge sharing between team members Nissen et al, 2016), and is the creation base for new knowledge (Tan, 2016). Problems under investigation are presented in new and innovative ways and solutions are suggested, evaluated and agreed upon. The notion of collaboration is fundamentally procedural in nature. It draws attention from diverse intellectual. Professional and cultural communities to meet and engage in a discussion that yields new ways of thinking, new ways of living and new ways of working (Beaulieu et al, 2018; Sliva et al, 2019). Collaborative decision-making is refers to a situation where people from varying backgrounds and with differing perspectives work together to solve a given problem. It is defined by Konate *et al,* (2015) as a joint effort towards a common goal; a process in which stakeholders with different perspectives about a given problem, constructively explore the differences and can search for solutions that go beyond their individual limited capabilities. With the advent of knowledge economy and the growing importance of knowledge societies, organizations are constantly seeking new ways of leveraging and sharing knowledge to support decision-making processes (Abdelrahman et al, 2019).

Due to the complexity in decision-making, collaborative decision-making plays an essential role at all levels in problem solving processes. It ideally involves a free exchange of ideas to allow creation of most innovative and strategic decisions (Kolfschoten *et al*, 2011). With collaborative decision-making, there is more engagement with the audience, and best practices can be employed and shared to ensure the best outcomes (Van de Ven, 2007). Collaboration can be a process or as a sequence of steps performed by a group of people to achieve a common goal. A collaborative process provides a mechanism for engaging stakeholders in an effort to identify and address a problem; for instance, a problem of food security (Lasker, et al, 2001). In the field of food security for example, stakeholders may be considered to be key players with skills, values, judgments and experience in food security enhancement. Stakeholders provide strength to decision-making and execution of generated resolutions/knowledge (Konate et al, 2015). Community engagement collaboration is associated with sharing of knowledge between local and global communities and creates an opportunity to engage in a dialogue translation of knowledge in which ascribing meaning is a collective process (Holland et al, 2010). Poor stakeholder involvement in knowledge generation has proved to be a challenge to problem solving process (Amiyo, 2012). Stakeholder involvement, the integration of different types of knowledge in knowledge production and the creation of meaningful interactions are critical factors in engaged scholarship and co-production of knowledge (Beaulieu et al, 2018). In this regard, adoption of a strategy that is problem-driven rather than theory-driven may be appropriate.

Collaboration stimulates comprehensive thinking and is a good foundation for fruitful ideas. It enables individuals to work together to achieve a defined and common business purpose through sharing of ideas. In the case of rural food insecurity, relevant stakeholders need to be involved to appropriately brainstorm, i.e. share their knowledge experiences on how for example, indigenous knowledge is useful for food security enhancement (Konate et al, 2015). Engaged scholarship research enhances knowledge co-production through collaborative inquiry between scholars and practitioners (Barger & Zalabak, 2008). Engaged collaboration enables scholars to work in and with communities to tackle socio-economic challenges, to resuscitate lost or dormant knowledge and to shape local and global identities (Holland et al, 2010). It is a compelling mode of applied anthropology that has scholars grappling with ethics of engagement and relevance of their work especially with regard to the impact it might have on the communities with which they work. Engaged scholarship tasks researchers to adopt a pluralistic view of science and practice and participate in conversation and discourse with different people with aim of producing new but complementally knowledge (Van de Ven, 2007). Nonaka, 1994; Van de Ven & Johnson, 2006) argue that there is little research that attempts to identify the impact that these values and beliefs have on individual faculty-level knowledge dissemination.

Ranganathan (2004) argues that the strength of collaborative decision-making is that for any problem, there is a high possibility that at least one other person has encountered the same problem before and perhaps has successfully developed a workable solution for it. In collaborative decision-making, multiple views are generated, which help to go beyond individual experts' limited capacity to search for solutions of the problem. Furthermore, a lot of ideas are generated through brainstorming and these ideas have to be converged and evaluated to get the best possible explanations of the problem (Kolfschoten et al, 2011; Konate et al, 2015). To make better decisions, it is important that everyone whose involvement will help produce high quality decisions, be brought on board and be give chance to give his/her views.

Group support system (GSS) may also be used to help in collaboration engineering. Kolfchoten et al (2011) describe collaboration support as tools, processes and services that support groups in their joint effort to generate knowledge for solving a given problem. Therefore, in knowledge oriented organizations, there is often a need for collaboration support tools. Tools and technology for group support exist in a variety of shapes, from complex computer systems (groupware) and group support systems, to simple boxes with manila cards and pencils. Briggs et al, (2009) refer to collaboration tools as instruments or apparatus used in performing an operation for easy movement of a group towards achieving its goal for example, whiteboards, flipcharts or collaboration software systems. Collaborative decision-making means merging of various separate ideas into significant knowledge advances than when basic or applied research is undertaken (Simon, 1976). It is important that every discussion group gets a facilitator who takes the role of process leader; offering group guidance in choosing collaborative activities, instructing and guiding members on how to use collaboration support techniques and tools (Vreede et al, 2003; Gaffney, 2009). The style and skillfulness of the facilitator has significant effect on the outcome of the collaboration processes[1] and knowledge generation.

CONCLUSION

This chapter shades light on how best knowledge societies (universities and research institutions) should always aspire to generate knowledge that is relevant to communities' needs and has far-reaching outcomes, which address the interests of all stakeholders. It presents a theoretical and practical approaches for creating knowledge-based society and knowledge economy for sustainable development. It is important to note that the purpose of knowledge production is not only to advance technological innovations but also to promote inclusive development. This underscores the role of inclusive knowledge production and sharing to achieve sustainable socioeconomic development. Fostering sustainable socio-economic development requires involvement of different stakeholders with their varying perspectives. However, it is worth noting that collaboration especially with diverse communities and people with varying backgrounds can be challenging. Building trust of communities that been viewing scholars/academics as experts and omniscient is not easy and may take time. Collaborative practices often require a great deal of agility in sensitizing participants and also, in responding to shifting social and political landscapes.

REFERENCES

Abdelrahman, M., & Papamichail, K. N. (2016). *The Role of Organizational Culture on Knowledge Sharing by using Knowledge Management Systems in MNCs*. In 22nd *America's Conference on Information Systems*, San Diego, CA.

Amiyo, R. M. (2012). *Decision Enhancement and Business Process Agility* (PhD Thesis). University of Groningen. The Netherlands.

Barreno, L., Elliot, P., Maducke, I., & Sarny, D. (2013). *Community engage scholarship and Faculty Assessment: A review of Canadian Practices.* http://engagedscholarship. ca/res/communityengagedscholarshipandfacultyassessment-a-review-of-canadian-practices

Barge, J. K. (2016). *Making the case for academic and social impact in organizational communication research.* Paper presented at the organizational communication traditions, transitions and transformations conference, Austin TX.

Barge, J. K., & Shockley-Zalabak, P. (2008). Engaged scholarship and the creation of useful organizational knowledge. *Journal of Applied Communication Research, 36*(3), 251–265. doi:10.1080/00909880802172277

Beaulieu, M., Breton M., & Brousselle A. (2018). Conceptualizing 20 years of engaged scholarship: A scoping review. *PloS ONE, 13*(2), e01193201..Pone.01193201 doi:10.1371/journal

Bock, G. W., Zmud, R. W., Kim, Y. G., & Lee. (2005). Behaviora Intention Formation in Knowledge Sharing: Examining the Roles of Extrinsic Motivators, Social Psychological forces and Organizational Climate. *MIS Quartely, 29*(1), 87–111. doi:10.2307/25148669

Briggs, R. O., Kolfschoten, G. L., Vreede, G. J., & Dean, D. L. (2010). Defining Key Concepts for Collaboration Engineering. In America conference on information systems, Acapulco, Mexico.

Costello, G., & Donnellan, B. (2012). Engaged Scholarship in the Innovation Value Institute. In *Irish Academy of Management Conference.* National University of Ireland.

Dattakumar, A., Chong, G., Malone, L., Sharma, R. s., & Valenzuela, J. F. (2016). Knowledge Societies and their role in sustainable Development. *2016 IEEE International Conference on Industrial Engineering and Engineering Management (IEEM)* 10.1109/IEEM.2016.7797962

Denzin, N., & Lincoln, Y. (2003). The Discipline and Practice of Qualitative Research. In Collecting and Interpreting Qualitative Materials (2nd ed.). Sage publications, Inc.

Dupre, S. & Mijnhardt W. (2015). *Creating knowledge society in a globalizing world (1450-1800).* Academic Press.

Dobrin, O., & Papa, I. (2007). Knowledge Society Features: The Academy of economic Studies, Bucharest, Romania. *AMFITEA. Economic Journal (London), 9*, 77–86.

Gaffney, G. (2000). *What is facilitation?* https://www.infodesign.com.au/ftp/facilitation.pdf

Holland, D., & Powell, D. E. (2010). Models of Engaged Scholarship: An Interdisciplinary Discussion. *Collaborative Anthropologies*, *3*(1), 1–36. doi:10.1353/cla.2010.0011

International Alliance of Research Universities (IARU). (2016). http://www.iaruni.org

Knol, J. A. (2013). *Decision Enhancement for Sourcing and Sharing in the Dutch Government* (PhD Thesis). University of Groningen, The Netherlands.

Kolfschoten, G., Lukosch, S., & Seck, M. (2011). Simulating Collaboration Processes to Understand and Predict Group Performance. *Proceedings of the 44th Hawaii International Conference on Systems Sciences*. 10.1109/HICSS.2011.376

Konate, J., Sahraoni, A., & Kolfschoten, G. L. (2014). *Collaboration requirements elicitation: A process-centered approach.* http://linkspringer.com/article/10.1007

Lloyd, S., Kinti, I., Simpson, A., & Hayward, G. (2005). Managing collaborative expertise: Issues and Challenges. In *Proceedings of OKLC 2005*. MA Hhtp. orgns. man.ac.uk/projects/include/experiment

Lasker, R. D., Weiss, E. S., & Miller, R. (2001). *Partnership Synergy: A practical framework for studying and strengthening the collaborative advantage.* http://www.jstor.org/stable/3350547

Melnikas B. (2010). Sustainable development and creation of the knowledge economy: The new theoretical approach. *Technological and Economic Development of Economy, 16*(3), 516-540. doi:10.3846/tede.2010.32

Mensal, R., & Tremblay, G. (2013). *Renewing the knowledge society's vision: towards knowledge societies for peace & sustainable development. In WSIS+10 Conference. United Nations Education Scientific and Cultural Organization.* UNESCO.

Mirembe, D. P. (2015). *The Threat Nets Approach to Information Systems Security Risk Analysis* (PhD Thesis). University of Groningen.

Mugadas, F., Muggadas, R., & Aslam, U. (2016). Exploring the challenges, Trends and Issues for Knowledge Management. A study of Employees in Public Sector Universities, Punjab, Pakistan. *Journal of Information and Knowledge Management Systems, 47*(1), 2017.

Nissen, A. H., Evald, R. M., & Clark, A. H. (2014). Knowledge Sharing in Heterogeneous Teams through Collaboration and Cooperation; Exemplified through Public-Private Innovation Pattern ships. *Industrial Marketing, 43*(3), 473–482. doi:10.1016/j.indmarman.2013.12.015

Nonaka, I., & Takeuchi, H. (1995). *The Knowledge-creating Company: How Japanese companies create the dynamics of innovation*. Oxford University Press.

Nonaka, I., & von Krogh, G. (2009). Tacit knowledge and knowledge conversion: Controversy and Advancement in Organisational Knowledge Creation Theory. *Organization Science, 20*(3), 635–652. doi:10.1287/orsc.1080.0412

Nonaka, I., Byosiere, P., Borucki, C. C., & Konno, N. (1994). Organizational knowledge creation theory: A first comprehensive test. *International Business Review, 3*(4), 337–351. doi:10.1016/0969-5931(94)90027-2

Nonaka, I., Reinmoeller, P., & Senoo, D. (1998). The art of knowledge. *European Management Journal, 16*(6), 673–684. doi:10.1016/S0263-2373(98)00044-9

Pohn, C., Rist, S., & Zimmmermann, P. F. (2010, May). Researchers' Roles in Knowledge Co-Production: Experiences from Sustainability Research in Kenya, Switzerland, Bolivia and Nepal. *Science & Public Policy, 37*(4), 267–281. doi:10.3152/030234210X496628

Ranganathan, A. (2004). *Using ICT to place IKS at the heart of education for sustainable Development*. https://www.ceeindia.org/esf/download/paper47.pdf

Simon, H. A. (1960). *The new science of management decisions*. Harper and Row. doi:10.1037/13978-000

Shelat, K. & Mbuya, O. (2018). *Building Climate Smart Farmers: Doubling of Income in Arena of climate Change*. Kindle edition.

Sliva, S. M., Greenfield, J. C., Bender, K., & Freednthal, S. (2019). Introduction to Special Section on Public Impact Scholarship in Social Work: A conceptual review and call to action. *Journal of the Society for Social Work and Research, 10*(4), 529–544. doi:10.1086/706112

Tan, C. N. (2016). Enhancing Knowledge Sharing and Research Collaboration among Academics: The Role of Knowledge Management. *Higher Education, 71*(4), 525–556. doi:10.100710734-015-9922-6

Terepyschyi, S. (2016). The concept of "knowledge society" in the context of information era. *Studia Warminskie, 53.*

Tweheyo, R. (2018). *Indigenous Knowledge and Food Security: Enhancing Decisions of Rural Farmers* (PhD Thesis). University of Groningen, The Netherlands.

Tweheyo, R., Lubega, J., & Baguma, R. (2018). A mobile Artefact for collecting and availing indigenous knowledge to farmers for food security enhancement. *6th International Conference on M4D Mobile Communication Technology for Development, Kampala Uganda.*

UNESCO. (2012) *Culture and Sustainable Development. The future we want.* www.unesco.org

UNESCO (2016). *Global Education Monitoring report. Indigenous knowledge and implications for sustainable development agenda.* UNESCO.

United Nations (UN). (2005). Understanding knowledge societies. Department of Economic & Social Affairs. UN Publishing Section.

Van de Ven, H. A. (2007). *Engaged Scholarship: A guide for Organizational and Social Research.* Oxford University Press.

Van de Ven, A. H., & Johnson, P. E. (2006). Knowledge for Science and Practice. *Academy of Management Review, 31*(4), 822–829. doi:10.5465/amr.2006.22527385

Vreede, G. J., Kolfschoten, G. L. & Briggs, R.O. (2006). ThinkLets: A collaboration Engineering Pattern Language. *International Journal of Computer Applications in Technology, 25*(2-3).

Weerakoon, C., McMurray A. J., Rametse N., & Arenius P. (2020). Knowledge Creation Theory of Entrepreneurial Orientation in Social Enterprises. *Journal of Small Business Management, 58*(4), 834-870. Doi: doi:10.1080/00472778.2019.1 672709

Wong, D. (2010). *Knowledge management catalyst for sustainable development.* Academic Press.

World Bank. (1997). *Knowledge and Skills for the Information Age, the first meeting of the Mediterranean Development Forum.* www.worldbank.org/afr/ik/basic.htmfpd/technet/mdf/objective/htm

World Bank. (1998). *Indigenous Knowledge for Development: A Framework for Action.* https://www.worldbank.org/afr/ik/ikrept.pdf

KEY TERMS AND DEFINITIONS

Collaborative Decision-Making: This is used in this chapter to refer to a process of engagement in which people from varying backgrounds and with different perspectives agree to work together to solve a given problem.

Engaged Scholarship: This is a research approach that involves researchers, practitioners and key stakeholders and leverages their varying knowledge perspectives to study and solve a given problem. It is viewed as a form of inquiry between academics and practitioners that enhances generation of useful knowledge.

Knowledge: Knowledge is expertise and skills acquired by a person through experience or education in theoretical or practical understanding of a subject. Knowledge is information in context which is interpreted and acted upon by those who must perform a given function. Organizational knowledge unlike individual or personal knowledge, is of value only if it is shared with those that are in need of it.

Knowledge Co-Production: This is used to refer to a form of knowledge production based on dynamic and interaction between academic and non-academic community practitioners. People with differing expertise come together with their varying ways of viewing and analyzing issues in the process of generating new and robust knowledge and technologies.

Knowledge Creation: This is a continuous process of generating and sharing of new ideas through social interactions, collaboration, education, and practice. Knowledge creation is usually supported by information and data sharing to inform decisions and serve as building blocks in problem solving.

Knowledge Society: Knowledge society is such a society that generates, processes, shares and makes knowledge available to all members. It is a society in which the creation, dissemination and utilization of information and knowledge are the most important factor of production. Intellectual capital is the most powerful producer of wealth in societies.

Socioeconomic Development: This may refer to the transformation of a society with regard to social and economic dimensions.

Sustainable Development: Sustainable development is development that meets present needs without compromising the ability of future generations to meet their own needs and capabilities.

ENDNOTE

[1]   https://www.infodesign.com.au/ftp/Facilitator.pdf.

Chapter 2
Knowledge Societies Landscape and Framework for Distinct Context Settings

Nuno Vasco Lopes
United Nations University, Portugal

ABSTRACT

The chapter attempts to do a comprehensive literature review on knowledge societies describing its main concepts, dimensions, aspects, and actors/players. In addition to the literature review, it proposes a framework to build knowledge societies. The framework presents seven dimensions, which have been extracted from the literature where each dimension is characterized by several aspects collected from the literature. The framework can be used by decision makers around the world as a useful tool for building robust knowledge societies in different context-specific environments.

1. INTRODUCTION

This chapter makes an overview of knowledge society's concept, followed by the qualitative analysis of the research literature on this subject. Most of literature on how knowledge is created and applied to benefit society, considers knowledge as an instrument for innovation ("Towards knowledge-based economies in APEC," 2000). The helix representation is a very common way to illustrate the main players and nature of a knowledge society. In the foundation of knowledge society's concept, the triple helix has raised as the first one helix system (see Figure 1), with three main actors government, academia and businesses (Leydesdorff & Deakin, 2011) (Verdegem, 2011a).

DOI: 10.4018/978-1-5225-8873-3.ch002

Figure 1. Triple Helix Model

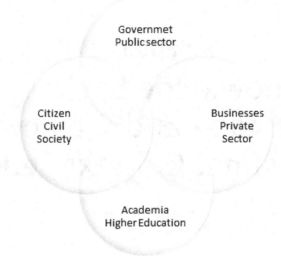

Since then have emerged the quadruple helix system (see Figure 2) (Carayannis, Barth, & Campbell, 2012) (Lindberg, Danilda, & Torstensson, 2011) and quintuple helix system (Carayannis et al., 2012), which is essentially an extension of the previous one with the incorporation of environment component as a critical attribute for sustainable development (see Figure 3).

Figure 2. Quadruple Helix Model

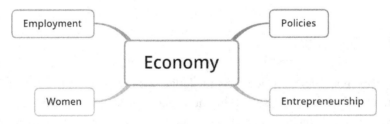

Figure 3. Helix Models for Knowledge Production

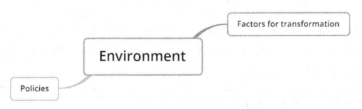

The basic Triple Helix with innovation at is core was mainly focused on economy grow through knowledge.

Quadruple Helix was significant jump towards knowledge societies by putting society at is core and stressing the need of coevolutionary processes between knowledge economy and knowledge societies. According to the Quadruple Helix, the economy structure lies in the following pillars: academia, companies, and government and talent communities. Together, with good information and communication infrastructures they create the ideal ecosystem for creativity and innovation. Governments provide laws, regulations and financial support for the definition and deployment of innovation activities. The talent communities generate new ideas and demand innovating goods and services. The concepts such as cocreation can be easily implement under this model. Figure 4, show an example how this can be putted into practice. The four actors in figure correspond directly to the Quadruple designations. This scenario is focus on the establishment of living labs for collaborative co-creation of innovative products/services.

Figure 4. Collaborative Co-creation platform for knowledge societies

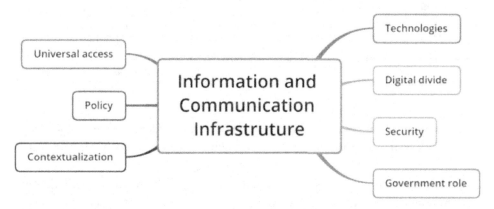

The Quintuple Helix was at its core the sustainable development highlighting the importance of having codevelopment and coevolution of society, environment and culture (see Figure 3). The Quintuple Helix puts the knowledge as the most important element in development of societies, through the circulation of knowledge between social communities, the know-how increases and that drives innovation, economy prosperity and progress. The key constituents of five helices are the 1) educational system, 2) economic system, 3) environment, 4) culture and 5) political system.

The helix systems identify the overall actors involved in knowledge societies production. Another important aspect of knowledge societies is what its main dimensions for its creation are. For knowledge creation several dimensions with different roles and nature can come into place to deploy, foster and promote its acquisition such as Governance, Education, Economy, Environment, Society, Information and Communication infrastructures. On this chapter, we are going to propose an assessment framework based on seven dimensions: 1) Governance; 2) Education; 3) Economy; 4) Environment; 5) Society; 6) Information and communication infrastructure and 7) Knowledge (see Table 1).

Table 1.

Actors Dimensions	Government	Academia	Business	Citizen	Dimension Score
Governance	*Score*	*Score*	*Score*	*Score*	**Total**
Education	*Score*	*Score*	*Score*	*Score*	**Total**
Economy	*Score*	*Score*	*Score*	*Score*	**Total**
Environment	*Score*	*Score*	*Score*	*Score*	**Total**
Society	*Score*	*Score*	*Score*	*Score*	**Total**
Inf. Com. Infra.	*Score*	*Score*	*Score*	*Score*	**Total**
Knowledge	*Score*	*Score*	*Score*	*Score*	**Total**
Actor Score	**Total**	**Total**	**Total**	**Total**	*Overall Score (Dimensions&Actors)*

The overall score could be also illustrated using a spider graph with the seven dimensions of the proposed framework and with a scale, for instance, between 1 and 10.

In the next sections will be described and explained the research methodology used to conduct the literature review as well as knowledge society dimensions identified in the Table 1.

2. LITERATURE OVERVIEW

The data collection process comprised of three main tasks: 1) determining the sources for relevant research literature, 2) defining keywords for identifying relevant publications from the relevant sources, and 3) searching the publications on the chosen literature source with the defined keywords.

The chosen keywords included: "Knowledge Society", "Information Society" and "Policy", combined as follows: *("Knowledge Society" OR "Information Society") AND "Policy")*.

This expression was applied to a search in Scopus against article titles, abstracts and keywords, and produced 41,842 publications.

The 41,842 papers identified at the outset of data collection were analyzed quantitatively to determine the knowledge Society and Information Society research landscape. The analysis focused on seven aspects: researchers, researcher disciplines, researcher disciplines, researcher countries, publication types, publication venues and publication growth.

The growth of Knowledge Society research started in 1970 when the first paper was published on the topic, but from then until 1995, the growth rate of research output in this area remained low with only 873 papers published during twenty-five years i.e. 35 papers in average per year. However, in the following years, the publication rate considerably increased as follows: between 1996 and 2004, in less than one decade, 3680 publications have been produced; between 2005 and 2012, in only seven years, the publications increased to 15548; and since 2013, the number of publications per year is on average 3102 publications/year.

Figure 5. Publication Growth

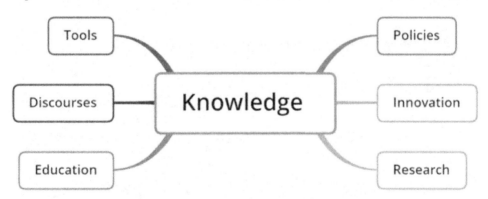

Based on researcher and institutional affiliations, the leading countries in the production of research on Knowledge Society are: USA, UK, Australia, Germany, Canada, Spain, Netherlands, Italy, Finland and Sweden in that order. The results, including the number of publications produced per country are depicted in Figure 6.

The results show that United Nations and United Kingdom have the highest number of publications both have more than fifty of percentage (53%, 15794 publications) of the total publications (29700 publication) of the 10 countries.

Figure 6. Countries

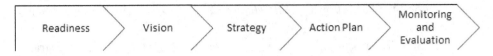

3. KNOWLEDGE SOCIETY DIMENSIONS

3.1. Governance Dimension

The governance dimension is concerned with formulation of the region's, state's or local division's intentions through laws, regulations, financing, policy and administration, and creates political and legal knowledge and capital. It plays the overarching coordinating and controlling role, but also uses knowledge to undertake these tasks.

Figure 7 below shows a conceptual map about the state of research for Governance Dimension. It shows the seven aspects about the governance dimension covered in the reviewed research papers and the specific issues highlighted about each aspect. The seven aspects include: policies, government role, favorable factors, approaches/ strategies, inclusion, women and challenges.

Figure 7. Conceptual Map of Governance Dimension

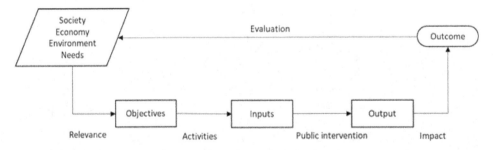

The specific issues under each of the seven aspects of the governance dimension that have been identified in the content of 204 research papers are described in the next paragraphs.

The Policies Aspect covers the policies recommended in the research papers reviewed for good governance towards a knowledge society. Table 2 shows eight policies related to the governance dimension that were given in the research papers reviewed namely; Education, content and the usability thereof, infrastructure other than ICTs, human capacity and respect for fundamental freedoms, Universal access, Media, Private Sector and Civil Society Organizations, Engagement with local communities and disadvantaged users, Research-Development and Innovation, employment environment and infrastructure and Language.

Table 2. Governance Dimension, Aspect 1 - Policies

SUBJECT	DESCRIPTION
Education	Universities are crucial nodes in the overall knowledge producing system, which, however, need to be repositioned and reformed (Krucken, 2003).
ICTs and connectivity, content and the usability thereof, infrastructure other than ICTs, human capacity and respect for fundamental freedoms	The five pillars of a knowledge society include: ICTs and connectivity; content and the usability thereof; infrastructure other than ICTs; human capacity; respect for fundamental freedoms (Lor and Britz, 2007).
Universal access	The Social Capital concept is useful in the design and implementation of a universal access policy (Mariscal, 2005).
Media	The information society will require a policy framework that encompasses all media and aims to be free from inconsistencies between policies in different media sectors (Schoof and Brown, 1995)
Private sector and civil society organizations	Via coherent and complimentary policies that engage both the private sector and civil society organizations, nations can move forward towards creating a knowledge society and at the same time by leveraging capabilities of ICT can address the social, economic and political issues on the ground (Rahman, 2008)
Engagement with local communities and disadvantaged users	If public libraries are to reach out to the excluded of the information society, they will need to move beyond a passive preoccupation with access and use technological change as a means towards more active engagement with local communities and disadvantaged users so that the public library will indeed be open to all (Dutch, 2001)
Research-Development and Innovation, employment environment and infrastructure	The transition to a knowledge-based society requires the placement of the research-development-innovation policy at the centre of economic policy and generally, implementing restructuring measures of the economic, social and institutional environment (Tocan, 2012) While huge potential for transition to a Knowledge Society exists in India, it would have to be preceded and accompanied by enabling policies such as investment in scientific research, standardization of working conditions, and the building up of physical and social infrastructure (Majmuder, 2007) R&D policy of supplying technologies for long-term period helps to achieve the construction and advancement of ICT industry, the efficient operation of Information & Telecommunication business and service, and the activation of information-utilization (Park, 2006). Research and policy efforts can offer a coherent approach to create the largest knowledge-based economy in the world (Zobel, 2003)
Language	A language policy predicated on Islamic philosophical norms is a necessary precursor to the development of a knowledge society in Islamic countries (Ismail, 2014).

The government role Aspect covers the roles government should play as the coordinator and controller of the development of a knowledge society that are recommended in the research papers reviewed. Table 3 shows two government roles that were given in the research papers reviewed namely; Participatory, regulatory & coordinating and in computerization and informatization & maintaining a favorable investment climate.

Table 3. Governance Dimension, Aspect 2 – Government Role

SUBJECT	DESCRIPTION
Participatory, regulatory & coordinating	The Singaporean government has taken a large participatory role and a smaller but significant regulatory and coordinating role in the development and diffusion of information technology throughout the country (Gurbaxani, Kraemer, Kind and Yap, 1990);
High level involvement in computerization and informatization & maintaining a favorable investment climate	In looking at IT (information technology) policy for Singapore, we see that the government has had a high level of involvement in the computerization and informatization of Singapore. In addition, it has played a strong role in developing the necessary IT infrastructure and maintaining a favorable investment climate to attract IT producers and sophisticated IT users to the island (Gurbaxani, Kraemer, kind and Yap, 1990).

The favorable factors Aspect covers the factors that can provide a conducive environment for governance agencies to effectively coordinate and positively control the development of a knowledge society. Table 4 shows three factors that were given in the research papers reviewed namely; the character of the state bureaucracy; real and perceived threats; and effective top-down policy coordination, Government's commitment, proactive policy and clear vision and Trusted computing.

Table 4. Governance Dimension, Aspect 3 – Favorable Factors

SUBJECT	DESCRIPTION
constitutional structure; the character of the state bureaucracy; real and perceived threats; and effective top-down policy coordination	A country's ability to successfully navigate the various phases of the critical information infrastructure protection programme is determined by a number of observable factors: constitutional structure; the character of the state bureaucracy; real and perceived threats; and effective top-down policy coordination (Nicander, 2010)
Government's commitment, proactive policy and clear vision	The Egyptian Government's commitment, proactive policy and clear vision are creating growth in the ICT market while contributing to building the country's information society (Wheeler, 2003)
Trusted computing	Trusted Computing technology is capable of enhancing the security of computer systems, and is another helpful means towards establishing trusted infrastructures (Sadghi, 2008).

The approaches/strategies Aspect covers the knowledge society governance approaches/strategies that are given in the research papers reviewed. Table 5 shows two approaches/strategies that were given in the research papers reviewed namely; Nurturing child computer users and Trusted computing.

Table 5. Governance Dimension, Aspect 4 – Approaches/Strategies

SUBJECT	DESCRIPTION
Nurturing child computer users	Various discourses of the 'child computer user' have been integral elements in the framing and justification of prevailing notions of the 'information society' in the 'adult world' and, more importantly, continue to underpin the ongoing political-economic construction of the UK as a technological society (Selwyn, 2003).
Trusted computing	Trusted Computing technology is capable of enhancing the security of computer systems, and is another helpful means towards establishing trusted infrastructures (Sadghi, 2008)

The inclusion Aspect covers issues related to making it possible for persons with disabilities to participate and benefit from the knowledge society under the governance dimension, that are given in the research papers reviewed. Table 6 shows two inclusion issues under the governance dimension that were given in the research papers reviewed namely; Engagement with local communities and disadvantaged users and Digital inclusion Indicators.

Table 6. Governance Dimension, Aspect 5 - Inclusion

SUBJECT	DESCRIPTION
Engagement with local communities and disadvantaged users	If public libraries are to reach out to the excluded of the information society, they will need to move beyond a passive preoccupation with access and use technological change as a means towards more active engagement with local communities and disadvantaged users so that the public library will indeed be open to all (Dutch, 2001)
Digital inclusion Indicators	Indicators/statistical data of digital inclusion help in the measurement and investigation processes of the WSIS outcomes, as well as help in the process of establishing information policies that meet the demands of the Information Society (Marques, 2013).

The women Aspect covers women issues under the governance dimension that are given in the research papers reviewed. Table 7 shows one issue i.e. Poor representation of women as experts, owners and designers.

Table 7. Governance Dimension, Aspect 6 - Women

SUBJECT	DESCRIPTION
Poor representation of women as experts, owners and designers	Women are poorly represented in the sector that constitutes the growth engine of the U.S. economy and that bears primary responsibility for the scientific and technological development of an Information Society. The human capital requirements of the Information Society demonstrate the need for women to strengthen their participation as experts, owners and designers of information technologies. Stronger representation by women in technical roles not only would help to redress a troubling human capital deficit, but is highly likely to modify and expand the range of technological applications, products, standards and practices to benefit all of society (Fountain, 2000).

The challenges Aspect covers governance challenges in the knowledge society that are given in the research papers reviewed. Table 8 shows two challenges namely; Privatization has a flip side and Under-employment in Europe and America.

Table 8. Governance Dimension, Aspect 7 - Challenges

SUBJECT	DESCRIPTION
Privatization has a flip side	Efforts to privatize the information highway, which have been and are still being implemented, undermine the network's long-range potential to encourage citizen-to-citizen discussion of public issues (Schaefer, 1995).
Under-employment in Europe and America	With the further development of global electronic networking informational tasks are likely to be increasingly mobile. While this will aid development outside the rich states, it will also reinforce the dynamic of income inequality and under-employment in Europe and America. Thus, the global information society represents a further challenge to the developed states' labor forces rather than their delivery from low cost manufacturing competition (May, 2000).

3.2. Society Dimension

The society dimension is composed of citizens, communities and non-profit organizations, creating social and cultural knowledge and capital including values, norms, identity, life styles, self-expression, etc.

Figure 8 below shows a conceptual map about the state of research for society dimension. It shows the seven aspects about the society dimension covered in the reviewed research papers and the specific issues highlighted about each aspect.

The seven aspects include: policies, employment, factors for transition, digital divide, inclusion, globalization and assessment.

Figure 8. Conceptual Map of Society Dimension

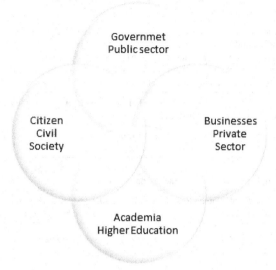

The specific issues under each of the seven aspects of the society dimension that have been identified in the content of 204 research papers are described in the next seven subsections.

The policies aspect covers policy issues in the society dimension associated with creation of social and cultural knowledge and capital in the knowledge society that were given in the research papers reviewed.

Table 9 shows seventeen policy issues in the society dimension that were given in the research papers reviewed namely; Access and content freedom, Privacy, Universal access, Equal access, Women, Democratic and social development of cyberspace, Social Policy, Happiness, Inclusion, Second-level-digital divide, Social Models, Second-level-digital divide, Language, Protection of linguistic and cultural diversity, society context, Increasing awareness of the need to focus on the social dimension and Humanistic epistemology.

The employment aspect covers employment issues in the society dimension associated with creation of social and cultural knowledge and capital in the knowledge society that were given in the research papers reviewed.

Table 10 shows three employment issues in the society dimension that were given in the research papers reviewed namely; Teleworking, Soft skills and Urban centric.

The factors for transition aspect covers transitional factors in the society dimension associated with creation of social and cultural knowledge and capital in the knowledge society that were given in the research papers reviewed.

Table 9. Society Dimension, Aspect 1 - Policies

SUBJECT	DESCRIPTION
Access and content freedom	From an ethical perspective, and more specifically from a perspective of social justice, while a technologically oriented concept of the information society may not be incompatible with severe state control, a more multi-dimensional knowledge society cannot develop under such circumstances. Hence, freedom is fundamental to participation in a knowledge society (Lor, 2007)
Privacy	There is need to devise a sensible, balanced privacy framework for the information society (Hunton and Brussels, 2002)
Universal access	Social Capital concept is useful in the design and implementation of a universal access policy (Mariscal, 2005)
Equal access	Equal access to telecommunications for individuals with disabilities in both the formulation and the implementation of policy is important (Jaeger, 2005).
Women	The model of Women Resource Centres illustrates the need for further development of predominant models for promoting innovation (Lindberg, 2012)
Democratic and social development of cyberspace	There is need for a fundamental shift in approach to e-regulation that may offer a more effective design for the democratic and social development of cyberspace (Venturelli, 2001)
Social policy	Communication policy has to shift from media policy to social policy (Burgelman,2000)
Happiness	Policies for Knowledge Based Economies (KBEs) should be informed by insights from happiness research (Engelbrecht, 2007)
Inclusion	Digital exclusion continues to demand a complex set of policy responses which go far beyond simply increasing levels of hardware provision and support (Selwyn, 2010)
Second-level-digital divide	There is an emerging second-level digital divide in some countries with high broadband penetration concerning access, skills and utilization. This has significant implications for policies aiming to narrow the digital divide. Hence, access, skills and utilization issues should be addressed separately (Park, 2014)
Social models	The analysis of individual civil participation in different kinds of civil formal organizations across Europe further confirms the existence of different European social models and hints to a possible positive parallelism between the effectiveness of economic policies and social policies aimed at fostering social participation (Vidoni, 2009)
Regional policies for African Countries	It is the improvement in the collective stock of knowledge of the African countries that would determine whether they could make a transition to a high productivity knowledge society (Agola, 2014).
Language	A language policy is viewed as a necessary precursor to the development of a knowledge society in Islamic countries (Ismail, 2014)
Society context	Policy making and implementation would benefit from and be better advised by measures that focus on the phenomenon (society) to which ICT is relevantly applied (i.e. within context); identifying change attributed to the ICT and depending on theory as their basis of development (Remenyi, 2007).
Protection of linguistic and cultural diversity	There is renewal of Western interest towards African consumers of scientific information. Therefore, policies concerning knowledge productivity and circulation are being set up within strategies of epistemological standardization. At the same time, the "linguistic and cultural diversity" fashion, which was supposed to protect local languages and knowledge, could eventually turn them into simple ethnic items (Abolou, 2006).

continues on following page

Table 9. Continued

SUBJECT	DESCRIPTION
Increasing awareness of the need to focus on the social dimension	Policy to date has been influenced by a strong technology dimension with an emphasis on the installation of necessary infrastructure and equipment. There is an increasing awareness, however, of the need to focus on the social dimension, as skepticism grows about wasted resources, poorly thought out projects and false expectations (Grimes, 2000)
Humanistic epistemology	A wisdom-based renaissance of humanistic epistemology is needed to avoid increasing social dysfunction and a lack of wisdom in complex technological societies (Rooney, 2005).

Table 10. Society Dimension, Aspect 2 - Employment

SUBJECT	DESCRIPTION
Teleworking	Teleworking, which was widely hyped as the best prospect for rural areas, continues to be predominantly an urban or suburban phenomenon (Grimes, 2000).
Soft skills	There is increasing centrality of soft skills, as capabilities, in the knowledge society (Donolo, 2013)
Urban centric	Despite the apparent potential for much of IS-related activity to be decentralized outside major urban areas, it is clear from the Irish experience that such a decentralized pattern has not evolved. With 83 per cent of Ireland's software employment concentrated in Dublin, the regions are facing an uphill battle to attract the necessary critical mass of software professionals in order to develop a software culture. The fact that Dublin has emerged as Europe's software localization centre also contributes to the level of concentration of software activity in Dublin (Grimes, (1999)

Table 11 shows two transitional factors in the society dimension that were given in the research papers reviewed namely; Social ability for growth and political learning and Social interaction.

The digital divide aspect covers digital divide issues in the society dimension related with creation of social and cultural knowledge and capital in the knowledge society that were given in the research papers reviewed.

Table 12 shows two digital divide issues in the society dimension that were given in the research papers reviewed namely; Second-level digital divide and Measurement.

The inclusion aspect covers inclusion issues in the society dimension related with creation of social and cultural knowledge and capital in the knowledge society that were given in the research papers reviewed.

Table 13 shows two inclusion issues in the society dimension that were given in the research papers reviewed namely; Equal Access and More than increasing levels of hardware and support needed.

Table 11. Society Dimension, Aspect 3 - Factors for Transition

SUBJECT	DESCRIPTION
Social ability for growth and political learning	So-called social ability for growth and political learning is the basic mechanism for overcoming the current institutional inertia. Those factors determine, also, the dynamics of transition to knowledge economy (Švarc, 2006)
Social interaction	The flow of interactions among the individuals of a group provide the necessary opportunities to share the existing knowledge and use it to further accumulate the (human) capital, which is the main productive input for the development of any knowledge economy. In this sense, the opportunities of social interaction are per se a resource and a dimension of knowledge (Vidoni, 2009)

Table 12. Society Dimension, Aspect 4 - Digital Divide

SUBJECT	DESCRIPTION
Second-level digital divide	An emerging second-level digital divide in some countries with high broadband penetration is emerging concerning access, skills and utilization. This has significant implications for policies aiming to narrow the digital divide and that access, skills and utilization issues should be addressed separately (Park, 2014)
Measurement	Several tools other than e-readiness ranking can be used to measure the breadth and depth of the digital divide. The paper brings to the fore the importance of addressing sub-Saharan Africa's digital divide peculiarities using extraordinary interventions (Mutula, 2008).

Table 13. Society Dimension, Aspect 5 - Inclusion

SUBJECT	DESCRIPTION
Equal access	Equal access to telecommunications for individuals with disabilities in both the formulation and the implementation of policy is important (Jaeger, 2006).
More than increasing levels of hardware and support needed	Digital exclusion continues to demand a complex set of policy responses which go far beyond simply increasing levels of hardware provision and support, and then assuming any 'gaps' to have been 'bridged (Selwyn, 2010).

The globalization aspect covers globalization issues in the society dimension related with creation of social and cultural knowledge and capital in the knowledge society that were given in the research papers reviewed. Table 14 shows one globalization issue in the society dimension that was given in the research papers reviewed namely; Information Society a global social problem.

Table 14. Society Dimension, Aspect 6 - Globalization

SUBJECT	DESCRIPTION
Information Society a global social problem	Information society is a global social problem because it corresponds to the themes of the era of globalization (Drori, 2007).

The assessment aspect covers assessment issues in the creation of social and cultural knowledge and capital in the knowledge society that were given in the research papers reviewed. Table 15 shows two assessment issues in the society dimension that were given in the research papers reviewed namely; Social context and Measurement.

Table 15. Society Dimension, Aspect 7 - Assessment

SUBJECT	DESCRIPTION
social context	Progress towards Information Society status is assessed in a social context that illustrates the gap that exists between aspiration and achievement in this regard (Martin, 2005)
Measurement	Several tools other than e-readiness ranking can be used to measure the breadth and depth of the digital divide. The paper brings to the fore the importance of addressing sub-Saharan Africa's digital divide peculiarities using extraordinary interventions (Mutula, 2008).

3.3. Education Dimension

The Education Dimension is composed of the activities of education and especially higher education stakeholders, academia, universities and research institutes, and creates human knowledge and capital as students, teachers, researchers, scientists, academic entrepreneurs, etc. The tremendous growth in resources invested in education in the last thirty years has significantly stimulated the capacity to turn information into knowledge and knowledge into know-how. These are being increasingly used to provide ever deeper understanding and insight into specific application areas in science, technology and society.

Figure 9 below shows a conceptual map about the state of research for Education Dimension. It shows that the research papers reviewed only covered policy aspects about the Education dimension in the knowledge society. The policy issues highlighted about education in the knowledge society include: support to teachers in transforming teaching, mismatch between rapid change of pace at the level of higher education

Figure 9. Conceptual Map of Education Dimension

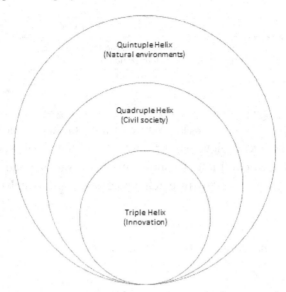

discourse and the reality at universities, new public policy for universities, adoption of global university models, factors for success, and new providers of higher education.

The specific policy issues highlighted about education in the knowledge society that were identified in the content of 204 research papers are described in the next six subsections.

The policy aspect covers policy issues in the education dimension associated with creation human knowledge and capital in the knowledge society that were given in the research papers reviewed. Table 16 shows six policy issues in the education dimension that were given in the research papers reviewed namely; Support to teachers in transforming teaching, Mismatch between rapid change of pace at the level of higher education discourse and the reality at universities, New public policy for universities, Adoption of global university models, Factors for success, and New providers of higher education (private higher education, distance education, cross-border providers, and the corporate sector).

3.4. Economy

The economy dimension consists of industry, firms, entrepreneurs and banks, and creates economic knowledge and capital in the form of entrepreneurship, machines, products, services, technology, finance, etc. A number of research papers covered different aspects of the economy dimension in the knowledge society. These research papers are summarized in figure 10 and described below.

Table 16. Education Dimension, Aspect 1 - Policy

SUBJECT	DESCRIPTION
Support to teachers in transforming teaching	Unless education policies give a high priority to supporting teachers in transforming teaching in schools to promote productive, interactive learning, students will not be able to acquire the knowledge and skills they need within a modern knowledge society (Sahlberg, 2010).
Mismatch between rapid change of pace at the level of higher education discourse and the reality at universities	The rapid change of pace at the level of higher education discourse is hardly met at the level of universities. Here, one has to take the path-dependent character of their structures, practices and identity concepts into account (Krücken, 2003).
New public policy for universities	Areas of development and conflict within the market university include: 1) autonomy and collegiality, 2) the market and the university, 3) ideology, 4) globalization and privatization, 5) pluralism, 6) the social context of knowledge, 7) science, research of knowledge, 8) knowledge as property, 9) the transfer of knowledge (Buchbinder, 1993)
Adoption of global university models	On the surface, a convergence of higher education and science policies seems to have occurred in the past decade or so. A closer look at organizational practices, however, might reveal more local variation in the adoption of these global university models for the knowledge society (Beerkens, 2008).
Factors for success	Two factors influencing the success of policies that aim to support higher education-to-work transition of youth in a knowledge society: (i) the extent to which the relationship between the type of transition process and the type of personal capital is self-reinforcing or compensatory; (ii) the nature and intensity of competition for jobs between students in higher education and degree holders (Lindberg, 2008)
New providers of higher education (private higher education, distance education, cross-border providers, and the corporate sector)	Trends in global higher education demonstrate a tendency to mass higher education with increasing demand for enrolments, especially in developing countries, as societies want to be active partners in the knowledge society. At the same time the public sector no longer manages to meet this growing demand and new providers of higher education are filling the gap: private higher education, distance education, cross-border providers, and the corporate sector. However, these new providers raise a number of issues and challenges in terms of equity, quality, and relevance (UNESCO, 2007)

Figure 10 below shows a conceptual map about the state of research for the economy dimension. It shows that the research papers reviewed covered different aspects about the economy dimension. The specific aspects highlighted about the economy in the knowledge society include: policy, employment, women, and entrepreneurship.

Figure 10. Conceptual Map of Economy Dimension

The specific issues under each of the four aspects of the Economy Dimension that have been identified in the content of 204 research papers are described in the next four subsections.

The policy aspect covers policy issues in the economy dimension associated with creation of economic knowledge and capital in the knowledge society that were given in the research papers reviewed. Table 17 shows twelve policy issues in the economy dimension that were given in the research papers reviewed namely; Domestic employment and education, Systematic analytical framework for policy development, Research-Development and Innovation, Science parks, National development, Financing, Entrepreneurship, Entrepreneurship, Integration of economic development policy with education policy, Low level of ICT positioning in the Latin America and lack of research-development and innovation policies/ strategies, Cooperation between EU & developing countries, indicators, and under employment in Europe and America.

Table 17. Economy Dimension, Aspect 1 - Policy

SUBJECT	DESCRIPTION
Domestic employment and education	The U.S. political economy requires modernization of domestic employment and education policies to sustain growth in the information society (Fountain, 2000)
Systematic analytical framework for policy development	It has now become fashionable for policy-makers to publish 'visionary' reports on the future 'Information society'. Unfortunately they equate 'vision' with unsupportable claims of potential societal benefit. A systemic analytical framework is suggested that can help in assessing the claims of what information infrastructures will provide, and in designing information society policies that reflect the needs and priorities of particular countries. It shows the fundamental importance of service applications in specific sectors, skill development at both producer and consumer levels, and structural reform in the application sectors. A checklist for policy-planners is provided (Melody, 1997).
Research-Development and Innovation	R&D policy of supplying technologies for long-term period helps to achieve the construction and advancement of ICT industry, the efficient operation of Information & Telecommunication business and service, and the activation of information-utilization (Park, 2006). The precautionary principle (PP) can serve as a framework of orientation to avoid socio-economically irreversible developments hence PP is a useful approach for: (i) policy makers to reconcile information society and sustainability policies and (ii) ICT companies to formulate sustainability strategies (Som, 2009) For Romania, the transition to a knowledge-based society requires the placement of the research-development-innovation policy at the centre of its economic policy and generally, implementing restructuring measures of the economic, social and institutional environment (Burja and Burja,2003) The model of Women Resource Centres illustrates the need for further development of predominant models for promoting innovation (Lindberg, 2012)
Science parks	A system of certification and quality assessment that might speed up the change in science parks from organizations formed by the industrial society to organizations serving the needs of the knowledge society. The use of new organizational theory on knowledge management, illustrated by Nonaka's concept of ba, presents a new solution to overcome the traditional thinking on how to organize science parks (Hansson, 2004)
National development	The breakthrough agreement in the Tunis Agenda emphasizes that any Internet Governance approach should be inclusive and responsive, and should continue to promote an enabling environment for innovation, competition, and investment (Paul, 2012)
Financing	The Tunis Agenda stresses that ways to finance ICT for development must take account of its growing importance both as a medium of communication and as a tool for achieving internationally agreed development objectives. The Agenda states that strengthened international cooperation should be encouraged along with national development policies to ensure full participation of developing countries (Paul, 2012)
Entrepreneurship	Although the new technologies are no substitute for entrepreneurship, the potential they present, within a more enlightened policy environment, should not be underestimated (Grimes, 2000)
Integration of economic development policy with education policy	In the 1990s, the Finnish economic development policy was integrated with the governmental higher education policy. This took place simultaneously with a rapid increase of institutional autonomy and with the introduction of new accountability mechanisms for the institutions (Hölttä, 2000)

continues on following page

Table 17. Continued

SUBJECT	DESCRIPTION
Low level of ICT positioning in the Latin America and lack of research-development and innovation policies/ strategies	Latin-America (including Caribbean countries) are still far from achieving levels above the world average, there being very few exceptions which thereby seem more to corroborate the rule. One difficulty seems to stem from the low level of ICT positioning in the region's countries, as well as the lack of research and development policies and innovation strategies for improving such countries' competitiveness (and that of the region taken as a whole) (Serna, 2010)
indicators	The Indian Knowledge Commission's National Knowledge Index (NKI) is facilitating the design, development and monitoring of the policies, processes and projects which are enabling the nation's capacity and ability to create new ideas, thoughts, processes and products and to translate these into economic wealth (Law, 2000)
Cooperation between EU & developing countries	There is need for co-operation between the European Union and the Developing Countries by automatically taking the 'Information Society', into account in all measures carried out. Initially, dialogue must be improved between those in charge of technology and industry, and those of development (Bruxelles, 2006).
Under-employment in Europe and America	With the further development of global electronic networking informational tasks are likely to be increasingly mobile. While this will aid development outside the rich states, it will also reinforce the dynamic of income inequality and under-employment in Europe and America. Thus, the global information society represents a further challenge to the developed states' labour forces rather than their delivery from low cost manufacturing competition (May, 2000)

The employment aspect covers employment issues in the economy dimension associated with creation of economic knowledge and capital in the knowledge society that were given in the research papers reviewed. Table 18 shows three employment issues in the economy dimension that were given in the research papers reviewed namely; low women representation, urban centric, underemployment in Europe and America.

The women aspect covers women related issues in the economy dimension associated with creation of economic knowledge and capital in the knowledge society that were given in the research papers reviewed. Table 19 shows one issue i.e. innovation.

The entrepreneurship aspect covers entrepreneurship issues in the economy dimension associated with creation of economic knowledge and capital in the knowledge society that were given in the research papers reviewed. Table 20 shows two entrepreneurship issues in the economy dimension that were given in the research papers reviewed namely; New ICT dependent business opportunities emerging and Policy

3.5. Environment Dimension

The Environment dimension consists of 'natural' environment and resources, including raw materials and the biosphere, which together create natural knowledge and capital.

Table 18. Economy Dimension, Aspect 2 - Employment

SUBJECT	DESCRIPTION
Low women representation	Women are poorly represented in the sector that constitutes the growth engine of the U.S. economy and that bears primary responsibility for the scientific and technological development of an Information Society. The human capital requirements of the Information Society demonstrate the need for women to strengthen their participation as experts, owners and designers of information technologies. Stronger representation by women in technical roles not only would help to redress a troubling human capital deficit, but is highly likely to modify and expand the range of technological applications, products, standards and practices to benefit all of society (Fountain, 2000)
Urban centric	Despite the apparent potential for much of IS-related activity to be decentralized outside major urban areas, it is clear from the Irish experience that such a decentralized pattern has not evolved. With 83 per cent of Ireland's software employment concentrated in Dublin, the regions are facing an uphill battle to attract the necessary critical mass of software professionals in order to develop a software culture. The fact that Dublin has emerged as Europe's software localization centre also contributes to the level of concentration of software activity in Dublin (Grimes, 1999)
Under-employment in Europe and America	With the further development of global electronic networking informational tasks are likely to be increasingly mobile. While this will aid development outside the rich states, it will also reinforce the dynamic of income inequality and under-employment in Europe and America. Thus, the global information society represents a further challenge to the developed states' labour forces rather than their delivery from low cost manufacturing competition (Grimes, 1999)

Table 19. Economy Dimension, Aspect 3 - Women

SUBJECT	DESCRIPTION
Innovation	The model of Women Resource Centres illustrates the need for further development of predominant models for promoting innovation (Lindberg, 2012)

Table 20. Economy Dimension, Aspect 4 - Entrepreneurship

SUBJECT	DESCRIPTION
New ICT dependent business opportunities emerging	New business opportunities that are highly dependent on broadband telecommunications are emerging such as multimedia, content and ICT industries, while opportunities are also arising in remote back-office, fulfilment services and digital support entities (Grimes, 1999)
Policy	Although the new technologies are no substitute for entrepreneurship, the potential they present, within a more enlightened policy environment, should not be underestimated (Grimes, 2000)

A number of research papers covered different aspects of the environment dimension in the knowledge society. These research papers are summarized in figure 11 and described below.

Figure 11 below shows a conceptual map about the state of research for the environment dimension. It shows that the research papers reviewed covered different aspects about the environment dimension. The specific aspects highlighted about environment in the knowledge society include: policy and factors for transformation.

Figure 11. Conceptual Map of Environment Dimension

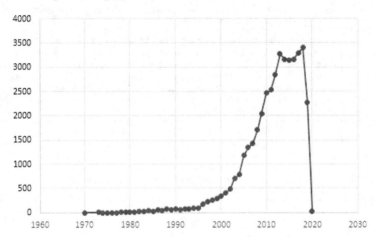

The specific issues under each of the two aspects of the Environment Dimension that have been identified in the content of the reviewed research papers are described in the next two subsections.

The policy aspect covers policy issues in the environment dimension associated with creation of natural knowledge and capital in the knowledge society that were given in the research papers reviewed. Table 21 shows two policy issues in the Environment dimension that were given in the research papers reviewed namely; sustainability and conscious societal use of IT.

Table 21. Environment Dimension, Aspect 1 - Policy

SUBJECT	DESCRIPTION
Sustainability	Precautionary principle (PP) is a useful approach for: (i) policy makers to reconcile information society and sustainability policies and (ii) ICT companies to formulate sustainability strategies (Som, 2009)
Conscious societal use of IT	There is need for a conscious societal use of information technologies and their potentials putting into consideration ecological considerations, economical, ethical and political concerns (Wala, 2012)

The factors for transformation aspect covers transformational factors for the creation of natural knowledge and capital in the knowledge society that were given in the research papers reviewed. Table 22 shows factor i.e. declining natural resources and rapid growth in population.

Table 22. Environment Dimension, Aspect 2 - Factors for Transformation

SUBJECT	DESCRIPTION
Declining natural resources and rapid growth in population	One of the factors contributing to transformation of Pakistan's agricultural society into an information society is declining natural resources and rapid growth in population (Mahmood, 2010)

3.6. Information and Communication Infrastructure Dimension

The Info and Communication Infrastructure Dimension captures all forms of ICT from technology infrastructures and electronic services to all sorts of media such as newspapers, TV and radio, social media, etc. It is responsible for creating both ICT technology and informational knowledge and capital such as news, communication and social networks, etc. More than ever, the information societies are concerned, not just with data as facts about the world, as had historically been the case, but increasingly with information as contextualized, organized and categorized data within a given society. The Info and Communication Infrastructure Dimension is part of the Knowledge Society and its contribution for knowledge transfer and creation in a Society resides in the transforming potential of new technologies and in new types of media communication. A number of research papers covered different aspects of the Info and Communication Infrastructure dimension in the knowledge society. These research papers are summarized in figure 12 and described below.

Figure 12 below shows a conceptual map about the state of research for the Info and Communication Infrastructure dimension. It shows that the research papers reviewed covered different aspects about the Info and Communication Infrastructure dimension. The specific aspects highlighted about Infocomm in the knowledge society include: Contextualization, Digital Divide, Government Role, Universal access, Technologies, Security and Policy.

The Contextualization Aspect addresses the importance of adapting the Infocomm resources to the specific context where they will be implemented and used. Table 23 shows seven contextualization issues in the knowledge society given in the research papers reviewed namely; ICTs in rural areas, contextualized ICT Strategy, focus on specific needs of specific Society, policy and reality matching, contextualization in globalization, framework to regional development and global transformation.

Figure 12. Research Qualitative Analysis, Dimension – Infocomm

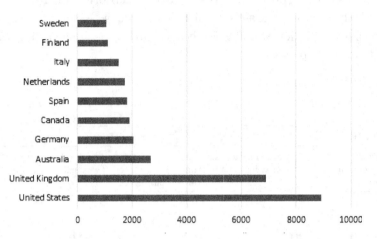

Table 23. Info and Communication Infrastructure Dimension, Aspect 1 - Contextualization

SUBJECT	DESCRIPTION
ICTs in Rural Areas	The limited success of ICTs in rural areas are due to the low spatial cover, cost and wrong political reasons. A different approach to include ICTs in rural areas in a strategical way is required, an approach concerned in human dimension (Grimes, 2000).
Contextualized ICT Strategy	The government should have a contextualized ICT strategy where the social and ICT infrastructures are embedded and the information system is not an event-time but a continuous an interactive ongoing process (Shin, 2007).
Focus on Specific Needs of specific Society	Countries can only benefit from information society if they met the specific need and priorities of their society (Melody, 1996).
Policy and Reality Matching	There is a long way to go to match policies and reality, find the right balance between technology and its impact on citizen and to enter smoothly and democratically in this new era (Kofler, 1998).
Contextualization in Globalization	There is a need to look at the context of each country before they enter in the globalization phenomena. Globalization brought liberalization and deregulation of communication industry. The democratization of information should translate into knowledge and therefore fill the economic gaps in society (Rahim & Pawanteh, 2011).
Framework to regional development	Before developing international information policies, it is necessary to design a framework to guide their development by taking into account the economic, political and cultural reality of the region (Bender, 2016).
Global Transformation	ICTs brought structural deep transformations in the economic, social and organizational framework of society thanks to its dramatic reduction in costs, digital convergence between communication and computer systems and rapid growth of Internet. ICTs were the first factor in history to introduce global economic transformations (Soete, 2001).

The Digital Divide aspect focuses on the social exclusion risk that the Info and Communication Infrastructure Dimension brings for less disadvantaged communities. Table 24 shows nine digital divide issues associated with the Info and Communication Infrastructure dimension in the knowledge society as given in the research papers reviewed namely; subsidized telecommunications, ICT strategies for marginalized people, pleonastic exclusion, public libraries for social inclusion, technology diffusion index, e-Readiness, new human capacity, conceptualize digital divide and policies for digital exclusion.

Table 24. Info and Communication Infrastructure Dimension, Aspect 2 – Digital Divide

SUBJECT	DESCRIPTION
Subsidized Telecommunications	In order to avoid digital divide the telecommunications should be subsidized because of its contribute to economic transformation (Mariscal, 2005).
ICT strategies for Marginalized People	It is urgent to develop ICT strategies able to bring marginalized people to arena (Mansell, 1999).
Pleonastic Exclusion	A new social phenomenon called pleonastic exclusion is emerging because some users are being excluded from the new media due to their educational and financial status (Servaes & Heinderyckx, 2002).
Public Libraries for social Inclusion	Public libraries could play an important role in supporting ICT and information society inclusion (Martin Dutch, 2001).
Technology Diffusion Index	The Technology Diffusion Index (TDI) makes it possible to conduct comparative studies on digital divide at regional, national or sub-nation levels (Howard, Anderson, Busch, & Nafus, 2009).
e-Readiness	Other tools than e-readiness ranking should be used to measure the digital divide. The preoccupation with digital divide of countries relies on the notion that better infostates stand better economic chances (Mutula, 2008) .
New Human Capacity	The newness of the technology by itself forces new human capacity and therefore a social problem of uneven access to digital technology naturally emerges (Drori, 2007).
Conceptualize Digital Divide	There is a lack of common ground at Government level in the conceptualization of the digital divide (Singh, 2010).
Policies for Digital Exclusion	The policy makers, ICT industry and other information society stakeholders face a big challenge in addressing the needs and interests of people. The digital exclusion demands a set of policies that go beyond increasing ICT access and support (Selwyn & Facer, 2010).

The Government Role aspect is related with the role that government can have in the incentive, promotion and implementation of Info and Communication Infrastructure in society. Table 25 shows four roles associated with the Info and Communication Infrastructure dimension that governments must play in the knowledge society as given in the research papers reviewed namely; regulation measures, establishing national ICT strategies, promoting reforms, and driving society transformations.

The Universal Access aspect is concerned with the right of everyone to have access to information as a critical aspect for inclusive social economic development. Table 26 shows five universal access issues associated with the Info and Communication Infrastructure dimension in the knowledge society that were given in the research papers reviewed namely; democratic requisite, spread of Internet Cafes, free media and universal access to information, accessibility and individualization.

Table 25. Info and Communication Infrastructure Dimension, Aspect 3 – Government Role

SUBJECT	DESCRIPTION
Regulation Measures	The government may influence with regulation measures and could promote the use of technology at all levels of society using different forms such as funding, incentives and subsidies, information and consultation, and partnerships projects. It can use the legal power for the diffusion of IT directives, setting technical standards, formalizing procedures and protecting copyright, and influencing the supply/demand goals through regulation (Gurbaxani et al., 1990).
Establish National ICT Strategies	Developing countries could be in a better position with establishment of national or regional ICT strategies (Mansell, 1999).
Promoting Reforms	The government role in promoting the industrial restructuring of information producers and distributers is highlighted as a practice in Singapore government (Kuo & Low, 2011).
Drive Society Transformations	The state has a very important role in transformation to knowledge societies through policy framing, providing incentives, active participation in spread education, creating research & training environment and best use of human resources (Majumder, 2007).

The Technologies Aspect addresses the most cited technologies for the development of knowledge societies. Table 27 shows four technologies in the Info and Communication Infrastructure dimension that are/will contribute to development of the knowledge society that were given in the research papers reviewed namely; increase the Internet Broadband Access, Software Technologies, ICT Accessibility and Mobile Phone.

The Security Aspect is concerned with security and privacy issues associated with the Info and Communication Infrastructure dimension in knowledge societies. Table 28 shows three security issues in the Info and Communication Infrastructure dimension that were given in the research papers reviewed namely; Research on Security, Children's Safety on the Internet and Data Privacy.

Table 26. Info and Communication Infrastructure Dimension, Aspect 4 – Universal Access

SUBJECT	DESCRIPTION
Democratic Requisite	With information policies it is possible to limit the information access to individuals, social groups and government organizations to have political gains. The access to information must be a pre-requisite in democratic societies (Jaeger, 2007).
Spread of Internet Cafes	The spread of Internet cafes in china symbolized the arrival of the information age in the country. The Internet cafes helped to narrow down the information gap between urban areas and rural areas (Hong & Huang, 2005)
Free Media and Universal Access to Information	Free media and universal access to information is critical for good governance (Mutula, 2004).
Accessibility	Design products and services for all should become part of regular education in all European member states. Therefore, it is now necessary to create a European market of accessible goods and services (Klironomos, Antona, Basdekis, & Stephanidis, 2006).
Individualization	Media use is changing the way of life for young people, including language, socialization, national, ethnic and mass culture. Young peoples' life is dominated by media use to the extent that their world is mediated through this channel. And this new social structure and forms of interaction will reinforce risk for the individualization of the young people (Morimoto & Friedland, 2010).

Table 27. Info and Communication Infrastructure Dimension, Aspect 5 – Technologies

SUBJECT	DESCRIPTION
Increase the Internet Broadband Access	Governments should choose policies that favor speed of broadband diffusion, adopt standards to increase the rate of broadband penetration and use mobile Internet to complement fixed Internet because it has the potential of increasing broadband penetration (Lee, Marcu, & Lee, 2011).
Software Technologies	Software technologies support ubiquitous effective knowledge and learning management solutions, helping the knowledge transfer and acquisition in society through information systems (AF Lytras & Ordóñez de Pablos, 2011).
ICT Accessibility	The importance of equal telecommunications access for people with disabilities to have an inclusive society for all. ICT accessibility is vital for the social inclusion of people with disabilities (Jaeger, 2006).
Mobile Phone	Propagating knowledge by means of a mobile phone is demanding in information societies (Mamlook, Aljumah, & Farooqui, 2011).

The Policy Aspect concerns information and ICT policies recommended for regulating the market and promoting the use of information and technologies in society. Table 29 shows ten policy issues in the Info and Communication Infrastructure dimension that were given in the research papers reviewed namely; Stimulate the Use of Internet, Ubiquitous Information Receiver for Everyone, European Top-Down

Model for Policy Formulations has a Strong Influence on Regional Development, Policy Process, Conceptual Framework for Knowledge Policies, Public Interest Attention on Information Policies, Regulation for Protecting underage, Policies for Promoting Digitalization, Information Policies and Research on ICT for governance.

Table 28. Info and Communication Infrastructure Dimension, Aspect 6 – Security

SUBJECT	DESCRIPTION
Research on Security	The research on security demands a deeper understanding of the complexity of IT systems and brings a lot of new technical and economic challenges (Sadeghi, 2008).
Children's Safety on the Internet	The concerns with children's safety on the Internet are one of the top worries expressed by parents. The young trust in the online environment remains untouched and it is crucial to recognize the rights of children on seeking for their safety (O'Neill, 2012).
Data Privacy	The EU data protection policy seems to be misconceived and misfocused. The foundations of EU data privacy regime should be revised and imaginary harms of data violation must be addressed by media and education (Bergkamp, 2002).

3.7. Knowledge Dimension

The Knowledge Dimension integrates and binds the other dimensions: Education, Economy, Environment, Info and Communication Infrastructure and Society, of knowledge society together. It is a cross-cutting characteristic for all Knowledge Society dimensions. Each dimension creates and transfers its own type of knowledge for a society as a whole, therefore building and stimulating the overall knowledge society. The knowledge dimension responsibility is to develop the knowledge societies at the economic, educational, environmental, technological and societal levels. A number of research papers cover the Knowledge Dimension from them six aspects have been identified: Research, Discourses, Policies, Innovation, Tools and Education, as the most relevant. These research inputs are described in the next sub-sections and summarized in Figure 13.

The Research Aspect highlights the importance of increasing the research activity on Information Society, Electronic Governance and security on information society to better understand the knowledge society benefits and risks. Table 30 shows three inputs for the Research Aspect.

Table 29. Info and Communication Infrastructure Dimension, Aspect 7 – Policy

SUBJECT	DESCRIPTION
Stimulate the Use of Internet	A set of policy actions to stimulate the use of Internet and Internet-based services should be adopted (Centeno, 2004).
Ubiquitous Information Receiver for Everyone	In terms of important policies for ICT market, everyone should have an ubiquitous information receiver and the government should decide if to continue expanding the ICT infrastructure for fixed access or substitute the fixed lines by mobile access (Chen & Watanabe, 2006).
European Top-Down Model for Policy Formulations has a Strong Influence on Regional Development	A top-down model used by European Union (EU) for policy formulation had a strong influence in the EU regional development (Dabinett, 2001).
Policy Process	Before adopting policies for acquiring ICTs and systems for society, it is important to know what the technologies and systems mean and its presumable impact (Klecun-Dabrowska & Cornford, 2000).
Conceptual Framework for Knowledge Policies	Conceptual Framework for Knowledge Policies - A conceptual framework for knowledge policies allows to formulate policies and analyze knowledge development giving support to policy-making decisions (Sharma, Samuel, & Ng, 2009).
Public Interest Attention on Information Policies	The information infrastructure management and technical decision making should be done under a deep democratic scrutiny and analysis; The implications of the information and telecommunication policies in the democratic system demand more public interest attention and more careful in its privatization (Schaefer Richard J., 1995).
Regulation for Protecting underage	A regulatory regime for the protection of underage against inadequate programmes harmful to their development as human being (Füg, 2008).
Policies for Promoting Digitalization	Digitization appears to have a higher influence on economic growth. Policies for promoting digitization need to be combined with industrial policies in order to generate economic growth and job creation (Katz, Koutroumpis, & Callorda, 2013).
Information Policies	The regulation of media and content services is important for the national information economy (Preston, 1997).
Research on ICT for governance	Research on ICT for governance and policy modelling including multiple stakeholders and large-scale experimentation should be ongoing (Misuraca, Broster, & Centeno, 2012)

Figure 13. Research Qualitative Analysis, Dimension – Knowledge

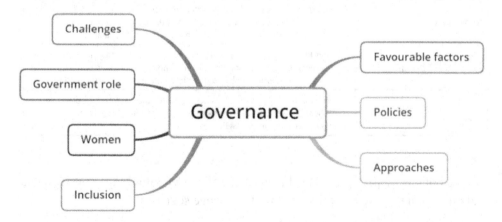

Table 30. Knowledge Dimension, Aspect 1 – Research

SUBJECT	DESCRIPTION
Information Society as a new Academic Field	In order to ensure that the information revolution leads to more benefits than damages, its understanding should be grounded in solid scientific work (Menou & Taylor, 2006)
Electronic Governance	Electronic Governance - Research and innovation investment in electronic governance could create value for the EU. A joint strategic research on ICT for governance in Europe is required (MISURACA, 2012).
Security at the Light of International Relations Theories	The existing literature on security issues in the information society is policy oriented without any contributions for international relations theories. The theory and practice on security in the digital age are so distant that they hardly can inform each other (Eriksson, 2006).

The Discourses Aspect refers to the major rationalities of Knowledge society and how they are used in different contexts and with different purposes. It could be observed a trend the A shift of the focus from the technology to information content and social and cultural issues. Table 31 shows five research inputs for the Discourses Aspect.

Table 31. Knowledge Dimension, Aspect 2 – Discourses

SUBJECT	DESCRIPTION
Information Society Discourses	Four major discourses are identified: threat/opportunity, technological determinism, market dominance and citizen vs consumer. These discourses favor the economic dimension at the expense of social and cultural dimensions. Paradoxically, it is through the social and cultural benefits of information society that the policy changes are being justified (Goodwin & Spittle, 2002).
Co-operative Information Society	There is a need for an alternative information society view. A view that is less-capitalistic and more co-operative of information society (Fuchs, 2010).
Right of Property	The development of the global information society is not towards free market, but rather it is at the enforcement of the rights of property of international media and telecommunication companies (Calabrese, 1997).
Conceptual Discourse	A wider knowledge conceptual discourse is needed. It is important to complement the government discourse on knowledge with an empirical programme in order to emphasize practices on the ground (Pfister, 2009).
Shift from Technology to Content	The economic growth alone does not guarantee the growth of information use. There is a need to shift the focus on information society from technology to content (Cornella, 1998).

The Policies Aspect describes the types of policies on knowledge development and utilisation that are recommended for knowledge societies.

A wide range of policies are appointed out namely: social cohesion, attract investment, regulate society, education, economic, inclusion and gender equality, from international organizations and professional and scientific communities. Table 32 shows fourteen research inputs for the Policies Aspect.

Table 32. Knowledge Dimension, Aspect 3 – Policies

SUBJECT	DESCRIPTION
Policies For Social Cohesion	To foster the growth of the European IS, policy makers must introduce priorities capable of enforcing the social cohesion such as increase the social dimension in IS policy implementation, develop new ways of IS awareness, develop a research agenda towards Knowledge society and refine the policies and the public campaigns (Ricci, 2000).
Professional Policy Discourses	Professional associations use knowledge policy discourses to promote themselves. Therefore, developing knowledge safeguarding standards for professional work is a big challenge for the knowledge society era (Karseth & Nerland, 2007).
Educational Policy	An alternative approach to educational policy based on social realist theory of knowledge is advanced. This alternative approach presupposes that there are social conditions under which knowledge is acquired more quickly (Young, 2010).
International Organizations	International organizations are fundamental because they can provide an arena where successful policies can be discussed and diffused. In this way, countries can move together in the ambition of achieving a knowledge society (Jakobi, 2006).
Aligned with Nacional Culture and Strategy	The paper recommends that the information society in Pakistan should be aligned with the overall strategic plan and culture of the country (Shafique & Mahmood, 2008).
Attract External Investment	The government should provide the appropriate environment through policies, enabling regulatory framework, free market economy and political stability to attract external investment (Tripathi, 2006).
Regulate Society	The transformation towards information society is not only a matter of regulating the media, but also regulating the society as a whole, firms, economics, governments and the way people live (Burgelman, 2000).
Education Policies	The development of education policies able to promote productive and interactive learning for students in order to them acquire the knowledge and skills needed for a knowledge society (Sahlberg & Boce, 2010).
Inclusive and Sustainable Policies	Policies could help in the development of an inclusive and sustainable information society and addressing the new challenges that rise with digitalization (Verdegem, 2011b).
Happiness Policies	The current state of knowledge policy is unsatisfactory but it is going in the right direction of including insights from happiness research. The happiness is the ultimate state of the economic activity, a closer relationship between knowledge and happiness policies should exist (Engelbrecht, 2007).
Economic Dimension	ICT activism and policy domains are being dominated by techno-economic dimensions (Franklin, 2007).
Protection from private Interests	The public sector must guarantee the fulfilment of public and private rights and duties. The European regions should have a policy that allow a coherent development of ICTs, which protects citizens from private interests (Alabau, 1997).
Social Exclusion	The inequality in information and knowledge acquisition creates further disproportionality in society. The globalization of the economy overlaps the national policies. The European Union policies for harmonization remain unfocused on the consequences a dual society would have in the future of individuals (Sarikakis & Terzis, 2000).
Gender Equality	The EU gender strategy has to be reframed to be able to challenge the market forces and power relations that underlie gender inequalities (Mósesdóttir, 2011).

The Innovation Aspect explores the favorable conditions which knowledge societies can offer for creating innovation and creativity. The creativity and innovation are key constituents for the economic survival of a knowledge society. Table 33 shows four research inputs for the Innovation Aspect.

Table 33. Knowledge Dimension, Aspect 4 – Innovation

SUBJECT	DESCRIPTION
Creativity and Innovation	Creativity and innovation are key elements in the information economy. The nations should create the right environment (policy, legal, institutional, educational, infrastructure and access) to enter in the global and innovative information society. There is a need to invest in creative human capital and not merely in the diffusion of gadgets and hardware (Venturelli, 2002).
Science Parks	The science parks must become active partners in the creation of knowledge networks between organizations and have a central role in the innovation and knowledge creation (Hansson, 2007).
Technology Convergence	There is a paradigm shift in innovation with the convergence between ubiquitous computing, ubiquitous communications and intelligent user interfaces (Blackman, 2004).
Harmonization of threats	There is the danger of harmonizing the cultural policy across nations thereby causing the loss of cultural and linguistic diversity. The threats to the right to create are growing and this danger to the right to create is even greater because most people are unaware of the new threats brought in by ICT (Braman, 1998).

The Tools Aspect presents the tools that can be used and how they can contribute to development of a knowledge society. Table 34 shows nine research inputs for the Tools Aspect.

The Education Aspect tackles the role that universities and other education institutions have in the development of Knowledge Societies. The learning and educational institutions reforms are also highlighted in this Education Aspect. Table 35 shows five research inputs for the Education Aspect.

4. A KNOWLEDGE SOCIETY FRAMEWORK

The framework can be also used to improve the knowledge societies dimensions and the overall knowledge society status/score with a five-steps methodology, which includes (see Figure 14):

1) Making a readiness study for contextualizing and diagnosing the current status and identifying possible actors and roles to be involved in designing and implementing the knowledge society goal

2) Develop a vision composed by a series of goals
3) For each goal design a strategy and a number of initiatives to achieve it
4) For each goal strategy make an action plan to operationalize it achievement
5) Monitoring and evaluation of action plans with qualitative and quantitative indicators

Table 34. Knowledge Dimension, Aspect 5 – Tools

SUBJECT	DESCRIPTION
Precautionary Principle	Precautionary Principle (PP) and sustainability share common a goal preserving social environment for future generations. PP can be seen as a framework for policy makers to support them in achieving sustainable development. PP can be used for making a sustainable strategic plan (Som, Hilty, & Köhler, 2009).
Knowledge Mapping	The knowledge mapping is a planning tool helpful to measure the impact of knowledge in all sectors of society. The epistemic landscapes is a precondition for the implementation of a sustainable knowledge society (Evers, Gerke, & Menkhoff, 2010).
Statistics	The statisticians should be at the center of how to measure the progress of knowledge societies (Giovannini, 2007).
Policy Framework	A policy framework for the knowledge society for helping to remove the unnecessary regulatory barriers, promote universal and public service, remove business restrictions and increase the pluralism of media (Schoof & Watson Brown, 1995).
Indicators of Society	Using indicators of society to evaluate its relative position towards a knowledge society (Gómez Barroso & Feijoo Gonzalez, 2010).
A Framework for Assessing Services	A framework that includes four segments: technology, supply, demand, and spatial impact scale, for assessing the electronic services and government best practices (Inkinen, 2012)
Society Measures	The traditional knowledge Society measures over the past years are mainly focused on infrastructural access but today the assessments have been extended to other dimensions than the infrastructure such as economic and social moving to technological and user aspects (Hanafizadeh, Hanafizadeh, & Khodabakhshi, 2009).
Knowledge Society Model	The Nordic knowledge society model is more based on economic competitiveness whereas the core European Union countries model makes a better combination of economic competitiveness and social cohesion (Green, Preston, & Janmaat, 2006).
Lessons Learnt	African countries need to identify the best practices and catch lessons learned from other emerging economies for helping them develop an information society (Cogburn, 2003).

The conceptual model derived from the methodology includes societal problems, knowledge society objectives, inputs with activities and programs and evaluation of outputs and outcomes, see Figure 15. This conceptual model illustrates a virtuous cycle that never ends. It is always in continuous improvement measuring the outcomes to see its impact and based on that evaluates again the needs to redefine the objectives and subsequent activities to achieve them, whenever it is justified or necessary.

Table 35. Knowledge Dimension, Aspect 6 – Education

SUBJECT	DESCRIPTION
Universities Role	From the very beginning universities were hybrid institutions with two types of roles; academic as a critical intellectual and academic official expert for the state (Simons, 2007).
Educational Language	The knowledge society discourse only explores the education from economical side and the will of citizens is subordinated to the will of the state and its economic interests. The actual educational language conveyed by the knowledge society does not give political tools for citizens to be able to live and act autonomously (Säfström, 2005).
Reform of Institutions	If we want to fully embrace an innovation and knowledge system, considering the reform or redesign of institutions should be put in place (Dufour, 2010).
Learning and education	Learning and education are key aspects for the development of information network society (Falch & Henten, 2000).
Lifelong learning	Lifelong learning is an essential process in developing human capital in a knowledge society (Das, 2011).

Figure 14. Methodology for Knowledge Societies

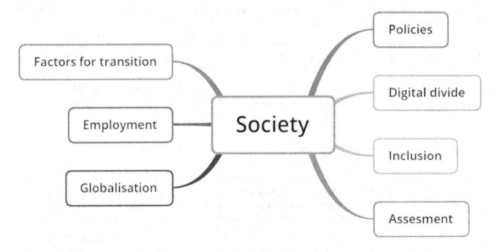

Figure 15. Conceptual model of the Knowledge Society Methodology

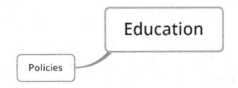

5. CONCLUSION

The innovation nature of knowledge societies has been the main driver for economic grow across countries. Figure 6 also shows this evidence, where some of most powerful economies in world appear in the top ten of knowledge societies research producers. The helix model has been used to represent the ideal ecosystem and identify the key actors, their relationship and roles in the knowledge creation. The helix metaphor in its basis represents the ideal ecosystem for achieving innovation, but along the times this metaphor has evolved with new elements been added. In quadruple helix the citizens (civil society) element has been added as a way for co-creation and co-development of knowledge societies. Collaboration platforms uniting those four elements (i.e. Government, Business, Academia and Citizens) to build knowledge societies have been proposed in literature. In the quadruple helix, the environment emerges as a new element, giving the ground to reach sustainable development. This element is critical and contributes directly to target the sustainable developments goals of the United Nations 2030 Sustainable Development Agenda.

In sum, this chapter, in addition to the literature review, has proposed a framework to build knowledge societies. The framework presents seven dimensions, which have been extracted from the literature. Where each dimension is characterized by several aspects collected from the literature. The framework can be used by decision-makers around the world as a useful tool for building robust knowledge societies in different context-specific environments.

The chapter attempts to do a comprehensive literature review on knowledge societies describing its main concepts, dimensions, aspects and actors/players. However, the author would like to highlight that although his effort, some concepts and literature, may have escaped to his scrutiny during the literature review. Therefore, this work is by nature limited to his human capacity, and to the time dedicated realize the job.

REFERENCES

Lytras, A. F. M., & Ordóñez de Pablos, P. (2011). Software Technologies in Knowledge Society. *J. UCS.* Retrieved from https://digibuo.uniovi.es/dspace/handle/10651/23937

Alabau, A. (1997). Telecommunications and the Information Society in European regions. *Telecommunications Policy*, *21*(8), 761–771. doi:10.1016/S0308-5961(97)00045-1

Bergkamp, L. (2002). EU Data Protection Policy. *Computer Law & Security Review*, *18*(1), 31–47. doi:10.1016/S0267-3649(02)00106-1

Blackman, C. (2004). Stumbling along or grave new world? Towards Europe's information society. *Foresight, 6*(5), 261–270. doi:10.1108/14636680410562963

Braman, S. (1998). The Right to Create: Cultural Policy in the Fourth Stage of the Information Society. *The International Communication Gazette, 60*(1), 77–91. doi:10.1177/0016549298060001005

Burgelman, J.-C. (2000). Regulating Access in the Information Society: The Need for Rethinking Public and Universal Service. *New Media & Society, 2*(1), 51–66. doi:10.1177/14614440022225706

Calabrese, A. (1997). Creative Destruction? From the Welfare State to the Global Information Society. *Javnost - The Public, 4*(4). Retrieved from https://javnost-thepublic.org/article/1997/4/1/

Carayannis, E. G., Barth, T. D., & Campbell, D. F. (2012). The Quintuple Helix innovation model: Global warming as a challenge and driver for innovation. *Journal of Innovation and Entrepreneurship, 1*(1), 2. doi:10.1186/2192-5372-1-2

Centeno, C. (2004). Adoption of Internet services in the Acceding and Candidate Countries, lessons from the Internet banking case. *Telematics and Informatics, 21*(4), 293–315. doi:10.1016/j.tele.2004.02.001

Chen, C., & Watanabe, C. (2006). Diffusion, substitution and competition dynamism inside the ICT market: The case of Japan. *Technological Forecasting and Social Change, 73*(6), 731–759. doi:10.1016/j.techfore.2005.07.008

Cogburn, D. L. (2003). Governing global information and communications policy: Emergent regime formation and the impact on Africa. *Telecommunications Policy, 27*(1–2), 135–153. doi:10.1016/S0308-5961(02)00088-5

Cornella, A. (1998). Information policies in Spain. *Government Information Quarterly, 15*(2), 197–220. doi:10.1016/S0740-624X(98)90043-0

Dabinett, G. (2001). EU Mainstreaming of the Information Society in Regional Development Policy. *Regional Studies, 35*(2), 168–173. doi:10.1080/00343400120033151

Das, A. K. (2011). Emergence of open educational resources (OER) in India and its impact on lifelong learning. *Library Hi Tech News, 28*(5), 10–15. doi:10.1108/07419051111163848

Drori, G. S. (2007). Information Society as a Global Policy Agenda: What Does It Tell Us About the Age of Globalization? *International Journal of Comparative Sociology, 48*(4), 297–316. doi:10.1177/0020715207079532

Dufour, P. (2010). Supplying Demand for Canada's Knowledge Society: A Warmer Future for a Cold Climate? *The American Behavioral Scientist, 53*(7), 983–996. doi:10.1177/0002764209356233

Engelbrecht, H. (2007). The (Un)Happiness of Knowledge and the Knowledge of (Un)Happiness: Happiness Research and Policies for Knowledge-based Economies 1. *Prometheus, 25*(3), 243–266. doi:10.1080/08109020701531379

Eriksson, J. (2006). The Information Revolution, Security, and International Relations: (IR)relevant Theory? *International Political Science Review/ Revue Internationale de Science Politique, 27*(3), 221–244. doi:10.1177/0192512106064462

Evers, H., Gerke, S., & Menkhoff, T. (2010). Knowledge clusters and knowledge hubs: Designing epistemic landscapes for development. *Journal of Knowledge Management, 14*(5), 678–689. doi:10.1108/13673271011074836

Falch, M., & Henten, A. (2000). Digital Denmark: From information society to network society. *Telecommunications Policy, 24*(5), 377–394. doi:10.1016/S0308-5961(00)00028-8

Franklin, M. I. (2007). NGOs and the "Information Society": Grassroots Advocacy at the UN?A Cautionary Tale. *The Review of Policy Research, 24*(4), 309–330. doi:10.1111/j.1541-1338.2007.00285.x

Fuchs, C. (2010). Theoretical foundations of defining the participatory, co-operative, sustainable information society. *Information Communication and Society, 13*(1), 23–47. doi:10.1080/13691180902801585

Füg, O. C. (2008). Save the Children: The Protection of Minors in the Information Society and the Audiovisual Media Services Directive. *Journal of Consumer Policy, 31*(1), 45–61. doi:10.100710603-007-9059-9

Giovannini, E. (2007). Statistics and Politics in a "Knowledge Society.". *Social Indicators Research, 86*(2), 177–200. doi:10.100711205-007-9137-z

Gómez Barroso, J. L., & Feijoo Gonzalez, C. A. (2010, January 1). Are Central and Eastern European Countries managing to develop the information society? In *Transformations in Business and Economics*. E.T.S.I. Telecomunicación (UPM). Retrieved from http://oa.upm.es/8819/1/INVE_MEM_2010_87332.pdf

Goodwin, I., & Spittle, S. (2002). The European Union and the information society: Discourse, power and policy. *New Media & Society, 4*(2), 225–249. doi:10.1177/146144480200400206

Green, A., Preston, J., & Janmaat, J. G. (2006). *Models of Lifelong Learning and the 'Knowledge Society': Education for Competitiveness and Social Cohesion.* doi:10.1007/978-0-230-20745-5_7

Grimes, S. (2000). Rural areas in the information society: Diminishing distance or increasing learning capacity? *Journal of Rural Studies, 16*(1), 13–21. doi:10.1016/S0743-0167(99)00027-3

Gurbaxani, V., Kraemer, K. L., King, J. L., Jarman, S., Dedrick, J., Raman, K. S., & Yap, C. S. (1990). Government as the driving force toward the information society: National computer policy in Singapore. *The Information Society, 7*(2), 155–185. doi:10.1080/01972243.1990.9960092

Hanafizadeh, P., Hanafizadeh, M. R., & Khodabakhshi, M. (2009). Taxonomy of e-readiness assessment measures. *International Journal of Information Management, 29*(3), 189–195. doi:10.1016/j.ijinfomgt.2008.06.002

Hansson, F. (2007). Science parks as knowledge organizations – the " ba " in action? *European Journal of Innovation Management, 10*(3), 348–366. doi:10.1108/14601060710776752

Hong, J., & Huang, L. (2005). A split and swaying approach to building information society: The case of Internet cafes in China. *Telematics and Informatics, 22*(4), 377–393. doi:10.1016/j.tele.2004.11.005

Howard, P. N., Anderson, K., Busch, L., & Nafus, D. (2009). Sizing Up Information Societies: Toward a Better Metric for the Cultures of ICT Adoption. *The Information Society, 25*(3), 208–219. doi:10.1080/01972240902848948

Inkinen, T. (2012). Best practices of the Finnish Government Information Society Policy Programme. *Transforming Government: People. Process and Policy, 6*(2), 167–187. doi:10.1108/17506161211246917

Jaeger, P. T. (2006). Telecommunications policy and individuals with disabilities: Issues of accessibility and social inclusion in the policy and research agenda. *Telecommunications Policy, 30*(2), 112–124. doi:10.1016/j.telpol.2005.10.001

Jaeger, P. T. (2007). Information policy, information access, and democratic participation: The national and international implications of the Bush administration's information politics. *Government Information Quarterly, 24*(4), 840–859. doi:10.1016/j.giq.2007.01.004

Jakobi, A. P. (2006). The Knowledge Society and Global Dynamics in Education Politics. *European Educational Research Journal*, 6(1), 39–51. doi:10.2304/eerj.2007.6.1.39

Karseth, B., & Nerland, M. (2007). Building professionalism in a knowledge society: Examining discourses of knowledge in four professional associations†. *Journal of Education and Work*, 20(4), 335–355. doi:10.1080/13639080701650172

Katz, R. L., Koutroumpis, P., & Callorda, F. (2013). The Latin American path towards digitization. *Info*, 15(3), 6–24. doi:10.1108/14636691311327098

Klecun-Dabrowska, E., & Cornford, T. (2000, January 1). Telehealth acquires meanings: information and communication technologies within health policy. In *Information Systems Journal*. Blackwell Publishing. Retrieved from http://eprints.lse.ac.uk/7366/

Klironomos, I., Antona, M., Basdekis, I., & Stephanidis, C. (2006). White Paper: Promoting Design for All and e-Accessibility in Europe. *Universal Access in the Information Society*, 5(1), 105–119. doi:10.100710209-006-0021-4

Kuo, C. Y., & Low, L. (2011). Information Economy and Changing Occupational Structure in Singapore. *The Information Society*, 17(4), 281–293. doi:10.1080/019722401753330878

Lee, S., Marcu, M., & Lee, S. (2011). An empirical analysis of fixed and mobile broadband diffusion. *Information Economics and Policy*, 23(3–4), 227–233. doi:10.1016/j.infoecopol.2011.05.001

Leydesdorff, L., & Deakin, M. (2011). The Triple-Helix Model of Smart Cities: A Neo-Evolutionary Perspective. *Journal of Urban Technology*, 18(2), 53–63. doi:10.1080/10630732.2011.601111

Lindberg, M., Danilda, I., & Torstensson, B.-M. (2011). Women Resource Centres—A Creative Knowledge Environment of Quadruple Helix. *Journal of the Knowledge Economy*, 3(1), 36–52. doi:10.100713132-011-0053-8

Majumder, R. (2007). *Emergence of Knowledge Society: The Indian Scenario*. MPRA Paper. Retrieved from https://ideas.repec.org/p/pra/mprapa/12808.html

Mamlook, R., Aljumah, A., & Farooqui, N. K. (2011). Knowledge on the Move. *Journal of Applied Sciences (Faisalabad)*, 11(16), 3062–3069. doi:10.3923/jas.2011.3062.3069

Mansell, R. (1999). Information and communication technologies for development: Assessing the potential and the risks. *Telecommunications Policy, 23*(1), 35–50. doi:10.1016/S0308-5961(98)00074-3

Mariscal, J. (2005). Digital divide in a developing country. *Telecommunications Policy, 29*(5–6), 409–428. doi:10.1016/j.telpol.2005.03.004

Martin Dutch, D. M. (2001). The Public Library, Social Exclusion and the Information Society in the United Kingdom. *Libri.* Retrieved from http://citeseerx.ist.psu.edu/viewdoc/summary?doi=10.1.1.178.5939

Melody, W. H. (1996). Toward a framework for designing information society policies. *Telecommunications Policy, 20*(4), 243–259. doi:10.1016/0308-5961(96)00007-9

Menou, M. J., & Taylor, R. D. (2006). A "Grand Challenge": Measuring Information Societies. *The Information Society, 22*(5), 261–267. doi:10.1080/01972240600903904

Misuraca, G. (2012). Envisioning digital Europe 2030: scenarios for ICT in future governance and policy modelling. *European Foresight Platform, 63.*

Misuraca, G., Broster, D., & Centeno, C. (2012). Digital Europe 2030: Designing scenarios for ICT in future governance and policy making. *Government Information Quarterly, 29,* S121–S131. doi:10.1016/j.giq.2011.08.006

Morimoto, S. A., & Friedland, L. A. (2010). The Lifeworld of Youth in the Information Society. *Youth & Society, 43*(2), 549–567. doi:10.1177/0044118X10383655

Mósesdóttir, L. (2011). Gender (In)equalities in the Knowledge Society. *Gender, Work and Organization, 18*(1), 30–47. doi:10.1111/j.1468-0432.2010.00533.x

Mutula, S. M. (2004). Making Botswana an information society: Current developments. *The Electronic Library, 22*(2), 144–153. doi:10.1108/02640470410533407

Mutula, S. M. (2008). Digital divide and economic development: Case study of sub-Saharan Africa. *The Electronic Library, 26*(4), 468–489. doi:10.1108/02640470810893738

O'Neill, B. (2012). Trust in the information society. *Computer Law & Security Review, 28*(5), 551–559. doi:10.1016/j.clsr.2012.07.005

Pfister, T. (2009). *Governing the Knowledge Society: Studying Lisbon as Epistemic Setting.* Retrieved from https://papers.ssrn.com/abstract=1553798

Preston, P. (1997). *Beyond the "Information Society": selected atoms and bits of a national strategy in Ireland. Dublin.* Retrieved from http://www.tara.tcd.ie/handle/2262/64423

Ricci, A. (2000). Measuring information society. *Telematics and Informatics, 17*(1–2), 141–167. doi:10.1016/S0736-5853(00)00002-2

Sadeghi, A.-R. (2008). *SOFSEM 2008: Theory and Practice of Computer Science* (V. Geffert, J. Karhumäki, A. Bertoni, B. Preneel, P. Návrat, & M. Bieliková, Eds., Vol. 4910). Springer Berlin Heidelberg. doi:10.1007/978-3-540-77566-9

Säfström, C. A. (2005). The European knowledge society and the diminishing state control of education: The case of Sweden. *Journal of Education Policy, 20*(5), 583–593. doi:10.1080/02680930500222386

Sahlberg, P., & Boce, E. (2010). Are teachers teaching for a knowledge society? *Teachers and Teaching: Theory and Practice.* Retrieved from https://www.tandfonline.com/doi/abs/10.1080/13540600903475611

Sarikakis, K., & Terzis, G. (2000). Pleonastic exclusion in the European Information Society. *Telematics and Informatics, 17*(1–2), 105–128. doi:10.1016/S0736-5853(99)00029-5

Schaefer Richard, J. (1995). National information infrastructure policy: A theoretical and normative approach. *Internet Research, 5*(2), 4–13. doi:10.1108/10662249510094740

Schoof, H., & Watson Brown, A. (1995). Information highways and media policies in the European Union. *Telecommunications Policy, 19*(4), 325–338. doi:10.1016/0308-5961(95)00006-R

Selwyn, N., & Facer, K. (2010). *Handbook of Research on Overcoming Digital Divides* (E. Ferro, Y. K. Dwivedi, J. R. Gil-Garcia, & M. D. Williams, Eds.). IGI Global. doi:10.4018/978-1-60566-699-0

Servaes, J., & Heinderyckx, F. (2002). The 'new' ICTs environment in Europe: Closing or widening the gaps? *Telematics and Informatics, 19*(2), 91–115. doi:10.1016/S0736-5853(01)00008-9

Shafique, F., & Mahmood, K. (2008). Indicators of the Emerging Information Society in Pakistan. *Information Development, 24*(1), 66–78. doi:10.1177/0266666907087698

Sharma, R. S., Samuel, E. M., & Ng, E. W. J. (2009). Beyond the digital divide: Policy analysis for knowledge societies. *Journal of Knowledge Management, 13*(5), 373–386. doi:10.1108/13673270910988178

Shin, D.-H. (2007). A critique of Korean National Information Strategy: Case of national information infrastructures. *Government Information Quarterly, 24*(3), 624–645. doi:10.1016/j.giq.2006.06.011

Simons, M. (2007). The 'Renaissance of the University' in the European knowledge society: An exploration of principled and governmental approaches. *Studies in Philosophy and Education, 26*(5), 433–447. doi:10.100711217-007-9054-2

Singh, S. (2010). The South African 'Information Society', 1994–2008: Problems with Policy, Legislation, Rhetoric and Implementation. *Journal of Southern African Studies, 36*(1), 209–227. doi:10.1080/03057071003607444

Som, C., Hilty, L. M., & Köhler, A. R. (2009). The Precautionary Principle as a Framework for a Sustainable Information Society. *Journal of Business Ethics, 85*(S3), 493–505. doi:10.100710551-009-0214-x

Towards knowledge-based economies in APEC. (2000). Retrieved from https://www.voced.edu.au/content/ngv%3A15963

Tripathi, M. (2006). Transforming India into a knowledge economy through information communication technologies—Current developments. *The International Information & Library Review, 38*(3), 139–146. doi:10.1080/10572317.2006.107 62715

Venturelli, S. (2002). Inventing e-regulation in the US, EU and East Asia: Conflicting social visions of the Information Society. *Telematics and Informatics, 19*(2), 69–90. doi:10.1016/S0736-5853(01)00007-7

Verdegem, P. (2011a, January 13). Social Media for Digital and Social Inclusion: Challenges for Information Society 2.0 Research & Policies. *TripleC: Communication, Capitalism & Critique. Open Access Journal for a Global Sustainable Information Society*. Retrieved from https://www.triple-c.at/index.php/tripleC/article/view/225

Verdegem, P. (2011b, January 13). Social Media for Digital and Social Inclusion: Challenges for Information Society 2.0 Research & Policies. *TripleC: Communication, Capitalism & Critique. Open Access Journal for a Global Sustainable Information Society*. Retrieved from https://www.triple-c.at/index.php/tripleC/article/view/225

Young, M. (2010). Alternative Educational Futures for a Knowledge Society. *European Educational Research Journal, 9*(1), 1–12. doi:10.2304/eerj.2010.9.1.1

Chapter 3
Rwanda as a Knowledge Society

Rehema Baguma
Makerere University, Uganda

Susana Finquelievich
University of Buenos Aires, Argentina

ABSTRACT

Generating and developing knowledge societies is a key element for sustainable development as defined in the 2030 Agenda for Sustainable Development Goals adopted by the United Nations in 2015. Based on a limited natural resource base, Rwanda chose to take an approach to development that differs from that of its neighbours by making ICTs the cornerstone of its development. With this focus, government of Rwanda (GoR) took a Pro-ICT led public policy that has led to several public reforms such as but not limited to liberalization of the telecom sector, enactment of laws to govern electronic messages, signatures, transactions, data protection, cyber-security and ICT usage, development of relevant infrastructure and establishment of key institutions such as the Rwanda Utilities and Regulatory Agency (RURA) and Rwanda Information Society Authority (RISA). These reforms have in turn led to a fast-growing ICT sector in Rwanda compared to that of the neighbours. To-date, Rwanda is one of the fastest growing African countries in ICT. In 2015, Rwanda emerged as the third best ICT country in Sub-Saharan Africa behind South Africa and Seychelles. In 2016, it moved one position up and emerged 2nd behind Seychelles. The fast-growing ICT sector has stimulated entrepreneurial creativity and growth across the economy. This chapter examines the best practices that Rwanda has applied in her journey to a knowledge society that could possibly help other countries in the region pursuing the same objective. The chapter also briefly reviews challenges and gaps in Rwanda's journey to a knowledge society and suggests recommendations for further improvement.
DOI: 10.4018/978-1-5225-8873-3.ch003

1. INTRODUCTION

Unlike most African nations, Rwanda has limited natural resources but Rwanda chose to take this limitation as an opportunity to take an approach to development that differs from that of its neighbours by making information and communication technologies (ICTs) the cornerstone of its development. With that goal, the government of Rwanda initiated the fourteen-year "National Information and Communication Infrastructure policy and plan (NICI) for 2006-2020. The overall aim of the NICI framework was to guide the country in the adoption and exploitation of modern ICTs to increase socio-economic development and create value for all citizens. The first NICI phase (2000 to 2005) focused on creating policies favourable to ICT initiatives. The second phase (2006 to 2010) concentrated on building the ICT backbone, including laying fibre-optic cables. The third phase (2011 to 2015) was aimed at speeding up the introduction of services to exploit the new technology[1]. The Pro-ICT public policy has led to several public reforms such as but not limited to: liberalization of the telecom sector, enactment of laws to govern electronic messages, signatures, transactions, data protection, cyber-security and ICT usage, establishment of key institutions such as the Rwanda Utilities and Regulatory Agency (RURA that has since adopted the International Telecommunications Union (ITU) ICT industry standards and the Rwanda Information Society (RISA) among others. Furthermore, the Government has also enhanced the ICT infrastructure by establishing a national data centre that centralizes information storage, management and protection, as well as use of cloud computing opportunities. Additionally, it has deployed a national fiber-optic backbone network that connects Rwanda to international sea cables increasing internet accessibility and affordability as well as connecting Rwandans to global networks.

Due to the varied reforms in the ICT sector, the country has registered a high growth rate of Internet usage compared to her neighbours and the global average. In the 2017 ITU global report on Measuring the Information Society, Rwanda was commended for a proactive strategic vision for the ICT sector that has made her achieve one of the highest levels of mobile broadband coverage in sub-Saharan Africa. In 2017, Mobile-cellular subscription per 100 inhabitants were 69.9 with Africa at 74.6 while LTE/WiMAX coverage (% of population) was 62 with Africa at 25.7 (ITU, 2017).

To-date, Rwanda is one of the fastest growing African countries in ICT. In 2015, it emerged 3rd best ICT country in Sub Saharan Africa behind South Africa and Seychelles (GIT Report, 2015). In 2016, it moved one position up and emerged 2nd behind Seychelles (GIT Report, 2016).

The ICT led development approach has stimulated entrepreneurial creativity and growth across the economy. In 2017, the "Ease of Doing Business" rankings, by which the World Bank gauges the intricacies of running a company in different countries, Rwanda emerged 41st out of 190 nations surveyed, up from 143 in 2009. In Africa, only Mauritius fared better (World Bank, 2017). A high rank indicates that a country has adopted laws favourable to starting and operating a company, in areas such as accessing credit, registering property transfers, paying taxes and enforcing contracts (World Bank, 2017). The World Bank report noted that while an entrepreneur had to go through nine procedures to start a business at a cost of 223 per cent of income per capita in 2005 in Rwanda, it now only took two procedures in three days at a cost of 8.9 per cent. Furthermore, the contribution of the service sector relative to agriculture to the overall GDP is increasing as a result of leveraging ICTs in all sectors of the economy. By 2011, services contributed 46% to GDP and consisted of wholesale and trade in various products, telecommunications, transport, and public administration (RDB, 2011).

The broader goal of the Government of Rwanda's ICT centred public policy is to transform Rwanda into a regional high-tech hub or "Singapore of Africa" as they sometimes refer to themselves.

The purpose of this book chapter is to document the best practices that Rwanda has applied in her journey to a knowledge society that could possibly help other countries in the region pursuing the same objective. The chapter also briefly reviews challenges and gaps in Rwanda's journey to a Knowledge society and suggests recommendations for further improvement. The rest of the chapter is organised as follows: best practices from Rwanda's journey to a Knowledge Society, challenges and gaps in Rwanda's journey to a Knowledge society, recommendations on the way forward for Rwanda's journey to a knowledge society and conclusion.

2. RWANDA'S JOURNEY TO A KNOWLEDGE SOCIETY-BEST PRACTICES

UNESCO defines a knowledge society as a society in which people have the capabilities not just to acquire information but to also transform it into understanding and/abilities, which empowers them to enhance their livelihoods and contribute to the social and economic development of their communities (UNESCO, 2015). The key functions of a knowledge society include: to democratize access i.e. to place within the reach of all persons the means to access and use ICTs for enjoyment of citizen rights, education, eradication of poverty, inclusion, transparency, trade, etc; to develop capacities to generate capabilities and skills to utilize ICTs for all sectors and groups of people; to build capacity for research and technological innovation for localised knowledge generation and its application for development; to achieve an adequate legal and regulatory framework covering necessary norms and regulations;

to encourage utilization of information and ICTs through relevant legal bodies and to create an adequate and stable legal setting (UNESCO, 2015).

The vision of the knowledge society is to use knowledge to further human condition. This vision is built upon principles of freedom of expression, cultural and linguistic diversity, universal access to information and knowledge, quality education for all, and enabled by the spread of digital technology and particularly upon Internet Universality principles of human rights, openness, accessibility and multi-stakeholder participation (UNESCO, 2015; UNESCO, 2019). Technology particularly ICT which plays an important role in the production and management of data, information, and knowledge is a key ingredient for a knowledge society. Information Technology is vital in all the stages of the information cycle namely: information capture (through sensors, databases such as immigration, customs, national ID systems); generation (through computations like data mining, statistical analysis); processing (encryption, compression, packaging); transmission (including all telecommunication methods); presentation (including visualization/display methods, audio, video) and storage (magnetic or optical or cloud).

The global technological revolution and the capabilities of ICTs for social and economic transformation has led to the coining of the term "Knowledge Based Economy" in reference to the current focus on integrating ICTs into all facets of social and economic activity. OECD defines a knowledge based economy as a society in which the creation, distribution, uses, integration and manipulation of information is a significant economic, political, and cultural activity (IGI Global). According to the OECD, a knowledge based economy is an expression coined to describe trends in advanced economies towards greater dependence on knowledge, information and high skill levels, and the increasing need for ready access to all of these by the business and public sectors (OECD, 2005).

The ultimate goal of the Government of Rwanda's ICT centred public policy is to transform Rwanda from an agrarian to a knowledge based society and economy. Below is a highlight of what Rwanda has done and is doing in her journey to becoming a knowledge society.

(a) **A strong will and determination from the current government to leapfrog the country from an agrarian to middle income knowledge based economy:** Government of Rwanda has positioned ICT as a crosscutting enabler for fast social, political and economic development of the country. Hence, the ICT sector has a strong and sustained political will. President Paul Kagame told the audience at the Transform Africa Summit of 2013 that Rwanda had decided to look at ICT as a utility like water and electricity. Due to the current strong political will, the ICT sector budget is at par with OECD countries (1.6 percent), far above the African average.

(b) **Establishment of the necessary regulatory framework:** The Government
of Rwanda has integrated ICTs into its public policy as a key driver for socio-
economic development and to fast track the country's transformation into
knowledge based economy. This is reflected in its policy agenda that includes
among others the following general and sector specific laws and policies:

- o **Vision 2050 Blueprint**- a successor of Vision 2020 that is aimed at
  ensuring high standards of living for all Rwandans based on the global
  commitments that Rwanda is part of including: the 2030 Sustainable
  Development Goals (SDGs); Paris Declaration on Climate Change
  (2030); Addis Ababa Action Agenda on Financing for Development
  (2030); East African Community Vision Agenda (2030); and the
  African Union Agenda 2063.

- o **Vision 2020-** gives the overall vision for Rwanda's development and
  establishes a goal to move Rwanda from an agrarian economy to an
  information-rich, service oriented, knowledge-based economy by 2020.
  It places ICTs at the centre of the transformation across all sectors.

- o **The 1st Strategy of an Integrated ICT-led Socio-Economic
  Development Policy:** This was adopted in 2001 to transform Rwanda
  into an IT literate nation. One of its key objectives was to enhance
  Rwanda's capacity to develop, produce, manufacture and assemble
  ICT products and services as a step towards developing a local globally
  competitive ICT service sector and industry.

- o **The 2nd Economic Development and Poverty Reduction Strategy
  (EDPRS II):** This strategy guides Rwanda's medium-term plans to drive
  sustainable economic growth and poverty reduction under five thematic
  areas of: Economic Transformation, Rural Development, Productivity
  and Youth Employment, and Accountable Governance. The EDPRS II
  rightly acknowledges the role that ICT can play in contributing to the
  targets of the five thematic areas.

- o **National Information and Communication Infrastructure (NICI)
  Program**: In 2000, the Government of Rwanda adopted and implemented
  the ICT for Development policy, usually known as National Information
  and Communication Infrastructure (NICI) Program[2]. The key objectives
  of this program are to transform the country into an IT-literate nation,
  promote and encourage the deployment and utilization of ICTs in each
  sector, improve the private and public services delivery, and improve
  the ICTs infrastructure in order to make Rwanda a regional ICT hub
  (NICI 2005, 2010, 2015). The NICI is divided into four stages to be
  implemented within the 20-year time-frame of Rwanda's 'Vision 2020':

- **NICI I**, lasting from 2001 to 2005, focused on the liberalization of the telecommunication industry and led to licensing private telecom companies and Internet Service Providers (ISPs) to operate within the country.
- **NICI II**, targeting 2006 to 2010, focused on deploying an ICT infrastructure throughout Rwanda. In 2010, the National Backbone Network Project led to a 3,000 km fiber optic backbone network. Kigali Metropolitan and Wireless Broadband Networks, the National Data Center and a Digital Broadcasting Network projects were launched.
- **NICI III**, scheduled to last from 2011 to 2015, focused on developing skills and knowledge.
- **NICI IV**, planned for 2016-2020, aims at consolidating previous results towards the overall goal of Rwanda's Vision 2020, that is to turn Rwanda into "a middle-income, information-rich knowledge-based society and economy by modernizing its key sectors using ICT" (Government of Rwanda 2000). Rwanda analyzes its success along three ICT key performance indicators, Availability of Mobile and Fixed Telephone Services, Internet Penetration, and Broadcasting Availability.

○ **The SMART Africa Initiative:** This was an implementation framework of the **Smart Africa Manifesto** with its secretariat in Rwanda. The Alliance has developed continent-wide goals and best practice for the implementation of Smart Africa. In turn, each adhering country was to develop and implement its own SMART country programmes aligned to the five principles of the Initiative. The National Digital literacy programme is one of the eight initiatives that each signatory country was required to implement in the framework of the SMART Africa initiative. Rwanda, being among the champions in ICT development is obligated to lead by example by implementing its own National Digital Talent Programme.

○ The **Smart Rwanda Master Plan - SRMP (2015-2020):** Aims to power Rwanda's socio-economic transformation towards a knowledge-based economy through innovative, information-driven and ICT–enabled solutions. Regarding ICT capacity building, the Master Plan highlights that Rwanda will embrace the policy approach to increase ICT skills in the general population and to undertake professional ICT certifications courses to increase their productivity. Students are supposed to graduate from high schools and universities with appropriate ICT proficiency certifications, national effort is supposed to be made to increase the available professionally qualified ICT professionals as well as attracting talent from Rwandans in the diaspora and foreign talent to support the growth and transformation of the country's economy.

o **The ICT in Education Master Plan:** Implements the SMART EDUCATION policy which complements the overall "SMART RWANDA" strategy. Its vision is to harness the innovative and cost-effective potential of world-class educational technology tools and resources, for knowledge creation and deepening, to push the boundaries of education, improve quality, increase access, enhance diversity of learning methods and materials, include new categories of learners, foster both communication and collaboration skills, and build capacity of all those involved in providing education.

o **Cyber security regulation:** This covers the Penal Code Law on Electronic Messaging, Signature and Transactions; National Computer Incident Response Team (CIRT) (Rw-CSIRT); Information Security Framework; draft national cyber security frameworks for the certification and accreditation of national agencies and public sector professionals, and draft National Cyber Security Policy.

o **The National Digital Talent Policy (DTP):** This was based on the fact that a digitally educated Rwandan citizenry ("Smart Citizen") is expected to be self-confident in manipulation of information technology devices, able to access e-services without intermediaries, interact with others in an environment where the process will be simple, intuitive, and fast.

o **An Implementation Strategy of the Digital Talent Policy (DTP) for Persons with Disabilities (PwDs) in Rwanda**: The Vision of the Strategy is to make Rwanda an inclusive knowledge based middle income economy by 2020. The aim is to provide guidance to the Ministry of Local Government, Community Development and Social Affairs (MINALOC) through the National Council for Disability (NCPD) about how the needs and interests of PwDs for digital literacy and skills development can be met in the implementation of the DTP. Its goal is to mainstream the needs and interests of PwDs into the activities of the DTP so as to make the entire implementation of the DTP inclusive.

o **Others:** Free Wi-Fi introduced across Kigali city, in schools, taxi stations and hotels, as well as on public buses under the SMART Rwanda initiative; laying of the 5,000 km of fibre-optic cable; a $140 million deal with Korea Telecom to deliver 4G LTE Internet to 95 percent of citizens in three years; and one Laptop per Child scheme which has so far seen 276,810 laptops distributed in 1456 schools' country wide.

c)   **Several Public Reforms to the ICT sector:** Rwanda continues to be one of the fastest growing African countries in ICT. In 2015, Rwanda emerged 3rd best ICT country in Sub Saharan Africa behind South Africa and Seychelles. In 2016, it moved one position up and emerged 2nd behind Seychelles (GITR, 2015; GITR, 2016). This steady progression is due to several public reforms such as liberalization of the Telecom sector, enactment of laws to govern electronic messages, signatures, transactions, data protection, cyber-security and ICT usage, establishment of key institutions such as the Rwanda Utilities and Regulatory Agency which was established in 2002 and has since adopted the International Telecommunications Union (ITU) ICT industry standards; establishment of the Rwanda Information Society (RISA) established in 2017 from the former IT department of Rwanda Development Board (RDB) with the mission of digitizing the Rwandan society through an increased usage of ICT as a crosscutting enabler for the development of other sectors.

d)   **Development of the ICT infrastructure**: Further to the establishment of the legal, regulatory and institutional framework that has led to several reforms, the Government has also enhanced the ICT infrastructure by establishing a national data centre that centralizes information storage, management and protection, as well as use of cloud computing opportunities. Additionally, it has deployed a national fiber-optic backbone network that connects Rwanda to international sea cables, increasing internet accessibility and affordability as well as connecting Rwandans to global networks. Between 2011-2013, three fibre-optic submarine cable companies-SEACOM, TEAMS and the Eastern Africa Submarine Cable System (EASSy) financed the extension of fiber-optic cables to every part of the country and increased fiber bandwidth capacity to benefit schools, health centres and other institutions. By December 2016, the number of active mobile-cellular phone subscribers had increased to 79.2%, from 70% in December 2014 while mobile payment subscribers were 9,735,694 (National ICT Sector profile, 2016). Due to the increasing mobile cellular phone subscriptions, different sectors especially financial institutions and utilities are increasingly digitizing and mobilizing their products and services, reducing costs and providing compelling new experiences for consumers. In terms of internet penetration, Rwanda has nine Internet Service Providers (ISPs) and one Network Service Provider (wholesaler). In 2014, the country had 3.7 million Internet users (36% penetration rate).

Of those, 55% use the Internet with mobile devices, 32% in cyber cafes and tele-centers, 10% in their institutions, and 3% at home via a fixed line (Rwanda Utilities Regulatory Authority 2014). In December 2017 there were 3,724,678 Internet users, 29.8% of the population, per RURA. For broadcasting, availability, Rwanda has fifteen Digital TV broadcasting stations and thirty FM radio broadcasters. In July 2015, all analogue transmitters were switched off migrating Rwanda completely towards digital TV.

e) **Opening up of ICT training:** Of the 7 Colleges that constitute the University of Rwanda, 4 offer one or more ICT courses. The College of Science and Technology (CST) offers (Bachelors and Masters) in computer engineering, electronics and Telecom engineering, computer science, information security, business information systems, ICT and information systems; the College of Medicine and Health Sciences (CMHS) offers a Masters in health informatics; the College of Business and Economics (CBE) offers a Bachelor of Business Information Technology and the College of Education (CE) offers a Bachelor of Education in Computer Science. In addition, of the 34 private Higher Learning institutions in the country, 17 offer ICT courses at certificate, diploma, bachelors and masters' levels mainly in the areas of IT, computer science, information systems and software engineering. Furthermore, the School of ICT in the College of Science & Technology at University of Rwanda and other ICT schools/departments in private institutions running ICT programmes have centres for international ICT certifications such as Cisco, Microsoft and Oracle certifications.

f) **Promotion of use of ICTs for better service delivery:** Government of Rwanda is also implementing ICT initiatives to improve delivery of different services including education, health care, security and financial services.

ICT in Education: The Government of Rwanda has initiated and implemented numerous ICT projects in education. The three most popular projects are: One Laptop per Child (OLPC)1, Rwanda research and Education Network (RwEdNet)2 and Knowledge Lab (kLab)3. One Laptop Per Child (OLPC) aims to enhance education by introducing ICT to primary schools. In particular, the project targets the development of pupils' computer skills. With an initial target to deliver one million XO laptops before 2017 (OLPC Rwanda Blog 2012), 200,000 XO Laptops covering 407 primary schools had been delivered by December 2013 (Ministry of Youth and ICT 2013). Slow implementation has been due to high production cost of USD 181 (more than half of the yearly average income of Rwandans that was not factored in or its impact underestimated. The Rwanda Research and Education Network (RwEdNet) aims to interconnect Rwanda's institutions of higher education with global education systems and research networks. The Knowledge Lab (kLab), launched with the help of both Korean International Cooperation Agency (KOICA) and Rwanda Development Board (RDB), provides them with free Wi-Fi, workspace and mentorship to young entrepreneurs3.

ICT in Governance: Over 95% of the Rwandan population has acquired national digital identity cards. A newly introduced smart card (e-ID) that combines the data from the current ID card, driving license, and passport serves as a travel document within the East African Community. The e-ID also stores biometric data such as digital picture, electric fingerprint and signature and helps the holder to carry just one card for several services. In 2010, more than 80 government institutions were connected together via a central system thereby enhancing transparency and reducing corruption (Ministry of Finance and Economic Planning 2011). In 2013, the Government of Rwanda introduced the document tracking and workflow management system 'e-Mboni', which is installed in 55 government institutions and on which 4,000 government employees have been trained. The purpose is to register all incoming and outgoing mail and documents and to ease tracking and long-term storage of the documents through streamlined and automated processes. Furthermore, by 2016, 43% of all government institutions were delivering their services online through the 'Irembo', a single platform through which business and citizens access integrated government services and over 53 government services were accessible through this portal.

ICT in Health: A central project is TRACnet. Replacing a largely paper-based system, since 2005, the TRACnet system is designed to collect, store, display and disseminate medical information, as well as to manage drug distribution and patient information related to the care and treatment of HIV/AIDS (Cishahayo 2011). Results from blood tests can be obtained much faster. HIV/AIDS physicians can monitor Anti-Retroviral (ARV) therapy drug stocks in real time and hospitals can send urgent requests to the central retroviral drug stocks in case of stock shortage. To tackle the insufficient number of physicians in the country, the plan has been to build five telemedicine centers to allow physicians and medical students exchange medical information for personal training and career development, and facilitate physicians' interaction with other medical specialists around the world. By mid-2015, three centers had been established. However, the of lack broadband connections and qualified personnel, led to more or less abandoning of the ICT systems deployed in the centers (Nchise et al. 2012[4]). By January 2018, a hundred-million-dollar fund was invested by the government to construct a broadband or fibre network infrastructure over a 2,796-mile vast land. 4G Internet coverage over the entire country makes it easier for technology developments to spring up in various Rwandan communities. In October 2016, Rwandan government created a partnership with Zipline, a Silicon Valley-based tech company to deliver blood and vaccines to hospitals and clinics via drones. Before the arrival of the Zipline[5], most hospitals outside of Kigali would have to travel several times in a week to procure blood from the primary source in Kigali[6].

Zipline is at the forefront of a logistics revolution, using battery powered autonomous aircraft to deliver just-in-time, lifesaving medical supplies around the world. At the moment, Zipline is delivering 20% of all the blood being transported outside of Kigali, Rwanda. The firm is expanding rapidly throughout the world and looking for individuals who are passionate about the nexus of public health and cutting-edge technology to change the world. The startup success story of Zipline is an indicator of the fact that any tech-related company searching for a market to grow in, can launch in Rwanda. Furthermore, the Open Medical Record System (OpenMRS) that was set up in 2006 facilitates nationwide tracking of patients' data, providing support for nutrition and child health, database synchronization tools, pharmacies, among others. OpenMRS is also used by community health workers to collect data for mBuzima, an electronic system that connects urban and rural hospitals to enable specialized treatment services remotely. Furthermore, the Health sector uses the Rwanda Health Management Information System (R-HMIS) in each of the country's over 500 health facilities together with RapidSMS to support clinical emergencies and track patients at community level. In addition, Government developed the Treatment and Research AIDS Centre (TRAC) system, a digital system that collects, stores, retrieves, displays and disseminates critical information about drug distribution and HIV/AIDS patient information to enable anti-retroviral treatment programme practitioners to submit reports electronically and have access to information. These and more e-health solutions are improving interventions, monitoring and reporting which has increased citizens' access to healthcare.

ICT in Agriculture: The 'eSoko' project, implemented in 2010, aims at transforming the Rwandan agribusiness. Esoko is an information and communication service for agricultural markets in Africa. It is a response to the explosive growth of cellular services across the continent. The company provides advice to farmers (market prices, weather forecasts, and growing tips) to help them increase yields and profits as well as solutions to businesses (marketing products, monitoring activities, and sourcing goods) to help them connect with farmers. The technology platform itself includes automatic and personalized SMS alerts, buy and sell offers, bulk SMS messaging, SMS polling, Android (operating system) surveys and more. A private initiative based in Accra, Ghana, Esoko was built and is supported by a team of local developers and consulting staff. In addition to the technology, Esoko provides extensive deployment support, strategic planning and field training to clients.

Using mobile and Internet networks, the system allows local farmers and traders to access information related to the prices of agricultural products and to provide statistics to support planning. However, the adoption of the system suffers from a high degree of illiteracy among farmers and traders in Rwanda. In addition, a collection of Apps designed to provide farmers with timely information on climate change, crops, livestock and diseases affecting them for informed decision making have been tested. One of the Apps will provide data on the state of weather, amount of rain and soil humidity, and livestock performance to ensure better farm management and productivity, as well as market information on produce. The Apps are intended to reduce the effects of climate change, and diseases on crops to improve crop yields[7]. The Apps are part of the project on "Agricultural Services and Digital Inclusion in Rwanda by the Food and Agriculture Organisation (FAO), the Ministry of Agriculture and Animal Resources (MINAGRI), and the Ministry of ICT. Additionally, there is an Agricultural Management Information System (AMIS), an exchange platform for all stakeholders of the agricultural and livestock sector, and E-soko, a project that seeks to empower farmers to enable them make more informed market pricing decisions.

ICT in Finance: In 2016, Kasha, a Rwandan e-commerce start-up which sells healthcare products confidentially to women was launched. In 2018, Kasha received a $100,000 grant to launch a pilot of its business in Kenya in 2019.

Currently, the government is focused on skills, private sector and community development, as well as improving and enhancing e-government and cyber-security.

f) **Promotion of ICT innovations:** Through national policies aimed at transforming the country into a knowledge-based economy, the Government of Rwanda has created initiatives to build skills, increase ICT use, and promote startups through creation of tech hubs that work with startups to foster entrepreneurship. An example of such Hubs is KLab located in the heart of Kigali City that provides an open space for IT entrepreneurs to collaborate and innovate. Others include: FabLab Rwanda-a space for members to turn innovative ideas into products specifically in the hardware and electronics domain, Impact hub, a global community, consultancy and a creative space that works at the intersection of innovation and society to collaboratively create impact with an entrepreneurial mind set and Co-Creation Hub Nigeria, a social innovation centre based in Nigeria that is launched a Design Lab in Kigali, Rwanda in 2019 to house Designers, Engineers and Product Developers to collaborate with top scientists globally to solve some huge social challenges.

In June 2018, the Rwanda government signed a $30 million loan with the African Development Bank (AfDB) for the National Research and Innovation Fund to boost the ICT sector. The goal of the fund is to provide equity financing to small and medium-sized technology companies, train technology-based entrepreneurs in business planning and management, and increase awareness of intellectual property rights8. *"We will continue to support research and technology by focusing on the link between our young innovators and the job market,'* affirmed the Prime Minister, Mr Edouard Ngirente while launching the Fund.

g)   **Public Private Partnerships:** To further promote innovation, skills development and entrepreneurship in the ICT sector, government has several partnerships with local and international private sector players. The latest on the block is Andela Learning Community (ALC) that started operations in the country (Kigali City) in October 2018. The ALC is a network of people technologists and tech enthusiasts across Africa dedicated to learning how to use technology to solve humanity's problems. The ALC facilitates learning through the aid of guided mentorship from learning community ambassadors. Their goal is to provide an ever-growing population of aspiring technologists with the resources and environments they need to become world-class problem solvers.

h)   **ICT Centres of Excellence:** A centre of excellence refers to a shared facility or an entity that provides leadership, best practices, research, support and/or training for a focus area. The term may also refer to a network of institutions collaborating with each other to pursue excellence in a particular area. In line with the focus on quality of education and Science, Technology, Engineering and Mathematics (STEM) by Vision 2050, the Government of Rwanda has supported the establishment of several centres of excellence in STEM. In ICT, the following have been established:

 ◦   **Carnegie Mellon University, Rwanda:** Rwanda is the headquarters of the ICT Centre of Excellence of the US-based Carnegie Mellon University, the leading ICT institution in the country with all teaching staff brought from the US based Carnegie Mellon University. It was the first of the five centres that Carnegie Mellon University will extend to Africa.

 ◦   **African Centre of Excellence for Innovative Teaching and Learning Mathematics and Science (ACEITLMS):** ACEITLMS aims at strengthening human capacity to deliver research-based quality teaching and learning of mathematics and science in Rwanda and across the region, in collaboration with regional and international institutions.

 ◦   **African Centre of Excellence in Internet of Things (ACEIoT):** The goal of ACEIoT is to educate and train African researchers in the field of IoT, who will develop and deploy innovative IoT-enabled services, to address development challenges across all regional high-priority domains such as remote monitoring and diagnosis technology to provide rural populations with access to quality healthcare; wide-area networked sensors for precision agriculture to improve yields; and smart metering in African households that could regulate the power usage and increase energy efficiency.

○ **African Centre of Excellence for Data Sciences (ACE-DS):** The ACE-DS is a regional centre of excellency whose core mission is to train post-graduate students with combined expertise in statistics, economics, business, computer science, and engineering to use big data and data analytics to solve development challenges.

i) **Using ICT to implement to implement the United Nations' Sustainable Development Goals**: The Government of Rwanda is using ICTs to implement more than a few of the United Nations' Sustainable Development Goals. The Digital Ambassodors Programme (DAP) project seeks to address SDG 5, SDG 8, SDG 10, and SDG 17, as it goes beyond access and digital literacy, with a strong focus on jobs and skills and aims to reduce inequalities within Rwanda.

j) **Expanding access to the Internet:** Expanding access to the Internet is a priority for the country, as it will aid in expanding economic opportunities for all citizens. The Rwanda Utility Regulatory Authority (RURA) in collaboration with other stakeholders are implementing measures towards Universal Access for all Rwandans. Some of the measures include e-learning and e-service centres in rural areas, subsidizing the cost of Internet in rural areas to ensure affordable access to Internet services and supporting people with disabilities to have equal opportunity and access to ICT[9].

3. CHALLENGES AND GAPS IN RWANDA'S JOURNEY TO A KNOWLEDGE SOCIETY

Despite the great strides Rwanda has made towards becoming a knowledge society especially in comparison to other African countries, there are some challenges and gaps that need to be addressed to make the country move faster on this journey. The key challenges observed in the analysis of the sources of data used in this chapter are described below:

Low digital literacy: Several studies have shown that ICT Literacy in Rwanda is still very low compared to what is expected though it is steadily increasing. The 4th Integrated Household Living Conditions Survey (EICV IV) established that computer literacy has increased in the past three years from 5.3% to 8.4% overall and almost doubled from 6.5% to 10.9% in the younger cohort. The low level of digital literacy among Rwandans is caused by a number of factors key of which include:

limited awareness about the wider potential of ICTs, limited use of ICT in teaching and learning, limited resources (digital devices and access to Internet) among others.

Limited awareness about the wider potential of ICTs: The Rwandan general population, Teachers, Learners and Parents are not utilizing optimally the digital skills they have. Just like in many other developing countries, most Rwandans mainly use ICTs and ICT applications like Internet, the Web and social media for social engagements like communicating with family and friends and entertainment instead of more productive endeavours like e-commerce, accessing government services, e-learning, etc. This has been attributed to limited awareness about the potential of such ICTs beyond social interactions and entertainment. One Instructor at a Teacher's College in Rwanda who attempted to use Facebook for learning faced several challenges and key of these was that students who had Facebook accounts did not welcome the idea because they were not aware that Facebook could be used for teaching and learning.

Limited use of ICT in teaching and learning: Although most Rwandan Higher Learning Institutions are trying to embrace online instructional strategies including use of social media (for example, in the College of Education of the University of Rwanda), more than a half of the Lecturers have been trained to use MOODLE, the Lecturers are not yet using MOODLE in teaching. Only a few upload their course materials onto MOODLE. This has been blamed on unreliable Internet connection for both Lecturers and Students. On the side of students, their use of technology in their learning process is limited to use of PowerPoint slides in classroom presentations. Some teachers especially in HLIs are using the Web (websites, video, music) to enhance learning but students and teachers also need to create online content to be utilized both in and out of the classroom. Strengthening use of ICT in teaching & learning would increase digital literacy and skills among products of the school system.

Limited Resources-particularly computers and or smart phones and Internet connection: Many Rwandans cannot afford computers and or smart phones due to their low levels of income. Secondly, although Rwanda was ranked the country with the most affordable Internet in least developed countries for the second year running, only 1.5 million out of the total population of 11.9 million have access to Internet. This has been largely attributed to the high cost of smart phones and low incomes. Though the mobile subscription rate is so high (8.8 million as of March 2016), few people have smart devices and for many others, they cannot afford Internet due to their low incomes. According to Rwanda Utilities Regulatory Authority (RURA), only 665,684 Rwandans had smartphones in the third-quarter of 2015. Despite efforts invested in expanding Internet infrastructure like the fibre optic network and the launch of the high-speed 4G LTE Internet, over 250 sector offices did not have Internet access along with numerous Cell level offices mainly in the remote areas with no reliable electricity in 2016 (Kanamugire, 2016). Yet, Services offered by different government institutions in a variety of sectors like education, utilities, mining, banking and others are supposed to be accessed online. Due to low digital literacy, adoption of e-government services has been very slow especially among farmers and traders.

Misalignment between ICT Education programs and national skill needs: Although there are several higher learning institutions offering ICT related courses, most of them concentrate on Information Technology, Computer Science or Computer Engineering, Information systems and software engineering yet, most of these programmes focus on basic aspects of computer management and engineering of software and use/applications of ICT. With an increase in access to Telecom infrastructure and use of shared infrastructure and services, mobile services and cybercrime education programmes are very necessary. Moreover, the five year programme for priority skills development to deliver EDPRS II prescribed skill units required from 2013-2018 to cover: telecommunication, computer networking, database, software engineering, mobile applications development, multimedia and digital design, information security and project management.

Mismatch between the capabilities of ICT graduates with that required by the industry: Although annually the education sector churns out over 1000 ICT graduates mainly at certificate, diploma, and bachelor's degree levels, the issue of quality of these graduates has been a recurring problem. Most graduates do not have the technical, market-oriented expertise required by employers in government and private sector (DTP, 2017).

Weak linkages between the ICT industry and ICT training institutions: Linkages between the ICT industry and ICT training institutions are weak. The 2012 ICT skills study established that only 3.7% of the ICT organizations had taken on interns (ICT skills study, 2012). Furthermore, none of the ICT establishments that participated in ICT skills study had any form of knowledge transfer partnership with any training institution.

Low enrolment of graduate, female and PwDs students into ICT programmes: Although ICT programmes seem to attract more students than many other fields in the country reflecting the fast growing nature and popularity of the sector, postgraduate diploma, master and PhD students constitute a very small number. Annually, HLIs in Rwanda train over 1000 graduates at bachelors, diploma and certificate level. But of these, those at the postgraduate level are not more than 5% (ICT skills study, 2012). For example, between 2009 and 2011, National University of Rwanda (NUR) and Kigali Institute of Technology (KIST) had only 120 post graduate diploma and master students in ICT and none at the doctoral level but had 1200 undergraduates. In terms of gender, the labor force in the ICT sector is still dominated by men especially technical positions such as software/application developers and analysts) due to low female enrolment into ICT programmes (ICT skills study, 2012). For Persons with

Disabilities (PwDs), their enrolment statistics are not yet captured. The 2012 ICT skills study only reported gender and age group disaggregated skill levels in the sector leaving out the PwDs dimension while the 4th Integrated Household Living Conditions Survey (EICV IV) only covered computer literacy rates for the general population, the younger cohort (youth) and according to gender.

Weak Research, Development & Innovations (RD&I) culture: Due to the low enrolment into graduate programmes, research output in the ICT fields is very low. In addition, the country does not have an ICT research and Innovations Strategy. The 2006 Science and Technology Policy is out-dated and gives little emphasis to ICT. The ICT part has 4 strategies covering use and integration of science and computer literacy in schools, intensification of training efforts in technical and scientific fields, promotion of publications, studies and investigations and establishment of a network of Science and Technology resource centres. It does not cover current needs of the sector such as low enrolment of graduate students, and development of innovations and knowledge in the areas prioritized for national development.

RECOMMENDATIONS

Rwanda has huge growth prospects for fast developing into a knowledge society and knowledge based economy with a world class IT industry and services to drive economic growth. To address the current challenges/gaps, the following further actions are recommended:

- **Improve the general education system:** There is need to reform the general education system and promote lifelong learning to create and constantly update e-skills. Suggested priorities include:
  - § Investing in education at all levels, and creating opportunities and incentives for private sector investment in education and lifelong training in e-skills. E-skills mean the effective application of ICT systems and devices. They vary from ICT specialists who have the ability to develop, operate, and maintain ICT systems, to basic ICT users, who are capable users of the mainstream tools needed in their working life.
  - § Focusing governmental interventions on key issues of quality, relevance, impact of education, and access for all.
  - § Integrating formal, informal, technical, and adult and distance education and training to provide a greater range of opportunities for life-long learning.

§   Creating policy and regulatory frameworks, including certification schemes, which may make lifelong learning opportunities attractive and easy for people to pursue.

- **Use ICT in teaching and learning at all levels of education:** UNESCO recommends four key curriculum areas that educational policy should address if ICT skills and literacy can be improved: ICT literacy – ICT skills are taught and learned as a separate subject; Application of ICT in subject areas – ICT skills are developed within separate subjects; infusing ICT across the curriculum – ICT is integrated or embedded across all subjects of the curriculum; ICT specialization – ICT is taught and learned as an applied subject to train for a profession.

- **Strengthen linkages between the ICT industry and training institutions:** There is need to promote academia/industry linkages especially concerning internships and apprenticeships between training institutions and the ICT industry to provide more opportunities for internship and apprenticeship. This will in turn improve the quality of graduates particularly in terms of technical and market-oriented expertise.

- **Increase enrolment into ICT programmes for graduate, female and PwDs:** There is need to increase enrolment into ICT programmes for graduate and special interest groups namely: females and PwDs. One of the key functions of a knowledge society is to democratize access i.e. to place within the reach of all persons the means to access and use ICTs for enjoyment of citizen rights, education, eradication of poverty, inclusion, transparency, trade, among others (UNESCO, 2015). Therefore, there is need to ensure adequate representation of different categories of Rwandan citizens in ICT education programmes.

- **Align ICT education programmes to national skill priorities and needs:** There is need to review the current national ICT curriculum and align ICT programmes taught in the country to national ICT skill priorities and needs. The Government of Rwanda has put ICT at the centre of the social, political and economic transformation to act as the main development catalyst. This requires a strong move towards online services, better protection of private information, more automation of economic and social activities, more collaboration between government departments, and a change in public service culture. Therefore, the future of government ICT should not just be about technology. It should also be about how government uses ICT to deliver better services in a cost effective way, create jobs and transform the Rwandan society and economy in a constantly changing environment. Hence, ICT programmes taught in the country need diversification beyond computer engineering and management, and software engineering.

- **Develop an ICT Research, Development and Innovations (RD&I) Strategy:** This strategy should provide national direction for increasing enrolment of graduate students (post graduate diploma, Masters and PhD) in the areas earmarked as necessary for national development. This will in turn increase the level of research output, innovations and specialists in ICT and in particular in the areas priotized for national development. The economy of Estonia, one of the successful case studies of a knowledge based society relies heavily on knowledge guided by its robust Research, Development and Innovations (RD&I) strategy that has four objectives: (i) Research in Estonia is of a high level and diverse; (ii) Research & Development functions in the interests of the Estonian society and economy; (iii) Research & Development makes the structure of the economy more knowledge-intensive; and (iv) Estonia is active and visible in international RDI cooperation (Estonian RD&I strategy, 2014).

CONCLUSION

The fast advancement of Rwanda towards a knowledge society and a knowledge based economy has been propelled by several best practices such as a strong political will, establishment of the necessary legal and regulatory framework, Several Public Reforms to the ICT sector like liberalisation of the Telecom sector, development of the necessary ICT infrastructure, opening up of ICT training and promotion of use of ICTs for better service delivery. However, there are still some challenges and gaps that need to be addressed to make the country move faster on this journey. Key of such challenges include: mismatch between the capabilities of ICT graduates with that required by the industry, weak linkages between the ICT industry and ICT training institutions, low enrolment of graduate, female and PwDs students into ICT programmes and weak Research, Development & Innovations (RD&I) culture. For Rwanda to continue progressing on her journey to a knowledge society and even move faster, existing challenges/gaps need to be addressed. Suggested strategies include: improving the general education system, use ICT in teaching and learning at all levels of education, strengthening linkages between the ICT industry and training institutions, increasing enrolment into ICT programmes for graduate, female and PwDs, aligning ICT education programmes to national skill priorities and needs and develop an ICT Research, Development and Innovations (RD&I) strategy.

REFERENCES

Estonian, R. D., & Strategy, I. (2014-2020). *Estonian Research and Development and Innovation Strategy 2014-2020 "Knowledge-based Estonia."* Accessed on 12th April 2019 rom: https://rio.jrc.ec.europa.eu/en/library/rdi-strategy-knowledge-based-estonia-2014-2020

Finquelievich, S. (2017). *Rwanda Knowledge Society Policy Handbook, Ministry of Education, Republic of Rwanda, United Nations Educational, Scientific and Cultural Organization Information for All Programme (UNESCO/IFAP).* Available at: https://unesdoc.unesco.org/images/0026/002614/261450E.pdf

Finquelievich, S. (2017). *Policies for Knowledge Society in Rwanda- Training Manual.* Available at: https://www.un.org/sustainabledevelopment/development-agenda/

Government of Rwanda. (2017). *Science & Technology in Rwanda. Science, Technology, Research and Innovation in Support of Economic and Social Development in Rwanda.* Available at: https://mineduc.gov.rw/fileadmin/user_upload/pdf_files/STI_in_Rwanda_Booklet_prepared_for_TWAS27th_Annual_Meeting_Final-1.pdf

Internet Society Report. (n.d.). Available at http://www.internetsociety.org/map/global-internet-report/?gclid=CjwKEAjwqZ7GBRC1srKSv9TV_iwSJADKTjaDLsYP5zz0FXsbW8lbb2kwHuSLSKw-gV29zhTkyPcX6hoC8a7w_wcB#global-internet-penetration

Ministry of Information Technology and Communications, Republic of Rwanda. (2017). *ICT Sector Strategic Plan (2018-2024) "Towards digital enabled economy".* http://www.mitec.gov.rw/fileadmin/Documents/Strategy/ICT_SECTOR_STRATEGIC_PLAN__2018-2024_.pdf

Nchise, A., Boateng, R., Mbarika, V., Saiba, E., & Johnson, O. (2012). The challenge of taking baby steps—Preliminary insights into telemedicine adoption in Rwanda. *Journal Health Policy and Technology.* Available at: https://www.healthpolicyandtechnology.org/article/S2211-8837(12)00079-2/abstract

Ntirenganya, E. (2017). How technology is primed to transform farming in Rwanda. *The New Times.* Accessed on 6th January 2019 from: https://www.newtimes.co.rw/section/read/223291

OECD. (2005). *Glossary of Statistical Terms.* Accessed on 2nd May 2018 from: https://stats.oecd.org/glossary/detail.asp?ID=6864

Rwanda: Government Gives a Sneak Peek into Vision 2050 Blueprint. (n.d.). https://allafrica.com/stories/201612190503.html

Rwanda Information Society Authority. (2019). https://www.risa.rw/home/

UNESCO-Korean Republic Funds-in-Trust (KFIT) Project. (2017). *ICT Transforming Education in Africa*. Ministry of Education, Republic of Rwanda. https://unesdoc. unesco.org/images/0026/002614/261449E.pdf

Uwamiyara, M., Cremer, S., & Loebbecke, C. (2015). ICT for Economic Development in Rwanda: Fostering E-Commerce Adoption in Tourism SMEs. *Proceedings of SIG GlobDev Eighth Annual Workshop*. Available at: http://www.globdev.org/files/SigGlobDev_2015_paper_3_0.pdf

World Bank. (2017). *Ease of doing business index (1=most business-friendly regulations)*. Accessed on 1st November 2019 rom: https://data.worldbank.org/indicator/IC.BUS.EASE.XQ

World Economic Forum. (2019). https://www.weforum.org/agenda/2017/02/rwandas-digital-ambassadors-are-boosting-computer-literacy/

ENDNOTES

1 Masimba Tafirenyika, From Africa Renewal: April 2011, https://www.un.org/africarenewal/magazine/april-2011/information-technology-super-charging-rwandas-economy
2 ICT for Economic Development in Rwanda Proceedings of SIG GlobDev Eighth Annual Workshop, Fort Worth, Texas, USA, December 13, 2015
3 ICT for Economic Development in Rwanda Proceedings of SIG GlobDev Eighth Annual Workshop, Fort Worth, Texas, USA, December 13, 2015
4 Abinwi Nchise, Richard Boateng, Victor Mbarika, Eugene Saiba, Oryema Johnson, The challenge of taking baby steps—Preliminary insights into telemedicine adoption in Rwanda, Journal Health Policy and Technology, Elsevier, 2012/12/31, available at: https://www.healthpolicyandtechnology.org/article/S2211-8837(12)00079-2/abstract
5 See Zipline, https://jobs.lever.co/flyzipline/affad69a-2019-4e1b-8806-c5c544d16587
6 "Is Rwanda the testing market for latest digital health technology? | Digital health sector in Rwanda, " Dr. Hempel Digital Health Network, January 2018, available at https://www.dr-hempel-network.com/health-policies-in-india/digital-health-sector-in-rwanda/

7   Emmanuel Ntirenganya (December 2017): How technology is primed to transform farming in Rwanda, The New Times, available at https://www. newtimes.co.rw/section/read/223291

8   https://en.financialafrik.com/2018/06/27/rwanda-launch-of-30-million-fund-to-boost-ict-sector/

9   Source: World Economic Forum, https://www.weforum.org/agenda/2017/02/rwandas-digital-ambassadors-are-boosting-computer-literacy/

Chapter 4
Transforming and Facilitating Quality Education in Developing Knowledge Economy:
The Indian Perspective

Ekta Sinha
University of Mumbai, India

ABSTRACT

In 2015, world leaders gathered at the United Nations (UN) to adopt 17 Sustainable Development Goals to achieve several extraordinary things by 2030. Among these 17 goals of sustainable development, 'Quality Education' has been recognized as the fourth most important thing in order to transform our world. Obtaining a quality education is the foundation to improving people's lives and sustainable development. India, which is now one of the fastest growing economies of the world, is continuously thriving to transform and facilitate quality education for all, irrespective of the gender, caste, and socio-economic status to leverage county's demographic dividend. Such initiatives have been helpful in creating and sustaining a knowledge society and economy where people learn and build their capabilities to add value through knowledge development, improvement, and innovation. The efforts taken by India to improve the creation, storage, and dissemination of knowledge have helped her to build human capital and face the challenges of dynamic and ambiguous environment. This chapter discusses critical activities contributing to the desired change, highlights prevailing structural and socio-economic issues, and in the course of the analysis identifies some critical areas for improvement.

DOI: 10.4018/978-1-5225-8873-3.ch004

INTRODUCTION

"Education is not the learning of facts, but the training of the mind to think." ___ *Albert Einstein*

"The Highest education is that which does not merely give us information but makes our life in harmony with all existence." ___ *Rabindranath Tagore*

"If your plan is for one year, plant rice. If your plan is for ten years, plant trees. If your plan is for one hundred years, educate children." ___ *Kuan chung (7th century B.C.)*

In 2015, world leaders gathered at the United Nation (UN) to adopt 17 Sustainable Development Goals to achieve several extraordinary things by 2030 (Sustainable Development Goals, n.d.). Governments, businesses and civil society together with the United Nations are mobilizing efforts to achieve the Sustainable Development Agenda by 2030. Among these 17 goals of sustainable development, 'Quality Education' has been recognized as the fourth most important thing in order to transform our world. Obtaining a quality education is the foundation to improving people's lives and sustainable development (United Nations, n.d.).

A society and economy driven by quality education and eventually by knowledge stands strong in the changing economic and social landscape and is capable enough to cater human welfare. When delivered and absorbed well, education cures a host of societal ills. For individuals, it promotes employment, earnings, health, and poverty reduction. For societies, it spurs innovation, strengthens institutions, and fosters social cohesion. When we talk of education there are two major stakeholders – 'Students' and 'Teachers'. It's important to focus on both to make the process of learning smooth and fruitful. It is to be noted that Each additional year of education increases wages by an average of 10% and an extra year of school raises a country's GDP on average by 0.5% annually (Desai, 2014).

Today we talk of knowledge economies, which are helpful in creating an environment where people learn and build their capabilities to add value through knowledge development, improvement, and innovation (Drucker, 1993). Knowledge is the driving force in the rapidly changing globalized economy and society (Gupta and Gupta, 2012). But like every other country, in India also education is influenced by the existing culture and framework of the society. For example, women in India are supposed to play family-centric roles and take care of the family and household chores. This scenario exists in almost every segment of the society but is a little more practiced and believed in rural parts of the nation. Inclination towards government jobs is another social bias that exists in India. This mindset inhibits the culture of innovation and entrepreneurship. Some societal and cultural practices such as, early marriage of a girl child and large number of children in the underprivileged family (more the children, more the earning members) impact Indian education system. But slowly with the help of government interventions, we are coming out of that rigid structures. Efforts towards promoting girls' education, quality of education and entrepreneurial education have started bearing fruits. India as a country has realized the value of generation and dissemination of knowledge. According to Gupta and Gupta (2012), the emergence of India as a knowledge-based service driven economy has made its human capital its major strength and opportunity for growth. Unlike China or other Asian economic giants, India's growth has not been led by manufacturing. Instead, the nation's pool of skilled workers has allowed India to move quickly up the economic value chain in several knowledge-based industries such as, information technology and consulting.

The education system in India has come a long way of evolution – from the Vedic days dating back to around 1700 BC to today's computer age and e-learning. Indian Upanishad (Dasgupta, 2001) states that there are four forms of education: learning from the teachers, learnings through self-reflection and introspection, learning through peer interaction and learning in time context through experience. From discovering *"Zero"* to uncovering mysteries of astronomical science; from promoting ethical ways of living through *"Srimad Bhagwat Geeta"* to Kautilya's *"Arthashastra"* that teaches us the ethical code of conduct in administration and accounting rules: and from scientists like Chandrashekhar Venkat Raman to Srivivas Ramanujan, Indian tradition has always accorded special importance to education (Sankaran, 2012). Indian economy has witnessed tremendous growth in the literacy rate in past 73 years; after independence. According to the data from National Institution for Transforming India (NITI Aayog), which is based on the 2011 census reports, the literacy rate for male in India is 82.14% and for female it is 65.46% as compared to 75.26% and 53.67% respectively in the year 2001. The overall literacy rate in 2011 has been found to be 74.04% as compared to 64.84% in 2001.

Indian education system works at three levels: Primary, Secondary and Tertiary (Figure 1) while moving towards knowledge economy. There are basically four types of institutions to look after the development of primary (elementary), secondary and tertiary (higher) education: (1) Central Government (Funds for the education at any level comes from the central government), (2) State Government (Funds for the education at any level comes from the state government), (3) Local Bodies/ Institutions (Funds for the education at any level comes from the local bodies or institutions), and (4) Private Institutions (Funds for the education at any level comes from the private ownership), (Educational Administration in India, n.d.). There are provisions where government provide aids to the institutions but doesn't give full financial support. Apart from these three levels (primary, secondary and tertiary) India also has the system of 'Adult Education'.

Let's see them one by one.

Figure 1.

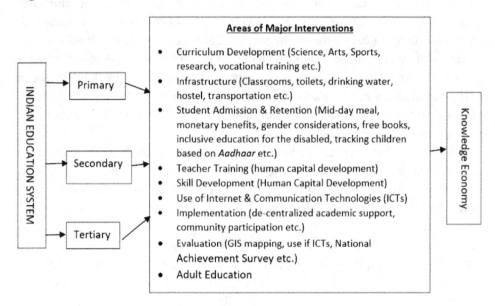

A. Primary or Elementary Education in India

There is a growing awareness, that expansion of primary education in terms of quality and quantity can't be resolved with a uniform and standard practice because of the diversity which exists. In particular, attracting and then retaining students in disadvantaged area is a big problem as testified by the low attendance and high drop-out rates (Govinda and Varghese, 1993; Maertens, 2013). This problem can be dealt with in two stages. First, to provide a network of schools for primary education in urban areas where demand is readily available and this stage is comparatively easy. Second, is to build a network of schools for primary education in those disadvantaged areas which, for some reasons like historical, economic and socio-cultural have been by-passed by the education developmental process. This stage is comparatively tough because only providing schools in those areas would not be enough rather it should be coupled with services that would correspond to the needs and living conditions of the disadvantaged groups.

In India the enrollment in primary education has increased due to the efforts made by the government. The Gross Enrolment Ratio (GER) for a class-group is the ratio of the number of persons in the class-group to the number of persons in the corresponding official age-group. Thrust on providing primary education has yielded results with the GER presently exceeding hundred. The progress is visible across the social categories and gender with GER for Scheduled Caste, Scheduled Tribe and girls shooting above hundred ("Educational statistics at a Glance", 2016). The GER for all persons in elementary education increased from 81.6% in 2000-01 to 96.9% (provisional figure) in 2014-15. At this level, the GER for boys and girls increased by 4.5 (from 90.3% to 94.8%) and 26.4 (from 72.4% to 99.2%) percentage point respectively during the stipulated period (Educational statistics at a glance, 2016).

In India the 'Right to education' (RTE) Act, 2009, confers the right to elementary education on all children, between age group of 6-14 years. The Act became operational in the country on 1st April, 2010 ("Ministry of Human Resource Development…", 2017, P- 30). According to the MHRD report 2016-17, the centrally (government of India) sponsored scheme of *Sarva Shiksha Abhiyan (SSA)*, which means *Education for all* Movement in English, supports states and union territories in their efforts to implement the RTE Act. Section 12(1)(C) of the RTE Act, mandates all private unaided schools and special category schools to reserve a minimum of 25% of seats for economically weaker sections. Under the SSA, the Government of India would reimburse the state expenditure towards 25% admissions to private unaided schools, based on per child cost norms notified by the state government, subject to a maximum ceiling of 20% of the size of the SSA annual work plan and budget. For the year 2016-17 the government expenditure towards this reimbursement was around 5,000 million, for around 1.2 million children. SSA interventions included, inter alia, opening of new schools and additional classrooms, constructing toilets and drinking water facilities, provisioning for teachers and academic resource support, free textbooks and uniforms, support for improving learning achievement levels, research, evaluation and monitoring. Such interventions have improved the primary enrolment for underprivileged children and have provided them with opportunities which would nurture their skill and knowledge. Following points give a brief description of the program interventions (MHRD report, 2016-17, pp 30-56): -

1. **Universal Access**: SSA is being implemented since 2001 for universalization of elementary education. Over the years 204,740 primary schools have been sanctioned. The RTE Act makes a specific provision for special training for age-appropriate admission for out-of-school children; children who discontinued their studies. Majority of out-of-school-children belong to disadvantaged communities, children with special needs, urban deprived children, children in other difficult circumstances (from difficult terrain, from displaced families and

areas affected by civil strife). SSA has a provision for residential facilities in sparsely populated or hilly and densely forested areas with difficult geographical terrains and in densely populated urban areas. SSA so far has provided 826 residential institutions with a capacity of around 90,855 children. Transportation or Escort facilities are also available for children in remote habitations or in urban areas where availability of land is a problem or children belonging to extremely deprived groups or children with special needs. For the year 2016-17, SSA had provided a provision of around 500 million for transport and escort facility to 0.161 million children. SSA also provides two sets of uniform to all girls and underprivileged children below poverty line (BPL). Provision of around 30 billion was made in the year 2016-17 towards providing free uniforms to 75,966,410 children.

2. **Bridging Gender Gaps in Elementary Education:** RTE-SSA provides a clear thrust and special focus on education for girls and children belonging to disadvantaged groups and weaker sections. Special training interventions are largely focused on girls and disadvantaged groups, because it is this category of children who are most deprived of opportunities to pursue their education. *Kasturba Gandhi Balika Vidyalaya* (KGBV), are residential schools for deprived girls and has been set up in educational backward blocks where schools are at great distances and are a challenge to the security of girls. There are 3600 functional KGBVs and construction of 215 KGBVs is in progress. Following the National Curriculum Framework (NCF), 2005 guidelines, states have consciously taken a decision to establish gender as a critical marker of transformation through increasing visual representation of girls and women and facilitating role reversals. Most of the states have incorporated the gender sensitization in their regular School Management Committee (SMC) training modules to deal with issues such as enrollment, retention, and completion of education of girls; creating suitable environment for girls in school and rapport with female teachers for discussing gender awareness. Department of School education and Literacy has prepared a Digital Gender Atlas (DGA) with the support of United Nations International Children's Emergency Fund

3. (UNICEF), which will help identify the low performing geographic pockets for girls, particularly from marginalized groups such as scheduled tribes and castes on specific gender related education indicators using government data such as Census 2011 and Unified district Information System for Education (U-DISE). The requirements of school infrastructure facilities have also been taken into consideration under SSA as well as availability of toilets and drinking water.

4. **Inclusive Education:** There is a positive trend of increased awareness among parents towards accessing education despite economic and social constraints.

Current efforts to promote elementary education among children from disadvantaged groups and weaker sections have been mix of both general efforts, which include: expanding infrastructure for physical access; incentives like uniform, books, cycles and tracking disaggregated data to reflect social groups. And specific/targeted efforts, which include: uniforms, books that were originally special provisions for disadvantaged children have been expanded to cover all children. RTE-SSA seeks to ensure that every child with special needs, irrespective of the kind, category and degree of disability is provided meaningful and quality education. The main components of SSA interventions for children with special needs include identification, functional and formal assessment, appropriate educational placement, preparation of individualized educational plan, provision of aids and appliances, teachers training, resource support, removal of architectural barriers, monitoring and evaluation and a special focus on girls with special needs.

5. **Improving Quality:** Department for Improving Quality of Elementary Education (DIQEE) has framed Grade-wise learning goals from class I-VIII are being framed and will be displayed on the notice board of all schools. It was decided that the National Achievement Survey would be conducted annually from 2017 instead of once in three years. This enabled regular assessment of learning levels of the children and helped to give insight into the pedagogical and policy changes required to improve these learning levels further. Grade-wise weak students would be identified for remedial classes. DIQEE has also framed guidelines for "Partnership between Schools" program with an aim of linking schools located in rural areas with private, aided or government schools in urban or semi-urban areas. The main objectives of the initiative include among other: to bring all students to one common platform, to share experiences and learn from each other, provide opportunities to the teaching fraternity to adopt better and more effective practices and to instill a spirit of sharing, caring and togetherness. All school going children in the age groups of 5 to 18 years in India are being covered under Aadhaar (a 12-digit unique identity number that can be obtained by residents of India, based on their biometric and demographic data). This would help in tracking of children so that they do not drop-out from school and also for monitoring their academic progress and for ensuring benefits to be disbursed to them in cash or kind under various schemes. Around 300 million children have already been covered under Aadhaar. The '*Padhe Bharat Badhe Bharat*' (in English "Educated India shall Progress"), a sub-program of the SSA, in class I and II focusing on foundational learning in early grades with an emphasis on reading, writing, comprehension and mathematics. The '*Rashtriya Aavishkar Abhiyan (RAA)*' (in English "National Invention Mission"), launched by late Dr. A. P. J. Abdul

Kalam, aims to motivate and engage children of the age group 6-18 years, in science, mathematics and technology by observation, experimentation, inference drawing and model building through both inside and outside classroom activities. Schools have been adopted for mentoring by Institutions of higher education like Indian Institute of Technology (IITs) and National Institute of Technology (NITs). In some states students have been taken for exposure visits to factories and research hubs. the total funding towards this initiative in 2016-17 was around two billion.

6. **Teacher Training:** Teachers are integral part of education system and to ensure their availability and quality should be the prime importance for any nation. To meet the shortage of teachers in elementary schools, around 2 million additional teacher posts have been sanctioned under SSA up to 2016-17. To upgrade skills of teachers, SSA provides for annual in-service training up to 20 days for all teachers. Some monetary benefits are also provided for the same. All training programs cover pedagogical issues, including content and methodology, aimed at improving teaching learning transactions in classrooms and learning process in schools. Training to improve managerial skills are also provided to the heads of schools for ten days. Capacity building of institutions and personnel in designing, developing, producing and delivering distance learning inputs and materials training of untrained teachers at the national, state, district and sub-district levels is being facilitated with assistance of Indira Gandhi National Open University (IGNOU) and other teacher education institutions in different states. The government of India had approved establishment of 75 district institutes of education and training, 16 colleges of teacher education, and seven institutes of advanced studies in education around the country in the year 2016-17. Additionally, block level institutes have been sanctioned to train teachers for minority and backward communities in different parts of the country. Teachers are research frontiers in their knowledge domains and thus well-equipped teachers would lead the knowledge economy based on knowledge creation and its proper dissemination.

7. **Academic Support System:** With the setup of 6,759 Block Resource Centers (BRCs) and 76,064 Cluster Resource Centers (CRCs), till September 2016 across the country, decentralized academic support, training and supervision to teachers and schools are being provided efficiently and effectively. Subject specific resource persons also visit schools to provide on-site training and support to teachers on pedagogic and content related issues. Under SSA grant up to 5 million is available to each district for strengthening computer aided learning in schools to support enhancement of children's learning. These enhancements aim at specifically improving the quality of learning processes and learning outcomes.

8. **School Management Committees & Community Participation:** SSA has always acknowledged the importance of 'community ownership' pertaining to effective functioning of government schools. As per norms it has been made mandatory for the schools to constitute School Management Committees (SMC) wherein the parents/guardians of students studying in the respective school are the members. It is worth mentioning that states and union territories have prepared their own training modules which are in different languages namely Bodo, Bengali, Assamese, Hindi, English, Gujarati and other local dialects according to the need. These SMCs look after enrolment, retention and completion of education of children, create suitable environment for girl students in school, effective utilization of funds provided either by government or received in the form of donation, monitoring the attendance of the students and teachers.

9. **Monitoring Institutes:** Only planning and excellent ideas on paper don't work unless implemented. And to ensure the proper implementation and functioning, evaluation is important. Institutions, including universities departments of education, social sciences and institutes of national stature have been assigned the work of periodic monitoring of SSA implementation in state and union territories. These monitoring institutes are required to make field visits and report on progress of SSA at the ground level every six months. This would result into better functioning.

10. **Mid-Day Meal:** Child malnutrition is a common problem in many developing countries, and there is a large amount of evidence that well-nourished children have better educational outcomes (Glewwe et al., 2013). With a view to enhance attendance and retention and simultaneously to improve the nutritional status of children, a centrally sponsored scheme of "Mid-day meal" was launched in 1995. This covered all school children studying in I-VIII classes in government and government-aided schools, special training centers, madarsas and maqtabs supported under SSA. Mid-Day meal addresses two major problems for children in India, viz. hunger and education. By improving the nutritional status of children studying in class I-VIII, the scheme encourages poor children to attend classes regularly and concentrate on classroom activities. Studies have shown that the impact of school meal on time in school are statistically significant (Damon et. Al., 2016, p: 45).

11. **Schemes for providing quality education in Madarsas:** Ministry of Human resource Development, Government of India, lays emphasis on providing equal opportunities to minorities (Muslims) as far as access to education is concerned. For the purpose, the ministry encourages madarsas/maktabs/dar-ul-uloom to introduce formal subjects i.e. science, mathematics, social studies, Hindi and English. They can opt to become accredited study centers with National Institute

of Open Schooling (NIOS). Children above 14 years are given opportunities to attain vocational training. Funding under such schemes are provided by central as well state governments to madarsas.

With improvement in the number of schools, facilities in schools and enrolment, the annual dropout rate at primary level has come down by 1.28 percentage point (from 5.62% in 2011-12 to 4.34% in 2013-14) for all categories of students. At this level, the dropout rate for boys and girls decreased by 1.36 (from 5.89% to 4.53%) and 1.2% (from 5.34% to 4.14%) percentage point respectively during this period (Educational statistics at a Glance, 2016). Such interventions, be it providing scholarship, building infrastructure and providing mid-day meals have resulted into increased elementary enrolments of students. A Study by Friedman et al. (2011) has also indicated that such interventions help in increasing participation. Emphasis on science, arts, math, technology, research & sports would result into holistic development of the students and this would help them learn better resulting into knowledge which could be applied suitably in emerging economy like India to create wealth (Drucker, 1993). However, even as we contemplate with satisfaction the above remarkable achievements, there is a need to improve quality education in schools, especially in rural areas. To assess area-wise learning outcomes in four subjects viz. English, Mathematics, Science and Social Science, it has been observed that in all subjects, urban students outperform rural students by a large margin.

B. Secondary Education in India

Secondary education is very important for the developing countries as it orients the target population towards, learning and building skilled human capital for the society and economy. Due to the increase in the primary enrollment, secondary education has also expanded. Also, indirect demand for secondary education is fueled by the demand for a highly skilled labor force in the global economy. However, access to secondary education without any bias has always been a challenge in India. There are several steps that the government of India has taken in order to make secondary education pervasive. For faster economic growth, it is not sufficient to exclusively concentrate on primary education. It is evidenced that early expansion of, and public investment in secondary education paid rich dividends in East Asia (World Bank, 1993, Tilak, 2001). Hence, secondary education is crucial for economic growth. Also, investment in secondary education yields considerable social and private returns, offering young people the chance to acquire attitudes and skills which in turn enables youth to develop job-oriented skills, participate fully in society, take control of their own lives, and continue learning (Lewin and Caillods, 2001; Duraisamy, 2002), hence creating knowledge economies driven by research and entrepreneurship.

Secondary education has a more significant effect on the redistribution of income, growth and reducing poverty than primary education (Tilak, 1989, 2005). Reforms in OECD countries during the early 1970s led to lower secondary education becoming compulsory and a part of basic education. Further, compulsory schooling age was set at 5-16 years during 1980s. The general focus was on improving the quality and relevance of education and redefining the role and responsibility of public education in the knowledge-based economy (Bregman, 2003).

To improve the state of secondary education in India, Government of India took the following initiatives: -

Rashtriya Madhyamik Shiksha Abhiyan (RMSA): The movement was initiated to improve the state of secondary education in India. it was launched in 2009. The scheme envisages to enhance the enrolment at secondary stage by providing a secondary school with a reasonable distance of habitation, with an aim to ensure GER of 100% by 2017-18 and universal retention by 2020. Important. This scheme provided, additional classrooms, laboratories, libraries, art and crafts room, toilet blocks, drinking water provisions, electricity/telephone/internet connectivity etc. Improvement in quality through appointment of additional qualified teachers, Internet and Communications Technologies (ICT) enabled education, curriculum reforms and teaching learning reforms, were ensured. Programmatic Support from external funding agencies to RMSA: The world bank, Department for international development (DFID) and European Union committed to extend their support to the implementation of the RMSA program during 2012-16. They provided support to the tune of 80 million pounds. For the year 2016-17, a total budgetary allocation of 30.7 billion had been made for integrated RMSA scheme. Under RMSA following significant initiatives have been taken to improve the quality of education: -

1. **Shaala Siddhi (National Program on School standard and evaluation):** It is a comprehensive instrument for school evaluation leading to school improvement. Developed by the national University of Educational Planning and Administration (NUEPA), it aims to enable schools to evaluate their performance in a more focused and strategic manner and help them to improve on the basis of evaluation reports. The program aims at establishing a set of standards and benchmarks for each school, by focusing on key performance domains. The results of the evaluations would be available on a public platform along with the school report card. According to the annual report (2016-'17) by the Ministry of Human Resource Development (2017), this program has been implemented in 25 states and union territories covering 25438 schools.

2. **Shala Darpan (School Management System):** This program was launched in 2015, with an objective to provide services based on school management systems to students, parents and communities. Under school information services,

the following list of services would be enabled: school profile management, student profile management, employee information, student attendance, leave management, report cards, curriculum tracking custom, SMS alerts for parents/administrators on student and teacher attendance. During the year, 2016-17, 3224 schools had been approved for implementing school management project on a pilot basis. This will ensure better and transparent administration in the school.

3. **Geographic Information System (GIS) Mapping:** To ensure universal access to schools including secondary schools within a reasonable distance of any habitation and without any discrimination, the geographic coordinates of schools along with school information available on Unified District Information System for Education (U-DISE->a database of information about schools in India). All states have conducted GIS mapping and shared geographical coordinates of schools with the National Information Centre (NIC) except the state of Jammu and Kashmir. This effort would add to the quality of planning and better utilization of resources available under SSA and RMSA. As per the MHRD report (2016-17), as on 31.12.2016, against the total of 1,522,925 (as per U-DISE 2015-16), 1,256,551 (81.55%) schools had been mapped on GIS portal.

4. **National Achievement Survey for class Tenth:** This kind of survey was undertaken by MHRD for the first time, in 2016. The survey investigated students' achievements in five subjects: English, Mathematics, Social Science, Science and Modern Indian Languages through a test based on robust scientific methods and rigorous adherence to technical procedures. In depth analysis of achievement scores and background variables (independent variables responsible for student's performance, e.g.- infrastructure and teacher) gives policy makers and curriculum developers and others better insights and accordingly, teachers training (pre-service and in-service) program would be designed to improve pedagogical aspects in relation to different subjects. Also, give states an idea about necessary curriculum reforms.

5. **Kala Utsav (Art Festival):** Is an initiative by MHRD to promote arts (music, theater, dance, visual arts and crafts) in education by nurturing and showcasing the artistic talent of school students at secondary stage in the country, for inclusive development. As part of 'Kala Utsav', competitions in the four themes of music, dance, theater and visual arts were held at district and state levels and the winning teams thereafter participated in the national level 'Kala Utsav 2016'.

6. **Focus on Science and Math:** Besides the focus on arts, Science and Math are being given equal importance. Under 'Rashtriya Avishkaar Abhiyan' (RAA), training of teachers, Science and Math kit, excursion trips to science centers and

museum for students, special teaching on science and math, science exhibition at district level and teaching of vedic math have been included. During the 2016-17 financial year, approx. 1.6 billion had been approved for the same.

7. **National Award for teachers using ICT for innovation in Education:** Under the ICT in schools, to promote computer enabled learning and usage of ICT in teaching in Government and Government aided secondary and higher secondary schools has provision for the above award to motivate teachers and educators for innovative use of ICT in teaching and learning.

According to Mouzakitis (2010), effective vocational education and training curriculum based on market research could play a significant role in today's age of globalization to meet challenges of dynamic environment. Thus, apart from the above-mentioned initiatives, Government of India has also introduced a centrally sponsored scheme of 'Vocationalization of Secondary and Higher secondary education'. The specific objectives of this scheme are to enhance the employability of youth through demand driven competency based, modular vocational courses, to maintain their competitiveness through provisions of multi-entry multi-exit learning opportunities and vertical mobility/interchange ability in qualifications; to fill the gap between educated and employable; and to reduce the dropout rate at the secondary level. The revised scheme while introducing vocational education at the secondary level, seeks to integrate vocational education with general education and provide horizontal and vertical mobility to the students. It envisages close partnership with the industry in the design, development, delivery, assessment and certification of skills content. Till 2016-17, 7448 schools have been covered under various vocational training programs under various areas such as: agriculture, apparel, automobile, beauty and wellness, banking services, construction, electronics, health, IT, logistics, media and entertainment. however, for the above training programs to be achieved there is a need to attract and retain more students, specially girl students. To do so, there is a centrally sponsored scheme of construction and running of girls' hostel for secondary and higher secondary schools. This provides girls with equal opportunity to continue their studies even if their schools are at a distance, parents' financial conditions and other social factors.

'National means-cum-merit scholarship' scheme has been constituted in order to support and award scholarships to meritorious students of economically weaker sections to arrest their dropout and encourage their studies at secondary and higher secondary level (Friedman et al., 2011). As examined by Karthick and Prakash (2013), in India, funds offered to families to purchase bicycles for their girl child so that their secondary school daughters could ride them to attend school, increased secondary school enrollment on average by 5.2 percentage points, and for girls who

lived more than three kilometers from the nearest school, the impact was about 9 percentage points.

A major scheme which encourages inclusive education for the disabled at the secondary stage is the scheme of 'Inclusive education for disabled at secondary stage' (IEDSS). The main objective of this scheme is to enable all students with disabilities, to pursue their secondary and higher secondary studies. The scheme includes assistance for two major components i.e. a) Assessment of medical/ educational needs- Provision of student specific facilities, like assistive devices, therapeutic service, books support services and development of learning material. b) Other Components include- appointment of special educators, special pay for general teachers trained in special education, constructions and equipping of resource rooms and making schools barrier free.

C. Higher Education in India

Typically, education reform that is targeted on serving knowledge-based economies emphasizes mathematics and science, information and communication technologies, basic knowledge and skills in literacy and development of interpersonal skills (Sahlberg, 2006). Moreover, a successful knowledge economy also requires advanced secondary and tertiary education provision able to boost labor productivity, research and innovation (Anon, 2004; World Bank, 2005). Higher education in India is of significant importance as successful knowledge economies compete on the basis of high value, not only low cost and high value is best guaranteed by well-trained and educated personnel and ñexible lifelong learning opportunities for all citizens (Sahlberg, 2006). The most frequently presented general idea for increasing economic competitiveness is to equip people with the skills and attitudes for economic and civic success in an increasingly knowledge-based economy (Hargreaves, 2003; Schweke, 2004).

India has the world's largest higher education system and it ranks second in terms of student enrolment in higher education. According to 2017 statistics, India has 35.7 million people enrolled in higher education (Indian Brand Equity Foundation, 2018). The Indian higher education system has undergone rapid expansion. During the year 2016-17 there were 795 Universities (47 Central,123 Deemed, 360 State Public, 262 State Private and 3 Institutions under Special State Legislature Act) and 42,338 Colleges, thus registering an increase of 38.74% in the number of universities and 19.13% increase in colleges ("University Grant Commission Annual Report", 2016-17). In recent years, India has undertaken massive structural and systemic changes that have started to yield encouraging results. According to a report titled, 'Higher Education in India: Vision 2030' (2013) by Federation of Indian Chambers of Commerce and Industry (FICCI), India consciously moved to a differentiated academic system with a three-tiered structure comprising of highly selective elite research universities at the top, comprehensive universities and specialized institutions in the middle, and an array of highly-accessible and high-quality colleges at the bottom.

1. **The first tier** is dedicated to further India's intellectual capital. They are centers of excellence for the creation of new knowledge, in research output and intellectual property. A selective set of talented, research-oriented students are taught by stellar faculty. Faculty and students at the university attract handsome research grants and nurture the greatest international diversity. Going beyond traditional scientific and applied research, these universities have exceptionally broadened the scope of India's research capabilities to new interdisciplinary areas which provide opportunity for the creation of new knowledge, relevant for India in the changing environment. For example, Indian universities are focusing on research in bioscience, climate change, leadership and inclusive development. Leveraging their cost and competitive advantage, Indian research universities have pioneered the model of blended research where they collaborate to produce cutting-edge research with other top-rank universities around the world. Further, these universities reach out to millions of other students through the Massive Open Online Courses (MOOCs) model.

2. **The second tier** of industry-aligned professional education institutions has seen the greatest growth over the last two decades. Focused on quality teaching and producing highly employable graduates, these institutions are a passport to white-collar jobs in a knowledge economy (Higher Education in India: Vision 2030 report, 2013). Such institutions use a perfect blend of technical knowledge and critical thinking and problem-solving skills to produce well-rounded industry leaders. Student learning outcomes are centre stage to this model. In effect, when a civil engineer educated under this model sets out to build a bridge he would not only approach it from an engineering angle, but would also assess the environmental impact of building the bridge, the socio-economic impact of improved infrastructure, the financing of the bridge and possibly all the related regulatory hurdles to be overcome to get the plans approved. The curricular focus in these institutions is on content delivery than on content creation, where faculty borrow from the best open courseware and customize it to the needs of their students (Higher Education in India: Vision 2030 report, 2013). Apart from experienced, research driven faculties, these universities draw experienced practitioners and industry professionals who are subject matter experts and can act as mentors to students in the early stages of their professional careers.

3. **The last cluster of highly-accessible universities** has been established to expand the reach of higher education to all eligible and deserving students

in the country. A wide range of courses aim to provide a holistic education to masses, and promote equity and access. Their distinguishing characteristic is a varied pool of students with significant regional, linguistic and cultural diversity. These colleges offer both part-time and full-time options.

4.   India has also developed an **Open University system** to encourage distance learning. Indira Gandhi National Open University (IGNOU) was the pioneer and now there are 14 open universities in India (Open Universities in India, 2019).

5.   Introduction to **'Choice Based Credit System'**, is one of the major measures taken by University Grant Commission (UGC- A Statutory Organization established for the promotion and coordination of University Education and for the determination of teaching, examination, research and extension in universities and maintenance of standards. Also provides grants to colleges & universities). This aims to enhance academic standards and quality in higher education through innovation & improvement in curriculum, teaching-learning process, examination and evaluation system. This system aims to ensure seamless mobility of students across the higher educational institutions in the country as well as abroad. This system gives students freedom to take courses of their choice, learn at their own pace, undergo additional courses and develop an interdisciplinary approach to learning (Ministry of Human Resource Development, 2017)

6.   UGC has also identified fifteen universities for granting the status of **'University with Potential for Excellence'**. UGC has been assisting these identified universities in teaching and in developing research culture in colleges. For the year 2015-16 around 800 million was released to colleges (Ministry of Human Resource Development, 2017) in order to setup a better teaching and research environment.

The differentiated system offers students a wider variety of unique and quality programs at both graduate and undergraduate levels. It clarifies student choices and effectively caters to a heterogeneous student population with varying needs and demands, while also providing them the option for inter-institution mobility through system wide credit transfer. In this way, while planned expansion has helped create capacity for ever-increasing numbers, the differentiated system has been instrumental in directing these numbers to the right stream and the appropriate kind of institution in order to effectively meet the needs of Indian society. Lastly, planned expansion has also helped solve for the problem of infrastructure and resources. Riding the wave of urban planning, India earmarked tracts of land in many tier-II cities to create 'education cities' which have today emerged to be thriving inner-city university campuses tightly integrated with their host cities. Unlike the erstwhile ideal of a mono-functional and isolated green-field campus removed from the city, providing academics and students the distance to reflect on humanity, these campuses are located in the heart of the city. They share a close relationship with the host city and are embedded in 'knowledge ecosystems' enabling them to perform better ("Higher Education…", 2013). Today we have 20 Indian Institute of Management (IIM), 23 Indian Institute of Technologies (IITs), and more than 25 National Institute of Technology (NITs). All these institutes nurture best minds to excel, innovate, research and transform economy through knowledge accumulation and dissemination.

ADULT EDUCATION

According to The International Standard Classification of Education (**ISCED**) 2011, adult education specifically targets individuals who wish to improve their technical or professional qualifications, further develop their abilities, enrich their knowledge with the purpose to complete a level of formal education, or to acquire knowledge, skills and competencies in a new field or to refresh or update their knowledge in a particular field. This also includes what may be referred to as 'continuing education', 'recurrent education' or 'second chance education'.

Apart from the three-tier educational structure, namely: primary, secondary and higher, there is one more wing of the Indian education system, to keep the flight of literacy soaring high- 'Adult Education'. According to the 2001 census report, male literacy was at 75.26%, while female literacy remained at an unacceptable level of 53.67% (MHRD, Department of School Education and Literacy, 2016). This improved tremendously in 2011 with a literacy rate of 82.14% for males and 65.46% for females (National Institution for Transforming India, 2011 census report on literacy). Undoubtedly, 'Adult Education' helped in achieving this stride via targeting primarily illiterate population. The focus is on imparting basic literacy. National Literacy Mission Authority (NLMA) has been set up as an independent and autonomous wing of the department of secondary education and literacy to promote literacy and adult education. It organizes workshops, conferences, mounts audio/video spots along with local language subtitles on prime slots of national and regional channels of TV and radio to create awareness among the target group.

ROLE OF DIGITIZATION IN EDUCATION

Indian education system at all the three levels have seen great rise, in terms of capacity building. To cater the demands of the increasing population and to improve administration of quality education, the role of technology has been crucial. There have been many strides that the government of India has taken to achieve access, equity and quality, one of them happens to be technology interventions. The 'DIGITAL INDIA' mission has been launched in the year 2015 to boost the digital access and connectivity in India to achieve greater transparency, efficiency and effectiveness. According to the report 'Higher Education in India: Vision 2030' (2013), by FICCI, the Indian higher education system has undergone massive expansion to become the largest in the world enrolling over 70 million students. Such expansion would have been unimaginable without the extensive use of ICT tools. To illustrate, if India were to create this additional capacity through increase in brick and mortar institutions alone, it would have had to build six universities and 270 colleges each and every month in the last 20 years – a feat that would have been impossible to achieve with India's limited resources. Instead, India chose to go the Massive Open Online Courses (MOOCs) way. Online platforms and ICT tools have helped take higher education to millions of deserving students in far-flung areas who would otherwise have no access to university education. Online education has become the first port of call for many students who were earlier left out of the higher education system, or had to settle for lower quality alternatives. The MOOCs model made it possible for the country to provide a quality education to the masses despite poor faculty-student ratios. Students today increasingly learn from leading faculty at elite institutions beyond the four walls of their classrooms as top-tier institutions have donned the mantle of being content generators. Professors collaborate across universities to collectively create and distribute for-credit curriculum for an online semester. Technology has not only been instrumental in addressing the demand-supply gap for quality education, but has fundamentally changed the nature of several educational processes. Gone are the days when students had to gather in a large hall only to hear a lecture. Today, classroom lectures and pre-recorded and uploaded to be accessed by students at their comfort. Class time is instead used for creating more in-depth learning experiences through group activities, problem solving and interactive learning. Online analytics provide faculty with data on how and at what pace each student is learning, enabling them to provide personalized support to aid student learning outcomes. The model also acts as a great democratize, allowing students to learn at their own pace – for instance, slow learners can go over certain content and exercises multiple times with special tools to aid their learning. Finally, the hybrid model (where part of the program is taught online and part in person) has become particularly popular among adult and working professionals looking to gain additional credentials. The model provides them with the flexibility to access course material as their schedule permits. In short, technology has been nothing short of disruptive for Indian higher education, solving for three of India's pressing problems – access, equity and quality - at once. This online education facilitates life-long and self-paced learning in order to develop 'human capital' (Sinha &

Bagarukayo, 2019), thus, contributing towards knowledge-based economy which foster creativity, rationality, flexibility and co-operation to strengthen economic competitiveness and support continuous growth.

Let's view some of the major technology interventions taken up by the Government of India, to improve Indian education system:

1. **National Mission on Education through Information and Communication technology (ICT):** the mission aims at providing high quality, personalized and interactive knowledge modules over the internet/intranet for the learners. The contents are being provided at low cost to the students. The mission also bridges the gap in skills needed to use the digital platforms for the purpose of teaching and learning. It plans to focus on appropriate pedagogy for e-learning, providing virtual laboratories to perform and experiment, on-line tests and certification, on-line availability of teachers for guiding and mentoring students and launch of fifty 24*7 direct-to-home (DTH) channels to deliver almost all the courses. Also, *SAKSHAT* is envisaged as one stop education portal to facilitate lifelong learning for the students, teachers and for all those who want to gain knowledge.

2. **Campus Connectivity:** A total of 438 universities have been connected through 1 Gbps optical fiber; 2,2026 colleges have so far been connected with 10 Mbps bandwidth. For 69 universities Local Area Network (LAN) work has been completed (Ministry of Human Resource Development, 2017). For campus connect, government share for each of the university & college in North-East region is 90% and for other states and union territories it is 75%. The remaining has to be paid by the respective institutions. The shares are being disseminated after performing the feasibility study.

3. **Integrated e-content Portal:** An integrated e-content portal named- e-acharya has been developed for all e-content projects, developed/funded under the National Mission of Education through ICT. There are more than 50 projects on e-content on various subject disciplines (Arts, science, Social-Science and Engineering) various Indian institutions. According to Ministry of Human Resource Development (2017), about 19,656 e-texts, 29,824 e-tutorials, 5,449 self-assessments, 9,217 web resources have been uploaded on the platform which includes 36,432 courses for under graduates and 12,813 courses for post graduate.

4. **Study Webs of Active Learning for Young Aspiring Minds (SWAYAM):** As per 'Digital India' initiative there has been greater thrust on developing and making available, Massive Online Open Courses (MOOCs) to the learners throughout the country. In-line with the above intension, SWAYAM was launched in 2017. This intends to provide integrated platform and portal for

online courses, using ICT and covering all secondary (9th class onwards) and higher education subjects and skill sector courses to ensure that every student in the country has access to the best quality higher education at affordable cost. The courses hosted on SWAYAM are developed in four quadrants- (i) Video lecture; (ii) Specially prepared reading material; (iii) Web resources; (iv) Self-assessment tests through tests and quizzes. SWAYAM courses are now open to foreign students also.

5.   **Global Initiative of Academic Networks (GIAN):** GIAN, promotes foreign collaborations in higher education. On selective basis foreign universities are allowed to contribute online courses on SWAYAM.

6.   **Talk to Teacher:** It is developed by IIT Mumbai, and is an initiative by the government to provide free access to a few selected graduate and postgraduate courses, taught at IIT Mumbai by distinguished faculty members and scholars at large. These courses can be accessed on a personal computer at a lower bandwidth.

7.   **Ask a Question:** This is a unique platform where students from science and engineering colleges all over India can ask questions and faculty from IIT Mumbai answers them. These questions can be asked during live interactive session or through online forum.

8.   **National Digital Library (NDL):** This library aims to integrate all the existing e-content available across educational institutions in the country. This will provide a single window access to different group of users. NDL does not store the full text rather it provides users with the links of respective content hosting sites. According to the statistics by Ministry of Human Resource Development (2017), there are 6,423,000 resources available on the portal and around half a million students are registered.

9.   **e-Yantra (Electronic Machines):** This initiative has been implemented to incorporate robotics into engineering education with the objective of engaging students through exciting hands-on application of mathematics, computer science and engineering principles. All the projects and code are available on e-Yantra website as open source content. Various initiatives under this program include: e-Yantra robotics competition, e-Yantra Summer Internship Program, e-Yantra Lab Setup Initiatives, e-Yantra Symposium and e-Yantra Resource Development Centre.

10. **Vidwan (A person with intelligence and wisdom):** The objectives of this scheme is to i) collect academic and research profiles of scientists and faculties working in leading academic and R&D organizations in India and abroad; ii) provide information about experts to peers, prospective collaborators, funding agencies, policy makers and research scholars in the country and establish communication between them; iii) identify peer reviewers for review of articles

and research proposals. The database aims to provide links to experts who can be selected for various committees and taskforces, established for monitoring and evaluation purposes.

11.   **Direct Benefit Transfer:** Digitization has helped the government to transfer monetary benefits like, grants under various schemes/ programs launched for primary, secondary and tertiary mode of education, directly to individuals' bank accounts electronically, minimizing tiers involved in fund flow, thereby reducing delays in payments, ensuring accurate targeting of the beneficiary and avoiding duplication.

The Digital India movement has made it possible for the citizens of India to engage qualitatively using digital platforms. The online platform also facilitates the education of girl student and minority group. The reach of such digital platforms has broken the geographical, economical and socio-cultural barriers. A study by Sinha and Bagarukayo (2019) reflected that learners utilize online digital platforms to up-scale their existing knowledge and to learn something new. The study also showed that learners valued the availability of world-class instructors and the convenience with which they could take up various courses. However, the study reflected that lack of personal attention and awareness were sources of considerable hindrance among Indian learners. The knowledge society is a learning society in which economic development and competitiveness depend on the will and skill of workers to keep on learning alone and from one another (Sahlberg, 2006) and ICTs based online education certainly helps to achieve this motive. Knowledge is most important factor of production in knowledge economies. ICTs provide a cost-effective and faster way to build capacity among learners by creating, storing and transmitting knowledge in a timely manner. Thus, facilitating a rapid globalization of economic activity in knowledge economies.

OTHER INTERVENTIONS IN ORDER TO TRANSFORM & FACILITATE QUALITY EDUCATION

Apart from the above-mentioned schemes, missions and programs there are some other major interventions that have been taken in order to improve, facilitate and transform the quality & availability of education in India across sections and tiers. They are as follows: -

1.   **National Skill development Mission (NSDM):** The National Skill Development Mission was launched in 2015. The Mission has been developed to create convergence across sectors and States in terms of skill training activities.

Further, to achieve the vision of 'Skilled India', the NSDM would not only consolidate and coordinate skilling efforts, but also expedite decision making across sectors to achieve skilling at scale with speed and standards. Seven sub-missions have been proposed initially to act as building blocks for achieving overall objectives of the Mission. They are: (i) Institutional Training; (ii) Infrastructure; (iii) Convergence; (iv) Trainers; (v) Overseas Employment; (vi) Sustainable Livelihoods; (vii) Leveraging Public Infrastructure (Ministry of Skill Development and Entrepreneurship, n.d.). The mission also aims at proving students with necessary technical and soft skills that enable them to become an entrepreneur and thus be job-givers rather than job-seekers.

2. **Standardized tests for Admissions:** Standardized tests have been introduced to streamline the process of screening and further admissions to various courses. Such standardization allows students to escape multiple exams to get a seat for the same course. Also, they just pay once and hence their expenditure is reduced. Every candidate all over India will have an equal opportunity of getting selected. It also induces greater transparency. The only drawback is, India being a culturally diverse country there are some language issues among the learners of various states. Though the usefulness of such tests has been questioned many times, their ubiquity globally is prompted by a variety of economic and political factors. Developed countries lead the world in producing and dispensing standardized tests to enhance education and eventual workforce productivity. While emerging economies follow the lead with the appeal of simplicity and cost-effectiveness (Wilcox and Ryder, 2002)

3. **Inclusion of sports:** Apart from paying considerable attention to studies and making it available for all, India has paid immense consideration towards development of sports also, within every tier of education system. As the importance of sports and fitness in one's life is invaluable. Playing sports inculcates team spirit and develops strategic thinking, analytical thinking, leadership skills, goal setting and risk taking. A fit and healthy individual leads to an equally healthy society and strong nation. "*Khelo India*" (India Shall Play), is a nation-wide mission to promote sports education and rather than calling it as extra-curricular activity, emphasis is on making it a core curricular activity.

4. **Revival of an ancient University:** Revival of the world's oldest university in Bihar, 'Nalanda University' (NU) became the headline of every major national and international newspaper, as for over 800 years NU was one of the best universities in the world. Students from across the globe came here to study in one of the greatest libraries in the world (Pareek, 2014). It used to be the original center of Buddhist religion, culture, and enlightenment. Nalanda drew students not only from all over India, but also from China, Japan, Korea,

Sumatra, and other Asian lands with Buddhist connections, and a few from elsewhere, including Turkey (Pareek, 2014). It was the only institution of higher learning outside China to which any Chinese in the ancient world ever went for education. After more than eight hundred years of successful teaching, Nalanda was destroyed in the 1190s by invading armies from West Asia, which also demolished the other universities in Bihar (Nalanda University, n.d.). It was a completely residential university believed to have 2,000 teachers and 10,000 students (Nalanda University, n.d.). Revival of the university of this stature was surely challenging but reviving the same culture of quality education would encourage cooperation and interchange of ideas across national borders, major characteristics on knowledge economies. The university was established by an act of the Indian Parliament in 2010 (Sen, 2015). There is also a proposal to revive another ancient university, 'Vallabhi University' in Gujarat (Rupera, 2017).

5. **Reviving indigenous practices:** No country can develop san nurturing its traditional heritage and practices. India also took cognisance of the fact and formed Ministry of AYUSH in the year 2014, with the aim of developing, education and research in ayurveda (Indian traditional medicine), yoga, naturopathy, unani, siddha, homoeopathy, Sowa Rigpa (Traditional Tibetan medicine) and other Indigenous medicine systems (Ministry_of Ayush, 2017). The *National Education Policy 2020,* also emphasises on promoting regional languages in school education so that heritage can be saved. India has recognised 22 languages in its constitution as scheduled languages for official encouragement.

IMPLICATIONS OF VARIOUS INTERVENTIONS IN DEVELOPING A KNOWLEDGE ECONOMY

Above mentioned measures have and are expected to contribute immensely towards improving existing education system in India by transforming and facilitating quality education. We need to understand that schooling or enrolling in formal education does not necessarily promote learning. Schooling is different from learning. Thus, it's important to outline and focus on the outcomes and processes that ensure education imparts learning (World Bank education Report, 2018) and above-mentioned interventions aims towards the same. These interventions have not only made education accessible to all without any bias of gender, caste and religion but have also used well-designed tools for student assessments to gauge the health of education systems and promotes classroom innovation. Education at all levels, and especially higher education, with its potential to enhance productivity through research is seen as the global panacea to economic policy. As one of the major areas of public policy investment, governments around the world, in both advanced and developing economies, are restructuring education systems, often in transparent terms that reflect the new policy template of the 'knowledge economy' (Peters & Humes, 2003).

Education anywhere should equip students to learn how to interpret types of written passages—from medication labels to job offers, from bank statements to great literature. They should understand how numbers work so that they can buy and sell in markets, set family budgets, interpret loan agreements, or write engineering software. They must have the higher-order reasoning and creativity that builds on these foundational skills. And they should have the socio-emotional skills—such as perseverance and the ability to work in teams—that help them acquire and apply the foundational and other skills (world education report, 2018), and only then will they be able to embrace the two major trends towards knowledge economy. First, globalization, which facilitates free trade, exchange of ideas, human resources and technologies across nations with falling cost and rising efficiency in transmission, retrieval and analysis of information and knowledge. Second, innovation, which again in particular has become a national determinant of wealth and the basis of comparative advantage. While knowledge is instrumental in improving the efficiency of production and distribution processes, it also helps to build quality and quantity of products. Further, it also helps to increase the choice of products and services for consumers and producers (Peters and Humes, 2003). India has taken great efforts to ensure proper creation, storage and dissemination of knowledge by facilitating quality education and making it available to each and every learner despite of their location, gender, socio-economic status and age. Learners who thought they were too old to learn anything are now picking up necessary skills to upgrade themselves. The above-mentioned interventions have contributed towards narrowing the socio-cultural and economic gaps, thus, facilitating the creation of a knowledge economy. These interventions have not only focused on technical aspects of education but have also promoted liberal art and life sciences for a holistic development of the learners. According to the Educational Statistics at a Glance (2016) report, the adult literacy rate (the percentage of population 15-24 years old who can both read and write with understanding a short simple statement on everyday life) has shown an upward trend for females as well as for males. In 2014, the adult literacy rate stood at 70.5% as compared to 61% in 2001. The bright line is that the increase in adult literacy rate was higher among females than males and the gender gap was also narrowing down. This surely could be considered as an achievement. With increased number of schools, improved facilities and enhanced enrolment, the annual dropout rate at primary level has come down for all categories of students. Studies by Handa (2002), Dumitrescu et al. (2011) and Burde and Linden (2013), showed that construction of new educational institutions helped to increase enrolment rates for boys as well as girls. Building new schools reduced an important indirect cost of attending school- the distance to the nearest school. More time spent traveling to school is time lost that could have been used for work or other activities, and greater distances may increase transportation costs and worries about safety (Damon et al., 2016, p: 44). India, by constructing new facilities and improving the existing ones, aims to increase the enrollment rates at all the levels of education. This in turn would lead to enhanced knowledge creation and subsequently its implementation to improve the economic landscape of the country.

Kazianga et al. (2013) evaluated the impact of providing "girl friendly" schools in rural villages. These schools had amenities that were attractive to girls, such as sources of clean water and separate toilets for boys and girls. Overall, such schools increased the enrollment rate of all children (average over boys and girls) by 18.5 percentage points, and separate estimates showed increases of 16.3 percentage points for boys and 21.9 percentage points for girls. Similar measures have been taken in India (as mentioned above), which have resulted in increased enrolment in educational institutions. High enrollment rate would result into increased knowledge-intensive activities which would contribute to an accelerated pace of technical and scientiðc advances, thus, facilitating the creation of knowledge economy.

Certain inhibition that exists in the society like corruption, inadequate social and financial inclusion can be taken care of with increased rate of education. Citizens can be educated and made aware of their rights and duties. Additionally, it becomes easy to inform educated people about the governments' provisions that are meant for their development (Bhattacharya, 2010).

Such interventions, would help to create a knowledge economy, which is characterised by meta-cognitive skills that are both broad and highly transferable, such as problem-solving and the ability to learn (Peters & Humes, 2003). With educational reforms and transformation, India aims to provide such knowledge workers an opportunity to engage themselves in continuous and life-long learning to upgrade and broaden their skills.

All thanks to the above interventions, according to Higher Education in India: Vision 2030, (2013) report:

- India is the single largest provider of global talent, with one in four graduates in the world being a product of the Indian system
- India was ranked among top 5 countries globally in cited research output during 2007-16, where countries from North America, the European and Pacific dominate both in terms of quantitative and qualitative research, a joint study by Council of Scientific & Industrial Research—National Institute of Science Technology and Development Studies (CSIR- NISTADS) and Indian

Institute of Science Education and Research (IISER) revealed (Sharma, 2017).

- 49 Indian institutions have made it to the list of 'Emerging Economies University Rankings' by London-based Times Higher Education (THE), a global organization that produces data, analysis and expertise on higher education. Of these, 25 institutions have been included in the list of top 200 universities (PTI London, 2019).

- Over the years, five Indian intellectuals have been awarded the Nobel Prize across categories. Rabindranath Tagore in 1913 for literature, C V Raman in 1930 for physics, Mother Teresa in 1979 for peace, Amartya Sen in 1998 for economics and Kailash Satyarthi in 2014 for peace as well.

- India is a regional hub for higher education, attracting global learners from all over the world with its systematic partnership (MOUs) with the developing counties, development of regional multi-county universities, campus abroad, Online courses offered, and distance education network (Khare, 2015).

- The country has augmented its Gross Enrollment Ratio (GER) to 50% while also reducing disparity in GER across states to 5 percentage points

- According to Chauhan (2017), India after USA is dominating the global growth of enrolment in MOOCs, started by several elite research universities, like, IITBX and IIMBX.

- Indian higher education institutions are governed by the highest standards of ethics and accountability, with every single one of them being peer-reviewed and accredited.

Thus, we can say that emerging economies like India can improve and narrow the economic and socio-cultural gap by transforming and facilitating quality education.

CRITICAL AREAS FOR IMPROVEMENT

Although there is wide recognition of the importance of knowledge and intangible capital in fostering economic growth and social change, devising useful measures of these assets has been difficult (Powell and Snellman, 2004). One focus could be on stocks of knowledge— human, organizational, and intellectual capital, while another focus could be on activities—R&D efforts, investments in information and communication technology and in education and training, and organizational reforms. Balancing the creation, storage and dissemination of knowledge can become challenging in India, given the existing socio-economic diversity.

Despite all the efforts from the government, the socio-economic status of Indian learners is critical to access to quality education. The demand-side factors which may be critical for poor students to continue their education, could be classified as direct cost, which include fees charged by educational institutions, expenses towards books and uniforms. Also, higher opportunity cost of labour to poor families where children are needed to work in the farms and sites prevent them to avail quality education even if the fees is nominal or free (Rani, 2007). So, to let such students invest their time and forego earnings to attend school, highly motivated and rewarding education system, which constitutes the supply side factors, are needed. Supply-side factors can be discussed at three levels at the i) public policy or macro level, which includes the infrastructures, location and school administration. ii) system level, which includes governance dimension such as, incentives and penalty to influence the performance of the schools, school governance, management mechanism and structures including supervision and inspection; ineffective or no teacher accountability, and at the iii) institutional level, which includes the academic factors on the one hand and leadership and cordial environment on the other hand influence the performance. It includes academic oriented approach and also good institutional leadership, good interpersonal relationship among headmaster, staff and students, and team-work. All of these factors need to operate together for better performance (Rani, 2007).

Corruption is another area of concern as it inhibits the quality of public spending. Mr. N. Vittal (2005), former Central Vigilance Commissioner said, "there are five basic reasons for corruption in India. (i) The scarcity of goods and services; (ii) red tape and complicated rules and procedures; (iii) the lack of transparency in decision-making; (iv) legal cushions of safety for the corrupt under the `healthy' principle that everyone is innocent till proved guilty; and (v) tribalism among the corrupt who protect each other." Corruption in the society has resulted in failure of several social development initiatives, like the Public Distribution System and mid-day meal (Bhattacharya, 2010). Thus, governments must ensure proper accountability to curb corruption.

Further, e-learning should be promoted and maximum awareness should be created among the learners. Sinha and Bagarukayo (2019) in their study found that lack of awareness and affordability are two major reasons which prevent learners to take up online educational courses. Although, the trend of online education has gained momentum in the past few years, it has been found that learners at the bottom of the pyramid have been struggling to meet the cost of online education. Governments must ensure that the education is inclusive and gives equal opportunities to every learner. Otherwise the prevailing classical method of learning with brick and mortar evidence will have to cater a very large number of learners that would need additional cost to build capacity (e.g. infrastructure) and would involve greater consumption of scarce resources.

Additionally, India has taken steps to standardized academic tests, and it has become an integral element of Indian education system. However, critics have time and again argued they (standardized tests) do not fully measure students' higher-order thinking skills (Schmoker, 2000). But supporters have argued that regardless of these shortcomings, standardized tests still enhance public trust by emphasizing accountability in terms of discrete, measurable outcomes (Schmoker, 2000). Some ways should be worked out in order to overcome the shortcomings of such tests, to raise and promote the higher order-skills of students and minimize undesirable effect of narrowing the curriculum to factual information or simplistic cognitive tasks (Wilcox and Ryder, 2002).

It is important to realise that academics play a significant role in imparting quality education, hence building a knowledge economy. Their well-being (physical, mental and emotional) cannot be ignored. Compensation is one of the very important components towards teachers' satisfaction and well-being. Unfortunately, faculty compensation in India is not very attractive, as compared to other sectors. Many intellectuals from premier institutes like, IITs and IIMs, choose to go abroad where infrastructure facilities are intellectually more stimulating or select a career in a multinational company at home (Bhattacharye, 2010). Government should address this problem in order to retain human capital and discourage brain drain, in order to give boost to the knowledge economy. Another major component is rewards and recognition. Time to time recognition keeps the teachers' morale high and motivates them to deliver their best. Third component is autonomy. Overregularization of work processes can inhibit the latent creativity of teachers as well as students. Thus, greater autonomy can be granted to individuals so that they can display their potential in their area of interests.

Despite India being one of the largest economies in the world, the nation's public education spending doesn't touch even the average of the amount spent by the rich club. In OECD countries, over 11% of the total government spending went to education, on average. However, in India, the same stood at 10.2% in 2016-17, centre and state combined (Gupta, 2019). In 2018-19, India's educational spend had risen to 10.6% of the total government expenditure, the report showed. According to OECD's latest findings, India lags behind several other nations such as the USA, Chile, Mexico, UK, Korea, Israel etc. in terms of total educational costs (Gupta, 2019). With spending 4.6% of its total GDP, India ranks 62nd in total public expenditure on education per student (Business Today, 2020). It is important for the governments (union and states) to allocate more funds towards education. Funds should also be available as research grants to promote the culture of innovation and entrepreneurship.

The above areas of concern need proper attention to eliminate the unnecessary hassles in the way of quality education. Authorities must ensure that the learning is inclusive and caters to every segment of the society. Existing socio-economic barriers, such as, lesser expenditure on the education of girl child by parents, early marriage of girls and poverty makes education of a less priority, even if it is free.

Governments can look forward to public-private models and collaborate with non-governmental organizations (NGOs) to reach out to remote areas and provide quality education to learners in most effective ways.

CONCLUSION

India is a very diverse country with 3190 languages 28 states and nine union territories. Managing people, with diverse cultures and sentiments is not easy. India will be the youngest nation by 2030 and the working population would be more. Despite the expected high growth rate of the Indian economy (Mourdoukoutas, 2017) with sectors like, agriculture, manufacturing and service promising great potential, India would have labour surplus. Generating employment for the skilled workforce may become a challenging task. But with the focus on quality education, India could become the global supplier of skilled manpower to labour deficient markets. Hence, skilling and educating people would be of prime importance to meet the demands of the domestic as well as international markets for efficient and effective human resources as ongoing globalization creates competition as well as opportunities for knowledge workers in developed economies.

The 'National Education Policy 2020' of India is expected to provide much needed thrust to the current reforms. The National Policy on Education was framed in 1986 and modified in 1992. Since then several changes have taken place that calls for a revision of the Policy. The Government of India aims to bring out a National Education Policy to meet the changing dynamics of the population's requirement with regards to quality education, innovation and research, aiming to make India a knowledge superpower by equipping its students with the necessary skills and knowledge and to eliminate the shortage of manpower in science, technology, academics and industry. For the first time, the Government of India has embarked on a time-bound grassroots consultative process, which will enable the Ministry of Human Resource Development to reach out to individuals across the country through over 0.275 million direct consultations while also taking input from citizens online (http://mhrd.gov.in/nep-new). However, Experience in many countries indicates that increased standardization of teaching and learning, may be counterproductive to the expectations of enhanced economic competitiveness. It is important for governments, institutions, academics and students to collaborate rather than compete. Networking, deeper co-operation and open sharing of ideas at all levels is needed to strengthen the role of education in creating a knowledge economy and overcome economic challenges (Sahlberg, 2006).

India as a major growing economy has taken and is still planning a lot of measures to leverage its young population and make it a dividend rather than a burden. This can be done by skilling and re-skilling learners, according to the need and demands of the industries. Proper synchronization between governments at various levels, academia and industry would be needed to facilitate and transform quality education in India further.

ACKNOWLEDGMENT

The author would like to thank the anonymous reviewers for their comments on the earlier version of this chapter.

REFERENCES

Anon. (2004). *55 Policy Recommendations for Raising Croatia's Competitiveness.* National Competitiveness Council.

Bhattacharya, S. (2010). Knowledge Economy in India: Challenges and Opportunities. *Journal of Information & Knowledge Management, 9*(3), 1-23.

Bregman, J. (2003). Summary of Se Summary of Secondary Education (SE) reform trends in OECD countries with an African perspective. Paper Presented at the *first Regional Secondary Education in Africa (SEIA) Conference in Uganda.*

Burde, D., & Linden, L. L. (2013). Bringing Education to Afghan Girls: A Randomized Controlled Trial of Village-Based Schools. *American Economic Journal. Applied Economics, 5*(3), 27–40. doi:10.1257/app.5.3.27

Business Today. (2020). *Union Budget 2020: How much will Modi govt spend on education?* https://www.businesstoday.in/union-budget-2020/news/budget-2020-how-much-will-modi-govt-spend-on-education/story/395077.html#:~:text=the%20education%20system.-,India%20spends%204.6%20per%20cent%20of%20its%20total%20GDP%20on,improve%20education%20quality%20in%20India

Chauhan, J. (2017). An Overview of MOOC in India. *International Journal of Computer Trends and Technology, 49*(2). https://www.researchgate.net/publication/320038196_An_Overview_of_MOOC_in_India

Damon, A., Glewwe, P., Wisniewski, S., & Sun, B. (2016). *Education in developing countries – what policies and programmes affect learning and time in school?* https://www.oecd.org/derec/sweden/Rapport-Education-developing-countries.pdf

Dasgupta, A. D. (2001). Corporate ethical dilemmas: Indian models for moral management. *Journal of Human Values, 7*(2), 171–191. doi:10.1177/097168580100700207

Desai, M. (2014). *Why improving education in India is the key to growth*. https://www.weforum.org/agenda/2014/12/why-improving-education-in-india-is-the-key-to-growth/

Drucker, P. F. (1993). *Postcapitalist Society*. HerperCollins Publishers.

Dumitrescu, A., Levy, D., Orfield, C., & Sloan, M. (2011). *Impact Evaluation of Niger's IMAGINE Program*. Mathematica Policy Research. Available at http://cipre.mathematica-mpr.com/our-publications-andfindings/publications/impact-evaluation-of-nigers-imagineprogram

Duraisamy, P. (2002). Changes in Returns to education in India, 1983-94: by gender, age-cohort and location. *Economics of Education Review, 21*(6), 609-622.

Educational administration in India. (n.d.). *Chapter II*. Retrieved from https://shodhganga.inflibnet.ac.in/bitstream/10603/86857/10/10_chapter%202.pdf

Educational Statistics at a Glance. (2016). *Report by Government of India, Ministry of Human Resource Development, Department of School Education & Literacy, New Delhi*. Retrieved from http://mhrd.gov.in/sites/upload_files/mhrd/files/statistics/ESG2016_0.pdf

Friedman, W., Kremer, M., Miguel, E., & Thornton, R. (2011). *Education as Liberation? No. w16939*. National Bureau of Economic Research. doi:10.3386/w16939

Glewwe, P., Hanushek, E., Humpage, S., & Ravina, R. (2013). School Resources and Educational Outcomes in Developing Countries. In P. Glewwe (Ed.), *Education Policy in Developing Countries*. University of Chicago Press. doi:10.7208/chicago/9780226078854.003.0002

Govind, R., & Varghese, V. N. (1993). *Quality of Primary Schooling in India, A case study of Madhya Pradesh. Report for International Institute for Educational Planning*. Paris and National Institute of Educational Planning and Administration.

Gupa, D., & Gupta, N. (2012). Higher Education in India: Structure, Statistics and Challenges. *Journal of Education and Practice, 3*(2), 17–24.

Gupta, P. (2019). *How much India spends on education: Hint, it's less than rich countries' average*. https://www.financialexpress.com/economy/how-much-india-spends-on-education-hint-its-less-than-rich-countries-average/1772269/

Handa, S. (2002). Raising primary school enrolment in developing countries. The relative importance of supply and demand. *Journal of Development Economics*, *69*(1), 103–128. doi:10.1016/S0304-3878(02)00055-X

Hargreaves, A. (2003). *Teaching in the Knowledge Society. Education in the Age of Insecurity*. Teachers College Press.

Higher Education in India. Vision 2030. (2013). *FICCI Higher Education Summit 2013*. Retrieved from https://www.ey.com/Publication/vwLUAssets/Higher-education-in-India-Vision-2030/$FILE/EY-Higher-education-in-India-Vision-2030.pdf

India Brand Equity Foundation. (2018). *Education and Training*. Retrieved from https://www.ibef.org/download/Education-and-Training-Report-Jan-2018.pdf

International Standard Classification of Education. (2011). Retrieved from http://uis.unesco.org/en/glossary-term/adult-education#slideoutmenu

Karthick, M., & Prakash, N. (2013). *Cycling to school: increasing secondary school enrollment for girls in India*. NBER Working Paper #19305.

Kazianga, H., Levy, D., Linden, L. L., & Sloan, M. (2013). The effects of "girl-friendly" schools: Evidence from the BRIGHT school construction program in Burkina Faso. *American Economic Journal. Applied Economics*, *5*(3), 41–62. doi:10.1257/app.5.3.41

Khare, M. (2015). India's Emergence as a Regional Education Hub. *International Higher Education*, *83*, 26-28. https://ejournals.bc.edu/ojs/index.php/ihe/article/download/9088/8195

Lewin, K., & Caillods, F. (2001). *Financing Secondary Education in Developing Countries: Strategies for Sustainable Growth*. UNESCO, International Institute for Educational Planning. doi:10.1007/BF03220050

London, P. T. I. (2019). *Indian universities move up in global ranking; 25 institutions in top 200*. Retrieved from https://www.thehindubusinessline.com/news/education/indian-universities-move-up-in-global-ranking-25-institutions-in-top-200/article26000998.ece

Maertens, A. (2013). Social Norms and Aspirations: Age of Marriage and Education in Rural India. *World Development*, *47*, 1-15. doi:10.1016/j.worlddev.2013.01.027

MHRD, Department of School Education and Literacy. (2016). *Adult Education*. Retrieved from https://mhrd.gov.in/adult-education

Ministry of Ayush. (2017). *About the Ministry*. Retrieved from http://ayush.gov.in/about-us/about-the-ministry

Ministry of Human Resource Development (MHRD). Government of India, Department of School Education & Literacy, Department of Higher Education. (2017). *Annual Report 2016-17*. Retrieved from http://mhrd.gov.in/sites/upload_files/mhrd/files/document-reports/HRD_AR%202016-17.pdf

Ministry of Skill Development and Entrepreneurship. (n.d.). *National Skill development Mission*. Retrieved from https://www.msde.gov.in/nationalskillmission.html

Mourdoukoutas, P. (2017). *Modi's India The World's 4th Fastest Growing Economy*. Retrieved from https://www.forbes.com/sites/panosmourdoukoutas/2017/06/22/modis-india-the-worlds-4th-fastest-growing-economy/#664b1d674120

Mouzakitis, S. G. (2010). The role of vocational education and training curricula in economic development. *Procedia: Social and Behavioral Sciences, 2*(2), 3914–3920. doi:10.1016/j.sbspro.2010.03.616

Nalanda University. (n.d.). Retrieved from https://www.nalandauniv.edu.in/about-nalanda/history-and-revival/

National Institution for Transforming India (NITI Aayog), Government of India. (2011). *Literacy rate- 7+ years (%)*. Retrieved from http://niti.gov.in/content/literacy-rate-7years on 23.8.18.

Open Universities in India. (2019). Retrieved from https://www.eduvidya.com/Open-Universities-in-India

Pareek, S. (2014). *The Ancient Indian University Which Is Taking Students Again After 800 Years!* Retrieved from https://www.thebetterindia.com/13918/ancient-nalanda-university-reopens-monday-know-lesser-known-facts-great-university/

Peters, A. M., & Humes, W. (2003). Education in the Knowledge Economy. *Policy Futures in Education, 1*(1), 1–19. doi:10.2304/pfie.2003.1.1.1

Powell, W. W., & Snellman, K. (2004). The Knowledge Economy. *Annual Review of Sociology, 30*(1), 199–220. doi:10.1146/annurev.soc.29.010202.100037

Rani, G. P. (2007). Secondary Education in India: Development and Performance. In *43rd Annual Conference of the Indian Econometric Society (TIES)*. Indian Institute of Technology.

Rupera, P. (2017). *Ancient Vallabhi University to be revived*. Retrieved from https://timesofindia.indiatimes.com/city/vadodara/ancient-vallabhi-university-to-be-revived/articleshow/60811468.cms

Sankaran, S. V. (2012). *From Vedas To Cloud: The Transformation Of Education In India*. Retrieved from https://www.forbes.com/sites/sap/2012/10/09/from-vedas-to-cloud-the-transformation-of-education-in-india/#763c1e4a646f on 22.8.2018

Schmoker, M. (2000). The results we want. *Educational Leadership, 57*(5), 62-65.

Schweke, W. (2004). *Smart Money: Education and Economic Development*. Economic Policy Institute.

Sen, A. (2015). India: The Stormy Revival of an International University. *The New York Review*. Retrieved from https://www.nybooks.com/articles/2015/08/13/india-stormy-revival-nalanda-university/

Sharma, C. N. (2017). *India ranks 5th in global research publication output: report*. Retrieved from https://www.livemint.com/Education/QYkn6doeciNSv2m7CzG7dP/India-ranks-5th-in-global-research-publication-output-repor.html

Sinha, E., & Bagarukayo, K. (2019). Online Education in Emerging Knowledge Economies: Exploring factors of motivation, de-motivation and potential facilitators; and studying the effects of demographic variables. *International Journal of Education and Development Using Information and Communication Technology, 15*(2), 5–30.

Sustainable development Goals. (n.d.). Retrieved from: http://www.undp.org/content/undp/en/home/sustainable-development-goals.html

Tilak, J. B. G. (1989). *Education and its Relation to Economic Growth, Poverty and Income Distribution: Past Evidence and Further Analysis*. World Bank Discussion Paper No.3, World Bank, Washington, DC.

Tilak, J. B. G. (2001). *Building Human Capital: What Others Can Learn*. World Bank Institute Working Paper, World Bank, Washington, DC.

Tilak, J. B. G. (2005). *Post-Elementary Education, Poverty and Development in India*. Working Paper Series, No.6, Centre of African Studies, University of Edinburgh, UK.

United Nations. (n.d.). *Sustainable development Goals-Quality Education*. Retrieved from https://www.un.org/sustainabledevelopment/education/

University Grant Commission Annual Report (UGC). (2016-17). Retrieved from: https://www.ugc.ac.in/pdfnews/9764381_Complete-AR-2016-17-English.pdf

Vittal, N. (2005, Sept. 24). Moral Values Must Prevail. *The Tribune*, p. 15.

Wilcox, K., & Ryder, R. (2002). Standardized Testing and Improving Educational Opportunity in Brazil. *The Educational Forum, 66*(3), 214–219. doi:10.1080/00131720208984831

World Bank. (2005). Expanding Opportunities and Building Competences of Young People. A New Agenda for Secondary Education. World Bank.

World development Report. (2018). *Learning to realize Education's Promise.* Retrieved from: https://www.worldbank.org/en/publication/wdr2018

ADDITIONAL READING

Banerjee, V. A., Banerji, R., Duflo, E., Glennerster, R., & Khemani, S. (2010). Pitfalls of Participatory Programs: Evidence from a Randomized Evaluation in Education in India. *American Economic Journal. Economic Policy, 2*(1), 1–30. doi:10.1257/pol.2.1.1

Bhattacharya, S. (2010). Knowledge Economy in India: Challenges & Opportunities. *Journal of Information & Knowledge Managmement., 9*(3), 203–225. doi:10.1142/S0219649210002620

Coleman, J. (2017). Lifelong Learning Is Good for Your Health, Your Wallet, and Your Social Life. URL: https://hbr.org/2017/02/lifelong-learning-is-good-for-your-health-your-wallet-and-your-social-life

Goal 4: Quality Education. URL: https://www.undp.org/content/undp/en/home/sustainable-development-goals/goal-4-quality-education.html

OECD. (2016). *Innovating Education and Educating for Innovation: The Power of Digital Technologies and Skills.* OECD Publishing., doi:10.1787/9789264265097-

Online Education in India. 2021. A Study by KPMG in India and Google, May 2017. URL: https://home.kpmg.com/in/en/home/insights/2017/05/internet-online-education-india.html

Sahlberg, P. (2006). Education reform for raising economic competitiveness. *Journal of Educational Change, 7*(4), 259–287. Advance online publication. doi:10.100710833-005-4884-6

Umashankar, V., & Dutta, K. (2007). Balanced scorecards in managing higher education institutions: An Indian perspective. *International Journal of Educational Management, 21*(1), 54–67. doi:10.1108/09513540710716821

KEY TERMS AND DEFINITIONS

Census: A survey of population done after every ten years in India. It includes all the demographic profile of the Indian citizens, like age, caste, religion, education, and income.

Entrepreneurship: The process of channelizing different factors of production or resources in order to create a business which provides innovative and sustainable solutions to the end user and narrows the gap between demand and supply. It is also known as 'Entrepreneurial Behaviour'.

Facilitate: To ensure easy access of the facility to the end user without any discrimination.

Family-Centric Roles: Roles, responsibilities and duties towards family takes the centre stage or becomes the priority. Family members and their needs are considered to be more important than anything else, thus taking precedence over other aspects of life, such as education.

Human Capital: People who know how to learn and who continue learning by upgrading existing skills and acquiring new skills. There is a strong relationship between human capital and economic growth. Because people come with a diverse set of skills and knowledge, human capital can certainly help boost the economy. This relationship can be measured by how much investment goes into people's education.

Intervention: Actions or set of actions which improves the current state of functioning. Timely and focused interventions help in achieving goals much easily. These interventions can be in the areas of Production, Capacity Building, Human Resources, and Technologies.

Knowledge Economy: The economy where the growth is directly proportional to the availability of the information, access to it, and quality of the information. Such economies rely on creation, assimilation, and dissemination of information to create value and promote innovation and sustained growth.

Liberal Arts: An area of learning which promotes and cultivates general intellectual abilities rather than technical skills. Like, painting, language, humanities, and drama.

Life-Skill: It refers to the large group of psychosocial and interpersonal skills that can help people make informed decisions, communicate effectively, and develop coping and self-management skills that may help lead a healthy and productive life. Life Skills education is a combination of learning experiences that aim to develop not only knowledge and attitudes but also facilitates positive actions with the potential to change surrounding environment and negative behaviour.

Research: It is a scientific process to discover and investigate underlying pattern(s) of an entity or phenomenon through experimentation, exploration, structured observation or in a descriptive manner. Research helps us to understand the phenomenon more deeply and draw conclusions which can be tested and results can be reproduced by using same investigating methods, techniques and tools.

Skill: The ability to do something nicely. There could be different skill or set of skill to do a task. Special training and knowledge can improve one's skills. Skills can be learned lifelong.

Sustainable Development: It is the process of utilizing scarce resources optimally in order to meet the present needs of development without compromising the needs of future. It can be measured on triple bottom-line framework: social, economic, and environmental.

Transformation: The process of profound change in appearance, functioning, nature and form in order to improve the current state in order to achieve profound shared goals.

Vocational: Education or training which is directed towards particular occupation. Such kind of education helps in proving the learner with the means to earn his/her livelihood. This training could be in different sectors like; manufacturing and service and helps the learner find a job or start something of his/her own.

Chapter 5
Knowledge Society, Globalization, and Impacts on Knowledge Management:
Perceptions of Brazilian Education Reality

Daiana Garibaldi Rocha

iD https://orcid.org/0000-0001-6738-772X
Universidade Fernando Pessoa, Portugal

ABSTRACT

Continuing knowledge, skills, and practice update through continuing education, which then becomes the lever of society and the recipe for a successful future. This chapter aims to initiate a discussion about the concepts of knowledge societies, globalization, and their perceptions and impact on knowledge management in relation to the Brazilian educational reality. From a theoretical-methodological perspective, continuing education is considered as a key element that can sustain knowledge management and foster knowledge societies. This question is the reason why this intensity of the offer of continuing education nowadays becomes pertinent, as well as to look at how the knowledge societies have seduced people to consume more and more knowledge. The conclusions raise the question of how societies of knowledge have become a contemporary imperative, justified by the acceleration of time in different spaces and driven by globalization. As knowledge management has contributed to this movement, it is necessary for professionals to be more flexible and resourceful, as well as about what can happen to the individuals who cannot keep up with the demands of the market and become disposable in society.

DOI: 10.4018/978-1-5225-8873-3.ch005

INTRODUCTION

Serrano and Fialho (2005), knowledge societies "praise information and knowledge as essential elements of organizational activity and establish new ways to understand and develop them" (p. 11), knowledge starts to be valued in the market.

In knowledge economy, education is a valuable commodity because it should last for one's entire life and always renew itself. People constantly need to look after themselves to be desirable in the market. Perhaps this justifies the currently growing emergence of institutions which offer programs of all types, not only in professional development.

The main idea in this chapter is to explore the concepts of knowledge societies, globalization and perceptions and impacts on knowledge management in light of the Brazilian educational reality. For this purpose, the concept of continuing education used and questioned.

To meet the objectives of this chapter, a qualitative theoretical-methodological analysis through the review of literature of the narrative type is used. Therefore, the chapter is organized as follows. Continuing education and knowledge societies open the chapter with a brief overview on changes in continuing education. The focus of interest in different periods, understanding permanence and displacement as ways to reorganize the subjects' experiences, but not without the marks and presences of the period that preceded it is emphasized. The study and underpinnings that support it and referrals of this trend to the known knowledge societies then are also presented.

In addition to labor and globalization, the reader is instigated to look at these concepts through a contemporary lens and how they are being placed in the market and. The view through thinking on cognitive capitalism, which provokes us to examine the commodification of continuing education through other perceptions is broadened. According to Costa (2009a), this is "an attempt to show the way things happen through a different angle and how they become what they are" (p. 17).

Some definitions about knowledge management and how all the other interwoven concepts are in constant change and relate to one another in knowledge societies are given. This represents some relevant and current points in the Brazilian educational and organizational scenarios.

CONTINUING EDUCATION AND KNOWLEDGE SOCIETIES

Continuing knowledge, skills and practice upgrade through continuing education is the lever of society and the recipe for a successful future. According to Camozzato and Costa (2013), "it is possible to assume we are dealing with subjectivities that seek constant *upgrades* to meet the social demands of current times" (p. 10). Its importance is linked to the subjects' possibility to constantly recreate themselves, which is an indispensable demand to compete in the market and acquire values and behavior required for human coexistence.

In the general sense of the volume *Learn to Be,* continuing education means understanding the relevant idea of preparing people to live in their time and follow changes in the world and labor. It is important to consider that the ideas of living and preparing yourself for your time, of being a responsible person, a citizen who can understand the constant changes in the world and, therefore, should be reading, studying and getting up-to-date are the focus of Faure's report (1972). Clearly, it does not have the same connotation that continuing education has today.

The concept of continuing education arose and strengthened itself with the ideas aforementioned. However, from the most recent changes in contemporary societies, it began increasingly to take shape and approach the idea that Robertson (2003) refers to as "knowledge society", in which the characteristics of competition and competitiveness prevail and permeate education as a whole.

The desire to be accepted by society is what drives individuals to pursue continuing education and this relates to the general meaning of knowledge economy, in which the culture of consumption is present and has qualified all fields of life. The acquisition of different kinds of knowledge and practices of all types incorporate into subjectivities some attributes, which make them more valuable in varied spheres of life and causes the commodification of people that Bauman mentions (2008a).

The notions of space and time, the evolution of scientific and technological knowledge, the innovations introduced in all areas of knowledge, the erosion of life models and interpersonal relations and, especially, the reinvention of economic needs have contributed to the importance given to the constitution of knowledge societies, with subjects who are increasingly more present and active through technologies and sharing knowledge in real time.

Following this line of reasoning, the next few pages, highlight the approaches to the interesting metaphor of "liquid" and "solid", by Bauman (2001), with the displacements of "permanent" to "continuous" which seem to correspond to the same logic and eventually produce new and diverse subjectivities. In the past, there was the solid education designed to subsidize the subjects' "whole life". Nowadays, the expression "education for the whole life" emphasizes the obsolescence and simultaneous constant recycling of knowledge and the multiplication of knowledge societies. Nothing is "forever", but rather like the liquid, which flows and changes all the time.

LABOR AND GLOBALIZATION

In academic studies already mentioned in different lines of research published in Brazil and Europe, the relationship between continuing education and labor stand out differently in two moments: from the decade of 1990 to mid-2002, with focus on the qualification of teaching, with studies focusing on education; and from 2003 to 2011, the concept is expanded to be considered not only a qualifier, but a need for professional improvement and acknowledgement, with emphasis not only in education, but in all areas of knowledge.

In his study, Ferraz (2001) says, "Teacher Education is called continuing education and should occur throughout the course of the teacher's life" (p. 7). Without demonstrating requirements and needs, it is clear, in the author's quote, how "natural" the process of continuing education was considered. Still within the area of education, more specifically teaching, we have Bruno's contribution (1998), which emphasizes teacher training as something mandatory within the field of teaching.

Even though the connection with social and educational changes was already mentioned in the decade of 1990, continuing education used to be offered predominantly as an option for possible improvement to teachers' work.

At the end of 2002, Cunha (2002) in his study mentions the importance of continuing education regarding today's society, in which "the economy and employment relations are changing, and the phenomenon of employability appears to require a permanent condition of occupying spaces in the productive sector" (p. 112).

The same author addresses the difficulties faced by IT professionals on the provision of courses, by saying that only through continuing education can professionals acquire knowledge and enable behavioral change.

From 2002 - 2003, continuing education clearly becomes a possibility for professionals to improve and perform changes of behavior in their work environments so as to be able to conquer new spaces in society and be flexible to occupy them.

From 2003, studies show that continuing education becomes both evident and needed. Continuing education is still often mentioned in the field of education and as continuous training. It is important to emphasize that the studies expand to other areas of knowledge. Some marketing issues that surround the practice to educate continuously in contemporary society have also emerged. Nascimento (2003) arouses questions involving continuing education, which are closely related to public policies. For him, the narratives of these policies with those of continuing education are not connected naively because there are many relations of language and power underpinning these concepts.

These reflections are important because they reinforce how knowledge societies have had an impact on trends of globalization and how much they are linked to contemporary social and cultural issues.

Under the Cultural Studies perspective, the doctoral thesis by Santos (2006), carried out a study based on Foucault's theory using the concept of manumission to connect it to freedom and use it as an inquiry tool to problematize the emergence of continuous teacher education in Brazil.Initially, the author characterizes the transition from a society of disciplines to the society of standardization, based on Foucault. After that, he contextualizes the beginning of teacher education in 19th-century Brazil. From headlines of *Revista Brasileira de Estudos Pedagógicos* (Brazilian Magazine of Pedagogical Studies), an object of study he analyzed, he describes the space-time problematics of school education and teacher education. He justifies his option for researching continuous education instead of non-continuous or permanent education, because such expression is already widespread in all fields of knowledge.

The main question raised by the author is the duration of the program, which seems to have become endless, and problematizes the discourses of this Brazilian educational policy in the 20th century. According to Santos (2006), "in order to allow teacher education to be spoken about, it was necessary to operate a discontinuity in the space-time experience (...)" (p.81). In this study, the author presents the emergence of continuous teacher education in Brazil, which, according to him, bridged the gap between modern and contemporary life.

As years go by, it is important to mention that studies have shown concern on the connection between continuing education and globalized world and how it has become indispensable to society. For Bauman (1999), "globalization" is the irremediable fate of the world, an irreversible process; it is also a process which affects us all in the same measure and the same way" (p.7). Paiva (2004) warned that continuing education is essential for any area of knowledge, in particular after the phenomenon of globalization.

Years later, another author, Abbiana (2009) reinforces the idea by saying that continuing education takes on a distinctive role in a changing world, because it seeks to meet specific needs of everyday teaching, such as social, ethical and technological demands.

Although globalization seems to be a concept connected to spatial issues, it is mainly seen as an economic concept and a cultural one as a result. Connecting the whole world in the era of globalization has been something useful for the economy.

It seems beyond doubt that globalization is not something new. Giddens (1990) has already highlighted that by saying that "globalization is not a recent phenomenon: modernity is inherently globalizing" (apud HALL, 2001, p. 68). However, we have been living in a new version of globalization today.

People have lived in a time in which consuming, selling, buying and wanting products and services go beyond what is considered necessary. The process of globalization discussed by Claclini (2003) encourages reflection on money and production of goods and messages that have spread across the world. In the case of continuing education, it seems that what matters now is to transform it into an essential *commodity* for the subjects' social, professional and cultural lives.

With the contemporary trend of globalization, even economic interests have grown, because sales became international. Santos (2006) says in his thesis that in the proliferation of education, "you can also glimpse that the continued education seems to represent an easy to sell product and of high profitability" (p. 30).

Economic globalization triggered what Bauman (1999) calls "human consequences". According to this author, globalization has produced a mixture of cultures.

The deeper meaning conveyed by the idea of globalization is the indefinite, undisciplined and self-propelled character of world affairs; the absence of a center, of a control board, of a commission director, of an administrative office. Globalization is the 'new world disorder' (p. 67).

Thus, it appears that economic interests, cultural changes and globalization are intertwined. For Houssaye (2007), "it is noted, with all evidence, an internationalization of education and training" (p. 297).

What happens in an era in which changes have been constantly happening and in which economy is mixed with culture in such peculiar fashion? There are human consequences and it is necessary to prepare subjects for life. According to Bauman (1999), "globalization does not relate to what all of us, or at least the most talented and enterprising of us desire or hope to do. It relates to what is happening to all of us" (p. 68). The wide web of globalization is shaped by various means and it is institutionalizing through knowledge societies and materializing itself in knowledge management.

The new century and globalization have accumulated different challenges for society Costa (2017). Some of these challenges include: dealing with new technologies and new ways of sharing knowledge in the classroom and increase scientific mobility.

The need for continuing education, justified by speed of time in different spaces - whether educationally acknowledged or not - in a contemporary society that increasingly requires specialists and flexible professionals, goes from being an option to becoming an inevitable alternative, an inescapable imperative.

Franciscone (2006) presents important considerations about the process of continuing education engagement in economic matters. According to the author, in the period of criticism to human capital, education was technical, centered on the teacher's role as knowledge keeper. The student had limited tasks, focused only on reproducing techniques. The goal was to train technical subjects that yielded more in the labor market. Citing Furter (1974), he adds that the evolution of the concept of continuing education is marked by three moments as a process of individual development and continued throughout life; as a system of education promoted by companies; as a cultural strategy in light of global development.

What matters for this chapter, in which continuing education is indispensable for global development, and becomes an important economic strategy that encourages consumerism.

Although the second moment is very close to the third, what differs is that in the second one, companies implement the logic of continuing education for greater business productivity and in the third moment, continuing education takes on a global perspective, which instigates each of the subjects to invest in themselves through training so as to boost economy.

Nowadays, since the beginning of the 21st century, information quickly moves and can be critiqued anytime by anyone from anywhere, which intensifies the need for knowledge and immediate and constant upgrading.

Globalized education is emerging as a personal investment to develop more flexible, dynamic and suitable individuals for the contemporary market.

Through this contemporary demand of competitiveness and constant knowledge upgrade, the impression from reading the studies is that continuing education seems to be gaining a central role in market-oriented societies of the current stage of capitalism. According to Moro (2007), continuing education has always been linked to interests of capitalist markets. Although market issues are not addressed in this study, the author emphasizes that continuing education should no longer be used to bridge gaps alone, but as something to encourage the process of understanding oneself and the world. That is, it is again mentioned as indispensable, which will probably end up being consumed by society.

Another important study is Oliveira's (2011), which noted "continuing education has a real value because of the content one acquires and because it is an indicator" (p. 4). By addressing the competence of executives in face of the structure of organizations, one of the goals is to provide flexibility before market situations. For this reason, Costa (2002) says that "in order to acquire this level of employability, it becomes clear to the professional the indispensability of permanent learning, of continuing education" (apud OLIVEIRA, 2011, p. 21), that is, the market increasingly values lifelong education.

KNOWLEDGE MANAGEMENT

It is undeniable that lifelong education is one of the significant trends of knowledge societies which is closely connected to labor and globalization. According to Serrano and Fialho (2005), lifelong learning is part of a cycle comprising aspects such as the development of skills and knowledge: knowledge management

Considering these concepts, knowledge management from the trend of new technologies has an important role because it represents the whole history of creation and dialectics of knowledge, covering from companies as creators of knowledge to the concept of knowledge management as global competition.

According to Gonzalez and Martins (2017), "organizational knowledge is considered, nowadays, an asset that, although intangible, generates competitive advantage to the organization". With the advent of new technologies, knowledge societies seek new managers for their organizations who have unique expertise to understand systems of varied values. These requirements are tied to new theories and practices of knowledge management.

Based on the new technology movement, knowledge management plays an important role in today's society, since it represents the whole history of creation and the dialectic of knowledge, ranging from the process of setting up companies to the concept of knowledge management itself as a factor of global competition.

This movement of new technologies also impacts and drives the educational area to move faster in order to prepare its professors to act in the classroom with these technologies. In the Brazilian reality, mainly in public basic education, due to lack of resources and government incentives, that only rarely appear in the purchase of equipment, lack of capacity and incentive of the professionals to use them in a diversified way in the classroom.

Before this complex picture, which involves the management of assets of different kinds, such as people, as well as tacit, explicit, individual, structural and organizational knowledge, it is relevant to highlight that the mere existence of knowledge is of little value if not accessible and shared with everyone. Ikujiro and Nonaka (2008) reinforce that "the transition to knowledge society raised the paradox from something to be eliminated and prevented to something to be accepted and cultivated" (p.19). The authors believe knowledge is made up of two opposing components: an explicit one and a tacit one. From this definition, it is understood that explicit knowledge is linked to procedures, databases and relationship with people, while tacit knowledge relates to experience, power of innovation and performance of everyday tasks.

New technologies connected to trends of globalization currently constitute networks of communities that transform technology into means and knowledge into capital, because according to Serrano and Fialho (2005), "knowledge increases when shared and does not depreciate as it is used" (p. 37).

Thus, the expression of knowledge management assumes varied meanings according to the context in which it is inserted. Mostly applied to Brazilian reality, knowledge management has been understood under the perspective of obtaining competitive advantages. It has become an intentional systematic, aiming to promote global performance of organizations, based on the creation and sharing of knowledge.

Knowledge management is related to the leverage of resources, either structural or human, that must be tied to clearly defined goals. This process leads to the accumulation of diversified experiences, thus increasing the development of people and products as well as their life cycles.

In practice, knowledge management seems to be an effort involving several aspects, whether human or technological, structural or arisen from cultural or social processes.

In the Brazilian scenario, knowledge management is closely related to management by competencies. This relationship seeks and reinforces the imperative of competitiveness, already discussed in this chapter, because it refers to a means by which companies advertise to place higher than their competition. This creates a chain of knowledge production supported by competences with greater dynamism to knowledge management, which makes it a common function in organizations, and no longer an emerging concept.

Currently, as a means to disseminate knowledge in organizations, distance learning has played a crucial role in building virtual learning environments that allow the sharing of tacit knowledge. According to Moore and Kearsley (2013) "in general, distance learning allows many new learning opportunities for a large number of people" (p. 29). In addition, other strategies are important, such as: mapping internal talents; structuring knowledge flow; managing intellectual resources; innovating and creating new knowledge.

Such strategies have contributed to Brazilian companies seeing knowledge as a tactical resource, contributing further to the concept of competences as a result of knowledge, skills and attitudes. For Stewart (2002), "new jobs are jobs of knowledge" (p. 37), which are concepts extensively explored in recent years in Brazil, both in education and in business.

Knowledge societies have not only encouraged knowledge management to become a continuous process – one which involves and determines knowledge as strategy, sharing, application in order to make business, they have also boost the levels of tacit and explicit knowledge.

Knowledge management adds to other organizational initiatives, in particular learning, which, along with quality and management processes, has a prominent role in the competitive market. Regarding management of business knowledge, Stewart (2002) reinforces" the economic reality shows that the association of IT and communication is finally improving worker's productivity of knowledge in a measurable way" (p. 123).

In this sense, the beginning of this section emphasizes what was said about knowledge management, in which the tools permeating new technologies are closely related to trends that assist in capturing, structuring and providing knowledge.

Thus, knowledge management is not only technology, but everything that permeates and composes the four pillars of knowledge, recommended by Delors (2001): learn to know, learn to do, learn to get along (learn to live with others); learn to be. And they are closely linked to the trends of cognitive capitalism.

COGNITIVE CAPITALISM: A REALITY IN BRAZIL

The transition from liberalism to neo-liberalism represented many changes in society. From production to consumption to consumption of production, now the emphasis is in competition, the best performance, quantity and innovation.

In this context, labor market changes its focus and so should the professionals' profiles. This current change has a constant intonation, which evokes upgrading as a savior of the competitive market. Therefore, going back to school became a basic requirement to remain in the labor market.

Upgrade, imperative, personal and professional development, and progress are common expressions, but when articulated to knowledge societies they take on a very specific meaning, flawed of marketing intentions.

Being part of knowledge societies goes beyond the upgrade. This is now connected to personal investment, renewed creativity, intensity of flexibility and staying in a workplace which is adept of constant changes while looking at innovation. According to Sennet (2011), "the very instability of flexible organizations imposes on workers the need for 'changing vases', that is, taking risks in their work" (p. 94). One cannot be still, it is necessary to innovate and create without interruption, production in this process turns out to be just a consequence. Corsani's studies (apud SARAIVA and VEIGA-NETO, 2009, p. 192) show that there is a shift from the evolution of the institution that manufactures goods to the institution that produces innovation. The use of physical force, representing the era of industrial capitalism, has shifted to the use of the brain, for today's cognitive capitalism.

Thus, in cognitive capitalism there is one more reason/imperative to be part of these societies. According to Saraiva and Veiga-Neto (2009), "in cognitive capitalism, invention becomes an ongoing process, the exception becomes the rule" (p. 192), and "the time of cognitive capitalism is a discontinuous time, marked by invention" (p.193), which draws enough attention because of the alignment of characteristics of knowledge societies with those of cognitive capitalism.

Cognitive capitalism to Vargas (2017) is an economy based on knowledge-intangible goods are derived from the production of knowledge-that, to be effective, has bio-political control over the subjects. Along with flexibility and creativity required by cognitive capitalism, knowledge management proposes to teach how to be flexible and creative through its inputs. Cognitive capitalism addresses management as the manager of instability. Saraiva and Veiga-Neto (2009) show that "it is necessary, first of all, a flexible brain, adaptable to changing conditions" (p. 194) to be able to survive in the midst of so much pressure and changes.

This link between cognitive capitalism and knowledge societies is the evidence that the commodification of lifelong education is taking power. Lazzarato says (2003), "every good is transformed into a commodity, and every activity is increasingly subject to the power of currency" (p. 61). Therefore, the combination of demands of cognitive capitalism with the process of continuing education becomes a means of guaranteed profitability for the institutions. Zayas (2012) says that "continuing education emerges as the society's need to adapt to new productive, economic, social and technological models" (p. 11), Moreover, it can be said that it arises to meet society's demands, provided that individuals have capital to invest.

Nowadays everyone seems to be born into a knowledge-based society that cherishes and encourages cognitive capitalism. According to Ball (2009), success or failure and having talent or not are issues which do not depend on who the person is, but on what they can become. If they do not possess skills and competencies that are compatible with the labor market, it is necessary to seek upgrade to become the person the market needs.

With this upgrade, it is possible to achieve, according to Zayas (2012), "promotion possibilities at work, (...) the improvement of quality of life, family or emotional cohesion, the best economic retribution" (p. 73). This quote is emphasized because continuing education inserted in knowledge societies is basically characterized as an 'extended life warranty', which, according to the author, is pursued by individuals when they seek upgrade to follow the trend of current globalization, with perspectives that go beyond professional demands, being quality of life and family and emotional cohesion, some of the items to be achieved in face of this proposal.

According to Bauman (2010), "this current cult to 'continuing education' is partly focused on the need to upgrade the 'state of the art' in professional information" (p. 54-55). It is undeniable that everyone should upgrade themselves, because being a competent and a flexible generalist is essential. To achieve that, it is all about choosing the best course with the most efficient methodology. However, in addition to paying for this product, Sennet (2006) warns us that "when we acquire qualifications, it does not mean that we have a durable asset" (p. 91) because the learning gained will certainly suffer changes in a short term. For Robertson (2008), this occurs because of the process of commodification of education into a product" (p. 36), that is, it is essential to make education a saleable product to move the economy of knowledge, because this economy needs to be on the move, it needs to be reinvented daily to be kept active.

The characteristics of contemporary capitalism, addressed by Sennet (2011), introduce changes in the world of labor. In the new capitalism, the labor market also wants mobile, flexible and innovative individuals and who are considered "good products".

According to Boutang (2003), in cognitive capitalism, "the substance of value lies in society, population, implicit knowledge, cognitive processes (...)" (p. 41), knowledge has value in the market. Robertson (2008) says, "as in every economy, 'the knowledge-based economy' is built. (...) as a result of discourses, practices and ideological, material and institutional struggles, and in development" (p. 41). Knowledge societies emerged in this process in order to build their own discourses to boost economy, which in the Brazilian reality moves billions every year. Ball (2009) mentions that the demand for lifelong learning begun increasingly earlier. People finish a course and already start another. They often attend more than one course at the same time. According to Gerzson (2007), "individuals suffer the anxiety of not lagging behind, being competent, qualified, talented in all areas" (p. 107), knowledge management takes on the responsibility to meet this demand.

In this chapter, the concept of cognitive capitalism is understood as the one moved by ideas, in which the emphasis is no longer on material objects alone and takes a sharp bend to focus on the consumption of messages and ideas.

Cognitive capitalism is associated with production of subjectivities and goods that are not necessarily material products. Instead, they are skills, knowledge and ideas that become productive so that the subjects who consume them place themselves in the market and in life. Under this perspective, cognitive capitalism is characterized by creating a world in which this kind of merchandise makes sense, in which the subjects need to be continuously learning, studying and upgrading in order to be competitive.

CONCLUSION

This chapter's conclusions invite the reader to think about how everything seems to be continuous nowadays concerning education, globalization and knowledge. The key concern of this chapter are the subjects who simply cannot keep up with the frantic composition of knowledge societies, either due to financial constraints, time restrictions or any other.

For Robertson (2013), "the choices always depend on the existence of those who cannot choose", because the value of one's choice depends on the choice of another, so choosing ends up becoming an action of not being able to choose. Being able is far from being enough!

Regarding thinking on knowledge societies, globalization and impacts on knowledge management presented in this chapter, aligned with Robertson's words, making choices in the contemporary might have become something inevitable. The emphasis on choosing seems to dismay all of us. Bauman (2001) says, "living in the midst of seemingly endless chances (...) has the sweet taste of 'freedom to become any one'" (p. 74). Once the options are varied, investing in different choices ends up selecting ones and downgrading others.

The subjects should resort to continuing education, because there seems to be no other alternative to become a valued commodity in knowledge societies. However, choosing to educate oneself continuously involves investments and, at that moment, many subjects for not having financial conditions, according to Bauman (2005b), become disposable. For this author, "the production of 'human reject', or more specifically, of human beings having been rejected, is an inevitable product of modernization, and an inseparable companion of modernity" (p. 12). Subjects with limitations and restrictions that prevent them to follow the proposed upgrades by knowledge management, become flawed consumers and candidates to market exclusion. These subjects identified as rejects are at risk of becoming invisible.

This article, besides showing the process of constituting knowledge societies, trends of globalization and influences caused in knowledge management, which, in an apparently subtle manner, seems to mobilize hundreds of subjects to consumption, allows a glimpse of contemporary uncertainties in which we find ourselves, the risks we face and our inability to project the future.

Commodification penetrates not only the subsistence of humans, in the farthest corners, but also fits in fields such as education and management, producing changes and electing and classifying the subjects as if they were businesses. However, the product itself is the creative idea.

Guided in a line of thought in which the facts are not stagnant, neither natural, but in an almost invisible border arising from the opposite, the opposite and almost never said, this study tried to present the main concepts of Knowledge society, globalization and knowledge management which currently intervene in the subjects' subjectivities (people who constantly seek continuous education).

This very exercise of thinking, rethinking and trying to understand leads to the realization of how difficult the transformation proposed by knowledge societies are not within everyone's reach. The very concept of continuing education, used many times in this chapter to illustrate and explain the reflections proposed, has become a saleable and valuable commodity and, as any other product, promotes exclusion, classification and selection of those who can and cannot enter the game of cognitive capitalism.

REFERENCES

Abianna, I. C. B. (2009). *Prática docente de profissionais-formadores em cursos de Educação continuada de professores: uma experiência de ação-reflexão* (Mestrado em Educação). Faculdade de Educação, Pontifícia Universidade Católica do Rio Grande do Sul, Porto Alegre.

Ball, S. (2009). Lifelong Learning, Subjectivity and the Totally Pedagogised Society. In A. C. B. Michael A Peters, M. Olssen, S. Maurer, & S. Weber (Eds.), *Governmentality Studies in Education*. Sense Publishers. doi:10.1163/9789087909857_013

Bauman, Z. (1999). Globalização, as consequências humanas. Tradução: Marcus Penchel. Rio de Janeiro: Zahar.

Bauman, Z. (2001). Modernidade Líquida. Tradução: Plínio Dentzien. Rio de Janeiro: Zahar, 2001.

Bauman, Z. (2005b). Vidas Desperdiçadas. Tradução: Carlos Alberto Medeiros. Rio de Janeiro: Zahar.

Bauman, Z. (2008a). Vida para consumo. A transformação das pessoas em mercadoria. Tradução: Carlos Alberto Medeiros. Rio de Janeiro: Zahar.

Bauman, Z. (2008b). A sociedade individualizada: vidas contadas e histórias vividas. Tradução: José Gradel. Rio de Janeiro: Zahar.

Bauman, Z. (2010). Capitalismo parasitário e outros temas contemporâneos. Tradução: Eliana Aguiar. Rio de Janeiro: Zahar.

Boutang, Y. M. (2003). O território e as políticas de controle no capitalismo cognitivo. In *Capitalismo cognitivo, trabalho, redes e inovação. Tradução: Eliana Aguiar*. DP&A.

Camozzato, V. C., & Costa, M. V. (2013). Vontade de pedagogia – pluralização das pedagogias e condução de sujeitos. Pelotas, Cadernos de Educação, 44, 22-44.

Canclini, N. G. (2003). *A globalização imaginada. Tradução: Sérgio Molina*. Iluminuras.

Costa, E. G. (2017). A globalização e as universidades latino-americanas. *Historia, Ciencias, Saude—Manguinhos*, 24(2), 538–540. doi:10.15900104-59702017000200014

Costa, M. V. (2009a). O consumismo na sociedade de consumidores. In M. V. Costa (Ed.), *A educação na cultura da mídia e do consumo*. Lamparina.

Cunha, V. A. (2002). *Profissional da informação na biblioteca pública contemporânea: o bibliotecário e a demanda por educação continuada* (Mestrado em Educação). Faculdade de Ciência da Informação, Universidade Federal da Bahia, Salvador.

Delors, J. (2001). Educação: um tesouro a descobrir: relatório para a Unesco da Comissão Internacional sobre Educação para o século XXI (5th ed.). São Paulo: Cortez; Brasília: UNESCO.

Faure, E. (1972). *Aprender a ser*. Bertrand.

Ferraz, A. (2001). *Educação continuada de professores: um estudo das políticas da secretaria municipal de educação de campinas - 1983/1996* (Mestrado em Educação). Faculdade de Educação, Universidade Estadual de Campinas, São Paulo.

Franciscone, F. (2006). *Educação continuada: um olhar para além do espelho, iluminando mente, corpo, coração e espírito do docente da educação superior* (Mestrado em Educação). Faculdade de Educação, Pontifícia Universidade Católica do Rio Grande do Sul, Porto Alegre.

Gerzson, V. R. (2007). A mídia como dispositivo da governamentalidade neoliberal: os discursos sobre educação nas revistas Veja, Época e Istoé (Doutorado em Educação). Faculdade de Educação, Universidade Federal do Rio Grande do Sul, Porto Alegre.

Gonzalez, R. V. D., & Martins, M. F. (2017). Knowledge Management Process: A theoretical-conceptual research. *Gestão & Produção*, *24*(2).

Hall, S. (2001). A identidade cultural na pós-modernidade. Tradução: Tomaz Tadeu da Silva e Guacira Lopes Louro. 6ª ed. Rio de Janeiro: DP&A.

Houssaye, J. (2007). Pedagogias: importação-exportação. In *Viagens Pedagógicas*. Cortez.

Ikujiro, H., & Nonaka, T. (2008). *Gestão do Conhecimento*. Tradução: Ana Thorell. Porto Alegre.

Lazzarato, M. (2003). Trabalho e capital na produção dos conhecimentos: uma leitura através da obra de Gabriel Tarde. In *Capitalismo cognitivo, trabalho, redes e inovação. Tradução: Eliana Aguiar*. DP&A.

Moore, M., & Kearsley, G. (2013). Educação a distância: sistemas de aprendizagem on-line. Tradução: Ez2Translate. 3 ed. São Paulo: Cengage Learning.

Moreto, J. A. (2002). *A Educação continuada do diretor de escola: avaliação da política implementada pela secretaria municipal da educação de campinas, no período de 1994 a 2000* (Mestrado em Educação). Faculdade de Educação, Universidade Estadual de Campinas, São Paulo.

Moro, V. (2007). *Educação continuada: um processo itinerante na construção de si com vistas à transformação da prática docente de professores de educação básica* (Mestrado em Educação). Faculdade de Educação, Pontifícia Universidade Católica do Rio Grande do Sul, Porto Alegre.

Nascimento, C. O. C. (2003). *O que querem os professores ante a educação contínua?* (Mestrado em Educação). Faculdade de Educação, Universidade Federal da Bahia, Salvador.

Oliveira, J. Q. (2011). *Percepções sobre a Educação continuada no formato MBA pelo executivo em sua carreira: um estudo de caso em São Paulo* (Mestrado em Administração). Faculdade de Administração, Pontifícia Universidade Católica de São Paulo, São Paulo.

Oliveira, S. G. D. (2007). *Políticas de formação continuada de professores que atuam no ensino fundamental* (Mestrado em Educação). Faculdade de Ciências Humanas, Letras e Artes. Universidade Tuiuti do Paraná, Curitiba.

Robertson, S. (2003). É o Teu Cérebro que Nós Queremos: A Bala de Prata da Sociedade do Conhecimento. *A Página da Educação, 129*(12).

Robertson, S. (2008). Professoras/es são importantes, não? Posicionando as/os professoras/es e seu trabalho na economia do conhecimento global. *Espaço do Currículo, 1*(1), 34-64.

Santos, J. D. (2006). Formação continuada: cartas de alforria & controles reguladores (Doutorado em Educação). Faculdade de Educação, Universidade Federal do Rio Grande do Sul, Porto Alegre.

Saraiva, K., & Veiga-Neto, A. (2009). Modernidade Líquida, capitalismo cognitivo e educação contemporânea. Educação e Realidade, 34(2), 187-201.

Sennett, R. (2011). A corrosão do caráter - consequências pessoais do trabalho no novo capitalismo (16ª ed.). Tradução: Marcos Santarrita. Rio de Janeiro: Record.

Serrano, A., & Fialho, C. (2005). *Gestão do conhecimento. O novo paradigma das organizações*. FCA Editora Informática.

Stewart, T. (2002). A riqueza do conhecimento: o capital intelectual e a nova organização. Tradução: Afonso Celso da Cunha Serra. Rio de Janeiro: Campus.

Vargas, E. J. (2017). La idea de universidad en vilo. Gestión de calidad, capitalismo cognitivo y autonomca. *Revista Colombiana de Educación, 72.*

Zabala, A., & Arnau, L. (2010). *Como aprender e ensinar competências.* Artmed.

Zayas, E. L. (2012). A elaboração de programas inovadores de educação permanente. In *O Paradigma da Educação continuada. Tradução: Alexandre Salvaterra.* Penso.

Chapter 6
Developing Knowledge Societies:
A Case of Women in Kanungu District

Peace T. Kyamureku
Rural Women and Youth Fund (RUTH Fund), Uganda

ABSTRACT

This chapter explores how the knowledge societies are being developed in different local, national, regional, and international societies and more in particular how the women and girls in Kanungu are developing their knowledge within the clans. The methodology followed to generate a set of questions: What are clans? and Does belonging to a clan group have an individual or group impact on their identity (as Bakiga/Banyankole/Bahororo/Bairu/Bahima) Ugandans? Why are women in Kanungu district organizing in paternal clans? How new is the trend? What is its origin? Are there women, girls who do not identify with clans? What are the basic socio-economic challenges confronting the girls and women of Kanungu? Has local government and development partners tried to deal with the challenges of women? With what results? Is organizing in Clan Groups matriarchy? Is it empowerment or cementing submissiveness? Is it increasing women work load? What is its effect on men-masculinity? In order to understand how the clan groups' learn, a feminist qualitative ethnographic approach was used. Women's personal stories were collected through focus group discussions and interviews to explore their experiences on the prospects and challenges of clan group activities. A sample of five women and five men randomly picked was used. Therefore, this chapter aims to stimulate sharing knowledge and learning about women's lives in rural areas; document women's narratives; show the economic development trends in Uganda; promote self-actualization, self-awareness, and pride among women as equal citizens of Uganda; and motivate reading and learning and contribute to creation of rural libraries.

DOI: 10.4018/978-1-5225-8873-3.ch006

INTRODUCTION

Uganda is a landlocked country in East Africa, with Sudan to the north, Kenya to the east, Lake Victoria Rwanda and Tanzania to the south, and Zaire (Congo) to the west. Her population was of diverse ethnic groups, who were organized either in kingdoms with hereditary kings (Buganda, Ankole, Toro, Bunyoro) or Chiefdoms (Kigezi, Teso, Acholi, Karamoja, Madi, West Nile, and other parts of Uganda). The indigenous communities were socially well organized because of systems where children were socialized to become active and useful members of society. Girls were trained to be good mothers and boys were trained to be heads of families.

Social economic developments in education, religious beliefs, health education and use of modern as opposed to traditional medicine, and, a transition from a subsistence to a cash economy, took place during the colonial period-(1895-1962) . The boys and girls had to learn skills that would make them fit into the changing environment that was being influenced by the Arab-European and African cultures and practices. One way to learn new practices was through women organizations and clubs, which were formed by women who had some western education. Christian based organizations like Mothers Union and Catholic Women taught girls and women sewing, knitting, child welfare, nutrition, house-keeping and cooking. The organizations were useful in development of knowledge, skills and learning of new cultural practices, but few seem to have taught women to challenge the unequal gender relations, have an identity of their own not dependent on male relatives (husband, father or brothers).

During the early colonial era, women and girls were mainly considered as home-makers and economic assets where families exchanged bride price. Few writers mentioned women and children, for example, *An Economic History of Ankole c.1895-c.1919* Master of Arts thesis by Peace Twine Kalekyezi. Men were trained and forced to grow cash crops-cotton or coffee and later on tea, to earn an income so that they could pay government tax. The economic trends greatly impacted on the political development. People who paid homage to local kings, started to be ruled by Chiefs of a central government that enforced its presence with tax collection.

Education[1] was introduced with religion and new beliefs were embraced changing some cultural practices, which continued to favour men against women. Education for women was introduced gradually as the British felt that the educated men needed educated women to influence society. The women that got some Western education were confined into care service jobs like teaching and nursing while majority of women stayed home to do unpaid work as wives and mothers while working on clan land cultivating or taking care of livestock and its products. Women continued to teach children customs and traditions concerned with family life revolve around assuring men's control of women's sexuality(in order to have offspring and lineage) and a woman's labour (in order to sustain the families). *The Rising Tide-Ugandan Women's Struggle for a Public Voice 1940-2002*, FOWODE, Edited by Winnie Byanyima and Richard Mugisha, 2003, *page 240.*

In 1966 the Buganda problem[2] got Uganda into phases of violence and unrest in different parts of the country. It was during such phases of unrest that women would get involved in economic and social practices that used to be areas for men. The Economic War of mid 1970's led to women getting into petty trading alongside men, many of who were engaged in smuggling essential commodities into the country and taking out cash crops for better prices. Education that was a vehicle for change was neglected and there was increase in school drop- out. Girls were considered only good for marriage. The few who were educated struggled to get and keep jobs and run families. The war affected Ugandans and Kigezi (Kanungu, Kisoro and Rukungiri) region felt the impact due to neighboring countries of Congo Zaire, and Rwanda where youth and men took political or and sometimes economic refugee.

A five (5) year guerrilla warfare (1981-1986) was not only a climax of Uganda's political problems, it was also a beginning of wars that affected the north while the south struggled out of under-development. The National Resistance Army/Movement (NRA/M) that came into leadership of Uganda started on rehabilitation of Uganda's economy, and building up democratic governance institutions.

"Although patriarchy, which oppresses poor rural women most (was) hardly challenged in the bush, the NRM promised to address past injustices and opened a window of opportunity to women through quota system at local government and parliamentary levels." Editors, Winnie Byanyima and Richard Mugisha-The Rising Tide, page ix.

1989 Uganda Constitutional Commission was set up, and later a Constituent Assembly was put in place to draft the first Uganda Constitution by Ugandans. The 1995 Constitution is commended as gender sensitive and progressive. It had Affirmative Action policies aimed at improving the situation of all marginalized groups (women, youth, Persons with Disabilities, workers and army). These developments coincided with the third UN Conference on Women (1985 in Nairobi), and the fourth UN Conference on Women (1995 in Beijing) where many decisions were made by government as a commitment aimed at uplifting the situation of women. The Constitution is still expected to contribute to implementation of laws to end discrimination and enhance gender equality.

Political, Social, Economic Status of Women in the 21st Century.

At the 62nd Commission on the Status of Women, Uganda Civil Society Report indicated that women have remained the most deprived and discriminated. The report highlighted women's land rights; women's voice, decision-making and leadership; poverty and inequality; health care and education as challenges to women in Uganda as in 2018.

Women have been denied rights to own land, even ancestral land, before marriage, in marriage and out of marriage. *"Some cultures still consider women as property to be inherited."* (62nd CSW Report) This is coupled with ignorance of the law by women on their land/property rights and land governance often exhibited during land acquisition/registration and ownership of land. Often men have sold off land without their spousal consent and in other instances women act as witnesses in the sale of their land with very minimal information on the implication of their actions to the future of land tenure security.

Women's voice, leadership and decision-making power may be present at the household, community, and the national level has a third women legislators. The capacity varies from individual to individual but as a collective Uganda is making some progress. Rural women and girls are still struggling to access and sustain quality and affordable health care. For rural women there are challenges of communicable diseases, limited information and knowledge on causes, prevention, management of non-communicable diseases, lack of proper sanitation and hygiene exposes women and girls to water sanitation health(WASH) related diseases. Education is key to women empowerment but it still has challenges, especially for the poor. Minimal education implies that one is prone to negative cultural practices like Female Genital Mutilation, child marriages, sexual violence, gender based violence and widow inheritance. These have often made rural women and girls more inferior, vulnerable and marginalised in both public and private spheres.

51% of the Uganda population who are women continue to be at the bottom margins of socio-economic and political development processes. 19% of the population is living in poverty with women forming the bulk. For example, 5 out of 10 households use *tadoba* (kerosene wick lamp) as source of lighting and 8 out of 10 households use the three stone fire place for cooking. 2 out of 10 households have access to piped water and 4 out of 10 households practice water harvesting. 6 out of 10 households have pit latrines, and 5 out of 10 households are located 1.5km from a tarmac road (Citizens' Survey on Uganda Vision 2040, Uganda National NGO Forum, May 2015).

83% of women are engaged in agriculture, the major economic activity in Uganda, but only 25.5% control the land they cultivate and only 27% of registered land is owned by women. The women in agriculture lack technical support, 2 out 10 people receive extension services, 7 out of 10 did not know of any efforts to promote nutrition at community level, the majority of Ugandans have no organized storage facilities, and 4 out of 10 keep their agricultural produce in their homes, an indicator to size of harvest. Failure to have storage leads to wastage and at times contamination of agricultural produce which cause health problems.

Uganda has one of the highest maternal mortality rates, 20 mothers die giving birth daily. This is inevitable in a patriarchal setting where early pregnancies and marriages are practices that are not recognized as negative traditional practices by many in the rural community. The Uganda Demographic Health Survey (UDHS) 2011 and National GBV survey 2010 showed that gender based violence (GBV) is wide spread and affects all people irrespective of their social, economic and political status. It occurs in families, communities, workplaces and institutions. However, GBV within families is often hidden from public sight and the victims usually suffer in silence either due to fear of repercussions of reporting or lack of awareness of their rights and the different forms of GBV.

In education, drop out of girls from school is increasing with teenage pregnancies accounting for 34%, poverty 28% (From Uganda Civil Society Position Paper for the 62nd Commission on the Status of Women, February 2018). It is unfortunate that education that was and still is a pillar of nation building is on the decline in Uganda and especially in rural areas. The poor quality of education is compounded by increased cheating in examinations at all levels. Attitude and value of education are further reflected in the poor quality of professionals (doctors - medical and veterinary, engineers, economists, legal personnel, judges and religious leaders). Facts show that 3 out of ten household reported ever paying a bribe to access a service, and 7 out of 10 persons had ever reported a complaint but only 1 out of 10 had ever had a complaint addressed (Citizen's Survey May2015). Where do women and girls seek for solace and justice?

Rural communities are marginalized and those most affected are women and youth. The rural women still believe men are their providers and that they have no rights. This is due to a number of factors among which are traditional beliefs, practices, distances from centers of power and social services. Few women can claim their rights, instead they take on men's roles, of caring for family and even paying school fees and they feel they are the ones to keep homes running. The poor are continuously being pushed away from developed areas where safe water, electricity, safe houses and roads are available . Urban poor and the rural based populations are not visible, especially to leaders because they are not easily accessible.

Rural women are referred to in international, regional conventions - the Beijing Platform for Action, CEDAW, the Maputo Protocol and the Social Development Goals (SDGs) indicate that unless there is more effort made to include every woman in development, gender equality and social justice targets for 2030 will not be achieved. However, Uganda committed herself to improve the situation of the rural communities and especially to support women and girls get out of poverty, to lead lives of dignity.

Men and women in rural areas complain that the elected leaders abandon and forget them after they have been voted into power. They feel isolated and isolation leads to exclusion from programs and plans and there is limited information and knowledge on government programs, policies and laws. Exclusion is about rights, about access and about opportunities for the rural communities. Women in rural communities experience low self-esteem, and lack voice to participate effectively in self and national development.

Due to gender inequalities and cultural beliefs, women and youth have limited decision making powers at house-hold and community levels They lack control over resources (time, personnel for labour and finances). Illiteracy and poverty are visible challenges in rural communities which have led women and female youth to depend on the male flock a situation that drives gender based violence. Emotional violence against women in marital relationships is common and some of the contributing factors include; men being jealousy when women talk to other men (59%), tracking women's movement outside the home (56%), suspicions of being unfaithful (34%), isolation of women from friends and family at 29% and 20% respectively.(UDHS 2011).Women and girls feel helpless and because they do not know their rights, they cannot speak up for themselves and others.

In spite of a gender sensitive constitution,[3] there is marginalization and discrimination within the women population. There are urban and rural, young and old, educated and illiterate, therefore there are women and girls who identify with the national Women's movement and some who do not and say they have never heard of it. The Rural Women's Day (15th October) is not yet recognized by government to draw attention to the plight of rural communities, and get them to enjoy rights to development, education, safe water, health and well-being. Rights of adequate housing, a clean environment, economic development and financial autonomy. There is no guaranteed access to an adequate standard of living and ending poverty, to land and inheritance, and peace. There are limited chances for women and girls in rural areas to have positions in decision-making and leadership either in homes, community and nation (WWSF-Women's World Summit Foundation, 2017).

The Kanungu Women Clan Groups[4] Role

History has shown that changes are part of life. Some changes are due to external factors (foreigners-whose beliefs and practices affected Africans) while others are due to local situations like political and economic wars. There have been many changes geographically in Uganda. For example, Kigezi was a colonial region of Uganda which over time disintegrated into four districts of Rukungiri (1974), Kisoro (1991), Kanungu (2001) and Kabale.

Kanungu district was formed from Rukungiri district in July 2001. It was a remote area in Uganda. Kanungu is in middle of districts of Rukungiri to the north, Kabale to the south east, Kisoro to the south, and the Democratic Republic of Congo to the west. It is after some incidents of killings of tourists in Bwindi Forest by Hutu Interahamwe from Zaire, burning of a family of six in Kinkizi East Kambuga (1999) and mass suicide or the Millennium mass massacre by Kibwetere cult (17th March 2000) drew attention to the district. It is a hilly area with soils and weather that promote agriculture in an estimated area of 122,000squire kilometers. The district leadership (Local Council 5- Josephine Kasya, the first woman chairperson in Uganda, Chief Administrative Officer-Elias Byamungu and Councillors) started off with a mission to serve the community through coordinated delivery of services which focus on national priorities and significant local needs, to promote socio-economic development of the district (The Giants of Kigezi Volume Number 2, 2003, page 31.).

It is in the Kanungu district that history is being made by women and girls who celebrate and claim their paternal clans, what we are calling the Women Clan Groups. Clan leaders appointed on merit but not hereditary, were responsible for peace and order in greater Kigezi (Historian Festo Karwemera, The Giants of Kigezi Volume Number 2, 2003, page 1).

- What are clans?

Clans are groups of people who have same origin, same cultural beliefs, same totems and tended to live together but would not have marriages of people of similar clans. The Bantu were/are organized in clans which were patriarchal in practice. There are documented examples of where a clan would take over property of a deceased clans' man disinheriting the widow and her children. Where clansmen did not ask for property the widow would be required to be inherited by a clansman preferably a brother to the deceased. Rebecca Mulira narrated how

In 1956, my father died and he left a lot of property to my mother. The clan people did not want this and decided to take everything from my mother....In the Will, that house was left to my mother so she refused to move...After a few months one Lovincer Kato lost her husband in an accident. The clan people took all her property and wanted to take the house as well. They took her cattle and all other things she had worked for with her husband.....(Editors Winnie Byanyima and Richard Mugisha, The Rising Tide, page 26).

Some examples of clans among Bakiga, Bahororo and Banyankole are – Basyaba, Bagahe, Bitira, Bakyimbiri, Basingo, Bazigaba, Bahinda, Bajengwe, Bajara, Banzira, Bashaaki, Basigi, and many others. They yielded power and at this time of changes, women could be enhancing their male relatives' power and significance.

- Does belonging to a Clan group have an individual or group impact on women identity (as Bakiga/Banyankole/ Bahororo/ Bairu/ Bahima)Ugandans?

Oshwera abuuza meaning that one should ask before getting married is a crucial question among Bantu of Western Uganda, and especially among rural communities. It is before marriages that questions are asked about clans and totems in order to avoid people who are related by blood to intermarry. Avoiding marrying from same clan reduces chances of communicable health problems and cultural complications, and so is given importance.

The Clan groups have some impact on one's identity, but it's of limited significance in a global environment. The fact that clans are among both Bakiga, Banyankole, Bahororo, there is no definition of identity that is enhanced for individuals. The concept of Bahima (cattle keepers) or Bairu (cultivators)is rare in Kanungu because there is more agriculture than cattle keeping. Economic occupation depends more on the environment, terrain and capacity to carry out manage because a lot has changed, in fact growing of tea has overshadowed everything else in Kanungu.

A sample of five women from Kanungu living and working in Kampala was asked about the trend of women organizing along their clans but no one had ever heard about it. The fact that daughters of Kanungu who are educated do not know about the trend, it means clan organizing will stay a local issue among neighbouring communities and has no impact on national identity. This seems to be a practice of rural women exclusively.

- What is the origin of women organizing in Clan Groups?

Some women in Kanungu (and Rukungiri) are organizing in their fathers' clans. This has been going on for over twenty years. Depending on the activities a group carries out, there was admiration by women to emulate the practice. The Clan Groups visit the sick, the elderly, share gifts and food. As death is said to be a uniting factor in life, groups take part in sending off /burying the loved ones. Funerals are spaces for sharing information, learning about what is appreciated in behavior as the living talk about the life of the deceased. No wonder, the visibility of a clan group at a funeral was admired by many and led to formation of new Clan Groups. When a group would lay a wreath and/or give a speech at a funeral, they would announce their contribution in form of food stuffs (matooke, posho and rice) and bottled water which make the burial ceremony special, and different from other village burials.

There are different types of organizing. In one village of Rukungiri women organized according to husbands' clan the *Baka Bagahe* (wives of Bagahe). However, it is not all wives are welcome to join the group, but the middle group of wives, without their mother-in laws or their daughter- in laws.

- Are there women, girls who do not identify with clans?

This question was more than not participating in Clan Group activities, and was about one not knowing ones' clan to be able to participate.

This was found to be a difficult area to discuss due to the cultural practice of silence on issues of sexuality. While communities of Kanungu tend to glorify males when they are popular with girls, they condemn females who are free with men. Cases of defilement are often not reported to authorities and where it results into pregnancy the victim of defilement and the mother suffer consequences of condemnation. The mother has a duty to get out of the problem, by advising and assisting the daughter to get an abortion, or convince the offender to marry the defiled girl. Few mothers take the case of defilement to authorities for appropriate action, which would mean police action, court and imprisonment. Many times defilement is due to incest which complicates the situation for a family. The crime brings shame to family and so the victim is forced to keep quiet about the injustice. Cases of rape are similar except that some cases are taken to authorities because the victim can testify, there is no stigma as in defilement. The court process is not friendly to rural communities due to inadequate knowledge about procedures, long distances to courts and affordability in terms of time and money. Few women and girls admit being born out of wedlock. The orphans claim the clans of the guardians who are either maternal or paternal relations. There are few single parents in rural areas due to the cultural practices and beliefs which protect family and every one belonging to a clan. The clan gatherings could trigger an increase in thoughts of belonging among the community. There have been cases where children (boys and girls) demand to know their clans and biological fathers. The use of DNA to determine paternity is not well known and would be expensive for rural communities. There is a link between early pregnancies and early marriages to avoid having children without clans. There is a strong belief that mothers should protect their daughters from getting pregnant before marriage.

- What are the basic socio-economic challenges confronting the girls and women of Kanungu?

When women and girls in Nyarurambi-Kanungu were asked about the challenges and community problems, these were the issues, not in any order of importance, for the youth it was/is school drop-out, unemployment, early marriages, unsafe abortions, unplanned pregnancies, alcoholism and drug abuse which in turn lead to mental health, violence and insecurity in homes and community, family neglect as women do not work when abusing alcohol which leads to food shortage and famine.

The women group gave the following challenges –domestic violence, food shortage due to infertile land, homeless women who end up in prostitution, and unsafe water.

Both groups took time to bring out challenges of human right violations (rape and defilement) and destitute children who are abandoned with grandparents. Majority of older persons live in poverty due to limited economic opportunities, ill-health and poorly equipped health services.

The above confirm that gender-based violence (GBV) is not easily talked about and is not visible to the public eye. One needs to put on gender lenses[5] to know there is gender based violence that is harmful to families, affecting women and children most because men tend to be the initiators of the violence. This may explain why some women organize in Clan Groups. It could be one way to overcome challenges of psychological, emotional, and economic violence that that are not visible, unlike physical violence where one can be bruised or tortured. For instance, among the married women aged 15 – 49 years who have access to cash; 53% decide its usage, 31% decide jointly as a couple, while 14% indicated that decision is made solely by the husbands.(UDHS 2011) A woman who is affected by this may need a trusted confidant. In a district where there is sometimes food insecurity and women are responsible to put food on the table, they need peer support and encouragement to lead stable lives. The activities of Clan groups provide this support, one can talk about her family issues and get advice without feeling ridiculed and out of place.

- Has local government and development partners tried to deal with the challenges of women? With what results?

Kanungu is one of the far-to-reach areas in Uganda. The local government and development partners have limited reach to rural women and girls because of distances, poor road network, lack of transport to reach those areas. Moreover, cultural practices hinder women visibility, and exposure. A government official will visit the Chairperson, a man, to discuss issues and women will rarely be consulted. Like most societies in Uganda, Kanungu is highly patriarchal and few women participate in development programs. The women elected leaders tend to behave like men and work with close friends leaving out many needy women who have no voice. The Clan Groups provide a platform to share some information from government by the few women who work with government.

- Is Women organizing in Clan Groups matriarchy?

"Matriarchy is not domination by mothers, it refers to mothers as being present at the beginning of life and culture," said Dr Sister Dipio who further alleged that matriarchal Africa will re-align society (In a Key Note address - *Writing to Re-Claim the Archaic African Matriarch,* at a FEMRITE Conference, at Uganda Museum on 24th July 2018.

Women celebrating in their clan groups is a depiction of matriarchy. They are re-aligning society to create a sense of human community, and transmitting aspects of African culture, especially exchanging gifts. In contrast, patriarchy is characterized by interest in exchange and profit.

Women have created a new way of bringing gifts into their homes because the old ways through dowry or bride price are declining/ fading. Girls are encouraged to complete schools and so spend more years before marriage. Some educated girls choose not to get married traditionally with dowry/ bride price, others cohabite and their partners never pay dowry/ bride price. Girls exchange value has depreciated and so women have found new ways of identity in a patriarchal society. Women would be proud of cows paid for them,[6] a trend that is changing. Dowry is at times paid in cash which may not be visible to public to make a woman proud.

- Is it empowerment[7] or cementing submissiveness? Is it increasing women work load? What is its effect on men-masculinity?

We cannot underestimate the impact of Women Clan Groups. We can compare them to women clubs and organizations in the early days of colonialism where the partially educated women played a role in empowering[8] fellow women who never went to school. There are still many women who never completed primary school education, and crave to be seen as educated. It is in hospitals or at school meetings where the illiterate women find problems following up discussions and instructions. A doctor gave a smartly dressed couple a sample bottle and told them in simple English-*Let her drink a lot to get the sample, urine.* Other patients came and left them waiting, until the lab technician asked what the problem was, in the local language. The couple replied they were waiting for a doctor to call them, they had to get the instruction again. It was embarrassing.

Parents who cannot read risk children dropping out of school because they never understand what the school requirements are. It is no wonder that the village Savings and Credit schemes have become popular because only the Secretary records what each woman deposits. There are many stories where women have lost their savings because of illiteracy. The Women Clan Groups can be of social support to encourage literacy. The activities of Clan Groups are increasing on women's workload and at times overlap with what joint groups of men and women are doing. For instance, the Bataka Groups were meant to help in funeral arrangements. Clan Groups are merely supplementing their work.

A group of men were asked what they thought about the activities of Clan Groups. Three of the five men in the group said their wives were not in any Clan group. The two men said the decision for joining any group was solely the decision of the women. One explained that his wife was already in other groups, like Emanzi group where men and women are trained in gender equality and gender roles. There are other groups which take up time and some women choose not to be involved in Clan Groups. There is need to observe and listen to men's reaction to the Women Clan Groups. The Clan Groups are not a threat to masculinity, in fact women are giving value to patriarchy.

It is too early to evaluates the impact of women organizing along clans to overcome gender inequalities in a patriarchal society. Women continue to be custodians of socialization, expected to transfer patriarchal ideologies that promote male domination and female subordination from one generation to another, as gate keepers of patriarchy. Clan groups may be one new way of doing this.

• What implications does it have on urban/rural[9]; poor/rich divides in society?

The Women Clan Groups have their activities in rural areas. Their functions or gatherings usually take half a day, which implies that participants do not live very far from each other. The organizers try to include those living in walk-able distance. The fact that the functions do not involve women who live in urban areas, the Clan Groups may not have a big impact on the urban/ rural divide.

There is a tendency of women who take part in the Clan Group activities to evaluate each other informally after a function. Comments and rumors are made on the type and taste of food[10], the people invited and how well they were served. This implies that there may be unity along clan lines but discrimination along economic lines. There is a poor/rich divide that is shown within the Clan Group activities, how it is handled will be a good lesson in inclusiveness. The poor may work harder and invest more in what the rich have, or the poor may fear to invite the rich to their functions or the rich may not attend functions of the poor. There is need for further observation to determine which way the poor/rich divide will take. On the national level, there is evidence that the gap between the poor and the rich is getting wider. This is a worrying trend as it leads to insecurity, mistrust and people living in fear of each other.

CASE STUDIES OF WOMEN AND CLAN GROUPS FROM NYARURAMBI, KIFUNJO, RUGYEYO KANUNGU DISTRICT

1. Alice was excited about her uniform – a long black skirt and a green T-shirt on which was written Bahara Ba Basigi which meant Daughters of Basigi. Alice was originally from Kabale, and moved to Kanungu with her male partner. They worked hard digging for people to get food to survive. Although Alice was hard working, independent and adventurous that did not earn her the respect. She was called by different derogatory names (Iwe mushumbawe / muhukuwe:You slave, Iwe murogi we: You witch) but when she was accepted in the group she was referred to as Muhara wa Basigi: Daughter of Basigi clan. She felt like a complete human being and not a foreigner any more. One could see she had identity in a group.

2. Beatrice is a member of Daughters of Bajara Development Group (Bahara Ba Bajara Tutunguke Group) which is two years old. She narrates benefits of being a member as –

    ◦   *Advise each other on family matters, behavior, not to abuse each other (okuherana)alcohol abuse/drunkardness, and how to get out of poverty.*

    ◦   *She learnt how to be responsible at house hold level, how to organize functions hosting each other, how to help each other in times of sickness, have got to know each others' family members better;*

    ◦   *She feels she has become more civilized, has overcome ignorance (obutamanya bwekinyakare); has acquired material /financial benefits (okushukirana ebyomunju).*

    ◦   *A space where she can report wrong doing, grievances, because she trusts the group to have powers to suspend/expel members who shame/ disgrace the clan (nibashwaza aboruganda).*

Beatrice is looking forward to owning a uniform for the group (a kitenge or African print material), and participating in the great get together.

CONCLUSION

There is awareness among rural women that the world they are living in is changing very fast. Villages that used to be sparsely populated are now congested, where food crops were in plenty, there is scarcity as witnessed in the 2017 famine. This can be compared to the period of colonialism when there were new ideas and challenges. In the 1960's the Ministry of Culture had women organized in Clubs in each county where they were *"taught sewing, knitting, repairing clothes, child welfare, nutrition, housekeeping, and cooking. They also sang, danced and played games.* Tripp.A.M,2000. *Women in Politics in Uganda,* Fountain Publishers, Kampala, page 36 claims that in *Kigezi, women embraced organizations for other purposes: development, getting rid of ignorance, and only 5% mentioned learning ways of caring for the family."* (eds. Winnie Byanyima and Richard Mugisha, page 6 and 7).

There are economic pressures in 21st society. There are new issues, new ways of doing things and a need to adjust attitude to life, practices and ways of living.

Kanungu is still inhabited mainly by indigenous people there are few tribes from different parts of Uganda. This means new ideas are brought in by the inhabitants, some girls and women, who have travelled in and out of the district. In spite of low education and illiteracy, they have gained knowledge and skills. They are admired and have things they can teach those who have been domesticated and have never gone beyond Kanungu district. To bridge the knowledge gap, women have decided to learn in Clan groups rather than formal Clubs. Just as in early days of Colonialism, women want to be exemplary, live in good houses, enjoy dressing in new modern fabrics and fashions. Eating new food stuffs is a necessity because of changes in land use, fertility, and climate change that have led to reduced production of traditional food crops.

However, the 21st century Clan groups are like the 1960's Clubs because they are also involved in singing, learning to be good citizens.

The immediate results of women and girls embracing their clans are exciting. They have acquired self-esteem and minimized unnecessary embarrassment they previously faced due to ignorance and lack of exposure. They have people centered skills for family benefits and have earned respect from their children, neighbors and community. Women are excited about freedom of movement, as they visit each others' homes, share delicious meals, show off the relatives and children. The visiting and entertaining comes at a cost. They are investing in creating social networks.

As women organize the functions, they have met the wider community –the service providers, like those hiring out tents, generators, chairs. They are able to negotiate prices and quality of products. They have networked with government officers, and some have been able to invite them to their homes. The functions have cemented relationships among women, their husbands and community leadership. In the short term, the trend will reduce enmity in society and lead to peaceful co-existence.

The clan gatherings or festivals are part of culture that make women and girls enhance their ability to make decisions that protect their interests. The interests of women for a long time were marriage for themselves and for their daughters. The Women Club Groups teach how to cook, serve, and organize the home. There is a big possibility that women acquire new items for the homes before hosting visitors. A home needs to look clean and so it can be painted or smeared with sand, chairs, tables, plates, serving spoons and even cups and glasses can be added to a home as a result of the half day function. The Clan group uniform is a treasured item. They draw on knowledge from past to look ahead for survival with identity, and sense of destiny. It is believed that without culture a community loses self awareness, self –respect and guidance.

People without culture feel insecure and are obsessed with the acquisition of material things and public displays, which give them a temporary security. if one accepts one's cultural heritage and defines oneself by it-that indeed, only that culture can provide self-knowledge and self- identity (Waangari Maathai, page 161-162).

Hard times make poor and marginalized women more prone to social injustices and hardship. Do new practices create positive competition? Since Kanungu gained status of a district, there are new developments that impact on men and women equally. There are roads, safe water, the environment has greatly changed with a lot of deforestation. There is more cash crop growing (tea) which has affected food crop growing and the comfort of women and girls who have to seek of other ways of keeping their homes fed rather than from working on the small plots of land left for food growing. Women have been forced to get ways of earning cash to buy home necessities. In a way, men have failed to cope managing families like they used to. They have taken up drinking and roaming in the urban/ town centers. Women have a reason to seek for social support from which to learn how to keep marriages working, how to deal with family relations, children's education and family welfare. Poverty affects women differently from men, the Clan Groups are a way of coping for the marginalized women.

Women of Kanungu are partly on the right track for self and community development in tackling adverse norms and promoting positive rol e models, building assets and property .(Report of the UN Secretary General's High Level Report, Seven Primary Drivers of Women's Economic Development,2016.[11]

- What implications does the practice have on policy developments for gender equality, women empowerment?

Culture is a double-edged sword that can be used as a weapon for empowerment or to threaten those that would assert their own self-expression or self-identity. It is therefore a fact that women and girls through the clan gatherings are claiming self –identity, self-confidence, self-knowledge and ability to be visible. However, there is no evidence that they take charge of their lives, and are empowered. They could be reinforcing women's traditional roles and teaching their children about culture as required by clan heads .There is enhanced clan identity, responsibility and peer clan learning. There is increased decision making by women but not in strategic areas rather in the day to day entertainment, practical needs of society. There is minimal link between the clan gatherings and sustainable development, if it is there, it is indirect and needs to be encouraged.

Policy makers should not miss an opportunity of building up on the knowledge generated and shared by these groups. The clan gatherings provide a platform on which government policies can be shared, debated and monitored. The platform will give the women and girls a sense of participating in government decision –making. It is a bottom-up grass-root approach to development. Government is cautious about emphasizing a change to unequal gender relations, and is supported by religious leaders who preach that men are heads of families and women should be submissive. Government focuses on providing necessary social services like health and education and water, with minimal care if they were accessible and affordable to a rural woman and youth. *Linking the struggles for gender equality, poverty eradication and ending oppression of all women and men is a challenge we must address* (Winnie Byanyima, The Rising Tide, page 185. This is also confirmed in the fact that for over fifty years, the Domestic Relations Bill or Marriage and Divorce Bill is still in Parliament not passed into a Family law that would clarify women's property rights and inheritance.

Recommendations and Lessons for Policy Development

Few African leaders recognize that what they call the Nation is a veneer laid over a cultureless state –without values, identity, or character….no African really knows what the character of that modern State might be beyond a passport and an identity card (Waangari Maathai, page 46). This is good governance in motion where even previously marginalized groups are brought into domain of decision-making which hither to may not have been the case (New Vision, October 16th, 2014.).

The study recommends that 1)Local government structures take advantage of clan gatherings to get views for development, and to share more progressive ideas, like human rights, property ownership and inheritance; 2) Women leaders who are not politically elected can be found among the clan group leaders, to guide on social, economic and environmental rights and accountable management of natural resources. There will be citizen participation in rural areas where Civil society organizations are weak or non –existent due to shrinking space and hard to reach environment; 3) Working through women and girls' clan groups will lead to development because they are self-reliant and owned by members who are not driven by gain but self-development. There is peer learning, monitoring and evaluation. These are the informal Community Based Organisations that should be included in policy making and planning for Sustainable development.

Voice and leadership in decision making are recognized as key elements of women's empowerment. They encapsulate women having the capacity to express their preferences, demands, views and interests, to gain access to positions of decision making that affect public or private power and resource allocation, and to exercise influence in leadership positions. Women's voice, leadership and decision-making power may be present at the household, community and national level, and, can be individual or collective.

Girls' retention and completion rates in education continue to remain low. This is attributed to persistent socio-cultural and economic barriers that keep girls out of school generally, but which are more pronounced for girls from disadvantaged and marginalized communities. These barriers include; 1) Lack of gender-sensitive teachers (especially men); 2) Displacement due to conflict; 3) Male teacher harassment and intimidation; 4) Cultural beliefs (preferential treatment of boys and early marriage) and practices such as household chores that keep girls too busy to attend school and 5) Lack of parental support for girls' education due to low literacy level of parents

GBV has diverse effects on the individual, families, community and country at large. These range from discrimination, stigmatization, and isolation often leading to loss of self-confidence, unpredict able and frightening environment, and a huge cost in terms of income lost due to ill health and diminished motivation to work by the victims. In addition, GBV leads to health complications particularly; obstetric fistula and other birth complications.

Culture is the means by which a people expresses itself, through language, traditional wisdom, politics, religion, architecture, music, tools, greetings, symbols, festivals, ethics, values and collective identity...Culture gives a people self-identity and character. It allows them to be in harmony with their physical and spiritual environment, to form the basis for their sense of self-fulfillment and personal peace.

ACKNOWLEDGMENT

The staff of Rural Women and Youth Fund Uganda who took time to contribute ideas, and time to the study are highly appreciated.

REFERENCES

Byanyima, W., & Mugisha, R. (Eds.). (2003). *The Rising Tide-Ugandan Women's Struggle for a Public Voice 1940-2002. FOWODE.*

Dipio. (2018). *Writing to Re-Claim the Archaic African Matriarch.* Keynote address at FEMRITE Conference.

Kalekyezi, P. T. (1982). *An Economic History of Ankole c.1895-c.1919* (Master of Arts thesis). Makerere University.

Maathai. (2009). *The Challenge for Africa. Arrow* Books.

Report of the UN Secretary –General's High –Level Panel on Women's Economic Empowerment. (2016). *Leave no one behind-A call to action for gender equality and women's economic empowerment.* UN.

New Vision. (2014). *Support Women's Efforts to attain Financial Independence.* Author.

World Survey on the Role of Women in Development. (2014). *Gender Equality and Sustainable Development states.* Author.

ENDNOTES

[1]   Both formal (school-based) and informal education in families and community went on hand-in hand, varying in details for individuals.

[2]   The Buganda crisis got many into exile and caused suffering for women in many families.

[3]   The Uganda Constitution of 1995 provided for Affirmative Action Policies to improve gender equality and opportunities.

[4]   This Chapter will use the term to refer to groups of women formed along their fathers' clans as they operated in Kanungu.

[5]   Gender lens is having skill and knowledge on how to men and women are socialized. It takes experience to detect that a woman could be affected by GBV. For instance with a bruised face a medical personnel needs to understand how to get truth on what caused it to advise to prevent more harm that could lead to deformity, mental breakdown or death. GBV affects health and economic well-being of a family, community and nation. It needs intervention of medical, law enforcement/police and local leaders to deal with it.

[6]   From interviews and observation women who bride price has not been paid feel they are not valued and are not stable in homes. They are not respected by some in laws. Men who have not paid are also treated with little respect as in the local saying (*omukwe atajugire*)an in-law who has not paid bride price. Such a group seeks for peer support to convince their partners that they are worth paying for.

7   Empowerment is having capacity to take action to improve ones' life, having a right to make choices that enhance ones' enjoyment of social, economic and political rights.

8   Empowering refers to building ones' capacity, knowledge, confidence, self-esteem and skills, for instance through training.

9   There used to be a small margin between urban and rural population because in the 1960's-80's, everyone would come from a rural part of Uganda. Men would work in urban areas living in government houses/ quarters, and the wives would be in rural homes. In 21st century, both women and men work in urban areas where they could have a home and rarely go back to rural areas. Thus, there is a divide economically, socially and culturally. Urban areas have mixed cultures (language and practices) whereas rural areas are populated by people bound by traditions and similar cultural practices.

10 The financially rich tend to have a variety of food stuffs (rice, chapatti)in addition to the locally grown foods(millet, potatoes, bananas).The rich will have modern beverages (sodas, beers) while the poor will use porridge from millet. These are differences in diet.

11 Check details in References.

Chapter 7

Information and Knowledge Needs of Artisans in a Knowledge Society:
A Case Study of Willow–Works Artisans in India

Showkat Ahmad Wani
DLIS, University of Kashmir, India

ABSTRACT

The chapter demonstrates the concept of information, knowledge, and the knowledge society. Stress was given to highlight the information and knowledge needs of artisans, problems faced by them, and how they can achieve socio-economic development in a knowledge society. The particular ascent was given to highlight the perceptions and beliefs of willow-works artisans of district Ganderbal, India. The sample of 100 artisans was surveyed and it was founded that majority of them are between the age group of 20-40 years; 63% among them are educated (ranging from 5th–PG above), and there are both genders which practice willow-works, but the majority of them are males. Their tenet is that knowledge can change their standard of living, if there are provisions in knowledge society for creating and disseminating the new knowledge among these artisans pertinent to technology, scientific cultivation of raw materials, marketing, availability of new markets, and potential exploitation by entrepreneurs.

DOI: 10.4018/978-1-5225-8873-3.ch007

INTRODUCTION

It is universally accepted that knowledge is the power to achieve the higher standards in ones living, by putting it in the right direction at right time. The society which makes extensive use of knowledge is termed to be the knowledge society. The societies which are economically and culturally dependent to create scientific and technical knowledge to use it as a competitive factor between the nations in general and companies, the market in particular. The dominant principle in a knowledge society is networking among knowledge producers, effectiveness in applying, controlling and evaluating & learning (Style, 2018). The main advantage of knowledge society includes the predominant large-scale production, transmission and application of knowledge, the massive investment in education, Research & Development. The majority of the labour forces of the state are knowledge workers and continuous innovation by organizations (Thomson Gale, 2008). The purpose of the knowledge society is the development of the society by concentrating on more usage of knowledge at every step in different settings by different people, to yield the maximum output with minimum input or achieving greater benefits with limited resources.

A Society is consists of diverse sections associated with different jobs like farmers, teachers, doctors, engineers and others etc. All of these have a dependence on the freshest, appropriate knowledge to perform their everyday tasks engaged. The output they produce is counted in terms of the development of the society in which they used to live. The standard of their living and the luxuries they enjoy all is indirectly considered as the outcome of knowledge they used to achieve the same, thus prime focus goes to call upon knowledge society. One of the important and a broad section of every society are of artisans & craftsmen. If this section of society may get benefited from knowledge, definitely the advancement of society is due. The concept of the knowledge society and its characteristics need, artisans and their information/ knowledge requirements all needs to be explained. Besides, it also needs to be emphasized that, does the artisan community gets impacted by knowledge society and if yes how they were? And what are their perceptions and tenets towards the knowledge society? How they can accomplish their developmental goals by accessing and utilizing the new knowledge. These are some questions which need to find answers. In this milieu, the present study has made an effort to find reliable answers to these questions. It has been tried to explain the concept of information/ knowledge, knowledge society & its characteristics, artisans information & knowledge needs, the problems they generally face, knowledge society & its impact on artisans and social-sustainable development. Besides, an empirical approach was also followed to identify the beliefs and views of willow-works artisans of district Ganderbal-191201 in the state of Jammu & Kashmir, INDIA on how their socio-economic sustainable development is possible in the knowledge society. More simply, how knowledge society will full fill their information/knowledge needs necessary for their development.

BACKGROUND

"Access to knowledge is, you know, a basic human right" (Elliot, 2014).

Introduction to Information/Knowledge

The concept of knowledge is defined by Cambridge Dictionary (2018) as the "understanding of or information about a subject that you get by experience or study, either known by one person or by people generally". Similarly, it can be said that knowledge is the result of knowing, which is the most specific process of human beings (Bolisani & Bratianu, 2018). There is a close relationship between the two terms of information and knowledge. Both can be interchanged to some extent, even the latter is the outcome of the utilization of information. The information can be defined as the facts and opinions received and provided in the course of the daily life of an individual (Osuala, 2001 cited by Akinola, 2016). Moreover, it can also be said that information is processed data, meaning full statements drawn from raw facts. Which have the sense to get perceived by an information seeker or information user, on the other hand, the knowledge is the reflective stage of information acquisition, understanding and application? The human mind always acts upon acquisition of task-specific information and reflect the experienced output in terms of information, skill and ideas which forms the emergence of knowledge. The concept of knowledge is more philosophical to understand that a general one, but its root is always laid with the concept of information.

The worth and value of information & knowledge are vast, everyone has realized its significance in the developmental process of his or her lives. All the sects of society are significantly dependent on the utilization of knowledge and information. It is believed that the information or knowledge is power, by which an individual or a group of persons make their ways in social bonds (Uhegbu 2001). Similarly, Information & knowledge is a precious resource and serves as an important apparatus for achieving the goals and objectives of individuals as well as of the organizations (Igbeka&Atinmo, 2002). The importance of knowledge and information has been realised by nations across the globe, earliest by the European nations. Where the utilization and application of new knowledge in all walks of social-economic development have shown drastic improvement and helped them in raising the standard of living of masses. The Research & Development institutes were set up to develop new knowledge in various fields of study to sophisticate the human life. The concept of information society got emanated out of the notion that major emphasis is given to generate, acquire and apply more & more information to solve the socio-economic problems faced by the societies. Similarly, the more progression in this terrain led to the appearance of the concept of knowledge societies. Where the focus is given to create, acquire and utilize huge and huge knowledge for solving the complex socio-economic problems and achieve the developmental goal in all walks of human life.

Concept of Knowledge-Societies

The humans in antiquity have transformed their lives everywhere in the world by using appropriate and need relevant information & knowledge. In all aspect of social development, information and knowledge have a significant impact on human lives. Capitalistic and industrial societies are the results of knowledge utilization. The society where the thrust is given to acquire and utilize the more and more knowledge is probably considered as knowledge-society. According to Thomson Gale (2008), the society which emphasizes creation, dissemination and utilization of information & knowledge and considers it as the vital factor of production and economic growth is termed as Knowledge-Society. In knowledge societies the value and significance of knowledge is par with other resources which are bound to increase the production of goods, channelizing the capital and building the strong foundation for nation building or enable the nations to increase the social-economic efficiency of its citizens. Similarly, the edifices of the modern economy are transformed through knowledge applications, constitutes the material basis and justification for designing an advanced modern society (knowledge –society). In the same vein, Roge Cowell showed that the main principles of building a knowledge society includes; (a) the potential of knowledge society is increased through its diversity and expanding its capacity, (b) It should have provision of facilitating the knowledge sharing & (c) industrial or organizational knowledge is not only confined to information but on practical skills, ideas, beliefs and experiences (Terepiszczy, 2016). In simple language, any knowledge society is the creation of human actions towards acquiring, utilizing or applying the new and advanced knowledge for satisfactory results to find the reliable solutions to problems faced or to achieve the targeted objectives either by an individual or by a group as a whole. Besides, there is also great stress given for generating new knowledge in a knowledge society to meet the future needs of knowledge or as forecasted.

Characteristics of Knowledge Societies

There are varied features of the knowledge society that makes its popularity in the present era a dominant one among all the concepts of pre and postmodern industrial societies. It has been said that knowledge society portrays the developmental climax of human society, is considered as the fundamental source for social power that succeeds all other sources responsible for the growth of human society (force-violence & money-wealth) etc. the dictum of Francis Bacon "knowledge is power" best prevails in all time and for knowledge society its foundation lies on it (Dobrin&Popa, 2007). Similarly, as asserted by Ashikuzzaman (2013) the characteristic of the knowledge society is as follows:

- Its members have achieved a higher standard of education in correlation to other societies and a growing proportion of its labour forces are employed as knowledge workers.
- Its industry manufactures products with integrated artificial intelligence.
- Its organizations –private, government and civil society are transformed into intelligent organizations.
- There is an increased organized knowledge in the form of digitalized expertise, stored in data banks, expert systems, organizational plans and other media.
- There are multiple centres of expertise and a poly-centric production of knowledge.
- There is a distinct epistemic culture of knowledge production and knowledge utilization.
- The price of most commodities is determined by the knowledge needed for their development and sale rather than by the raw material and physical labour that is needed to produce them.
- A large portion of the population attains higher education.
- A vast majority of the population have access to information and communication technology and the Internet.
- A large portion of the labour forces is knowledge workers, who need a higher degree of education and experience to perform their job well. Both individuals and the state invested heavily in education, research & development; and
- Organizations are forced to innovate continually.

Moreover, one can simply recognize what actually knowledge society is, by understanding its indicators. The well-known indicators for the same are: (a) by measuring the use & access of modern ICTs, (b) level of educational development, (c) strength of the scientific community and their achievements, (d) the amount of investment on R & D as a percentage of GDP, (e) the production and exportation of high-technology, (f) the number of patent fields and offices in the country and (g) the total research output published in scientific publications. These are the basic signs of showing whether society is knowledge-society or not. One important fact can also be ascertained in recognizing the knowledge society is whether the common masses especially the weaker sections are getting improvement in their standard of living or not. Because, the large number of countries have a major portion of their population residing in rural areas. Which are somehow below the standard of living than the masses living in urban areas? Ensuring an equal and universal growth and development of masses both in rural as well as urban areas must be the main goal of any knowledge society. In rural areas, the large numbers of people are less educated and are pursuing the job of arts & crafts for earning their livelihood. The knowledge society should have its due provision for these artisans as well to uplift them from the vices-circle of poverty to help them achieve their social sustainable development.

Artisans and Craftsmen (Concept)

An artisan or a craftsman is a person with skills in hand practising a particular craft pertinent to which he possesses his skills and knowledge. There are several arts and crafts practised by artisans and craftsmen in different regions of the world, thus led to the categorization of artisans based on their practising a particular craft or art; like carpet artisans, willow workers, wood carving artisans and paper mashie artisans etc. Each craft demands a particular kind of skill set from an artisan who practices it, and inversely each artisan gets an identity by practising a particular craft. Artisans create things by hand, which are functional or decorative in nature, includes a vast number of items used in the daily life of mankind. Similarly, it has been defined that "an artisan is a producer of a product that is handmade and involves a skill that is not part of a mechanical chain of production. An artisan is a skilled producer working primarily with his/her hands to make articles of daily use. Artisans are people who craft items/products or provide services, of both utilitarian and decorative value using their hands and traditional implements/tools. An artisan is a person who works with his/her hands to make products of utilitarian value from locally available natural resources" (Participant of the workshop organized by Society for Rural-Urban and Tribal Initiative, 1987 as cited by Shah & Patel, 2016). In the same vein, English oxford living dictionaries (2018) defined "Artisan" as "a worker in a skilled trade, especially one that involves making things by hand". As per this definition, an artisan adapts traditionally recognised skill sets and tools to make artistic items/craft items. In a simple language, we can define an artisan or a craftsman a person who used to practice a particular art or craft by employing his knowledge skill sets for the whole completion of product formation into the desired way as aimed. In information or knowledge society priorities are always given to produce, acquire and apply the new knowledge by every individual pursuing his concerned daily job. Artisans and craftsmen are too in the same boat and are in need of advanced knowledge for performing their daily routine works (arts & crafts creation) to raise their standard of earning and living.

MAIN FOCUS OF THE CHAPTER

The scope of the study will remain limited to the exploration of the concept of a Information/knowledge, knowledge society, artisans, information & knowledge needs of artisans and the suggested possible methods which can be adopted by them to achieve their socio-economic development. Besides, an empirical ascent was also given to ascertain the beliefs and perceptions of willow-works artisans of district Ganderbal in the state of J&K-INDIA.

Problem

Artisans & craftsmen are the vital part of every society and mostly these people remain less developed as compared to the rest of other sections of people like (business class and Govt. employees etc.). If a society especially which is considered to be a knowledge society is aimed at all rounded development of its masses. It must emphasize the weaker sections (like artisans & craftsmen) to uplift them to achieve their development. Particularly by making them able to be the active part of knowledge society where more emphasis is given to the larger use of knowledge to reach the developmental goal and improve the standard of living. There is a need to shed light on the concept of a knowledge society and its role towards artisans, artisan's information/ knowledge needs in a knowledge society. How they are impacted by it and how they will be benefitted by using the maximum, innovative knowledge and what are the perception & beliefs held by artisans regarding knowledge society. In this milieu, the study tried to discuss the same with shreds of evidence from literature and also tried to check the perceptions and beliefs of willow-works artisans of Ganderbal district (191201) in the state of J&K, India.

Objectives of the Study

- To investigate and explain the concept of Information & knowledge, knowledge societies and its characteristics, artisans and their problems etc.
- To find out the basic information & knowledge needs of artisans.
- To find the possible ways by which can be adopted by artisans & craftsmen to get profited from knowledge utilization in a knowledge society
- To examine the perceptions and beliefs of artisans regarding knowledge societies, particularly of willow-works artisans of district Ganderbal-191201, J&K-India.

Methodology

In order to achieve the objectives of the study, the relevant literature was scrutinized pertinent to the concept of Information & knowledge, knowledge societies and its characteristics, the concept of artisans and their problems, their information/ knowledge needs and the utilization of knowledge & its impact on the overall development of the society. For incorporating the practical flavours in this chapter, the perceptions and beliefs of willow-works artisans of Ganderbal district in the state of J&K, India were checked. The questionnaires and some schedules were distributed among 100 artisans, with mainly focused to get data upon gender & age of these artisans, their educational qualification and their beliefs & perceptions they possess regarding the knowledge society and their socio-economic development. All the collected data was tabulated in MS-excel for analysis and interpretation. The final findings were then depicted in figures and tables of this study. It reveals that knowledge society has significantly a dominant role in the present era in enabling the artisans to achieve their developmental goals by offering them a valuable latest innovative knowledge both technical as well as theoretical in nature.

Implications

The study will acquaint the target audience of the book with the concept of knowledge societies, its characteristics and its impact on the development process, particularly the development of the weaker section of the society like artisans & craftsmen. Besides, it will also enable them to know about the problems faced by the artisans and possible solutions for the same. Moreover, the users of this chapter will also get a practical view on what are the perceptions & beliefs held by willow-works artisans of Ganderbal district in the state of J&K, India. The specific implication of the study is to help the policymakers, knowledge disseminators and Craft institutes to understand the knowledge requirements of artisans & craftsmen, tailor the relevant knowledge skill sets which can yield the highest benefit for this community. Similarly, it will make a call upon the Govt. agencies to frame the policies to secure the knowledge provisions of the artisan community. Thus, it can be said that the chapter will be a significant contribution to this book.

Artisans Problems and Their Information/ Knowledge Needs in a Knowledge Society

The impact of knowledge societies or of knowledge on the artisans and craftsmen can be ascertained by observing understanding the problems faced by artisans & craftsmen and their information & knowledge needs.

Main Problems and Issues Faced by Artisans and Their Solutions

The artisans and craftsmen face a lot of problems pertinent to perform their daily jobs as well as in fulfilling their dream of acquiring a higher standard of living. Majority of problems are directly linked with their information needs or the knowledge required to innovating their craft weaving. Similarly, according to Raynolds& Bennett (2015) for the majority of the world's artisans, living in poverty is a daily reality. This is the major problem faced by artisans concerned with any art/craft throughout the world; reasons may be huge. Artisans have a difficult time in their current environment. They are hindered in their ability to offer their goods and services in the same manner as the more established business ventures (Myers, 2015). It has been founded that, "artisans suffer from a significant educational deficiency. Hence, it may be argued that artisans are challenged due to a lack of educational background" (Kalinina, 2016). Literature reveals that artisans are facing problems due to illiteracy or lack of education. Which mars there business intelligence compared to other competitors who were literate and are able to develop intellectual capabilities, leads the business in their favour. Akilandeeswari and Pitchai (2016) state that, Pottery industry artisans face problems at every stage of their operation, from buying of raw materials, production of craft, raising of finance and marketing of goods. So this industry is not in a position to secure the internal and external economies of scale. The major problems which have been identified in this sector are: Raising adequate finance, Inadequate Raw material and old production methodology, inappropriate technology and improper Infrastructure, Lack of training for new changes, Lack of Marketing Network, Increase in Competition. Similarly, the artisans face a lack of infrastructure, stagnation and miss-alignment with a rapidly changing market, intense competition, the decline of the natural materials on which they depend, and the lack of the information and skills needed to benefit from new market opportunities. Artisans are confronted by new challenges that include those associated with technology, communication and intellectual property. According to him, artisan's information needs are as under. Need for direct market linkages and feedback loops, Need for skills training and Project management and logistics infrastructure (Emani, 2013). It can be generalised that the artisan community faces a lot of problems which mars their development process and leads them to degrade their artistic zeal and the art itself. So the trump card which can change the whole game for the betterment of artisans is knowledge provisions made available for them in a knowledge society. Artisans can solve their problems easily if they have accurate and sufficient information/ knowledge on the right time to take a wise decision. The above problems faced by artisan's shows that they need information/ knowledge relevant to their job from beginning to end. This includes:

- Technological knowhow
- Marketing information/knowledge
- Business opportunities' available
- Raw materials costs and availability
- Skill and training information/knowledge

Technological Knowhow

By technological know-how, we mean that artisans need information about latest techniques used and practised by experts of a particular craft to which an artisan is concerned with. As today is the age of technology and each sector of a state is directly or indirectly influenced by new technologies craft industry is too influenced by the same. An artisan must be aware of what are the newly emerged innovation in his craft is and how to adapt the same to make better creations out of these innovations. So that high returns of his craftwork/artistic work can be achieved or received.

Marketing Information/Knowledge

Artisans are not only concerned with making craft items for leisure, but they were also keen to attain the high monetary returns for their craft items. For that purpose, they need marketing information & knowledge. It is considered that marketing is the ultimate goal of every business to retain in the competitive economy. Similarly, it must be the end goal of the craft industry too. Artisans need to acquire marketing information for their products, Which includes where is the best market for selling their craft items, where is the highest profit earning avenues, what our customer requirements, what is the selling trend of craft items in different markets. And what are the rivalry business strategies of other competitors, how to reach a wider customer network? Simply artisans need marketing information, as needed by market researchers.

Business Opportunities Available

Most of the artisans are not directly concerned with selling and marketing of their craft products. But they were only confined to create or manufacture the craft items and sell them to mediators or middlemen. Who used to find the actual market of these craft items and in return receives huge profit by putting their ambitions on the shoulders of artisans. More simply middlemen exploit the artisans by providing them little sums for their craft items and sell these items on higher prices to end customers, i.e. they invest least and get huge returns. Artisans must need information & knowledge about business opportunities available, i.e. they should be aware of how to handle their whole business without the interference of middlemen. So that actual worth of the art & craft items could be achieved. Information & knowledge about business opportunities available includes like, information about business trade fairs, exhibitions, and govt schemes pertinent to these craft promotions etc.

Raw Materials Costs and Availability

Each crafted item requires an adequate amount of raw materials for its creation. Similarly, every raw material costs a sufficient amount of money. It is observed that raw materials differ both in quantity and quality, which determines its costs and availability. Artisans need information & knowledge pertinent to raw materials quality, quantity, costs and availability. When the artisan is aware of the costs and availability of raw materials required for manufacturing the desired craft items, he can adopt the cost-efficient approach during the production of craft items.

Skill and Training Information/Knowledge

Nobody is perfect in life is perfect. The man is learning become a learned one by exercising a particular task or activity. Every skill is acquired through practical demonstration and training. An artisan is a person who is concerned with practical work needs to acquire the most perfect skills for creating innovative artistic & craft items. It is worthy to say that artisans need information & knowledge about different skills and training. Which includes information & knowledge pertinent to distinguishing, which skill is most helpful in creating and designing a particular craft item, how to acquire and adopt a particular skill, where to get a trade relevant training, from whom to get same etc. besides above-discussed knowledge & information needs of artisans. They need information related to the latest trends in the market like brands, designs and vice versa. Simply, it can be said that artisans need information & knowledge by which they can regenerate their identity in society. The above-mentioned problems faced by the artisans & craftsmen are commonly experienced by the majority of artisans throughout the globe. If these problems are addressed properly and the special provisions for disseminating a required knowledge to the artisans in a knowledge society are made. Then they can definitely raise their socio-economic development or standard of living. More simply, knowledge society should ensure the social-sustainable development of artisans & craftsmen as par with other sections of society.

SOLUTIONS AND RECOMMENDATIONS

Knowledge Societies and Information/Knowledge Provisions That Leads to Sustainable Development of Artisans

The knowledge societies focus upon the widespread creation, collection and distribution of information & knowledge among its members. There are four basic attributes of knowledge society on which its existence relies upon these include: (a) knowledge is vital and main engine of economic development, (b) the knowledge society emerges when the professional groups and corporations share information & knowledge with others without hiding anything, (c) In every knowledge society there is an increase in the number of people and social groups, who are concerned to produce knowledge and are recognized by the society for the same (d) the systems of knowledge sharing (informal societies, schools, universities) are established for the benefit of all members of the society, knowledge society can exist (Dupré & Mijnhardt, 2015). It is now entirely accepted that knowledge is the main agent of socio-economic development of all section of the society. The section of people who are commonly known as artisans and craftsmen are also knowledge users, thus depends on it to perform different tasks. As the existing era is more concentrated towards creating knowledge societies, where the creation of new knowledge is a routine job. There should be a special provision of fulfilling the knowledge requirements of the artisan community as well. The following stipulations can be made available in a knowledge society, by which artisans & craftsmen can raise their socio-economic sustainable development like:

- Recognizing the worth of artisans & craftsmen
- Mass educational initiatives
- Technological diffusion among the artisans & craftsmen
- Establishment of community specific R&D institutions
- Making socio-economic policies
- Channelizing the available resources

Recognizing the Worth of Artisans and Craftsmen

In modern technology-driven knowledge societies people (artisans & craftsmen) who are preserving the cultural legacy of different regions, sects, and different countries are not recognized par with other communities like Doctors, engineers, & other business class professionals. This is the biggest flaw that artisan & craftsmen are facing the world over, only certain in rear cases are getting their due worth in the same. In every known society, their recognition should be a top priority by the policy makers/ administration.

Mass Educational Initiatives

Education is one of the major factors that contribute to achieving the overall development of the masses in a country. Artisans & craftsmen have generally remained away from this blessing which compels them to face the other problems that hinder their socio-economic sustainable development. There is a vital need to educate the artisan community both formally or informally & technically to help them achieve the goal of development. The knowledge society must have a provision of offering a mass educational initiative so that artisans & craftsmen can nourish their intellectual development.

Technological Diffusion Among the Artisans and Craftsmen

Artisans & craftsmen are using traditional labour consuming tools and techniques to perform their jobs, which results in less production and high stain on their health. In a knowledge society, there should be a provision that artisans & craftsmen relevant technologies (machines and other gadgetries) are produced. Similarly, the knowledge pertinent to them should be diffused among the artisans & craftsmen community so that they can adopt these new tools & techniques to ensure their socio-economic sustainable development.

Establishment of Community Specific R&D Institutions

The Research & Development institutes have a significant impact on the overall development of the nations. If they are established with the objective to cater needs of a particular community (Like, artisan community). The development scenario of that particular community will be an ideal one for others living in poverty. The community-specific R & D institutes have a greater role to play in creating new unique knowledge, long yielding positive results for uplifting the poor masses. Besides, they can initiate the research on root caused problems and help in finding reliable solutions for the same. The existing resources of that community can also be utilized in an efficient manner rather than wasting them due to lack of knowledge.

Making Socio-Economic Policies

The obligation of government and administrative structures are pivotal in all phases of socio-economic sustainable development of all people including the artisans &

craftsmen. Making the socio-economic policies is a routine matter of concern for the administration. But, the majority of the policies they have framed are a failure due to inappropriate planning and lack of result oriented knowledge for implementing and utilizing the resources. In the knowledge society, all walks of human life are dependent on appropriate usage of need specific information & knowledge. So, the policymakers should have firm faith in making the socio-economic policies as per the facts and knowledge obtained by community R&D institutes, to address the existing problems of the artisans & craftsmen.

Channelizing the Available Resources

The vast numbers of resources are available for the uplifting the artisan community. But, all of them are not fully utilized in the desired manner. The willow-works artisans need marshes as raw materials for making their craft items. But, due to limited production of marshes, they face the problem of price hike on raw materials, thus earning less profit on their crafts weaved. This very problem can be solved by cultivating the marshes on wastelands, unused government lands and other possible areas by the people so that the abundance of raw materials with low-price will be made available to artisans & craftsmen to enable them to fetch more wages. Similarly, the knowledge societies should have a provision to generate bunches of ideas to channelize the all possible and existing resources to ensure the socio-economic sustainable development of the artisans & craftsmen community of a society.

Empirical Findings of the Study

In order to access the ground-level situation of the artisan community and their perception of how Information & knowledge in knowledge societies, will affect their socio-economic development. The sample of one hundred willow-works artisans of district Ganderbal-191201 (State-J&K, India) was surveyed to collect the data about their gender, age, educational qualification, knowledge issues faced, & to identify their belief regarding how they can achieve socio-economic development in a knowledge society.

Gender Wise Distribution of Willow-Works Artisans in District Ganderbal-191201 (State-J&K, India)

The willow-works artwork is a major livelihood driver of district Ganderbal for the artisans concerned with it. The pilot study was initiated to check its distribution and study exhibits that this craft is practised by both genders (male & females). It was also founded that, out of 100 artisans (17%) are females and (83%) artisans are males in different villages of Ganderbal-district. Although the sample was limited only to one hundred artisans the figures may or may not remain the same for others. Fig-1 depicts a clear picture.

Figure 1.

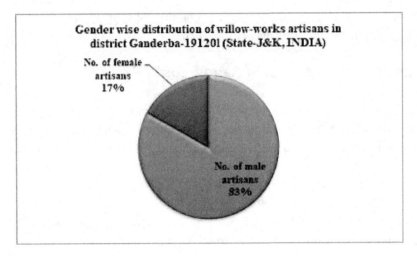

Educational Qualification of Willow-Works Artisans in District Ganderbal (State-J&K, India)

Education is a vital component for the all-round development of an individual. Similarly, for the artisans, it is more important in terms of achieving their socio-economic growth. The study tried to check the educational qualification of willow-works artisans of Ganderbal-district. The collected data exhibited that 37 artisans are illiterates out of 100 artisans surveyed, followed by 31 artisans who are between 5th to 10th pass, 27 artisans between 12th to graduate and 5 artisans between PG and above. It can be said that except illiterates, the rest of three categories of artisans have an educational qualification which is a positive sign that they are able to understand the power of knowledge and can utilize the same if guided where to apply it. Fig-2 offers a lucid view.

Age Wise Distribution of Willow-Works Artisans in District Ganderbal-191201 (State-J&K, India)

The study also made an attempt to check the age of willow-works artisans of district Ganderbal, with a purpose to ascertain the current scenario of the artisan community

Figure 2.

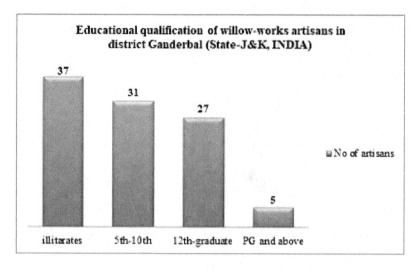

and forecast the future trend. The data analysis showed that there are 49 artisans out of 100 artisans between the age group of 31-40 years, followed by 30 artisans, which are between the age group of 20-30 years, 14 artisans between 41-50 years and 6 artisans between the age group of 50-above. It can be clearly evidenced that the majority of the artisans are young enough to continue the willow-works art. But the condition is that their interest and curiosity should be reinforced by the authorities. That can be done by offering them new result-oriented knowledge about how to achieve heights in socio-economic development and by making certain policies based on research conducted on the problems they are experiencing. Fig-3 gives clear glimpses of artisan's age.

Willow-Works Artisan's Responses Over Questions Posed Regarding Certain Issues

In order to find out certain issues faced by willow-works artisans of Ganderbal district and the role of knowledge to tackle them, some questions were catechized to them for answer. These questions and their responses are tabulated below. It reveals that a good number of artisans are able to understand that, knowledge is the major agent for their development. Table-1 shows a whole scenario of questions & responses of artisans.

Figure 3.

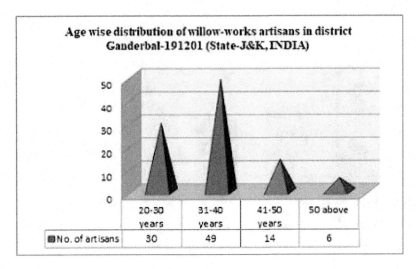

Table 1. Willow-works artisan's responses over questions posed regarding certain issues

Q.no	Question	No of responses out of 100 artisans	
1	Do you feel need of latest knowledge pertinent to your work?	**Yes**	**No**
		67	33
2	Do you realize that education is must for development?	89	11
3	Are you satisfied with your artistic job?	34	66
	The reasons for your dissatisfaction are: a) low income	**Agree**	**Disagree**
		78% artisans	22% artisans
	b) modernisation	90% artisans	10% artisans
	c) less recognition of your art	58% artisans	42% artisans
4	Is there any economic gap between your community and the others?	81% artisans	19% artisans
5	In knowledge society socio-economic development prevails, do you agree?	93% artisans	7% artisans
6	If you are able to get knowledge on all facets relevant to your art-work, do you try to utilize all this knowledge for your development?	99% artisans	1% artisans
7	Where from you acquire knowledge you require. a) From Colleagues	**Yes**	**No**
		86% artisans	14% artisans
	b) Parents	51% artisans	49% artisans
	c) Master experts	32% artisans	68% artisans
	d) Craft or art institutes	2% artisans	98% artisans
	e) None of the above	0%	0%

Willow-Works Artisans Belief, How They Can Achieve Socio-Economic Sustainable Development in Knowledge Society

The artisans are well-aware of, how they can achieve their socio-economic sustainable development. As they can better observe and judge the problems they face and what reliable solutions will solve those problems. Similarly, the study also tried to gather unique responses or check beliefs of artisans on how their socio-economic sustainable development is possible in a knowledge society. The beliefs of willow-works artisans of district Ganderbal were tabulated. It was founded that they believe the latest knowledge pertinent to technology, scientific cultivation of raw materials, marketing, new markets and possible exploitation threats by entrepreneurs will definitely help them to achieve their development. So, the knowledge pertinent to the same should be provided to them in a knowledge society. Besides, they also held the belief that the government of their region can play a significant role in uplifting their community by addressing all the necessary problems & issues they face either directly or indirectly. For clear understanding see table-2.

Table 2. Willow-works artisans belief, how they can achieve socio-economic sustainable development in knowledge Society

S.no.	Belief
1	The knowledge should be provided regarding new techniques and tools to us
2	Knowledge regarding production of raw materials should be provided (like, how to cultivate marshes in scientific way)
3	Knowledge pertinent to new designs long sustainable in markets should be provided
4	Knowledge regarding marketing and availability of new markets should be provided to us
5	The knowledge regarding possible exploitation by entrepreneurs should be provided
6	Govt. should have intervention in terms of making new feasible and result oriented policies for the uplifting of our community
7	Our overall issues faced should be solved by the administration (like, problems viz: shortage of power supply, drinking water, transport, education & health etc.)

FUTURE RESEARCH DIRECTIONS

The present study has only focused upon explaining the concept of information & knowledge, knowledge society & its characteristics, artisans & their problems, information & knowledge needs of artisans and the knowledge society and its impact on artisan's socio-economic sustainable development. Similarly, for the practical part, the study has only surveyed the willow-works artisans of district Ganderbal, in the state of J&K, INDIA. Besides the only sample of 100 artisans were surveyed, so there beliefs & opinions regarding knowledge society and their sustainable socio-economic development may or may not represent the views of all artisans. Thus the study suggests that future research can be conducted on knowledge societies and other communities other than artisans, their issues and impact of knowledge society on their social & economic development. In the same manner, for a practical approach to research, the beliefs and perceptions of other communities or other artisans as well can be focused upon to achieve the target objectives.

CONCLUSION

There is no doubt that knowledge has an immense power to shape the future of masses in society. The poor people have a major dependence on it to combat the challenges they face in daily life and to enhance or achieve their socio-economic development. As the concept of a knowledge society is widely known in the present era to all, artisans are too were aware of it. The present study made an endeavour to check & analyse the expectations and beliefs of willow-works artisans of Ganderbal district in the state of J&K, INDIA. It was found that they are aware that knowledge availability and utilization will surely make their development possible. They also mentioned that knowledge regarding all walks of life and all facets of their artwork can make a significant socio-economic development of these artisans. It was also founded that the majority of artisans are both educated and young enough to continue the nourishment and preservation of the cultural legacy of their art in general and that of their area in particular. Only their need is proper knowledge guidance and ensured social & economic growth. They also make their obligation upon administration to intervene in fulfilling their knowledge requirements and framing development oriented socio-economic policies. In short, it can be said that information & knowledge availability in a knowledge society has a significant impact on sustainable development of artisan.

REFERENCES

Akilandeeswari, S. V., & Pitchai, C. (2016). Swot analysis for the improvement of pottery industry in Tamil Nadu. *International Journal of Management and Social Sciences*, 4(7), 1–6. http://www.indianjournals.com/ijor.aspx?Target=ijor:ijmss&volume=4&issue=7&article=001

Akinola, A. (2016). *Information need, access, and use for social welfare and family planning by rural dwellers in Ido and Akinyele local government areas of Oyo State, Nigeria.* Retrieved from:https://digitalcommons.unl.edu/cgi/viewcontent.cgi?Article=3919&context=libphilprac

Ashikuzzaman, M. (2013).Characteristics and Indicators of Knowledge Society. *Library & information Science Network.* Retrieved from: http://www.lisbdnet.com/characteristics-of-knowledge-society/

Bolisani, E., & Bratianu, C. (2018). The Elusive Definition of Knowledge. In *Emergent Knowledge Strategies* (pp. 1–22). Springer. doi:10.1007/978-3-319-60657-6_1

Cambridge Dictionary. (2018). *Meaning of "knowledge" in English dictionary.* Cambridge University Press. Retrieved from: https://dictionary.cambridge.org/dictionary/english/knowledge

Dobrin, O. C., & Popa, I. (2007). Knowledge society features. *Repec.* Retrieved from:https://www.researchgate.net/publication/4982032_Knowledge_society_features

Dupré, S., & Mijnhardt, W. (2015). The Making of a Knowledge Society (1450-1800). *Creating a Knowledge Society in a Globalizing World (1450-1800).* Retrieved from: https://knaw.nl/shared/resources/actueel/bestanden/creatingaknowledgesocietyinaglobalizingworld14501800.pdf

Elliot. (2014). Access to knowledge: a basic human right. *Creative Commons.* Retrieved from:https://creativecommons.org/2014/01/07/access-to-knowledge-a-basic-human-right/

Emani, S. (2013). *Application of bi-directional ICT channels to increase livelihoods for artisans in rural India* (Doctoral dissertation). Massachusetts Institute of Technology. Retrieved from:https://dspace.mit.edu/bitstream/handle/1721.1/90068/890141347-MIT.pdf?Sequence=2

English Oxford Living Dictionaries. (2018). *Definition of artisan in English.* Oxford University Press. Retrieved from: https://en.oxforddictionaries.com/definition/artisan

Igbeka, J. U., & Atinmo, M. I. (2002). Information seeking behaviour and information utilization of agricultural engineers in Nigeria based on their different places of work. *Nigerian Libraries, 36*(1), 9-22.

Kalinina, A. (2016). *Artisans' limitations for developing own businesses: case of Querétaro, Mexico* (Bachelor's thesis). University of Twente. Retrieved from:http://essay.utwente.nl/70221/1/Kalinina_BA_BMS.pdf

Myers, K. A. (2015). *In the Shadow of Cortés: Conversations Along the Route of Conquest.* University of Arizona Press. Retrieved from: https://books.google.co.in/books?Hl=en&lr=&id=hr9tcgaaqbaj&oi=fnd&pg=PR5&dq=Myers,+K.+A.,+Loaeza,+P.+G.,+%26+Wray,+G.+C.+(2015).+In+the+shadow+of+Cort%C3%a9s:+Conversations+along+the+route+of+conquest.+Tucson:+The+University+of+Arizona+Press.&ots=5lqjg67lse&sig=dwhm-WLEZ3uy5H_jkx0ruq3qjue

Raynolds, L. T., & Bennett, E. A. (Eds.). (2015). *Handbook of Research on Fair Trade.* Edward Elgar Publishing. doi:10.4337/9781783474622

Shah, A., & Patel, R. (2016). *E-Commerce And Rural Handicraft Artisans* (No. 2016-12-07). Retrieved from: http://www.voiceofresearch.org/Doc/Dec-2016/Dec-2016_7.pdf

STYLE, University of Brighton. (2018). *Knowledge Society.* STYLE, University of Brighton. Retrieved from: https://www.style-research.eu/resource-centre/glossary/knowledge-society/

Terepiszczy, S. (2016). The concept of" knowledge society" in the context of information era. *Studia Warmińskie, 53*, 77-84. Retrieved from: https://www.infona.pl/resource/bwmeta1.element.desklight-66c870ff-31db-4717-b833-a37083baef03

Thomson Gale. (2008). Knowledge Society. *International Encyclopedia of the Social Sciences.* Retrieved from:https://www.encyclopedia.com/social-sciences/applied-and-social-sciences magazines/knowledge-society

Uhegbu, A. N. (2001). Deterrents to information service for community development. *Library Review, 50*(5), 237–242. doi:10.1108/00242530110394493

KEY TERMS AND DEFINITIONS

Artisans and Craftsmen: Those people who possess artistic skills and apply the same for productions of art and craft items.

Beliefs and Perceptions of Willow-Works Artisans: The opinions and perceptions which willow-works artisans held regarding something (like, about knowledge society).

Knowledge Societies: The societies where more emphasis is given to production, utilization, and distribution of new knowledge.

Problems and Issues of Artisans: The hindrances that bars the socio-economic development of artisans' community.

Social-Sustainable Development: The development of a society where standard of living is good and long durable.

Technological Diffusion: The deliberate attempt to acquaint the masses with new technologies.

Willow-Works Artisans: Those artisans who practise willow-works art/ craft.

Worth of Artisans: The value an artisan in a society means worth of an artisan.

Chapter 8

Education and Knowledge Under the Impact of Economic Stress:
Rhodesia 1965–1979 vis–a–vis Zimbabwe Since 2002

Innocent Chirisa
University of Zimbabwe, Zimbabwe

Gift Mhlanga
University of Zimbabwe, Zimbabwe

Abraham Rajab Matamanda
iD https://orcid.org/0000-0001-5260-5560
University of the Free State, South Africa

Roselin Ncube
Women's University in Africa, Zimbabwe

ABSTRACT

This chapter intends to have answer the questions: How did Ian Smith structure his government and economy and survive sanctions for sixteen years (1965-1979) and become innovative? Why, under almost similar conditions, did Robert Mugabe fail to bring the economy do its toes? In cases, what was the role of knowledge societies and what role did they play to bridge the gap between society and them towards meaningful development? The study uses desktop review as the basis of getting data and information useful in building this theoretical case study of Zimbabwe in the period 1965 to 2018. The robustness of an economy under a stringent

DOI: 10.4018/978-1-5225-8873-3.ch008

economic environment is a function of its ability to tap and harness the prowess of its knowledge societies. It is recommended that strong links between the private, public, and knowledge sectors are required and this must happen in an environment with trust, transparency, accountability, rule of law, and commitment translating into a powerful connubio for transformation.

INTRODUCTION

The Rhodesian Government under Ian Douglas Smith registered a lot of good results on the ground than the Robert Mugabe Government under economic sanctions. It is theorized that the reason why the Rhodesian Government thrived very well under stringent economic conditions was not so much because of the sympathy of the other white governments around it. Rather, it was the strict and full-of-direction endogenous arrangements that involved serious partnerships in knowledge creation and management involving universities, businesses, community workers and the public sector. Specifically, the technical, vocational education and training (TVET) system under the Rhodesian economic climate were so designed that psychomotor skills were much developed and the exchange of ideas into products was well crafted. The major mistake by the Robert Mugabe Government, under sanctions, was to emphasis higher and tertiary education at university with much theoretical emphasis and little channeling and discipline that produce tangible and saleable products on the market.

There was now much emphasis on imports rather than imports substitution. Although relief came with dollarizing in 2009, the honeymoon was too short, as the country fell prey to internal financial mismanagement and external poaching of the financial asset base of the United States of America dollars. Mugabe continued to blame his external 'foes' on 'illegal sanctions' against his government – the smart sanctions - for the challenges that his government has cause even within the economy. Confidence in both the public and private sector dropped. Knowledge involves putting emphases on practical solutions and experimentations based on creativity and readiness to package innovations into useful products and goods. Financial discipline within the private, public and the knowledge sectors is a major requisite for sustainability. It is even observed that Rhodesia came up with many useful products from the locally available resources. It was facing war within and sanctions without but still was able to thrive.

In this regard, a comparative analysis of the present and the Smith regime socio-economic policies is called for. Basing on the endogenous growth models, economic growth is a function of capital accumulation, employment and total factor productivity (TFP). In this case, TFP is positively influenced by such factors as institutions and improvement in human capital development (Bosworth and Collins, 2003). This is the role of the government to direct the economy into growth and hence blossomy. On the other hand, Rostow's theory of economic growth is anchored by the principles of trade whereby a nation-state nurtures its economy to growth through free trade.

The chapter is organized into seven sections as follows. The conceptual framework presents a discussion on the key concepts guiding the chapter and these include the concept of knowledge creation, innovation and sanctions. Second, the theoretical underpinnings section discusses the theories that guide this study and including Stolper-Samuelson theorem, public choice approach and human capital theory. Third, the literature review section presents a global, regional and national overview of the impact of sanctions and education on national economic performance. Fourth, the methodology and methods that have been used to gather information and their justification is discussed in the methodology section. Fifth, the results are presented in the results sections that focuses on the case of Rhodesia and Zimbabwe and how sanctions and education have been in both epochs together with the innovations that have been adopted to spearhead economic growth. Sixth, the discussion and synthesis of the results follow. Lastly, the study is concluded and the policy options are outlined.

CONCEPTUAL FRAMEWORK

National developments encompass governmental activities that promote socio-economic growth. Thus, these developments are mostly public goods that cannot be provided for by the private sector due to their basic characteristics of non-rivalry and non-excludability. Consequently, the government provides for such public amenities, such as infrastructure (both soft and physical) and security. Transport infrastructure, such as road and railway networks is critical for economic development in the sense that they connect one place to the other, one country to the next one, that is a pre-requisite for trade. In this vein, in this era of globalization, the development of communication infrastructure is also a necessity if a nation is to develop economically. Sustainability, as a concept, chose conservatism of resources, that is, the present beneficial enjoyment of resources with the future generation factored in as a beneficiary also. If a government initiates sustainability agenda, national resources, economic growth and social development are guaranteed

The ontological perspective of knowledge creation is based on four particular processes: socialization, externalization, combination and internalization (SECI) and that is known as the SECI model in psychological cycles (Nonaka and Takeuchi, 1995). Knowledge is created individually and through interaction between explicit and tacit knowledge. Thus, creating knowledge requires the existence of a person or group of people who originate new ideas, new concepts and/or an innovative product. Knowledge is achieved through research, innovation projects, experiments and observations. Firestone *et al.* (2003) claim that knowledge production begins with the request of knowledge, that is then followed by individual or group learning, then information acquisition and application for evaluation of knowledge and ultimately, the building of organizational knowledge (Ceptureanu and Ceptureanu, 2010). Knowledge also leads to innovation and plays an important role in economic growth (Ghanbari and Ahmadi, 2017).

Innovation involves both knowledge creation and diffusion of existing knowledge (Rogers, 1998). It is the ability to discover new relationships, of seeing things from new perspectives and to form new combinations from existing concepts. In this vein, specialized support and competitive pressure result in innovation. In this regard, specialized support encompasses the availability of capital to entrepreneurs, well-educated and the availability of skilled workers (Martin and Milway, 2005). On the other hand, the pressure that emanates from aggressive and capable competitors threatens complacency and the sophisticated customers demanding innovative goods and services at low prices panel-beats firms into being innovative and hence increasing productivity. Increased openness and thus foreign competition, encourages more domestic innovation through stronger incentives for defensive and expansionary research and design (Akcquit, 2018).

There are positive and negative economic sanctions. Negative sanctions are the best-known economic instruments of diplomacy. They are imposed to inflict an economic damage to one or more countries. On the contrary, positive sanctions foster cooperation among countries. Nonetheless, this study focuses on the impact of international negative sanctions on the Zimbabwean peninsula during and after colonialism and therefore "economic sanctions" imply negative sanctions in this context. Economic sanctions including boycotts, embargoes and financial sanctions. Boycott refer to restrictions of imports of one or more goods from the target country to reduce the target country's foreign exchange earnings and its ability to import goods. Embargos hand restrict exports of certain products to the target country. The measure is enforced through a system of export licenses and supporting measures. Financial sanctions restrict or suspend lending and investing into a particular target economy and sometimes freezing foreign assets of the target economy (Caruso, 2003).

The knowledge sector is concerned with the impartation and sharing of knowledge from one party to the other. Higher education could lift Africa out of its problems of development because the knowledge sector is a major driver for innovation and technological advancement. Investment in higher education ensures technological diffusion, reducing the knowledge gap among parties (Bloom *et al.*, 2006). Trust is a complex interpersonal and organizational construct. It is a subjective phenomenon that comes into being through a reliable and favorable predictability of reactions by involved parties (Duck, 1997). It is claimed that trust occurs "when parties holding certain favorable perceptions of each other allow this relationship to reach the expected outcomes" (Wheeless and Grotz, 1977, 251). It is an efficient means for lowering transaction costs in any social, economic and political relationship (Fukuyama, 1995; Levi and Stoker, 2000). Concerning public trust between a government and its subjects, it depends on credible policy-making (Blind, 2006). Transparency is a governance feature that allows for the public to assess an authority's activities. Thus, one aspect of transparency is access to information by the public. A link exists between institutional corruption and poor governance in both the private and public spheres. Consequently, if the governance style is opaque and is augmented by income disparities and accountability shortcomings, the impulse for private economic gains surpasses the concern for the well-being of a particular society (Gerring and Thacker, 2004). Public and private sector accountability therefore begins with the clear application of standards and access to information (UNDP, 2004). Accountability as one of the features of good governance compels authorities to be answerable to any party concerning their activities. It implies holding individual officials and organizations responsible for performance measured as objectively as possible, on the basis of such pillars as financial, administrative and political accountability (UNDP, 2004:21).

The phrase 'rule of law' describes a situation upon that a nation-state is guided by law to exercise justice and freedom. It implies that no citizen is above the law since the latter is a construction of all citizens. Therefore, the law dictates since it is the voice of all people. Whatever a citizen does, its suitability and appropriateness is judged the law of a particular nation-state (Minn, 2009). Rule of law is guided by three principles: dignity, equality and human rights of all persons (Kennedy, 2006). Commitment implies the political will of authorities to achieve their objectives and goals. This infers a resistance to divert from pre-set goals. Therefore, where there is commitment their credibility follows. In other words, there would be no time inconsistency problem since economic agents and all involved parties would enjoy their expectations being met. The word '*connubio*' has its roots in Italy and is literary translated as marriage or union. In this case, the phrase presupposes that a complete economic change to the better is a result of many factors. Thus, for an economic upturn to occur, there is a necessity of an amalgamation of various factors. For the Zimbabwean economy to grow, not only technological advancement is called for but other variables, such as political will and good governance (Nyarota, 2016).

THEORETICAL UNDERPINNINGS

The public choice approach was promulgated by Kaempfer and Lowenberg (1988) who are of the view that economic sanctions may be imposed not for a common and noble cause but rather serving the interest of a particular group of influential people within the sender state. The pressure groups are assumed to have a hold on policy-makers through financing the latter's political affiliations. Therefore, even if the pressure group members are few as compared to the opposing group, their plight would be endorsed as a policy through their lobbying capabilities. The interest groups are driven by a myriad of motives that are mostly centralized on pecuniary benefits from the imposition of the sanctions. For instance, an embargo on exports of a target country benefits producers of import-competing goods in the sender country, at the same time having a negative impact on producers of the sanctioning state that use imports from the target state as intermediate inputs (Kaempfer and Lowenberg, 1988). This predicates that the variation in the economic spoils in the sender state compels the interests of a more influential group to be implemented at the expense of the interests of the weaker pressure group. Consequently, a skewed income distribution would ensue.

The Stolper-Samuelson theorem asserts that when sanctions are imposed on imports, the direct result is that it favors the factors used intensively in the import-competing sector. This implies that if a target country is put under embargos, for example, the demand for goods produced internally increases due to a reduction in competition with foreign goods that were once imported before the sanctions. Cooper (1989) on the other hand proves that economic agents using domestic factors for the production of goods would be better off due to sanctions than those who import intermediate goods for the production of their products. Thus the sanctions result in an increase in the return to capital thereby favoring capitalists. If the capitalists have an economic gain through sanctions; they have an incentive to manipulate politicians and arm-twist them to prolong their beneficial undertakings. The effect of this manipulation is to slow down the pace of political change, while making the income distribution more unequal. Wang (1991) uses the Harris-Todaro model that comprises a two-sector model, the agricultural and manufacturing sectors, to show that export and import embargoes have asymmetrical effects on national income and on income distribution. This proves that the impact of sanctions differs depending on a targeted state's level of trade openness and also on the intensity of labor or capital in the economy (Black and Cooper, 1988).

From time immemorial, political entities and individuals have used economic sanctions as a means to gain an advantage in domestic and foreign affairs. In other words, economic sanctions are tools used by domineering nations to indirectly control politically and economically weaker nations (Askari et al, 2003: 4). Thus, when the seemingly docile states resist the machinations of the powerful polities, the sanctions are imposed as a measure to punish a country for failure to concur in a sender country's policy (Askari et al 2003: 16). Sanctions are used by a sender country as a tool to interfere in the internal affairs of another sovereign government without immediate introduction of military force (Hufbauer et al, 2007). In the Zimbabwean context, a once ZANU-PF legislator, Reuben Marumahoko, insisted that sanctions were imposed to assist the MDC-T to get into power so that farms that were distributed to Blacks for resettlement will be given back to the Whites (GoZ, 2001).

The human capital theory hinges on the premise that knowledge is a factor that promotes economic development through technological advancement. Therefore, an arbitrary sharing of knowledge improves the innate ability of labor to increase productivity (Becker, 1992). The economic prosperity and functioning of a nation depend on its physical and human capital stock (Schultz, 1971). The phrase "human capital" represents the investment the labor-force undertakes that enhance their economic productivity. The human capital theory emphasizes how education increases the productivity and efficiency of the labor-force by increasing the level of cognitive stock of economically productive human capability (Olaniyan and Okemakinde, 2008). The provision of formal education is a productive investment in human capital that is considered as equally necessary as the physical capital in increasing and sustaining productivity (Babalola, 2003).

The Ak model is a model of economic growth that acknowledges that technological advancement is a necessary variable in economic growth; submitting that the technology is endogenously determined (Munongerwa, 2016). In its simplest explanation, this model by Frankel (1962) points out that thrift, capital accumulation and efficient allocation of resources are the key factors to economic growth. Novelty and innovation are included in the explanation of economic growth (Aghion and Howitt, 2006). Thus, when capital is accumulated, 'learning by doing' generates technological progress that raises the marginal product of capital. Consequently, the natural tendency of diminishing marginal returns of capital is offset. As the model is a sequel to the Solow Swan model, it also assumes: the conditions of perfect competition in the economy; and a long run growth rate that depends on the savings (Aghion and Howitt, 2010).

LITERATURE REVIEW

A research determined the factors that contribute to economic growth in Zimbabwe. It applied an econometric approach to assess the sources of economic growth during the period 1980 to 2014. Using advanced regression analysis, the results suggested a significant decline in productivity and capital stock during the period from 2000 to 2008. It was observed that between 1990 and 2008, the contribution of capital to economic growth was, on average, negative. On the other hand, labor force participation as a significant variable for the analysis was proved to be static during the same period, implying that it was not a binding constraint to Zimbabwe's economic growth. In this regard, the main contributing variables for the decline in economic growth for Zimbabwe were mainly attributed to decline in the capital stock and productivity (Nyarota *et al.*, 2015). An empirical study using data from sixty-eight countries that stretched for thirty-four years, that is, data that covers the period 1976-2012 had to assess how economic sanctions imposed by the United Nations and the United States affect the target states' GDP growth. Specifically, the study shows that on average, the effect of sanctions by the United Nations decreases the real per capita GDP growth rate of a target country by 2.3 to 3.5 percent points.

Additionally, comprehensive UN sanctions lead to a reduction in GDP growth by at least 5 percent. On the other hand, the impact of US sanctions has a weaker impact on the economy of a target country, taking into consideration that they only decrease GDP growth over a period of seven years by 0.5 – 0.9 percent points on average (Neuenkirch and Neumeier, 2014). Another study estimated the impact of eight industrialized countries' sanctions against the South African Apartheid regime between the period 1978 and 1999. The results of the study suggest that the United States Anti-Apartheid Act, the Act that legalized the economic sanctions on the regime, had the strongest influence on South African exports (Evenett, 2002). This concurs with Hufbauer et al. (2009) who claim that the imposition of economic sanctions significantly reduces the volume of bilateral trade between the imposing and the target state. An augmented gravity model with dummy variables was used to investigate the impact of sanctions on U.S. trade flows. Different classifications of the sanction variable were tested to determine whether the results are sensitive to such regression manipulations. Unsurprisingly, the results showed that the sanctions have a significant impact on U.S. exports, imports and total trade. This was the same result when the impact of comprehensive economic sanctions imposed by the US was estimated (Hufbauer *et al.*, 1997).

Through the use of gravity-approach, the influence of political relations on trade flows among countries was investigated. For the analysis, an index to denote co-operation and hostility between countries was constructed and added t to the standard gravity equation. Thus, individual indicators were construed for the 'amount' of conflict between a pair of nations and on the other hand on the amount of co-operation between the nations. Through this way, a cross-sectional gravity model that dealt with bilateral trade flows of forty countries in 1986 was analyzed. The findings for the study revealed that the diplomatic climate strongly influences the pattern of international trade flows among nation-states (Van Bergeijk, 1994).

METHODOLOGY

The study used a qualitative approach to collect and analyze the data for this research whereby documentary research method is employed. Documentary research methods are a cost-effective way of gathering and analyzing information from documents that refer to the study of phenomenon (Bailey, 1994). For this research therefore, the data was collated from various secondary sources that include journal papers, governmental archives and publications, blogs, conference publications, reports and newspapers. Such documentary sources are most appropriate for providing background information and an understanding of policy issues, actors, histories and dynamics between two states or when comparing different time periods of a particular nation (Sibanda, 2012). The term 'documents' refers to a wide variety of data sources that can be grouped as such, personal, official, private, mass media and the internet (Bryman, 2004). The argument of discrediting documentary research method as being biased is countered by Fischer (2003) who points out that a researcher will always bring the baggage of their social life into research despite the research design used. Therefore, the validity of the data is ensured through collating the data within the four criteria of credibility, authenticity, representativeness and meaning (John, 1990).

RESULTS

In the case of Rhodesia/Zimbabwe, the trigger for the economic sanctions was humanitarian reasons during the Unilateral Declaration of Independence (UDI) era and during the post-independence era when Mugabe was in power. The Smith government was put under sanctions because it had pronounced its own independence from Britain in a bid to circumvent and delay majority rule in Zimbabwe.

The first wave of the sanctions included a ban on the purchase of Rhodesian sugar and tobacco. These two commodities constituted 71% of the value of exports to Britain. Additionally, export credit guarantees and any other trade benefits with Britain were terminated. Thus, the sanctions sought to cripple the trade flow between Britain and Rhodesia. This was exacerbated by the removal of Rhodesia from the sterling area and the Commonwealth preference system. It is noteworthy that besides the trade embargoes and boycotts on Rhodesian trade with Britain; financial sanctions were also imposed on the country through denying the Smith regime access to the London capital market, its major source of financing. Also by December of the same year, Rhodesia Reserve Bank assets in London, worth approximately 10 million pounds sterling, were frozen. Additionally, the payment of dividends, interest and pensions to Rhodesian citizens was blocked.

Since Britain had veto power in the United Nations, on 20 November 1965, its national interests were also expediently served and, thus, the Security Council adopted voluntary sanctions on Rhodesia. Subsequently, all member countries in UN were requested to break economic relations with the country, stressing the need to embargo the sale of arms, military material and petroleum. Nonetheless, the voluntary sanctions were relatively not effective since some of the super-powers had economic interests in Rhodesia through their transnational companies. Moreover, the fact that Britain still refused to concede that the Rhodesian situation constituted 'a threat to international peace and security', grounds for mandatory economic sanctions under Chapter VII of the UN Charter rendered the efforts less effective. Nonetheless, by December 1965, Britain had expanded its embargo list, adding Rhodesian copper, chrome, asbestos, iron and steel, maize and beef. This constituted 95 per cent of the value of Rhodesian exports to Great Britain.

It is of interest to note that it took over a year after UDI for the Security Council to impose selective mandatory sanctions against Rhodesia, acknowledging that the country's state of affairs constituted a threat to the peace. Consequently, the mandatory sanctions affected approximately 60 per cent, by value, of Rhodesia's exports and 15 per cent, by value, of its imports (military equipment, aircraft, motor vehicles and petroleum). The selective mandatory sanctions implied that if any member country failed to adhere to the pronouncement, it would be a violation of Article 25 of the UN Charter. However, there were several cases of sanction busting by other member states, such as the United States of America.

Rhodesian Economy, Innovations and Survival (1965-1979)

In the short-term the economic sanctions on Rhodesia resulted in considerable damage to the Rhodesian economy as evidenced by a stunted growth as an aftermath of the sanctions imposition. This may be explained by the fact that the sanctions terminated the country's source of revenue when there was an embargo on its agricultural products, especially tobacco. Moreover, since the country depended on the export of minerals, such as chrome with countries, such as the United States, the sanctions curtailed the country's direct source of income. Nonetheless, after the first few years of hardship and readjustment, the Rhodesian economy began to recover. This recovery is owed to the policies that were employed by the government to deal with such a situation to sustain the economy.

Since 1965, foreign economic interests in Rhodesia helped in harboring the Smith regime against the unpleasant consequences of the economic sanctions. Thus, European and American companies were able to invest in Zimbabwe during UDI period through their subsidiaries operating from South Africa (Austin, 1975). The fact that South Africa dealt with the Smith Regime in many inextricable ways, it was difficult to detect foreign investments channeled through this neighboring country. This relationship made it possible for oil to be ferried through South Africa when the Mozambique ports were closed to the Regime. Another provision in the Emergency Powers Regulation of 1969 was that, it was unlawful for the foreign companies to retrench their workers without the permission of the Minister of Labor. Thus, the government was able to shield the labor-force from the harsh realities of the economic sanctions.

Although such labor-force adjustment regulations were inclined towards the protection of the whites mostly, there was no excess discrepancy in unemployment rate between the UDI period and the period before the sanctions were invoked. The Smith regime also adopted an effective blockage of capital flight. Through a series of actions taken under the Emergency Powers Regulations of 1969 the Rhodesian government insisted that profits, except for certain South African subsidiaries, cannot be repatriated. As a result of this regulation, foreign companies were made to reinvest their profits in the country. These funds were invested in the expansion of mining and the manufacturing sector. Resultantly, between 1967 and 1974, the GDP grew at an annual rate of more than eight percent in real terms. Through the cascading effect from agricultural and manufacturing sectors, the Rhodesian economy rebounded to being self-sufficient.

There were no clearly defined community workers during the Smith Regime, except for the missionaries. After the arrival of European settlers in 1890, missionaries found it easier to spread their influence among the indigenous people (Kanyongo, 2005). Through their community work, the Christian missionaries conducted the first formal education in Zimbabwe. In this regard, mission schools were the source of formal education for indigenous people. In this context, the missionaries were excising their community support through imparting of knowledge despite the challenges expounded by the white minority regime. In the same vein, the missionaries were the pioneers offering pre-service training for teachers (e.g., at Waddilove Mission, Howard Mission, St. Paul's Musami, Nyadire Mission).

The establishment of the University College of Rhodesia and Nyasaland in 1957 was the first-ever colonial government initiative toward providing university education in pre-independent Zimbabwe. However, access to university education was determined more by phenotype than the academic abilities of individuals as evidenced by only about 0.2% of all African students who were academically qualified for university education. However, after the imposition of sanctions, the Smith regime implemented a new education system where around 37.5% of primary school graduates were channeled toward a vocationally oriented Junior F2 secondary education (Dorsey, 1989). Thus, the vocational training of the Africans was centered Africans to be trained in such blue-color jobs as farming, carpentry and mechanics. The need for skilled native labor by the white settlers caused the colonizers to reconsider the educational program (Mart, 2011). While the Africans were developing an interest in Western-style literary education, the colonial government began to realize the necessity of training Africans for service to the white man (Urch, 1971). Through innovation endeavors and technological advancement, the Smith regime was able to sustain the economy of the country during the UDI era. Consequently, there was a rapid stimulation of food processing, textiles, clothing and footwear manufacturing and other import-substitution industries. Moreover, some incentives were introduced to induce the diversification of agriculture towards large scale production of maize, cotton, soya beans and beef.

The Zimbabwean Sanctions (2002 to date)

The Zimbabwean economy has experienced booms and depressions, as explained in the business cycle theories. Between 1980 and 1990, the economy of the country was on a rise, albeit, on a small scale, benefiting from the UDI economic residuals. The economic structural adjustment period between 1990 and 2000 saw the economy being turbulent due to structural and institutional reasons, making it more appropriate to describe the economy to be on the decline. The economic sanctions that were impose on the country had a negative impact of further putting the economy into turmoil, the ultimate trough being in 2008 where the country's monthly inflation rate was reckoned to be 79,600,000,000% (Hanke, 2008).

During the Zimbabwean 2002 parliamentary elections, the Zimbabwean government revoked the observer status of Pierre Schorri, the then head of EU's electoral observer mission after he denounced the poor human rights abuse in the country (the BBC News Africa, 2002). The EU responded by suspending the development cooperation between Zimbabwe and the EU. This was the harbinger of the economic sanctions that were subsequently imposed on the country. The Council of Ministers of the EU reacted by invoking Article 96 of the Cotonou Agreement, governing partnership between the EU and African-Caribbean-Pacific countries.

Consequently, the EU Council Decision of 18th February 2002 conferred that financial support for all projects except for those in direct support to the Zimbabwean population would be suspended. The only financing that would be availed to the Zimbabwean government is that around social sectors, such as health, education micro-projects and agriculture (EU, 2002). In this case, the then Mugabe government had been dealt a financial blow as the foreign financial life-line was cut-off. It is noteworthy that as the EU had diverted its interest to the social cause only, over EUR 128 million directed at providing support for government capacity building and policy reforms were halted (EU, 2002). These were targeted sanctions as they did not directly affect the livelihood of the ordinary Zimbabwean. The targeted sanctions were meant to prevent adversity on ordinary people and sometimes to provide support and encouragement to reform constituencies (Cortright and Lopez, 2002:17).

Following the adoption by the Zimbabwean government of the Information and Protection of Privacy Act (AIPPA), an Act that limited media freedom and broadcasting licensing, the US President issued the Executive Order Number 13288 under ZIDERA. This further imposed restrictions on targeted individuals (Govt of USA, 2013). Furthermore, through this Act, Zimbabwe was not granted eligibility for the African Growth and Opportunity Act (AGOA), a piece of legislation introduced in 2000 to facilitate access to the US markets for Sub-Saharan Africa. Following these events, that may be dubbed cascading silent sanctions, in 2002 the Commonwealth decided to indefinitely suspend Zimbabwe's membership. The Zimbabwe reacted to this by pulling out of the organization. The final blow to this adverse chain on Zimbabwean foreign relations was the executive decision by the IMF to suspend, Zimbabwe's voting rights in June 2003 as a result of the government's incapacity to repay the arrears contracted with the international financial institution. This curtailed the possibility for Zimbabwe to borrow further resources and technical assistance from the institution (IMF, 2003). Additionally, World Bank also suspended loans and programs to support the balance of payment of Zimbabwe since 2001 due to the same reasons of the Zimbabwe government failing to meet arrears payments.

The private sector has suffered a terminal blow due to the scarcity of foreign currency for a sustainable functionality of the industrial sector. The industries that survive on imports of intermediate products as their inputs face dire challenges as the operations costs are increased by scarcity of foreign currency. This resulted in their products being incompetent as compared to foreign goods that are imported. This saw the government engaging in protectionist policies through the Statutory Instrument 64 of 2016 to reduce imports into the economy and encouraging import-substitution production. On the other hand, in the foreign market, the goods that are exported are as well incompetent, a result of dollarization that makes the goods more expensive in the foreign market since the US dollar is "strong" as compared to regional currencies, such as the South African Rand. Overall, Kanyenze *et al.* (2017), foreign direct investment (FDI) has remained depressed over the years. For example, Zimbabwe's FDI inflows amounted to US$1.7 billion between 1980 and 2013, compared to US$7.7 billion for Zambia and US$15.8 billion for Mozambique.

The public sector, one of the economic pillars, that lends a supportive role to the private sector. The public sector in Zimbabwe is maligned by corruption and bad governance. For example, it is stated in the 2016 Budget Statement that the Zimbabwe Electricity Transmission and Distribution Company (ZETDC), was granted a provision of US$482 million for its operations, yet the organization's debtors as at 30 September 2015 owed it US$1 billion and this figure was growing as a result of the prevalent culture of not paying for services. On the other hand, Kanyenze *et al.* (2017), overall requirements for infrastructural development for 2016 were projected at US$2.7 billion. In this regard, this is a reflection that state enterprises in the Zimbabwean economy have long ceased to yield value.

The most effective way of boosting economic growth, reducing poverty and improving people's health is by investing in education. Education is a differentiated aspect of socialization and denotes the formal process of developing human skills and other attributes cognitively, technically, physically and socially. In this regard, the tertiary education, universities and technical colleges being its custodians should have a mandate for socio-economic development (Wosley, 1970). Between 1985 and 2003, Zimbabwe's public expenditure on higher education was more than other developing countries in Africa and 24% of the higher education students being in the science and technology field (World Bank, 2000, 2007). In Zimbabwe, the policy governing higher education is the National Council for Higher Education Act of 1990, that was then amended in 1994 and 2006. The Act delineates the maintenance of appropriate standards with regards to teaching, courses of instruction, examinations and academic qualifications in all institutions of higher learning.

Nonetheless, it is of great concern that the Act emphasizes on theoretical professionalism at the expense of vocational education and technical training. For example, it was only in the first quarter of 2018 that most of the programs taught at the University of Zimbabwe were granted some attachments. Moreover, it is of great concern that the universities in Zimbabwe have deny students' access to communication and deliberation (Cheater, 1991) through the University of Zimbabwe Act of 1990, that was exported to other state-owned universities. Thus, the mandate of tertiary institutions to be the hubs of socio-economic development is more theoretical than practical since the beneficiaries of such education are not contributing to economic growth. It is argued that the quality of education offered in higher tertiary institutions has deteriorated owing to higher enrolment since the increase in enrolments has not been complemented by increases in the number of lecturers and other support staff (Zembere, 2018).

The indigenization policy became part of the Zimbabwean government to counter the economic sanctions imposed on the country. The main objective of the policy was to re-orient the economy to being inward-looking, that is, to stabilize the economy through indigenous means rather than being foreign-dependent. Consequently, the Mugabe government put it into law that the larger percentage of investment spoils by foreign investors would, by right of sovereignty, be preserved for Zimbabwe. Specifically, the indigenization law required foreign investors with more than US$500,000 to cede 51% of shares to indigenous Zimbabweans. The policy had a drastic effect of lowering FDI into the country. the CZI Manufacturing Sector Survey of 2015, 87% of the respondents in 2014 and 90% in 2015 indicated that the environment in Zimbabwe is deterrent to FDI, with the percentage of firms that made capital investment using FDI very low at 5%. This was owed to unclear signaling through such policies as the indigenization laws. Therefore, before indigenization, there is need for a strong, independent economy that can only be sustained by sustained by innovation and good governance.

Government of Zimbabwe knows the importance of technological advancement and economic sustainability. For example, a Scientific and Industrial Research and Development Centre (SIRDC) was established in 1993 by an Act of Parliament. The mandate of SIRDC is to provide technological solutions for sustainable development through such institutes as biotechnology, electronics and energy technology. Moreover, it is claimed that the 24% of higher education students in the field of science and technology compares well with the average of 25% in developed countries (Kariwo. 2007:45). Nonetheless, much of Zimbabwe's research effort is directed at improvements in agriculture and the government's budget for agricultural research is administered by the Agricultural Research Council. However, despite the clear road-map in economic development through innovation initiative, the country still lags behind in effecting such institutions to function smoothly and to full capacity. Thus, although the foundations for sustainable development have been lain through such institutions that promote innovation through technological advancement, the noble cause is truncated by scarcity of the necessary resources.

DISCUSSION

Ironically, the political party that benefitted from the sanctions imposed on the Smith regime, ZANU-PF, is itself now suffering from the same fate of economic sanctions by the same super-powers. Nonetheless, the sanctions impacted differently on the two regimes (Maravanyika, 2005). Concerning the Smith Regime, the sanctions are considered to be a failure in that instead of crumbling the economy to coerce the regime to politically surrender, the opposite was witnessed. On the other hand, concerning the Mugabe regime, the sanctions had an effect of worsening the human rights abuse of the opposition members and the ordinary Zimbabwean despite the fact that the economy deteriorated, that is the primary goal of imposing economic sanctions. The environment surrounding the imposition of financial sanctions on Zimbabwe ensured a maximum drawback on economic growth. After the government gave grants to liberation war heroes, a Z$50,000 that was unbudgeted for, the IMF was against it. This negative attitude was further perpetrated by Zimbabwe lending military assistance to DRC. This was as well an impromptu, out–of-budget decision on the Zimbabwean government. The foreign financial institution reacted by pulling out the financial assistance on the grounds that the government was misusing the foreign aid. Therefore, when the financial sanctions were imposed on Zimbabwe, it was a doomsday scenario in that balance of payment problems was already experienced. By and large, the stunted economic growth cannot be explained by the sanctions alone but rather the fact that it is a manifestation of the dependency syndrome whereby the government relies on financial aid for economic growth. Africa is not realizing its potential due to the fact that the necessary innovation initiative is being suppressed by the provision that the economic hardships experienced are usually diluted away by foreign aid. This is where the Smith regime is different from the Mugabe regime: the former managed to stand on its own economic initiative while the latter resorted to the "Look-East Policy". Thus, the Zimbabwean government struck a deal with East-Asian countries, substituting the Western financial institutions for them, feeding on the dependency syndrome (Moyo, 2009). The Policy back-fired in that instead of the Asian countries bailing Zimbabwe out of the economic quagmire, the countries was plunged deeper into economic mayhem as evidenced by the 2008 hyper-inflation and Chiadzwa diamonds scandals.

The two governments dealt with the sanctions differently. The Smith regime implemented policies that ensured that the Rhodesian economy would not crumble down. It is on record that the government entreated into policy that profits earned within Rhodesia would not be ploughed outside the country. In this regard, instead of a deteriorating scenario concerning the manufacturing sector, the economy was boosted. In this regard, it is on record that the economy grew by 1.2%. Although some may argue that the net value of 1965 GDP was the same as that prior to the inception of the economic sanctions, it is better than deterioration. On the other hand, the Mugabe regime responded to the sanctions by invoking the foreign exchange laws that date back to the 1977 Exchange Control Act (Chapter 170) to alleviate balance of payment problems. The amended Act (Chapter 22:05) says that if an entity earns any money while resident in Zimbabwe, that money must be brought into the country. In this case, externalization of funds in Zimbabwe is an offence as prescribed in terms of Section 4 (c) of the Act. Subsequently, Mugabe's successor, President Emmerson Mnangagwa, put to book culprits of externalization in March 2018. However, although this move was consequential result of good intentions, it was marred by corruption. Thus, ill-governance was one of the short-comings in the Mugabe government that intensified the effects of economic sanctions.

The difference on how the sanctions impacted is explained by the fact that the sanctions themselves were different in nature: the UDI sanctions were mostly trade sanctions while the ZIDERA sanctions were financial sanctions. Without condoning the development policies during the Mugabe era, it is noteworthy that financial sanctions have far-reaching repercussions than trade sanctions. In this case, the Zimbabwe government was yet to enjoy the benefits of the economic structural adjustment program through ZIMPREST, that as yet needed funding from the IMF. Therefore, when the IMF withdraw the financial and technical funding in Zimbabwe, the latter's economy was dealt a fatal blow. Concerning the UDI trade sanctions, the Smith regime was given a warning that if they ever opposed the British one man one vote policy, the ties bilateral relationship with Britain would be severed off.

Moreover, it was only after the harvest and sale of the golden leaf, tobacco, that the British government imposed the targeted sanctions on Rhodesia. Through this analysis, it is imperative to submit that the Smith regime was more prepared for the sanctions than the Mugabe sanctions since fore-warned is fore-armed. Moreover, the young economy of the Mugabe government was not yet ready to be weaned from foreign financial aid, hence the disastrous outcome of the sanctions. The fact that the foreign financial institutions closed doors in helping the government led to inflated domestic debt through the use of government bonds. This consequently led to the crowding out effect whereby only the government could source credit locally, slamming away the private sector for the same facilities. Therefore, domestic investment was reduced, a scenario that further chased away investors, hence a diminishing economic growth rate.

Moreover, the ZIMASSET blueprint enshrined the indigenization policy. An economic strategy that is resonated in the blueprint is value addition and beneficiation. The major argument in this blueprint is that since the economy is reeling down from the impact of economic sanctions and therefore, one strategy that can be implemented is the application of technological advancement and innovation to ensure value addition and beneficiation. In other words, the government resorted to home-grown strategies to overcome the stifling economic environment of isolation due to the sanctions. This is the same route that was taken by the Smith regime to ensure that the private sector and the public sector satisfies the domestic market independent of imports. Through value addition and beneficiation initiative, the Rhodesian economy boosted the industrial sector. However, due to the trade sanctions, the processed goods could not be exported. On the other hand, the lack of external competition resulted in sub-standard goods being produced. Still the Smith regime was able to revolutionize the manufacturing sector, adapting it to cover the gap made by import embargoes. On the other hand, the Zimbabwean government could not sufficiently exploit the dictates of the ZIMASSET blueprint and so it failed to meet the envisaged goals.

The other aspect in the analysis of sanctions concerning the two regimes is education. The Smith regime emphasized vocational and technical training and professional education. The white minority had the privilege of having technical and professional education. Nonetheless, the Africans were granted partial education that emphasized on blue-color jobs to reduce competition in white color jobs with the white minority. Thus, although Africans wanted a liberal curriculum that would enable them to get White collar jobs in towns, the government was opposed to the notion. However, there were also private colleges that were mostly supported by church organizations, that had strong links with the industrial sector. Therefore, the labor force during the Smith regime was always regimented and compartmentalized, implying that there was no shortage of labor at every level of the general labor-force hierarchy. However, during the reign of Mugabe, the problem that aggravated Zimbabwe was not lack of labor but rather under-employment that was intertwined with high unemployment rate. Thus, over-qualified labor-force was working below its potential as the economy was shrinking, while at the same time willing and able people were searching for jobs without respite, implying that the supply of labor had flooded the labor market, resulting in firms under-paying the labor-force.

CONCLUSION AND POLICY OPTIONS

It is evident that there is a gap between tertiary knowledge base and the community. Universities, for example, are recognized as the sources of knowledge creation and therefore they regurgitate out learned professionals from time to time. These professionals are poured into the already flooded job market because the market is not expanding due to a shrinking industrial sector. Thus, these stakeholders, together with the government as the custodian of the welfare of the citizens, have to channel up a way forward to expand the economy. The university lecturers, their mandate as social workers, have to be given research grants to fathom the link between the industrial sector and the labor supply. Innovation and technological advancement beget an expansion of the economy by exploring new avenues of resource manipulations. This way, value addition and beneficiation are recognized.

The other key factor to be considered in revamping the economy of Zimbabwe is the cooperation between the government, civil society and the private sector. Zimbabwe's development strategy needs to map up a concrete standing on the role of government and within the public sector, a framework for decentralization (Hurungo 2010). Thus, there is need for a 'partnership' among these three stakeholders, defining where the private sector and civil society should take the lead, for example. The Global Competitiveness Report (2012/13) aptly observes that there is a policy disconnection that stems from the unwillingness of policy-makers to tackle the challenges identified, opting rather to focus on soft factors that do not necessarily add value in lifting competitiveness rankings. Consequently, if there is cooperation among the three stakeholders, the competitiveness of the country would be enhanced. For example, concerning foreign aid, if there is cooperation between the non-governmental organizations, civil societies and the government, economic development is improved, as alluded to in the 2005 Paris Declaration on Aid Effectiveness and the 2008 Accra Agenda for Action (OECD, 2008).

REFERENCES

Afesorgbor, S. K., & Mahadevan, R. (2016). The Impact of Economic Sanctions on Income Inequality of Target States. *Economics Working Papers*, *4*.

Aghion, P., Bergeaud, A., Lequien, M., & Melitz, M., (2017). *The Impact of Exports on Innovation: Theory and Evidence*. 2017 AEA Meeting Presentation.

Aghion, P., Dewatripont, D., & Patrick, R. (1999). Competition, Financial Discipline and Growth. *The Review of Economic Studies*, *66*(4), 825–852. doi:10.1111/1467-937X.00110

Aghion, P., & Howitt, P. (2006). Appropriate growth policy: A unifying framework. *Journal of the European Economic Association*, *4*(2-3), 271–278. doi:10.1162/jeea.2006.4.2-3.269

Aghion, P., & Howitt, P. (2010). Economics of Growth. Wiley-Blackwell Publishing Asia.

Akcigit, U., Sina, T.A., & Giammario, I. (2018). Innovation and Trade Policy in a Globalized World. *International Finance Discussion Papers, 1230*.

Alinsky, S. (1971). *Rules for Radicals: A pragmatic primer for realistic radicals New York*. Vintage.

Askari, H., Forrer, J., Teegen, H., & Yang, J. (2003). *U.S. Economic Sanctions: An empirical Study*. Occasional Paper Series, CSGOP-03-01, The George Washington Center for the Study of Globalization.

Askari, H. G., Forrer, J., Teegen, H., & Yang, J. (2003). *Economic Sanctions: Examining their Philosophy and Efficacy*. Praeger Publishers.

Austin, R. (1975). *Racism and apartheid in southern Africa: Rhodesia*. The UNESCO Press. Available online: www.rbz.co.zw

Babalola, J. B. (2003). Budget Preparation and Expenditure Control in Education. In J. B. Babalola (Ed.), *Basic Text in Educational Planning*. Ibadan Awemark Industrial Printers.

Bailey, K. (1994). *Methods of Social Research* (4th ed.). The Free Press.

Baldwin, D. (1979). Power Analysis and World Politics. Princeton: Princeton University Press.

BBC News Africa. (2002). *Zimbabwe Forces Out Top EU Observer*. Available online: news.bbc.co.uk

Becker, G. S., & Murphy, K. M. (1992). The Division of Labor, Coordination Costs and Knowledge. *The Quarterly Journal of Economics, 107*(4), 1137–1160. doi:10.2307/2118383

Blind, P. K. (2006). Building trust in government in the twenty-first century: Review of Literature and Emerging Issues. In *7th Global Forum on Reinventing Government Building Trust in Government 26-29 June 2007*. UNDESA.

Bond, B., & Manyanya, M. (2003). *Zimbabwe's Plunge: Exhausted Nationalism, Neoliberalism and the Search for Social Justice*. Weaver Press Ltd.

Bosworth, B., & Collins, S. (2003). The Empirics of Growth: An Update. *Brookings Papers on Economic Activity, 2*(2), 113–206. doi:10.1353/eca.2004.0002

Bryman, A. (2004). *Social Research Methods*. Oxford University Press.

Ceptureanu, S., & Ceptureanu, E. (2010). Knowledge Creation / Conversion Process. *Review of International Comparative Management, 11*(1), 150–157.

Chikomba, C. E. M. (1988). The role of the University of Zimbabwe in Adult, Primary and Secondary Education. *Michigan State University Conference Proceedings*, 12-26.

Chinamasa, E. (2012). Factors influencing lecturer research output in new universities' in Zimbabwe. *Zimbabwe Journal of Educational Research, 24*(2), 14–25.

Chombo, I. (2000). Higher Education and Technology in Zimbabwe: Meaningful development in the New Millennium. *Zimbabwe Journal of Educational Research, 12*(3), 6–26.

Clemens, M., & Moss, T. (2005). Costs and causes of Zimbabwe's crisis. Washington, DC: Centre for Global Development Press.

Colin, J. (1968). *The lonely African*. Claredon.

Cooper, H. J. (1989). On income distribution and economic Sanctions. *The South African Journal of Economics, 57*(1), 14–20. doi:10.1111/j.1813-6982.1989.tb00174.x

Cortright, D., & Lopez, G. A. (2002). *Smart Sanctions: Targeting Economic Statecraft*. Rowman and Littlefield Publishers.

Cross, E. (2016, July 17). The Economic and Political Crisis in Zimbabwe. *The Zimbabwean*. Available online: www.thezimbabwean.co

Delevic, M. (1998). Economic sanctions as a foreign policy tool: The case of Yugoslavia. *International Journal of Peace Studies, 3*(1), 1–94.

Drezner, D. W. (1999). *The Sanctions Paradox: Economic Statecraft and International Relations*. Cambridge University Press. doi:10.1017/CBO9780511549366

Drezner, D. W. (2000). Bargaining, Enforcement and Multilateral Sanctions: When Is Cooperation Counterproductive? *International Organization, 54*(1), 73–102. doi:10.1162/002081800551127

Drezner, D. W. (2003). How smart are smart sanctions. *International Studies Review, 5*(1), 2–7. doi:10.1111/1521-9488.501014

Duck, S. (1997). *The Handbook of Personal Relationships: Theory, Research and Interventions*. Wiley.

European Parliament. (2011). Impact of sanctions and isolation measures with North Korea, Burma/Myanmar, Iran and Zimbabwe. Directorate – General for External Policies, Policy Department, May 2011.

Evenett, S. J., & Keller, W. (1998). *On Theories Explaining the Success of the Gravity Equation*. NBER working paper no. 6529.

Firestone, J. M., & McElroy, M. W. (2003). *Key issues in the new knowledge management*. Butterworth-Heinemann.

Fischer, F. (1998). Beyond Empiricism: Policy Inquiry in Postpositivist Perspective. *Policy Studies Journal: the Journal of the Policy Studies Organization, 26*(1), 129–146.

Fowale, T. (2010). Zimbabwe and Western Sanctions: Motives and Implications. *The American Chronicle, 09*(June), 7–11.

Frey, B. (1984). *International Political Economics*. Basis Blacwell.

Fukuyama, F. (1995). *The Social Virtues and the Creation of Prosperity*. Free Press.

Gerring, J., & Thacker, M. C. (2004). *Political Institutions and Corruption: The Role of Unitarism and Parliamentaris*. Cambridge University Press.

Ghanbari, A., & Ahmadi, M. (2017). The Effect of Innovation on International Trade: Selected Medium-High-Technology Industries, Evidence on Iran, *Iran. Economic Review (Kansas City, Mo.), 21*(1), 21–44.

Gono, G. (2006). An analysis of socio economic impact of Sanctions on Zimbabwe. *Supplement 7. Reserve Bank of Zimbabwe, 3*, 4.

Gray, P. H. (1986). Non Competitive Goods and Gains of Trade. *The International Trade Journal, 1*(2), 107-128.

Haas, R. N. (1997). Sanctioning Madness. *Foreign Affairs, 76*(6), 3–9.

Hakim, C. (1982). *Secondary Analyzis in Social Research, A Guide to Data Sources and Methods with Examples*. Allen and Unwin.

Hammar, A., & Raftopoulos, B. (2003). Zimbabwe's Unfinished Business: Rethinking Land, State and Nation. In A. Hammar, B. Raftopoulos, & S. Jensen (Eds.), *Zimbabwe's Unfinished Business: Rethinking Land, State and Nation in the Context of Crisis*. Weaver Press.

Hanke, S. H. (n.d.). *R.I.P. Zimbabwe Dollar*. The Cato Institute. Available online: www.cato.org

Hufbauer, G. C., Elliott, K. A., Cyrus, T., & Winston, E. (1997). *US Economic Sanctions: their impact on Trade, Jobs and Wages, working paper*. Institute of International Economics.

Hufbauer, G. C., & Oegg, B. (2003). *The impact of Economic Sanctions on US Trade: Andrew Rose's Gravity Model, International Economics Policy briefs*. Institute for International Economics.

Hufbauer, G. C., Schott, J., Elliott, K. A. & Oegg, B. (2007). *Economic Sanctions Reconsidered*. Academic Press.

Hughes, M. (2000). Potential, Procedures and Pitfalls of Analyzing Internal Newspapers. *Corporate Communications*, 19–25.

Huni, M. (2012, July 15). Candid talk with Professor Ncube. The Sunday Mail.

Hurungo, J. (2010). *An Inquiry into How Rhodesia Managed to Survive Under Economic Sanctions: Lessons for the Zimbabwean Government. Paper Prepared for the Trade and Development Studies Centre*. Trades Centre.

IMF. (2003). *Press Release: IMF Suspends Zimbabwe's Voting and Related Rights*. Available online: www.imf.org

IMF Executive Board Uphold Sanctions against Zimbabwe. (n.d.). *Press Release No. 06/45*. Available at https://www.imf.org/external/np/sec/pr/2006/pr0645.htm

Jenkins, C. (1997). The Politics of Economic Policy-Making in Zimbabwe. *The Journal of Modern African Studies, 35*(4), 575–602.

Kaempfer, W. H., & Lowenberg, A. D. (1988). The Theory of international economic sanctions: A Public Choice approach. *The American Economic Review, 78*(4), 786–793.

Kanyenze, Kondo, & Martens. (2006). The search for sustainable human development in Southern Africa. Alternatives to neo-liberalism in Southern Africa (ANSA).

Kanyenze. (2011). Beyond the Enclave. Towards a Pro-Poor and Inclusive Development Strategy for Zimbabwe. Weaver Press.

Kariwo, M. T. (2007). Widening access in higher education in Zimbabwe. *The Journal of Educational Research, 20*(3), 23–50.

Kennedy. (2006). *Written Constitutions and the Common Law Tradition*. 20th Sultan Azlan Shah Law Lecture, Kuala Lumpur, Malaysia.

Kurebwa, J. (2000). *The Politics of Multilateral Economic Sanctions on Rhodesia (Zimbabwe) during the Unilateral Declaration of Independence Period, 1965 to 1979* (Unpublished PhD thesis). University of Zimbabwe.

Levi, M., & Stoker, L. (2000, June). Political Trust and Trustworthiness. *Annual Review of Political Science, 3*(1), 475–507.

Maravanyika, O. E. (1990). *Implementing educational policies in Zimbabwe*. World Bank discussion paper no. 91. Africa Technical Department Series. Washington, DC: World Bank.

Marongwe, N. (2004). Socio-economic conflicts of the Fast Track Resettlement Programme. In Medicine Masiiwa, Post-independence land reform in Zimbabwe: Controversies and Impact on the Economy. Harare: Friedrich Ebert Stiftung and Institute of Development Studies, University of Zimbabwe.

Mart, C. T. (2011). British colonial education policy in Africa. *Internal Journal of English and Literature, 2*(9), 190-194. Available online http://www.academicjournals.org/ijel

Martin, R., & Milway, J. (2005). *Commercialization and the Canadian Business Environment: A Systems Perspective*. Institute for Competitiveness & Prosperity.

Minn, J. (2009). Rule of Law: What Does it Mean? *Journal of International Law, 18*(2), 293–303.

Moyo, D. (2009). *Dead aid: Why aid is not working and how there is a better way for Africa*. Farrar, Straus and Giroux.

Mpofu, B. (2016, Mar. 11). Local Banks' Nostro Accounts Depleted. *Zimbabwe Independent*. Available online: www.theindependent.co.zw

Munongerwa, C. (2016). An evaluation of the relevance of the AK model to developing countries such as Zimbabwe. *Afro Asian Journal of Social Sciences, 7*(2), 2229–5313.

Munyati, C. (2016, Apr. 21). Zimbabwe's Liquidity Crisis: The Curse of China's Slowdown and a Strong Dollar. *The Source*. Available online: source.co.zw

Neuenkirch, M., & Neumeier, F. (2014). The Impact of UN and US Economic Sanctions on GDP Growth. *Research Papers in Economics*, *8*(14).

Nherera, C. (1999). *Capacity building in educational research in Southern Africa. Empirical insights into Qualitative research*. Human Resources Research Centre.

Nonaka, I., & Takeuchi, H. (1995). *The Knowledge-creating Company. How Japanese Companies Create the Dynamics of Innovation*. Oxford University Press.

Olaniyan, D. A., & Okemakinde, T. (2008). Human Capital Theory: Implications for Educational Development. *European Journal of Scientific Research*, *24*(2), 157–162.

Omolewa, M. (2006). Educating the "Native": A Study of the Education Adaptation Strategy in British Colonial Africa, 1910-1936. *Journal of African American History*, *91*(3), 267–287. doi:10.1086/JAAHv91n3p267

Pape, R. A. (1997). Why economic sanctions do not work. *International Security*, *22*(2), 90–136. doi:10.1162/isec.22.2.90

Psacharopoulos, G., & Woodhall, M. (1997). *Education for Development: An Analysis of Investment Choice*. New York Oxford University Press.

Rodney, W. (1972). How Europe Underdeveloped Africa. Bogle – L'ouverture Publications.

Sakamota, A., & Powers, P.A. (1995). Education and the dual labour market for Japanaese men. *American Sociological Review, 60*(2), 222-246.

Schultz, T. W. (1971). *Investment in Human Capital*. The Free Press.

Sockwell, D. W. (2007). The Solow Growth Model. *The Journal of Economic Education*, *38*(4), 483–483. doi:10.3200/JECE.38.4.483

Solt, F. (2014). *The Standardized World Income Inequality Database*. Working paper. SWIID Version 5.0. Downloaded on 7th Nov 2014 from https://myweb.uiowa.edu/fsolt/papers/Solt2015a_pre.pdf

Solt, F. (2015). Economic inequality and non-violent protest. *Social Science Quarterly*, *96*(5), 1314–1327. doi:10.1111squ.12198

Strack, H. (1978). *Sanctions: the case of Rhodesia*. Syracuse University Press.

Urch, E. G. (1971). Education and Colonialism in Kenya. *History of Education Quarterly*, *11*(3), 249–264. doi:10.2307/367292

US Department of the Treasury. (2013). *Zimbabwe Sanctions Program, Office of Foreign Asset Control*. Available online: www.treasury.gov

Van Bergeijk, P. A. G. (1994). *Economic Diplomacy, Trade and Commercial Policy, Positive and Negative sanctions in a new World Order*. Edward Elgar Publishing.

Wang, L. F. (1991). Trade sanctions, sector-specific unemployment and income distribution: A dual approach. *South African Journal of Economics*, *59*(2), 72-76.

Wheeless, L.R., & Grotz, J. (1977). The Measurement of Trust and Its Relationship to Self-Disclosure. *Human Communication Research*, *3*(3), 250-257.

Wood, R. M. (2008). A Hand upon the Throat of the Nation: Economic sanctions and state repression, 1976–2001. *International Studies Quarterly*, *52*(3), 489–513. doi:10.1111/j.1468-2478.2008.00512.x

Wooldridge, J. M. (2010). *Econometric Analysis of Cross Section and Panel Data*. MIT press.

World Bank. (2002). *World Development Indicators*.

World Bank. (2007). *Zimbabwe Manpower Development and Training Project, Staff Appraisal report number 7005-Zim*. Population and Human Resources Department.

Worsley, P. (1970). *Introducing Sociology. Hamondsworth* Penguin.

Zembere, M. (2018). *Democratic citizenship education in Zimbabwe's higher education system and its implications for teaching and learning* (PhD dissertation). Stellensboch University.

KEY TERMS AND DEFINITIONS

Commitment: A conscious effort aiming for success of a pledge.

Community Workers: People who engage the community for development.

Connubio **for Transformation:** Amalgamation of forces that result in total change.

Economic Sanctions: Measures resultant from severed foreign economic relationships among countries.

Endogenous Arrangements: Commitments by a nation that are independent of outside influence.

Financial Discipline: Restraint in the use finance.

Innovation: Discovery of new ideas and initiatives.

Knowledge Creation: Knowledge designing.

Knowledge Sector: Higher education institutions.

National Developments: Activities that ensure national wellbeing.

Private Sector: Independent profit-making sector of the economy.

Public Sector: State-owned enterprises.

Rule of Law: A situation where the law is observed without exception.

Sustainability: A condition that propels the use of a particular resource.

Transparency: Openness.

Trust: Earned conviction.

Chapter 9

Influence of Information Systems and Technology on Hospitality Business Performance in Albania

Lerida Shkrepa
Epoka University, Albania

Alba Demneri Kruja
(iD) https://orcid.org/0000-0002-6902-1489
Epoka University, Albania

ABSTRACT

The transition from a closed economy to an open, market economy created new opportunities for the development of tourism in Albania. Tourism is known as one of the industries with the largest use of information technology (IT), but for various reasons, application of information systems (IS) in Albanian hotels is lower compared to other countries in Balkan region and other countries in Europe. Many processes and operations are handled in old and traditional ways. Most of the entrepreneurs do not know the benefit of using IS in the daily processes of the hotels. However, the demand of hospitality services dictates the need of using contemporary IS to gain competitive advantage and to survive in the market. IS and technology impacts competitiveness, management of information flow, and the decision-making process. They have influenced performance of the hotel sector through changing the nature of tourism services and the target market. This chapter aims to establish the extent of usage of these systems in the overall performance of the hotels in Tirana, the capital of Albania.

DOI: 10.4018/978-1-5225-8873-3.ch009

INTRODUCTION

Nowadays tourism is viewed as one of the largest and dynamically developing sectors of external economic activities in the world. Tourism remains a critical economic activity, which continues to grow (Phillips & Moutinho, 2014). The sector has a crucial impact on the economy of Albania and its total contribution to GDP for 2017, as reported by WTTC (2018), was 26.2%.

Tourism is an important sector for the Albanian economy and employment rates in the country (Kruja & Berberi, 2020). Its contribution is supported by many hospitality activities including restaurants and hotels which accommodate and serve tourists. For companies to compete and to give dynamism to the national economy, innovation together with technical development should be encouaged. However, this sector has many barriers that include lack of infrastructure, lack of professionalism, informality and sometimes the product does not meet the customer's expectations (Noti, 2014). Accommodative businesses have experienced a growth since Albania entered in the free trade market. Apart from political factors, there are many social and economic factors that leave Albania behind compared to other countries in the region.

Competitive prices and the diversity of natural and cultural tourism have encouraged ongoing development and an increase in foreign investments in the country. Impact of technology in this sector has been a long-studied subject where researchers try to understand how technology shapes service processes, and whether such enactment improves customer satisfaction and sector performance (Law et al., 2014; Melian-Gonzalez, & Bulchand-Gidumal, 2016; Ferizi & Kruja, 2018; Kruja et al., 2019).

An important component in daily operations of hotel businesss is the IT that they use in their main activities. Researchers claim that to be competitive in today's "high tech environment" world, organizations need to offer specialized services and develop an innovative strategy that employs new technologies especially information systems (IS) (Jing, et al., 2003; Lim, et al., 2004; Abugabah & Sanzogni, 2009; Ahmeti & Kruja, 2020; Kruja & Hysi, 2020; Kruja, 2020). According to Fichman (2004) information technology (IT) innovations have impacted every aspect of organizational life. DiPietro & Wang (2010), specify three fundamental dimensions of IT's influence to the hospitality industry: (1) IT utilization for business process automation and cost reduction; (2) improved communication within the hotel; and (3) marketing and customer relationships enhancement. Other authors argue that IT implementation has a focus to contribute to performance and growth by increasing productivity, competitiveness, efficiency, and effectiveness (Hameed & Counsell, 2012; Lee & Xia, 2006). Therefore, the services offered by tourism sector should be more creative and innovative in utilizing human potential and technology.

In hospitality services, IS can be widely used in all the departments (Kim & Ham, 2007). Awais et al. (2012) define IS as a combination of IT and human resources that use technology to perform business processes. More potential foreign guests can be reached through internet by investing in online marketing and online booking in international websites. Front office applications create convenience in managing room reservations, their availability, check ins and check outs of the guests (Noti, 2014). Point of sales computers are widely used to register sales. Many computer software supporting accounting and finance processes can also be useful in the procurement process.

Tourism is considered everywhere as an activity with massive development and high economic efficiency. Even though Albania has all the needed premises to develop tourism, this branch is not sufficiently developed. Regardless of the high potential for touristic development, the quality of services is stil low compared to other countries in the region. Albania's positioning near the Mediterranean Sea, the climate, natural wonders for every season, coastline and mountain scenery have not been enough for the country to be ranked among other European countries. United Nations World Tourism Organization (UNWTO) forecasts that the arrivals of tourists to Central/Eastern Europe are expected to grow rapidly and by this rapid growth in 2020 nearly one between three visitors to Europe will most probably choose a Central or Eastern Europe destination (World Bank, 2009). This indicates that the opportunities for Albanian tourism sector to expand are high (Kruja, 2012).

A touristic product to be complete should include not only the natural attractions but also the facilities, infrastructure, and proper services to their customers. A prominent part of the hospitality sector is the quality of accommodative spaces and level of service. As hospitality industry becomes more technology-dependent, Albanian hospitality sector is known to stay slow in adapting new technologies into its service systems (Kruja et al., 2019, p. 139). Bravo et al. (2015, p. 247) point out that "improvement in performance after the introduction of an IS may not be solved merely by tackling the features of the technology but also by simplifying the tasks or reviewing the users' knowledge gaps". They suggest managers should consider "individual" (knowledge of the task and the technology), "task" (ease) and "technology" (usefulness and ease) factors to boost performance (Bravo et al., 2015).

The purpose of this chapter is to help the managers to be aware of the importance of IT utilization and integrating IS in their businesses by answering the following questions: 1) What is the level of IT utilization in hospitality businesss in Albania?; 2) How integrated are IS components in hospitality businesss?; 3) What are the attitudes of managers towards the utilization of ICT?; 4) What are the hotel processes supported by IS? and 5) Do IT utilization and IS integration in hotel processes have any impact in overall hotel performance?

IT, IS and Hotel Performance

IT is a tool intended to generate value, whether productivity enhancement, cost reduction, competitive advantage, improved supplier relationships, etc (Melville, et al., 2004). Bharadwaj (2000), indicated that implementation of IS and having human IT resources can lead to benefits such as taking advantage of the synergies that result from interaction of resources and creating a customer-oriented mentality. Jessup and Valacich (2008) define IS as an academic study of systems with a specific reference to information and the complementary networks of hardware and software that people, and organizations use to collect, filter, process, create and also distribute data." Lewrick et al. (2010) argue that innovation is "the production, diffusion, and use of new and economically useful knowledge, a key factor for competitiveness and growth. Knowledge is the key element of the innovation systems and the institutions which have an important role in its development include: universities and other academic institutions that develop and transfer knowledge; government organizations; and innovative businesss (Kruja, 2013).

Hospitality businesss need IT to perform their basic activities and to use the resources efficiently. Previous researchers have found a positive impact of IT aspects on hospitality businesss performance (Gregory et al., 2005; Chiang & Jang, 2006; Law & Hsu, 2006; Buhalis & Law, 2008; Buhalis & Egger, 2008). Law & Jogaratnam (2005) point out in their study that in hospitality industry the IT can change the nature of products, organizations, processes and competitiveness, and those organizations that suffer the lack of success in mastering IS would find difficulty in managing the intense information and the competition.

The performance of the hotel's strategic management has been found to have a positive association with the interaction of the managers with information systems (Winata & Mia, 2005). The application of IS helps businesses to manage the information effectively and dynamically and impacts in gaining competitive advantage through assisting managers in decision making processes to make the right decisions, especially in investment. According to Kim & Ham (2007), IS plays an important role as a quality improver and impacts customer behavior. Small and medium hospitality organizations gain advantages in management by using many IS such as property management systems, decision support systems or financial systems. Hotel management information systems (MIS) create new priorities and help the staff to work better and easier. In customer-related aspects, the application of MIS facilitates the interaction among customers and employees to collect indicators of customer satisfaction, their feedback and likelihood to return. Reservation information systems have been an innovation in hospitality industry, by selling the services before they are provided. Other softwares used in the hospitality business include front-office applications and restaurant management systems.

Phillips and Louvieris (2005) sougt in their research to find the best performance measurement practice in hospitality small and medium businesss. Their focus was to study the power of the balanced scorecard (BSC) practice to strengthen and inflate performance measurement. Their research used a case study approach in exploring the critical factors that measure the performance. They concluded that IS impact even the proper measurements of performance. In financial aspects, the critical factors are the digitalization and collection of appropriate information using information systems that convert the information in relevant spreadsheets with departmental cost details and sales generation.

Pranicevic et al. (2011) used the BSC approach to evaluate the impact of IS in hotel performance on the Croatian coastal hotels. They found enough evidence to conclude that there exists a relationship between levels of IS applied and most of the non-financial performance measurements. Hardware and software renovation, security information systems, access to proper internal and external information and managerial support level represent the critical success factors that are applicable in the hospitality industry.

Noti (2014) examined the impact of IT in Albanian hospitality businesses and established that entrepreneurs in Albania have a positive attitude towards positive qualities of IT. His data analysis concluded that there is a statistical relationship between information systems and performance of hospitality businesses, but it is not very strong. Accommodation units use computer software to cover main activities such as reservations in the front office, room availability, food and beverages and check in and check outs of the guests. There is a group of owners/managers that have a negative opinion about IT because of their age which makes it difficult for them to adapt with the newest technologies however, most of the managers resulted to be satisfied with the convenience in the decision-making process facilitated by IS as well as they realized that IS impacts positively the performance of the businesses (Noti, 2014).

Ferizi & Kruja (2018) focused on examinining the internal success factors of the hospitality industry in Albania, with the focus on coastlines, and identifyed those factors critical to performance. Among the six internal success factors is technological innovation (investing in new technology systems such as offering a good quality of internet, as well as increasing the level of the hotel MIS).

Lam & Low (2019) study found that hotels are data-aware but not ready for the digital era ot just technologically but also in terms of their processes, people, culture, and mindset. Kruja, et al. (2019, p. 157) suggest to "develop arguments and publications that will tangibly show the gains of users by adapting this technology to the hotels".

RESEARCH METHODOLOGY

Sample and Data Collection

The main objective of this chapter was to emphasize the utilization level of IT and IS in Albanian hotels processes and their impact on general performance. Even though touristic businesss operate all over Albania, Tirana as its capital receives guests throughout the year not only during the summer or winter season. For this reason, among all the cities, Tirana was chosen as a case of this study.

The focus was on IT usage and many hotels in Albania do not need to invest in technology because they operate as micro businesses with a limited number of rooms and services. To have a realistic result, hotels with less than two rating stars were excluded from the sample. Other hotels that were established in less than a year were not included in the study. The person that answered the questionnaire had to be the manager or the owner of the hotel and had to be interviewed face to face. A short introduction of the study was necessary to help them understand the purpose and to explain the anonymity and their right to not answer if they did not want to. After gathering all the data, the questionnaires were reviewed for any unclear responses and responses about customer satisfaction were compared to reviews in online websites such as Trip Advisor and Booking.com et. Out of the 37 questionnaires distributed randomly only 30 were considered valid based on the sampling criteria.

Variables

The structure of the questionnaire was based on the literature review and previous studies about the same topic. Most of the questions were based on the questionnaire prepared by Pranicevic et al. (2011). However, some of the questions were edited to fit the characteristics of Albanian hotels. The questionnaire contained 20 questions and was divided into four parts. In the first part, the managers/owners were asked about hotel characteristics and in the second part about the level of satisfaction for some performance measurements. The critical factors that impact the performance of small and medium businesss were determined based on the study of Wu (2009). The third and fourth parts included questions about the level of information systems used in their hotel activities such as food cycle, guest cycle, sales, marketing, and procurement. Items and scale used to measure each variable of the study are presented in Table 1 below.

Table 1. Variables used in the study

Variables	Items	Scale of measurement
IS level in hotel processes	Food cycle	1 to 3
	Procurement	
	Background	
	Sales and marketing	
	Guest cycle	
IT level	Info access inside	1 to 3
	Info access from outside	
	Protection	
	IT knowledge	
	IT integration	
	Website	
Hotel performance	Growth in sales	1 to 5
	Growth in market share	
	Growth in profit	
	Return on investment	
	Customer satisfaction	
	Employee satisfaction	

Hypothesis, Conceptual Framework and Methods

This research aimed at assessing a measurement model of the impact/relationship/ added value of hotel`s IT level and IS level implementation in hotel processes on their performance. The study's conceptual framework is reported below (Figure 1). IT level is measured by the level degree of info access from inside as well as from outside; protection; IT staff knowledge; IT operational integration and website activeness. IS level in business is measured by the degree level of involvement in hotel operational processes such as food cycle; procurement; background; sales and marketing; and guest cycle. While hotel performance is measured through the level of growth in sales; market share; profit; return on investment (ROI); customer satisfaction; and employee satisfaction.

In this research the purpose is to identify whether the increase in IT level and IS level of the hotel processes in the hospitality industry in Tirana has a positive effect their performance. Based on this objective the following set of hypotheses were formulated and tested:

Hypothesis H1: There is a significant impact of IT usage in overall hotel performance.
Hypothesis H2: There is a significant impact of IS applied in business processes in overall hotel performance.

To test the hypothesis statistical tests such as one-way ANOVA and ANCOVA were used. These tests try to find if there is any statistically significant difference between independent groups and in this case, they tried to find out if the hotels' overall performance differed based on IT and IS levels.

Figure 1. Conceptual framework of the study

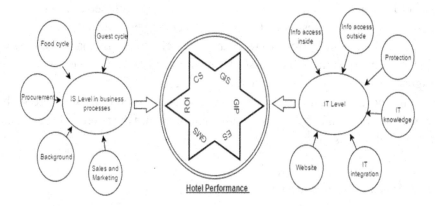

RESULT Analysis

When the data set was completed the following step was analysis of the data to achieve the objectives of the study. The analysis was done using the SPSS Statistics software. A problem occurred while performing statistical tests such as one-way ANOVA and ANCOVA. To have a better result each group of hotel performance, IT and IS level should have a frequency higher than one. In the data set many groups had only one data. As a result, it was necessary to group the variables to have a correct result of ANOVA and ANCOVA tests. Performance measurements range from 0 to 30 and the results of 30 hotels were distributed in 5 groups as follows: 11 to 13, 15 to 18, 19 to 21, 22 to 24 and 25 to 27. The same method was used in the level of IT utilization, by diving the data in 5 groups with the same range as performance.

Descriptive Analysis

One of the criteria of the study was that only the manager or the owner should answer the questionnaire. A lot of hotels in Albania are family businesses, the reason why they do not invest in hiring a manager. However, the results show that out of 30 people that answered the questionnaire 90% were managers of the hotel and only 10% were owners that managed their business on their own (Table 2).

Forty percent (40%) of the hotels started their business 15 years or earlier. Twenty seven percent (27. %) of the hotels had started 8 to 15 years ago and 20% were 3 to 7 years in business. The youngest hotels, with an age less than 3 years represented 13% of the sample.

According to the results, 10% of the hotels that were included in the study were classified as micro businesses with less than 10 employees. Seventy percent (70%) had a range of employees from 10 to 49 and were classified as small businesss and 20% of them were medium businesses with a range of 50 to 249 workers.

Eighty percent (80%) of the hotels used Hotel MIS that covered different operations and 20% did not use Hotel MIS and instead used other software such as Excel to store and organize the flow of information within the hotel. Table 2 presents a summary of the results

Table 2. Summary of the descriptive statistics

Variable	Item	Frequency	Percentage
Position	Manager	27	90
	Owner	3	10
Business size	Micro	3	10
	Small	21	70
	Medium	6	20
Business age	Less than 3 years	4	13.3
	3-7 years	6	20
	8-15 years	8	26.7
	More than 15 years	12	40
MIS usage	Yes	24	80
	No	6	20

Managers/owners answered about their satisfaction related to some performance measurements including growth in sales, growth in market share, growth in profit, and return on investment, and customer and employee satisfaction. According to the answers received, 36.7% of the managers of the hotels agreed that the average sales of the hotel's service have grown from year to year13.3% of the hotels had experienced a growth in the percentage of total sales volume in the market,46.7% of the managers were satisfied with the profit growth and only 23.4% agreed that the hotel is using the resources in an efficient manner. Seventy 70% of the hotels offered a good service to the customers, who gave a great feedback about their experience.

In order to attain a more realistic result towards achieving the objectives of the research, managers were asked about the level of IS used in their hotels to which 50% of the hotels use a non integrated application to access information within the hotel and 43.3% use individual applications. In adition, 93.3% offered access to their information via a website and 70% had secured contents. Based on managers' answers, 60% hired employees with basic IT knowledge and 40% had staff with more advanced IT literacy and the ability to evaluate the system and to suggest improvements. In 63.3% of the cases, applications were connected to the local network, and 73.3% of the hotels had the functionality of online booking in their website.

One of the most important factors in using technology in a business is the level at which these applications help the managers to supervise many activities inside the business. According to the hotels in the study, without taking into consideration the level of IS that they use, the managers rated the facility that IS creates in the information flow, required materials flow and monetary flow as follows 70% of the mangers were too satisfied with the help of IS in supervising the flow of data within their business. To handle and have access to the materials required in business, 56.7% agreed that IS was very useful. This evaluation changes in the case of cash flows inside and outside the hotel and 40% of the managers indicated that IS is not very helpful in incoming and outgoing of cash. However, 33.3% of them were satisfied with the help of IS in monetary flows and operating activities of the hotel.

In subsequent questions, the managers were asked about specific activities within the hotel since for different operations, specific applications can be used. The results sowed that 13.3% of the hotels do not offer food and beverage services to their customers, 30% use point of sale computers to register sales and 46.7% of the hotels have invested in intelligent cash registers that record the sales and inventory changes. The procurement process which includes preparation of demand, purchasing the materials, receipt, and final payment in 93.3% of the hotels is covered by applications that are not integrated with the hotel information system. Background process, which involves the systematic accounting processes and financing the resources, it is managed in 63.3% of the cases using software that is not integrated with the hotel MIS. In 30% of the hotels, the software is integrated with the hotel MIS. All the hotels that were included in the research are presented online with the on-line booking functionality. To accommodate the guests, 90% of the hotels use front office applications and only 6.7% have invested in utilizing the functionality of booking on-line which is integrated with the front office application.

IT/IS use and Performance of Hotels

To measure the performance of hotels, several indicators were taken into consideration. Managers rated their satisfaction on a scale from 1 to 5 for growth in sales, growth in market share, growth in profit, and return on investment, customer, and employee satisfaction. The summation of these variables gave the level of hotel performance. Performance was measured on a range from 0 to 30 and then distributed in 5 groups that represent 5 levels. Fifty three percent (53%) were satisfied with the performance of the hotel based on the indicators mentioned above. Twenty seven percent (27%) of the hotels' performance was within the 15-18 range and 20% of the managers rated the hotels' performance in a lower level indicating that the hotels needed improvements.

To study if there is an impact of information systems in the hotel performance it was necessary to measure the level of IT utilization in the business. The level of IT usage in hotel and level of IS used in hotel processes were measured using indicators and their values were separated in 5 groups. The higher the value the better the level of IT. Forty percent (40%) of the hotel owners had invested in information technology; forty four percent (44%) of the managers rated the level of IT utilized as average and 16% of the hotels were behind with investments in IT.

The level of information systems usage was measured on a range of 0 to 15 where 15 represented the highest level of information systems application. Only 10% of the hotels have made enough investments to use IS in hotel processes such as food cycle, procurement, accounting, sales and marketing and guest cycle process. It is important to emphasize that 77% of the hotels use information systems but at a low level. The applications they use for different processes are not integrated with the hotel MIS.

According to the results, the performance of the hotels was on average 19 on a range of 12 to 27. Regarding the level of IT usage, the hotels applied on average a level of 19 and this level varied from 11 to 26. Meanwhile concerning the level of IS used in the hotels studied, it was on average 8.2 on a range of 6 to 14. Table 3 gives a summary of the results about performance of the hotels versus use of IT/IS.

The main objective of this study was to find out if there is a significant impact of information systems in hotel performance. The level of information systems was measured by the level of IT usage and the level of IS applied in hotel processes. The study had two hypothesises namely:

Hypothesis H1: There is a significant impact of IT usage in overall hotel performance.
Hypothesis H2: There is a significant impact of IS application in business processes in overall hotel performance.

Table 3. Hotel performance, IT usage and IS process means (n=30)

	Hotel Performance	IT Usage	IS Process
N	30	30	30
Mean	19.2667	19.9333	8.2000
Std. Deviation	3.97348	4.99609	1.97222
Skewness	-.148	-.512	1.725
Kurtosis	-.931	-.938	3.505
Minimum	12.00	11.00	6.00
Maximum	27.00	26.00	14.00

To test the two hypothesises of the study, a one-way ANOVA test was performed. The test compared the means of two or more groups of the dependent variables and one of the independent variables, and tested the null hypothesis that the data in all groups are drawn from the population with the same mean values (Howell, 2002).

The results of the one-way ANOVA (Table 4) show that there is a significant difference between groups (F=9.471 and p=0.000). The test of homogeneity is not significant at the 0.05 level. As determined by the analysis, IT usage has a significant impact on performance because different levels of IT usage have different levels of performance. Tukey post hoc test detected that the overall performance was statistically significant in the hotel with level 5 of IT usage (3.88 ± 0.78) and level 4 (3.33 ± 1.15) compared to level 3 (2.87 ± 0.99), level 2 (1.6 ± 0.89) and level 1 (1.4 ± 0.54). There is no statistical significant difference between groups of level 1 and level 2 ($p=0.996$), level 2 and level 3 ($p=0.106$), level 2 and level 4 ($p=0.077$) level 3 and level 4 ($p=0.934$), level 3 and level 5 ($p=0.147$), level 4 and level 5 ($p=0.870$).

Table 4. ANOVA results for hotel performance and IT usage

Performance	Sum of Squares	df	Mean Square	F	Sig.
Between Groups	28.536	4	7.134	9.471	.000
Within Groups	18.831	25	.753		
Total	47.367	29			

One-way ANOVA analysis (Table 5) showed that there is a significant difference between groups of performance levels and IS level (F=7.481 and p=0.000). The test of homogeneity was not significant at the 0.05 level. As revealed by ANOVA analysis, IS level used in hotel processes had a significant impact on performance because different levels of IS applied had different levels of performance. From the test output, it was established that the overall performance was statistically significant and high in the hotels with level 14 of information systems utilized (4.5 ± 0.70) and level 9 (3.87 ± 0.64) compared to level 8 (1.04 ± 0.42), level 7 (1.88 ± 0.92) and level 6 (1.75 ± 0.95).

Table 5. ANOVA results for hotel performance and IS processes

Performance	Sum of Squares	Df	Mean Square	F	Sig.
Between Groups	28.853	5	5.771	7.481	.000
Within Groups	18.514	24	.771		
Total	47.367	29			

The output of ANCOVA analysis indicateed that there is a statistically significant difference in overall hotel performance between the levels of IT usage in the hotel when adjusted for size and age (*p*=0.03). The result it was supported by the result of Levene's test of homogeneity (equality of error variances) which is not significant at the 0.05 level (*p*=0.302). The same test was performed for the impact of IS used in different processes on hotel performance once their means have been adjusted for age and size of the hotel and the results showed that there is a statistically significant difference in performance between the levels of information systems by use of age and size as a covariate. According to Levene's test of homogeneity the error variance of the dependent variable was equal across groups.

FUTURE RESEARCH DIRECTIONS

This study attempted to contribute to the performance of the hospitality industry by focusing specifically on the impact of IT usage and IS process implementation on hotel businesss. One of the limitations of the study was the low number of observations included in the sample. For future studies, a larger sample is recommended. Additionally, this chapter focused on the hotels of Tirana but since the tourism sector impacts the entire Albanian economy, other studies should focus on other aspects of the tourism sector in Albania.

CONCLUSION AND IMPLICATIONS

Tourism is an important sector with a great influence on Albania`s economy, highly contributing to its GDP and employment. Previous studies indicate that there exist a willingness of managers/owners on IT/IS implementations, but they are not data savy in technology usage (Noti, 2014; Ferizi & Kruja, 2018; Lam & Low, 2019; Kruja et al., 2019). Kruja et al. (2019) urge further researching and advocating the benefits of hotels by adapting technology in their systems. Meanwhile Bravo et al. (2015) emphasize that managers should not focus only on tackling features of technology, but also considering individual and task factors to boost performance.

The aim of the research was to establish the extent hotels in Tirana were using IT/ IS in their business processes and the benefits associated with. Internet is a network with low costs and of a great value in service because necessary information can be delivered through it to customers such as, the price of the service, special offers and availability of the products/services. Hence, IT contributes to the strategic management of hospitality businesss and a lot of them have invested in IT and IS applications that facilitate their operations and service to customers. For this research, the hotel businesses in Tirana were chosen to be investigated given that it is a city destination receiving guests all year round.

Most of the hotel businesss that participated indicated a medium level of information technology applied in their daily processes. In Albanian hotels, it is used as a marketing tool, a fact that is supported by the results of the study which indicated that all the hotels had an on-line booking service and most of the hotels represented their business online through a website. Eighty percent (80%) of the entrepreneurs had invested in a hotel MIS but they did not have an IT specialist. It is the company or the person that had developed and at the same time was maintaining their software. To order and purchase goods needed in the hotels, they still use the traditional methods of procurement and most of the software used for accounting and finance was not integrated with the hotel information management systems. All the managers agreed to the fact that the use of different applications in various hotel processes eased their daily work and provided new opportunities for business development. The statistical analysis indicated that there was a significant impact of information system and technology on the performance hotels studies.

Many hotels currently use IT hardware, software and IS applications such as point of sale and intelligent cash registers to record the sales of food and beverages. However, the process of purchasing the materials and products needed from suppliers is not supported by IT/IS and managers find it easier to make the orders through traditional means. The accounting and finance service were largely covered by specific and high-quality applications but unfortunately in most of the cases were not integrated with hotel management software. Internet/the Web was used as a marketing tool by all the hotels that were part of this study. All of them offered on-line booking through other websites such as booking.com or Trip Advisor or their websites. However, front office applications of them was not integrated with the on-line booking functionality and the employees had to make the changes manually. Furthermore, only 6.7% had invested in integrating this functionality with their hotel management system.

Based on the output of the one-way ANOVA and ANCOVA analysis, it was established that there was a statistically significant impact of the use of IS in the hotels on their overall performance. Different levels of IS had different levels of performance and the hotels with a higher level of IS utilization had more effective processes than those that had lower levels of IT/IS use. However, most of the hotels that provided on-line booking did not include on-line payment. Additionally, online booking was not integrated with the hotel management system despite the benefits associated with such an integration such as increased efficiency of employees managing the bookings.

This research provides various contributions addressing crucial theoretical and practical implications. First, study findings contribute to literature on technology impact on hotel process performance with evidence from Tirana, a city destination on a developing country. Second the study offers practical implications towards policy makers, local government, destination management authorities, IT/IS providers, and hotel managers/owners. The study findings highlight the necessity of an effective, and efficient IT/IS implementation by the hotels to boost their performance through decreased operational costs, increased markets, and better served customers. This sector is decisive for the country, as it has abundance of natural resources and a lot of capacities to serve domestic and foreign customers throughout the year. An apropriate governmental policy planning is needed for technological infrastructure support of hotels. At the same time an increase of awareness of managers/owners in IT/IS implementation benefits is needed, thus system providers and destination management authorities should continuously communicate and collaborate with hotel manager/owners and local government towards achieving not only increased awareness but also implementation. Finally, the research recommends managers/owners to further invest in in hotel management systems, integrating all of their operations and managing them through the system, and consider hiring professional staff with good IT knowledge to professionally manage their IT sevices.

REFERENCES

Abugabah, A., & Sanzogni, L. (2009). Information Systems and Performance: An analytical approach to understand IS value in business organizations. *International Conference on Information Systems.*

Ahmeti, E., & Kruja, A. (2020). Challenges and Perspectives of Supply Chain Management in Emerging Markets: A Case Study Approach. In A. Dwivedi, & M. S. Alshamrani (Eds.), Leadership Strategies for Global Supply Chain Management in Emerging Markets (pp. 132-146). IGI Global. doi:10.4018/978-1-7998-2867-9.ch006

Awais, M., Irfan, M., Bidal, M., & Samin, T. (2012). Helpful Business Value of Advance Bal Information System. *International Journal of Computer Science Issues, 9*(2), 415–422.

Bharadwaj, A. S. (2000). A resource-based perspective on information technology capability and firm performance: An empirical investigation. *Management Information Systems Quarterly, 24*(1), 169–196. doi:10.2307/3250983

Bravo, E. R., Santana, M., & Rodon, J. (2015). Information systems and performance: The role of technology, the task and the individual. *Behaviour & Information Technology, 34*(3), 247–260. doi:10.1080/0144929X.2014.934287

Buhalis, D., & Egger, R. (2008). *E-tourism: Case studies.* Butterworth Heinemann/Elsevier.

Buhalis, D., & Law, R. (2008). Progress in information technology and tourism management: 20 years on and 10 years after the Internet - The state of e-tourism research. *Tourism Management, 29*(4), 609–623. doi:10.1016/j.tourman.2008.01.005

Chiang, C., & Jang, S. C. (2006). The effects of perceived price and brand image on value and purchase intention: Leisure travelers' attitudes toward online hotel booking. *Journal of Hospitality & Leisure Marketing, 3,* 49–69.

DiPetro, R. B., & Wang, Y. R. (2010). Key issues for ICT applications: Impacts an implications for hospitality operations. *Worldwide Hospitality and Tourism, 2*(1), 49–67. doi:10.1108/17554211011012595

Ferizi, V., & Kruja, A. D. (2018). Coastline Hospitality Industry Performance, Challenges, and Opportunities: Evidence From Durres Coastline. In D. Batabyal (Ed.), Managing Sustainable Tourism Resources (pp. 14-38). IGI Global.

Fichman, R. G. (2004). Going beyond the dominant paradigm for information technology. *Journal of the Association for Information Systems, 5*(8), 314–355. doi:10.17705/1jais.00054

Gregory, S. R., Kline, S. F., & Breiter, D. (2005). Group sales and marketing in convention hotels: Internet and web usage. *Journal of Travel & Tourism Marketing, 18*(1), 67–77. doi:10.1300/J073v18n01_07

Hameed, M. A., & Counsell, S. (2012). Assessing the influence of environmental and CEO characteristics for adoption of information technology in organizations. *Journal of Technology Management & Innovation, 7*(1), 64–84. doi:10.4067/S0718-27242012000100005

Howell, D. C. (2002). Statistical methods for psychology (5th ed.). Academic Press.

Jessup, L., & Valacich, J. (2008). *Information Systems Today* (3rd ed.). Pearson Prentice Hall.

Jing, J., Quan, Q., & Paul, J. (2003). Information Technology Investments and Firms' Performance: A Duopoly Perspective. *Journal of Management Information Systems, 20*(3), 121–158. doi:10.1080/07421222.2003.11045773

Kim, W., & Ham, S. (2007). The impact of information technology implementation on service quality in the hotel industry. *Information Technology in Hospitality, 4*(4), 143–151. doi:10.3727/154595306779868430

Kruja, A. (2012). The Impact of Tourism Sector Development in the Albanian Economy. *Economia. Seria Management*, 204-218.

Kruja, A. (2013). Entrepreneurship and knowledge-based economies. *Revista Românească pentru Educaţie Multidimensională, 5*(1), 7-17.

Kruja, A. D. (2020). Enterprise investments, innovation and performance: Evidence from Albania. *International Journal of Innovation in the Digital Economy, 11*(1), 68–80. doi:10.4018/IJIDE.2020010105

Kruja, A. D., & Berberi, E. (2020). Tourism and Handicraft Industry: Opportunities and Challenges of Operating in the Albanian Market. In I. Chirino-Klevans (Ed.), Cases on Global Leadership in the Contemporary Economy (pp. 119-136). IGI Global.

Kruja, A. D., Hysa, X., Duman, T., & Tafaj, A. (2019). Adoption of Software as a Service (Saas) in Small and Medium-Sized Hotels in Tirana. *Enlightening Tourism, 9*(2), 137–167. doi:10.33776/et.v9i2.3625

Kruja, A. D., & Hysi, K. (2020). Influence of Practice Management Software on Dental Services: A Case Study Approach. In B. Nogalski, A. A. Szpitter, A. Jabłoński, & M. Jabłoński (Eds.), Networked Business Models in the Circular Economy (pp. 241-267). IGI Global. doi:10.4018/978-1-5225-7850-5.ch011

Lam, C., & Law, R. (2019). Readiness of upscale and luxury-branded hotels for digital transformation. *International Journal of Hospitality Management, 79*(May), 60–69. doi:10.1016/j.ijhm.2018.12.015

Law, R., Buhalis, D., & Cobanoglu, C. (2014). Progress on information and communication technologies in hospitality and tourism. *International Journal of Contemporary Hospitality Management, 26*(5), 727–750. doi:10.1108/IJCHM-08-2013-0367

Law, R., & Hsu, C. H. (2006). Importance of hotel website dimensions and attributes: Perceptions of online browsers and online purchasers. *Journal of Hospitality & Tourism Research (Washington, D.C.), 30*(3), 295–312. doi:10.1177/1096348006287161

Law, R., & Jogaratnam, G. (2005). A study of hotel information technology applications. *International Journal of Contemporary Hospitality Management, 17*(2), 170–180. doi:10.1108/09596110510582369

Lee, G., & Xia, W. (2006). Organizational size and IT innovation adoption: A meta-analysis. *Information & Management, 43*(8), 957–985. doi:10.1016/j.im.2006.09.003

Lewrick, M., Omar, M., Raeside, R., & Saier, K. (2010). Education for entrepreneurship and innovation:`Management capabilities for sustainable growth and success. *World Journal of Entrepreneurship, Management and Sustainable Development, 6*(1/2), 1–18. doi:10.1108/20425961201000001

Lim, J., Richardson, V., & Roberts, T. (2004). Information technology investment and firm performance: A meta-analysis. *Proceedings of the 37th Hawaii International Conference on Systems Sciences.*

Melian-Gonzales, S., & Bulchand-Gidumal, J. (2016). A model that connects information technology and hotel performance. *Tourism Management, 53*(April), 30–37. doi:10.1016/j.tourman.2015.09.005

Melville, N., Kraemer, K., & Gurbaxani, V. (2004). Review: Information technology and organizational performance: An integrative model of IT business value. *Management Information Systems Quarterly, 28*(2), 283–322. doi:10.2307/25148636

Noti, E. (2014). *Ndikimi i teknologjise se informacionit ne sipermarrjet turistike ne Shqiperi*. Tirana University.

Phillips, P., & Louvieris, P. (2005). Performance Measurement Systems in Tourism, Hospitality, and Leisure Small Medium-Sized Enterprises: A Balanced Scorecard Perspective. *Journal of Travel Research, 44*(2), 201–211. doi:10.1177/0047287505278992

Phillips, P., & Moutinho, L. (2014). Critical review of strategic planning research in hospitality and tourism. *Annals of Tourism Research, 48*, 96–120. doi:10.1016/j.annals.2014.05.013

Pranicevic, D. G., Alfirevic, N., & Stemberger, M. I. (2011). Information system maturity and the hospitality enterprise performance. *Economic and Business Review for Central and South-Eastern Europe, 13*(4), 227.

Winata, L., & Mia, L. (2005). Information technology and the performance effect of managers' participation in budgeting: Evidence from the hotel industry. *International Journal of Hospitality Management, 24*(1), 21–39. doi:10.1016/j.ijhm.2004.04.006

World Bank. (2009). *Albania: Building Competitiveness in Albania.* Europe and Central Asia Region: World Bank. Retrieved from World Bank: http://siteresources.worldbank.org/EXTAR2009/Resources/6223977-1252950831873/AR09_Complete.pdf

WTTC. (2018). *Travel & Tourism Economic Impact 2018.* World Travel & Tourism Council.

Wu, D. (2009). *Measuring performance in small and medium enterprises in the information and communication technology industries.* RMIT University.

KEY TERMS AND DEFINITIONS

Hotel Performance: Encompasses areas of business outcomes such as financial performance, product market performance and shareholder return.

Information Systems (IS): Systems study with a specific reference to information and the complementary networks of hardware and software that people, and organizations use to collect, filter, process, create, and distribute data.

Information Technology (IT): A tool intended to generate value, whether productivity enhancement, cost reduction, competitive advantage, improved supplier relationships, etc.

Management Information Systems (MIS): An information system that facilitates the interaction among customers and employees to collect indicators of customer satisfaction, their feedback etc. used, for decion-making, coordination, control, and analysis purposes.

Technological Innovation: Providing new products and processes or technological advancements of already existing products and services.

APPENDIX 1: STUDY SURVEY

I. General Information

1.   Job position:
     ☐ Owner .... ☐ Manager
2.   Size of the enterprise:
     Micro .... Small .... Medium .... Large
     ☐ 1-9 .... ☐ 10-49 .... ☐ 50-249 .... ☐ 250 or more
3.   Company Age:
     ☐ Less than 3 years ...... ☐ 3 -7 years ...... ☐ 8- 15 years
     ☐ More than 15 years

II. Hotel Performance

4.   How much are you satisfied with following performance measurements of
     your company?

Strongly Disagree(1) ... Disagree(2) ... Neutral(3) ... Agree(4) ... Strongly Agree(5)

Performance Indicators	Low .... Middle .... High
Growth in sales	1 ...... 2 ...... 3 ...... 4 5
Growth in market share (GMS)	1 ...... 2 ...... 3 ...... 4 5
Growth in profit	1 ...... 2 ...... 3 ...... 4 5
Return on Investment	1 ...... 2 ...... 3 ...... 4 5
Customer satisfaction	1 ...... 2 ...... 3 ...... 4 5
Employee satisfaction	1 ...... 2 ...... 3 ...... 4 5

III. IT Usage Level

5.   Is it used in any hotel management information system?
     ☐Yes .... ☐No
     If no, explain why? _____

     _____

6.   Rate the level of IT in the following processes as:
     Low(1) .... Medium(2) .... High(3)

7. Information access within hotel:
    a) paper-based notes 1
    b) an application not integrated with other applications 2
    c) an application integrated with others applications or within Intranet 3
8. Access to hotel information from outside:
    a) fax / telephone 1
    b) e-mail (email) 2
    c) Web site 3
9. Protection of contents:
    a) no 1
    b) in most cases 2
    c) yes 3
10. IT literacy of staff:
    a) basic IT literacy (able to use and understand application functionalities) 1
    b) advanced IT literacy (able to evaluate existing functionalities and propose required improvements) 2
    c) creative IT literacy (able to use applications to innovate and improve business processes) 3
11. Integration of components of Information Systems:
    a) there is no connection between applications 1
    b) applications are connected to the local network/ Intranet 2
    c) the activities are carried out on the Web only 3
12. Website interactivity items:
    a) Static information about the offer (including "offline" contact information) 1
    b) Registration and website personalization, including availability information 2
    c) Online booking, with or without online payment 3

IV. IS Usage Level in Operations

13. Rate the extent at which IS help managers to supervise:
    a) flow of required information within the hotel 1 - 2 - 3
    b) flow of required materials within the hotel 1 - 2 - 3
    c) monetary (cash) flows within the hotel and with the hotel's partners 1 - 2 - 3

14. Food and beverage to guests (food cycle process):
    a) point of sales computers to register food and beverage sales 1
    b) intelligent cash registers to register food and beverages sales and changes in inventories 2
    c) pocket-based devices to register food and beverage sales, register changes in inventory and 3 send orders directly to hotel kitchen

15. Hotel procurement process:
    a) application not integrated with other applications 1
    b) application integrated with the hotel information system 2
    c) contact with suppliers in a hotel procurement is carried out within an extranet, virtual private 3 network, or a similar network facility

16. Background processes (accounting, finance, ...):
    a) they are supported by applications, not integrated with other applications 1
    b) they are supported by applications integrated into the hotel information system 2
    c) they are supported by web applications 3

17. Sales and marketing:
    a) hotel booking is carried out only by traditional distribution channels (phone, fax, presentations 1 at fairs, personal contacts)
    b) hotel is presented on-line, but there is no on-line booking functionality 2
    c) hotel is presented on-line, with the on-line booking functionality 3

18. Accommodating guests (guest cycle process):
    a) front office application, not integrated with other applications 1
    b) central reservation system, integrated with the front office application 2
    c) on-line reservation functionality, integrated with the front office application 3

19. Do you agree that the information technology opens new opportunities for the hotel?
    a) I do not agree
    b) I partially agree
    c) I agree

20. If a hotel management system is not used, are you interested in providing one?
    _____
    _____
    _____

APPENDIX 2: STATISTICAL RESULTS

Table 6. One-way ANOVA

Performance	N	Mean	Std. Deviation	Std. Error	95% Confidence Interval for Mean		Minimum	Maximum	Between-Component Variance
					Lower Bound	Upper Bound			
1.00	5	1.4	.548	.245	.72	2.08	1.0	2.0	
2.00	5	1.60	.894	.400	.49	2.71	1.0	3.0	
3.00	8	2.88	.991	.350	2.05	3.70	2.0	4.0	
4.00	3	3.33	1.155	.667	.46	6.20	2.0	4.0	
5.00	9	3.89	.782	.261	3.29	4.49	3.0	5.0	
Total	30	2.77	1.278	.233	2.29	3.24	1.0	5.0	
Model Fixed Effects			.868	.158	2.44	3.09			
Model Random Effects				.524	1.31	4.22			1.10

Table 7. Test of Homogeneity of Variances

Performance			
Levene Statistic	df1	df2	Sig.
1.275	4	25	.306

Table 8. Multiple Comparisons: Tukey HSD

(I) Usage		Mean Difference (I-J)	Std. Error	Sig.	95% Confidence Interval	
					Lower Bound	Upper Bound
1.00	2.00	-.20000	.54890	.996	-1.8120	1.4120
	3.00	-1.47500*	.49477	.045	-2.9281	-.0219
	4.00	-1.93333*	.63381	.039	-3.7948	-.0719
	5.00	-2.48889*	.48408	.000	-3.9106	-1.0672
2.00	1.00	.20000	.54890	.996	-1.4120	1.8120
	3.00	-1.27500	.49477	.106	-2.7281	.1781
	4.00	-1.73333	.63381	.077	-3.5948	.1281
	5.00	-2.28889*	.48408	.001	-3.7106	-.8672
3.00	1.00	1.47500*	.49477	.045	.0219	2.9281
	2.00	1.27500	.49477	.106	-.1781	2.7281
	4.00	-.45833	.58756	.934	-2.1839	1.2673
	5.00	-1.01389	.42172	.147	-2.2524	.2246
4.00	1.00	1.93333*	.63381	.039	.0719	3.7948
	2.00	1.73333	.63381	.077	-.1281	3.5948
	3.00	.45833	.58756	.934	-1.2673	2.1839
	5.00	-.55556	.57859	.870	-2.2548	1.1437
5.00	1.00	2.48889*	.48408	.000	1.0672	3.9106
	2.00	2.28889*	.48408	.001	.8672	3.7106
	3.00	1.01389	.42172	.147	-.2246	2.2524
	4.00	.55556	.57859	.870	-1.1437	2.2548
Dependent Variable: Performance						

*. The mean difference is significant at the 0.05 level.

Table 9. Descriptives

Performance		N	Mean	Std. Deviation	Std. Error	95% Confidence Interval for Mean		Minimum	Maximum	Between-Component Variance
						Lower Bound	Upper Bound			
6.00		4	1.75	0.96	0.48	0.23	3.27	1.00	3.00	
7.00		9	1.89	0.93	0.31	1.18	2.60	1.00	4.00	
8.00		6	2.50	1.05	0.43	1.40	3.60	1.00	4.00	
9.00		8	3.88	0.64	0.23	3.34	4.41	3.00	5.00	
11.00		1	4.00					4.00	4.00	
14.00		2	4.50	0.71	0.50	-1.85	10.85	4.00	5.00	
Total		30	2.77	1.28	0.23	2.29	3.24	1.00	5.00	
Model	Fixed Effects			0.88	0.16	2.44	3.10			
	Random Effects				0.52	1.44	4.09			1.07

Table 10. Test of Homogeneity of Variances

Performance			
Levene Statistic	df1	df2	Sig.
.558[a]	4	24	.695
a. Groups with only one case are ignored in computing the test of homogeneity of variance for Performance.			

Table 11. Univariate Analysis of Variance

Usage	Mean	Std. Deviation	N
1.00	1.4000	.54772	5
2.00	1.6000	.89443	5
3.00	2.8750	.99103	8
4.00	3.3333	1.15470	3
5.00	3.8889	.78174	9
Total	2.7667	1.27802	30
Dependent Variable: Performance			

Table 12. Levene's Test of Equality of Error Variancesa

F	df1	df2	Sig.
1.286	4	25	.302
Tests the null hypothesis that the error variance of the dependent variable is equal across groups.			
Dependent Variable: Performance			

a. Design: Intercept + Size + Age + Usage

Table 13. Tests of Between-Subjects Effects

Source	Type III Sum of Squares	df	Mean Square	F	Sig.
Corrected Model	30.993[a]	6	5.166	7.256	.000
Intercept	1.626	1	1.626	2.284	.144
Size	1.436	1	1.436	2.017	.169
Age	.380	1	.380	.534	.472
Usage	15.181	4	3.795	5.331	.003
Error	16.374	23	.712		
Total	277.000	30			
Corrected Total	47.367	29			
Dependent Variable: Performance					

a. R Squared = .654 (Adjusted R Squared = .564)

Tabe 14. Descriptive Statistics

Process	Mean	Std. Deviation	N
6.00	1.7500	.95743	4
7.00	1.8889	.92796	9
8.00	2.5000	1.04881	6
9.00	3.8750	.64087	8
11.00	4.0000		1
14.00	4.5000	.70711	2
Total	2.7667	1.27802	30
Dependent Variable: Performance			

Table 15. Tests of Between-Subjects Effects

Source	Type III Sum of Squares	df	Mean Square	F	Sig.
Corrected Model	29.337[a]	7	4.191	5.114	.001
Intercept	4.101	1	4.101	5.004	.036
Size	.043	1	.043	.053	.820
Age	.329	1	.329	.401	.533
Process	13.525	5	2.705	3.301	.023
Error	18.030	22	.820		
Total	277.000	30			
Corrected Total	47.367	29			
Dependent Variable: Performance					

a. R Squared = .619 (Adjusted R Squared = .498)

Compilation of References

Abdelrahman, M., & Papamichail, K. N. (2016). *The Role of Organizational Culture on Knowledge Sharing by using Knowledge Management Systems in MNCs*. In 22nd *America's Conference on Information Systems*, San Diego, CA.

Abianna, I. C. B. (2009). *Prática docente de profissionais-formadores em cursos de Educação continuada de professores: uma experiência de ação-reflexão* (Mestrado em Educação). Faculdade de Educação, Pontifícia Universidade Católica do Rio Grande do Sul, Porto Alegre.

Abugabah, A., & Sanzogni, L. (2009). Information Systems and Performance: An analytical approach to understand IS value in business organizations. *International Conference on Information Systems*.

Afesorgbor, S. K., & Mahadevan, R. (2016). The Impact of Economic Sanctions on Income Inequality of Target States. *Economics Working Papers, 4*.

Aghion, P., & Howitt, P. (2010). Economics of Growth. Wiley-Blackwell Publishing Asia.

Aghion, P., Bergeaud, A., Lequien, M., & Melitz, M., (2017). *The Impact of Exports on Innovation: Theory and Evidence*. 2017 AEA Meeting Presentation.

Aghion, P., Dewatripont, D., & Patrick, R. (1999). Competition, Financial Discipline and Growth. *The Review of Economic Studies, 66*(4), 825–852. doi:10.1111/1467-937X.00110

Aghion, P., & Howitt, P. (2006). Appropriate growth policy: A unifying framework. *Journal of the European Economic Association, 4*(2-3), 271–278. doi:10.1162/jeea.2006.4.2-3.269

Ahmeti, E., & Kruja, A. (2020). Challenges and Perspectives of Supply Chain Management in Emerging Markets: A Case Study Approach. In A. Dwivedi, & M. S. Alshamrani (Eds.), Leadership Strategies for Global Supply Chain Management in Emerging Markets (pp. 132-146). IGI Global. doi:10.4018/978-1-7998-2867-9.ch006

Akcigit, U., Sina, T.A., & Giammario, I. (2018). Innovation and Trade Policy in a Globalized World. *International Finance Discussion Papers, 1230.*

Akilandeeswari, S. V., & Pitchai, C. (2016). Swot analysis for the improvement of pottery industry in Tamil Nadu. *International Journal of Management and Social Sciences, 4*(7), 1–6. http://www.indianjournals.com/ijor.aspx?Target=ijor:ijmss&volume=4&issue=7&article=001

Akinola, A. (2016). *Information need, access, and use for social welfare and family planning by rural dwellers in Ido and Akinyele local government areas of Oyo State, Nigeria.* Retrieved from:https://digitalcommons.unl.edu/cgi/viewcontent.cgi?Article=3919&context=libphilprac

Alabau, A. (1997). Telecommunications and the Information Society in European regions. *Telecommunications Policy, 21*(8), 761–771. doi:10.1016/S0308-5961(97)00045-1

Alinsky, S. (1971). *Rules for Radicals: A pragmatic primer for realistic radicals New York.* Vintage.

Amiyo, R. M. (2012). *Decision Enhancement and Business Process Agility* (PhD Thesis). University of Groningen. The Netherlands.

Anon. (2004). *55 Policy Recommendations for Raising Croatia's Competitiveness.* National Competitiveness Council.

Ashikuzzaman, M. (2013).Characteristics and Indicators of Knowledge Society. *Library & information Science Network.* Retrieved from: http://www.lisbdnet.com/characteristics-of-knowledge-society/

Askari, H., Forrer, J., Teegen, H., & Yang, J. (2003). *U.S. Economic Sanctions: An empirical Study.* Occasional Paper Series, CSGOP-03-01, The George Washington Center for the Study of Globalization.

Askari, H. G., Forrer, J., Teegen, H., & Yang, J. (2003). *Economic Sanctions: Examining their Philosophy and Efficacy.* Praeger Publishers.

Austin, R. (1975). *Racism and apartheid in southern Africa: Rhodesia.* The UNESCO Press. Available online: www.rbz.co.zw

Awais, M., Irfan, M., Bidal, M., & Samin, T. (2012). Helpful Business Value of Advance Bal Information System. *International Journal of Computer Science Issues, 9*(2), 415–422.

Babalola, J. B. (2003). Budget Preparation and Expenditure Control in Education. In J. B. Babalola (Ed.), *Basic Text in Educational Planning.* Ibadan Awemark Industrial Printers.

Bailey, K. (1994). *Methods of Social Research* (4th ed.). The Free Press.

Baldwin, D. (1979). Power Analysis and World Politics. Princeton: Princeton University Press.

Ball, S. (2009). Lifelong Learning, Subjectivity and the Totally Pedagogised Society. In A. C. B. Michael A Peters, M. Olssen, S. Maurer, & S. Weber (Eds.), *Governmentality Studies in Education.* Sense Publishers. doi:10.1163/9789087909857_013

Barge, J. K. (2016). *Making the case for academic and social impact in organizational communication research.* Paper presented at the organizational communication traditions, transitions and transformations conference, Austin TX.

Barge, J. K., & Shockley-Zalabak, P. (2008). Engaged scholarship and the creation of useful organizational knowledge. *Journal of Applied Communication Research, 36*(3), 251–265. doi:10.1080/00909880802172277

Barreno, L., Elliot, P., Maducke, I., & Sarny, D. (2013). *Community engage scholarship and Faculty Assessment: A review of Canadian Practices.* http://engagedscholarship.ca/res/commu nityengagedscholarshipandfacultyassessment-a-review-of-canadian-practices

Bauman, Z. (1999). Globalização, as consequências humanas. Tradução: Marcus Penchel. Rio de Janeiro: Zahar.

Bauman, Z. (2001). Modernidade Líquida. Tradução: Plínio Dentzien. Rio de Janeiro: Zahar, 2001.

Bauman, Z. (2005b). Vidas Desperdiçadas. Tradução: Carlos Alberto Medeiros. Rio de Janeiro: Zahar.

Bauman, Z. (2008a). Vida para consumo. A transformação das pessoas em mercadoria. Tradução: Carlos Alberto Medeiros. Rio de Janeiro: Zahar.

Bauman, Z. (2008b). A sociedade individualizada: vidas contadas e histórias vividas. Tradução: José Gradel. Rio de Janeiro: Zahar.

Bauman, Z. (2010). Capitalismo parasitário e outros temas contemporâneos. Tradução: Eliana Aguiar. Rio de Janeiro: Zahar.

BBC News Africa. (2002). *Zimbabwe Forces Out Top EU Observer.* Available online: news. bbc.co.uk

Beaulieu, M., Breton M., & Brousselle A. (2018). Conceptualizing 20 years of engaged scholarship: A scoping review. *PloS ONE, 13*(2), e01193201. .Pone.01193201 doi:10.1371/journal

Becker, G. S., & Murphy, K. M. (1992). The Division of Labor, Coordination Costs and Knowledge. *The Quarterly Journal of Economics, 107*(4), 1137–1160. doi:10.2307/2118383

Bergkamp, L. (2002). EU Data Protection Policy. *Computer Law & Security Review, 18*(1), 31–47. doi:10.1016/S0267-3649(02)00106-1

Bharadwaj, A. S. (2000). A resource-based perspective on information technology capability and firm performance: An empirical investigation. *Management Information Systems Quarterly, 24*(1), 169–196. doi:10.2307/3250983

Bhattacharya, S. (2010). Knowledge Economy in India: Challenges and Opportunities. *Journal of Information & Knowledge Management, 9*(3), 1-23.

Blackman, C. (2004). Stumbling along or grave new world? Towards Europe's information society. *Foresight, 6*(5), 261–270. doi:10.1108/14636680410562963

Blind, P. K. (2006). Building trust in government in the twenty-first century: Review of Literature and Emerging Issues. In *7th Global Forum on Reinventing Government Building Trust in Government 26-29 June 2007.* UNDESA.

Bock, G. W., Zmud, R. W., Kim, Y. G., & Lee. (2005). Behaviora Intention Formation in Knowledge Sharing: Examining the Roles of Extrinsic Motivators, Social Psychological forces and Organizational Climate. *MIS Quartely, 29*(1), 87–111. doi:10.2307/25148669

Bolisani, E., & Bratianu, C. (2018). The Elusive Definition of Knowledge. In *Emergent Knowledge Strategies* (pp. 1–22). Springer. doi:10.1007/978-3-319-60657-6_1

Bond, B., & Manyanya, M. (2003). *Zimbabwe's Plunge: Exhausted Nationalism, Neoliberalism and the Search for Social Justice.* Weaver Press Ltd.

Bosworth, B., & Collins, S. (2003). The Empirics of Growth: An Update. *Brookings Papers on Economic Activity, 2*(2), 113–206. doi:10.1353/eca.2004.0002

Boutang, Y. M. (2003). O território e as políticas de controle no capitalismo cognitivo. In *Capitalismo cognitivo, trabalho, redes e inovação. Tradução: Eliana Aguiar.* DP&A.

Braman, S. (1998). The Right to Create: Cultural Policy in the Fourth Stage of the Information Society. *The International Communication Gazette, 60*(1), 77–91. doi:10.1177/0016549298060001005

Bravo, E. R., Santana, M., & Rodon, J. (2015). Information systems and performance: The role of technology, the task and the individual. *Behaviour & Information Technology, 34*(3), 247–260. doi:10.1080/0144929X.2014.934287

Bregman, J. (2003). Summary of Se Summary of Secondary Education (SE) reform trends in OECD countries with an African perspective. Paper Presented at the *first Regional Secondary Education in Africa (SEIA) Conference in Uganda.*

Briggs, R. O., Kolfschoten, G. L., Vreede, G. J., & Dean, D. L. (2010). Defining Key Concepts for Collaboration Engineering. In America conference on information systems, Acapulco, Mexico.

Bryman, A. (2004). *Social Research Methods.* Oxford University Press.

Buhalis, D., & Egger, R. (2008). *E-tourism: Case studies.* Butterworth Heinemann/Elsevier.

Buhalis, D., & Law, R. (2008). Progress in information technology and tourism management: 20 years on and 10 years after the Internet - The state of e-tourism research. *Tourism Management, 29*(4), 609–623. doi:10.1016/j.tourman.2008.01.005

Burde, D., & Linden, L. L. (2013). Bringing Education to Afghan Girls: A Randomized Controlled Trial of Village-Based Schools. *American Economic Journal. Applied Economics, 5*(3), 27–40. doi:10.1257/app.5.3.27

Burgelman, J.-C. (2000). Regulating Access in the Information Society: The Need for Rethinking Public and Universal Service. *New Media & Society, 2*(1), 51–66. doi:10.1177/14614440022225706

Business Today. (2020). *Union Budget 2020: How much will Modi govt spend on education?* https://www.businesstoday.in/union-budget-2020/news/budget-2020-how-much-will-modi-govt-spend-on-education/story/395077.html#:~:text=the%20education%20system.-,India%20spends%204.6%20per%20cent%20of%20its%20total%20GDP%20on,improve%20education%20quality%20in%20India

Byanyima, W., & Mugisha, R. (Eds.). (2003). *The Rising Tide-Ugandan Women's Struggle for a Public Voice 1940-2002.* FOWODE.

Calabrese, A. (1997). Creative Destruction? From the Welfare State to the Global Information Society. *Javnost - The Public, 4*(4). Retrieved from https://javnost-thepublic.org/article/1997/4/1/

Cambridge Dictionary. (2018). *Meaning of "knowledge" in English dictionary.* Cambridge University Press. Retrieved from: https://dictionary.cambridge.org/dictionary/english/knowledge

Camozzato, V. C., & Costa, M. V. (2013). Vontade de pedagogia – pluralização das pedagogias e condução de sujeitos. Pelotas, Cadernos de Educação, 44, 22-44.

Canclini, N. G. (2003). *A globalização imaginada. Tradução: Sérgio Molina.* Iluminuras.

Carayannis, E. G., Barth, T. D., & Campbell, D. F. (2012). The Quintuple Helix innovation model: Global warming as a challenge and driver for innovation. *Journal of Innovation and Entrepreneurship, 1*(1), 2. doi:10.1186/2192-5372-1-2

Centeno, C. (2004). Adoption of Internet services in the Acceding and Candidate Countries, lessons from the Internet banking case. *Telematics and Informatics, 21*(4), 293–315. doi:10.1016/j.tele.2004.02.001

Ceptureanu, S., & Ceptureanu, E. (2010). Knowledge Creation / Conversion Process. *Review of International Comparative Management, 11*(1), 150–157.

Chauhan, J. (2017). An Overview of MOOC in India. *International Journal of Computer Trends and Technology, 49*(2). https://www.researchgate.net/publication/320038196_An_Overview_of_MOOC_in_India

Chen, C., & Watanabe, C. (2006). Diffusion, substitution and competition dynamism inside the ICT market: The case of Japan. *Technological Forecasting and Social Change, 73*(6), 731–759. doi:10.1016/j.techfore.2005.07.008

Chiang, C., & Jang, S. C. (2006). The effects of perceived price and brand image on value and purchase intention: Leisure travelers' attitudes toward online hotel booking. *Journal of Hospitality & Leisure Marketing, 3*, 49–69.

Chikomba, C. E. M. (1988). The role of the University of Zimbabwe in Adult, Primary and Secondary Education. *Michigan State University Conference Proceedings*, 12-26.

Chinamasa, E. (2012). Factors influencing lecturer research output in new universities' in Zimbabwe. *Zimbabwe Journal of Educational Research, 24*(2), 14–25.

Chombo, I. (2000). Higher Education and Technology in Zimbabwe: Meaningful development in the New Millennium. *Zimbabwe Journal of Educational Research, 12*(3), 6–26.

Clemens, M., & Moss, T. (2005). Costs and causes of Zimbabwe's crisis. Washington, DC: Centre for Global Development Press.

Cogburn, D. L. (2003). Governing global information and communications policy: Emergent regime formation and the impact on Africa. *Telecommunications Policy, 27*(1–2), 135–153. doi:10.1016/S0308-5961(02)00088-5

Colin, J. (1968). *The lonely African*. Claredon.

Cooper, H. J. (1989). On income distribution and economic Sanctions. *The South African Journal of Economics, 57*(1), 14–20. doi:10.1111/j.1813-6982.1989.tb00174.x

Cornella, A. (1998). Information policies in Spain. *Government Information Quarterly, 15*(2), 197–220. doi:10.1016/S0740-624X(98)90043-0

Cortright, D., & Lopez, G. A. (2002). *Smart Sanctions: Targeting Economic Statecraft*. Rowman and Littlefield Publishers.

Costa, E. G. (2017). A globalização e as universidades latino-americanas. *Historia, Ciencias, Saude—Manguinhos, 24*(2), 538–540. doi:10.15900104-59702017000200014

Costa, M. V. (2009a). O consumismo na sociedade de consumidores. In M. V. Costa (Ed.), *A educação na cultura da mídia e do consumo*. Lamparina.

Costello, G., & Donnellan, B. (2012). Engaged Scholarship in the Innovation Value Institute. In *Irish Academy of Management Conference*. National University of Ireland.

Cross, E. (2016, July 17). The Economic and Political Crisis in Zimbabwe. *The Zimbabwean*. Available online: www.thezimbabwean.co

Cunha, V. A. (2002). *Profissional da informação na biblioteca pública contemporânea: o bibliotecário e a demanda por educação continuada* (Mestrado em Educação). Faculdade de Ciência da Informação, Universidade Federal da Bahia, Salvador.

Dabinett, G. (2001). EU Mainstreaming of the Information Society in Regional Development Policy. *Regional Studies, 35*(2), 168–173. doi:10.1080/00343400120033151

Damon, A., Glewwe, P., Wisniewski, S., & Sun, B. (2016). *Education in developing countries – what policies and programmes affect learning and time in school?* https://www.oecd.org/derec/sweden/Rapport-Education-developing-countries.pdf

Das, A. K. (2011). Emergence of open educational resources (OER) in India and its impact on lifelong learning. *Library Hi Tech News, 28*(5), 10–15. doi:10.1108/07419051111163848

Dasgupta, A. D. (2001). Corporate ethical dilemmas: Indian models for moral management. *Journal of Human Values, 7*(2), 171–191. doi:10.1177/097168580100700207

Dattakumar, A., Chong, G., Malone, L., Sharma, R. s., & Valenzuela, J. F. (2016). Knowledge Societies and their role in sustainable Development. *2016 IEEE International Conference on Industrial Engineering and Engineering Management (IEEM)* 10.1109/IEEM.2016.7797962

Delevic, M. (1998). Economic sanctions as a foreign policy tool: The case of Yugoslavia. *International Journal of Peace Studies, 3*(1), 1–94.

Delors, J. (2001). Educação: um tesouro a descobrir: relatório para a Unesco da Comissão Internacional sobre Educação para o século XXI (5th ed.). São Paulo: Cortez; Brasília: UNESCO.

Denzin, N., & Lincoln, Y. (2003). The Discipline and Practice of Qualitative Research. In Collecting and Interpreting Qualitative Materials (2nd ed.). Sage publications, Inc.

Desai, M. (2014). *Why improving education in India is the key to growth.* https://www.weforum.org/agenda/2014/12/why-improving-education-in-india-is-the-key-to-growth/

DiPetro, R. B., & Wang, Y. R. (2010). Key issues for ICT applications: Impacts an implications for hospitality operations. *Worldwide Hospitality and Tourism, 2*(1), 49–67. doi:10.1108/17554211011012595

Dipio. (2018). *Writing to Re-Claim the Archaic African Matriarch.* Keynote address at FEMRITE Conference.

Dobrin, O. C., & Popa, I. (2007). Knowledge society features. *Repec.* Retrieved from:https://www.researchgate.net/publication/4982032_Knowledge_society_features

Dobrin, O., & Papa, I. (2007). Knowledge Society Features: The Academy of economic Studies, Bucharest, Romania. *AMFITEA. Economic Journal (London), 9,* 77–86.

Drezner, D. W. (1999). *The Sanctions Paradox: Economic Statecraft and International Relations.* Cambridge University Press. doi:10.1017/CBO9780511549366

Drezner, D. W. (2000). Bargaining, Enforcement and Multilateral Sanctions: When Is Cooperation Counterproductive? *International Organization, 54*(1), 73–102. doi:10.1162/002081800551127

Drezner, D. W. (2003). How smart are smart sanctions. *International Studies Review, 5*(1), 2–7. doi:10.1111/1521-9488.501014

Drori, G. S. (2007). Information Society as a Global Policy Agenda: What Does It Tell Us About the Age of Globalization? *International Journal of Comparative Sociology, 48*(4), 297–316. doi:10.1177/0020715207079532

Drucker, P. F. (1993). *Postcapitalist Society.* HerperCollins Publishers.

Duck, S. (1997). *The Handbook of Personal Relationships: Theory, Research and Interventions.* Wiley.

Dufour, P. (2010). Supplying Demand for Canada's Knowledge Society: A Warmer Future for a Cold Climate? *The American Behavioral Scientist, 53*(7), 983–996. doi:10.1177/0002764209356233

Dumitrescu, A., Levy, D., Orfield, C., & Sloan, M. (2011). *Impact Evaluation of Niger's IMAGINE Program.* Mathematica Policy Research. Available at http://cipre.mathematica-mpr.com/our-publications-andfindings/publications/impact-evaluation-of-nigers-imagineprogram

Dupre, S. & Mijnhardt W. (2015). *Creating knowledge society in a globalizing world (1450-1800).* Academic Press.

Duprė, S., & Mijnhardt, W. (2015). The Making of a Knowledge Society (1450-1800). *Creating a Knowledge Society in a Globalizing World (1450-1800).* Retrieved from: https://knaw.nl/shared/resources/actueel/bestanden/creatingaknowledgesocietyinaglobalizingworld14501800.pdf

Duraisamy, P. (2002). Changes in Returns to education in India, 1983-94: by gender, age-cohort and location. *Economics of Education Review, 21*(6), 609-622.

Educational administration in India. (n.d.). *Chapter II*. Retrieved from https://shodhganga.inflibnet. ac.in/bitstream/10603/86857/10/10_chapter%202.pdf

Educational Statistics at a Glance. (2016). *Report by Government of India, Ministry of Human Resource Development, Department of School Education & Literacy, New Delhi*. Retrieved from http://mhrd.gov.in/sites/upload_files/mhrd/files/statistics/ESG2016_0.pdf

Elliot. (2014). Access to knowledge: a basic human right. *Creative Commons*. Retrieved from:https:// creativecommons.org/2014/01/07/access-to-knowledge-a-basic-human-right/

Emani, S. (2013). *Application of bi-directional ICT channels to increase livelihoods for artisans in rural India* (Doctoral dissertation). Massachusetts Institute of Technology. Retrieved from:https:// dspace.mit.edu/bitstream/handle/1721.1/90068/890141347-MIT.pdf?Sequence=2

Engelbrecht, H. (2007). The (Un)Happiness of Knowledge and the Knowledge of (Un)Happiness: Happiness Research and Policies for Knowledge-based Economies 1. *Prometheus, 25*(3), 243–266. doi:10.1080/08109020701531379

English Oxford Living Dictionaries. (2018). *Definition of artisan in English*. Oxford University Press. Retrieved from: https://en.oxforddictionaries.com/definition/artisan

Eriksson, J. (2006). The Information Revolution, Security, and International Relations: (IR)relevant Theory? *International Political Science Review/Revue Internationale de Science Politique, 27*(3), 221–244. doi:10.1177/0192512106064462

Estonian, R. D., & Strategy, I. (2014-2020). *Estonian Research and Development and Innovation Strategy 2014-2020 "Knowledge-based Estonia."* Accessed on 12th April 2019 rom: https://rio. jrc.ec.europa.eu/en/library/rdi-strategy-knowledge-based-estonia-2014-2020

European Parliament. (2011). Impact of sanctions and isolation measures with North Korea, Burma/Myanmar, Iran and Zimbabwe. Directorate – General for External Policies, Policy Department, May 2011.

Evenett, S. J., & Keller, W. (1998). *On Theories Explaining the Success of the Gravity Equation*. NBER working paper no. 6529.

Evers, H., Gerke, S., & Menkhoff, T. (2010). Knowledge clusters and knowledge hubs: Designing epistemic landscapes for development. *Journal of Knowledge Management, 14*(5), 678–689. doi:10.1108/13673271011074836

Falch, M., & Henten, A. (2000). Digital Denmark: From information society to network society. *Telecommunications Policy, 24*(5), 377–394. doi:10.1016/S0308-5961(00)00028-8

Faure, E. (1972). *Aprender a ser*. Bertrand.

Ferizi, V., & Kruja, A. D. (2018). Coastline Hospitality Industry Performance, Challenges, and Opportunities: Evidence From Durres Coastline. In D. Batabyal (Ed.), Managing Sustainable Tourism Resources (pp. 14-38). IGI Global.

Ferraz, A. (2001). *Educação continuada de professores: um estudo das políticas da secretaria municipal de educação de campinas - 1983/1996* (Mestrado em Educação). Faculdade de Educação, Universidade Estadual de Campinas, São Paulo.

Fichman, R. G. (2004). Going beyond the dominant paradigm for information technology. *Journal of the Association for Information Systems, 5*(8), 314–355. doi:10.17705/1jais.00054

Finquelievich, S. (2017). *Policies for Knowledge Society in Rwanda- Training Manual.* Available at: https://www.un.org/sustainabledevelopment/development-agenda/

Finquelievich, S. (2017). *Rwanda Knowledge Society Policy Handbook, Ministry of Education, Republic of Rwanda, United Nations Educational, Scientific and Cultural Organization Information for All Programme (UNESCO/IFAP).* Available at: https://unesdoc.unesco.org/images/0026/002614/261450E.pdf

Firestone, J. M., & McElroy, M. W. (2003). *Key issues in the new knowledge management.* Butterworth-Heinemann.

Fischer, F. (1998). Beyond Empiricism: Policy Inquiry in Postpositivist Perspective. *Policy Studies Journal: the Journal of the Policy Studies Organization, 26*(1), 129–146.

Fowale, T. (2010). Zimbabwe and Western Sanctions: Motives and Implications. *The American Chronicle, 09*(June), 7–11.

Franciscone, F. (2006). *Educação continuada: um olhar para além do espelho, iluminando mente, corpo, coração e espírito do docente da educação superior* (Mestrado em Educação). Faculdade de Educação, Pontifícia Universidade Católica do Rio Grande do Sul, Porto Alegre.

Franklin, M. I. (2007). NGOs and the "Information Society": Grassroots Advocacy at the UN?A Cautionary Tale. *The Review of Policy Research, 24*(4), 309–330. doi:10.1111/j.1541-1338.2007.00285.x

Frey, B. (1984). *International Political Economics.* Basis Blacwell.

Friedman, W., Kremer, M., Miguel, E., & Thornton, R. (2011). *Education as Liberation? No. w16939.* National Bureau of Economic Research. doi:10.3386/w16939

Fuchs, C. (2010). Theoretical foundations of defining the participatory, co-operative, sustainable information society. *Information Communication and Society, 13*(1), 23–47. doi:10.1080/13691180902801585

Füg, O. C. (2008). Save the Children: The Protection of Minors in the Information Society and the Audiovisual Media Services Directive. *Journal of Consumer Policy, 31*(1), 45–61. doi:10.100710603-007-9059-9

Fukuyama, F. (1995). *The Social Virtues and the Creation of Prosperity*. Free Press.

Gaffney, G. (2000). *What is facilitation?* https://www.infodesign.com.au/ftp/facilitation.pdf

Gerring, J., & Thacker, M. C. (2004). *Political Institutions and Corruption: The Role of Unitarism and Parliamentaris*. Cambridge University Press.

Gerzson, V. R. (2007). A mídia como dispositivo da governamentalidade neoliberal: os discursos sobre educação nas revistas Veja, Época e Istoé (Doutorado em Educação). Faculdade de Educação, Universidade Federal do Rio Grande do Sul, Porto Alegre.

Ghanbari, A., & Ahmadi, M. (2017). The Effect of Innovation on International Trade: Selected Medium-High-Technology Industries, Evidence on Iran, *Iran. Economic Review (Kansas City, Mo.)*, *21*(1), 21–44.

Giovannini, E. (2007). Statistics and Politics in a "Knowledge Society.". *Social Indicators Research*, *86*(2), 177–200. doi:10.100711205-007-9137-z

Glewwe, P., Hanushek, E., Humpage, S., & Ravina, R. (2013). School Resources and Educational Outcomes in Developing Countries. In P. Glewwe (Ed.), *Education Policy in Developing Countries*. University of Chicago Press. doi:10.7208/chicago/9780226078854.003.0002

Gómez Barroso, J. L., & Feijoo Gonzalez, C. A. (2010, January 1). Are Central and Eastern European Countries managing to develop the information Society? In *Transformations in Business and Economics*. E.T.S.I. Telecomunicación (UPM). Retrieved from http://oa.upm.es/8819/1/INVE_MEM_2010_87332.pdf

Gono, G. (2006). An analysis of socio economic impact of Sanctions on Zimbabwe. *Supplement 7. Reserve Bank of Zimbabwe*, *3*, 4.

Gonzalez, R. V. D., & Martins, M. F. (2017). Knowledge Management Process: A theoretical-conceptual research. *Gestão & Produção*, *24*(2).

Goodwin, I., & Spittle, S. (2002). The European Union and the information society: Discourse, power and policy. *New Media & Society*, *4*(2), 225–249. doi:10.1177/146144480200400206

Government of Rwanda. (2017). *Science & Technology in Rwanda. Science, Technology, Research and Innovation in Support of Economic and Social Development in Rwanda*. Available at: https://mineduc.gov.rw/fileadmin/user_upload/pdf_files/STI_in_Rwanda_Booklet_prepared_for_TWAS27th_Annual_Meeting_Final-1.pdf

Govind, R., & Varghese, V. N. (1993). *Quality of Primary Schooling in India, A case study of Madhya Pradesh. Report for International Institute for Educational Planning*. Paris and National Institute of Educational Planning and Administration.

Gray, P. H. (1986). Non Competitive Goods and Gains of Trade. *The International Trade Journal*, *1*(2), 107-128.

Green, A., Preston, J., & Janmaat, J. G. (2006). *Models of Lifelong Learning and the 'Knowledge Society': Education for Competitiveness and Social Cohesion.* doi:10.1007/978-0-230-20745-5_7

Gregory, S. R., Kline, S. F., & Breiter, D. (2005). Group sales and marketing in convention hotels: Internet and web usage. *Journal of Travel & Tourism Marketing, 18*(1), 67–77. doi:10.1300/J073v18n01_07

Grimes, S. (2000). Rural areas in the information society: Diminishing distance or increasing learning capacity? *Journal of Rural Studies, 16*(1), 13–21. doi:10.1016/S0743-0167(99)00027-3

Gupa, D., & Gupta, N. (2012). Higher Education in India: Structure, Statistics and Challenges. *Journal of Education and Practice, 3*(2), 17–24.

Gupta, P. (2019). *How much India spends on education: Hint, it's less than rich countries' average.* https://www.financialexpress.com/economy/how-much-india-spends-on-education-hint-its-less-than-rich-countries-average/1772269/

Gurbaxani, V., Kraemer, K. L., King, J. L., Jarman, S., Dedrick, J., Raman, K. S., & Yap, C. S. (1990). Government as the driving force toward the information society: National computer policy in Singapore. *The Information Society, 7*(2), 155–185. doi:10.1080/01972243.1990.9960092

Haas, R. N. (1997). Sanctioning Madness. *Foreign Affairs, 76*(6), 3–9.

Hakim, C. (1982). *Secondary Analyzis in Social Research, A Guide to Data Sources and Methods with Examples.* Allen and Unwin.

Hall, S. (2001). A identidade cultural na pós-modernidade. Tradução: Tomaz Tadeu da Silva e Guacira Lopes Louro. 6ª ed. Rio de Janeiro: DP&A.

Hameed, M. A., & Counsell, S. (2012). Assessing the influence of environmental and CEO characteristics for adoption of information technology in organizations. *Journal of Technology Management & Innovation, 7*(1), 64–84. doi:10.4067/S0718-27242012000100005

Hammar, A., & Raftopoulos, B. (2003). Zimbabwe's Unfinished Business: Rethinking Land, State and Nation. In A. Hammar, B. Raftopoulos, & S. Jensen (Eds.), *Zimbabwe's Unfinished Business: Rethinking Land, State and Nation in the Context of Crisis.* Weaver Press.

Hanafizadeh, P., Hanafizadeh, M. R., & Khodabakhshi, M. (2009). Taxonomy of e-readiness assessment measures. *International Journal of Information Management, 29*(3), 189–195. doi:10.1016/j.ijinfomgt.2008.06.002

Handa, S. (2002). Raising primary school enrolment in developing countries. The relative importance of supply and demand. *Journal of Development Economics, 69*(1), 103–128. doi:10.1016/S0304-3878(02)00055-X

Hanke, S. H. (n.d.). *R.I.P. Zimbabwe Dollar.* The Cato Institute. Available online: www.cato.org

Hansson, F. (2007). Science parks as knowledge organizations – the " ba " in action? *European Journal of Innovation Management, 10*(3), 348–366. doi:10.1108/14601060710776752

Hargreaves, A. (2003). *Teaching in the Knowledge Society. Education in the Age of Insecurity.* Teachers College Press.

Higher Education in India. Vision 2030. (2013). *FICCI Higher Education Summit 2013.* Retrieved from https://www.ey.com/Publication/vwLUAssets/Higher-education-in-India-Vision-2030/$FILE/EY-Higher-education-in-India-Vision-2030.pdf

Holland, D., & Powell, D. E. (2010). Models of Engaged Scholarship: An Interdisciplinary Discussion. *Collaborative Anthropologies, 3*(1), 1–36. doi:10.1353/cla.2010.0011

Hong, J., & Huang, L. (2005). A split and swaying approach to building information society: The case of Internet cafes in China. *Telematics and Informatics, 22*(4), 377–393. doi:10.1016/j.tele.2004.11.005

Houssaye, J. (2007). Pedagogias: importação-exportação. In *Viagens Pedagógicas.* Cortez.

Howard, P. N., Anderson, K., Busch, L., & Nafus, D. (2009). Sizing Up Information Societies: Toward a Better Metric for the Cultures of ICT Adoption. *The Information Society, 25*(3), 208–219. doi:10.1080/01972240902848948

Howell, D. C. (2002). Statistical methods for psychology (5th ed.). Academic Press.

Hufbauer, G. C., Elliott, K. A., Cyrus, T., & Winston, E. (1997). *US Economic Sanctions: their impact on Trade, Jobs and Wages, working paper.* Institute of International Economics.

Hufbauer, G. C., Schott, J., Elliott, K. A. & Oegg, B. (2007). *Economic Sanctions Reconsidered.* Academic Press.

Hufbauer, G. C., & Oegg, B. (2003). *The impact of Economic Sanctions on US Trade: Andrew Rose's Gravity Model, International Economics Policy briefs.* Institute for International Economics.

Hughes, M. (2000). Potential, Procedures and Pitfalls of Analyzing Internal Newspapers. *Corporate Communications,* 19–25.

Huni, M. (2012, July 15). Candid talk with Professor Ncube. The Sunday Mail.

Hurungo, J. (2010). *An Inquiry into How Rhodesia Managed to Survive Under Economic Sanctions: Lessons for the Zimbabwean Government. Paper Prepared for the Trade and Development Studies Centre.* Trades Centre.

Igbeka, J. U., &Atinmo, M. I. (2002). Information seeking behaviour and information utilization of agricultural engineers in Nigeria based on their different places of work. *Nigerian Libraries, 36*(1), 9-22.

Ikujiro, H., & Nonaka, T. (2008). *Gestão do Conhecimento.* Tradução: Ana Thorell. Porto Alegre.

IMF Executive Board Uphold Sanctions against Zimbabwe. (n.d.). *Press Release No. 06/45.* Available at https://www.imf.org/external/np/sec/pr/2006/pr0645.htm

IMF. (2003). *Press Release: IMF Suspends Zimbabwe's Voting and Related Rights.* Available online: www.imf.org

India Brand Equity Foundation. (2018). *Education and Training.* Retrieved from https://www.ibef.org/download/Education-and-Training-Report-Jan-2018.pdf

Inkinen, T. (2012). Best practices of the Finnish Government Information Society Policy Programme. *Transforming Government: People. Process and Policy, 6*(2), 167–187. doi:10.1108/17506161211246917

International Alliance of Research Universities (IARU). (2016). http://www.iaruni.org

International Standard Classification of Education. (2011). Retrieved from http://uis.unesco.org/en/glossary-term/adult-education#slideoutmenu

Internet Society Report. (n.d.). Available at http://www.internetsociety.org/map/global-internet-report/?gclid=CjwKEAjwqZ7GBRC1srKSv9TV_iwSJADKTjaDLsYP5zz0FXsbW8lbb2kwHuSLSKw-gV29zhTkyPcX6hoC8a7w_wcB#global-internet-penetration

Jaeger, P. T. (2006). Telecommunications policy and individuals with disabilities: Issues of accessibility and social inclusion in the policy and research agenda. *Telecommunications Policy, 30*(2), 112–124. doi:10.1016/j.telpol.2005.10.001

Jaeger, P. T. (2007). Information policy, information access, and democratic participation: The national and international implications of the Bush administration's information politics. *Government Information Quarterly, 24*(4), 840–859. doi:10.1016/j.giq.2007.01.004

Jakobi, A. P. (2006). The Knowledge Society and Global Dynamics in Education Politics. *European Educational Research Journal, 6*(1), 39–51. doi:10.2304/eerj.2007.6.1.39

Jenkins, C. (1997). The Politics of Economic Policy-Making in Zimbabwe. *The Journal of Modern African Studies, 35*(4), 575–602.

Jessup, L., & Valacich, J. (2008). *Information Systems Today* (3rd ed.). Pearson Prentice Hall.

Jing, J., Quan, Q., & Paul, J. (2003). Information Technology Investments and Firms' Performance: A Duopoly Perspective. *Journal of Management Information Systems, 20*(3), 121–158. doi:10.1080/07421222.2003.11045773

Kaempfer, W. H., & Lowenberg, A. D. (1988). The Theory of international economic sanctions: A Public Choice approach. *The American Economic Review, 78*(4), 786–793.

Kalekyezi, P. T. (1982). *An Economic History of Ankole c.1895-c.1919* (Master of Arts thesis). Makerere University.

Kalinina, A. (2016). *Artisans' limitations for developing own businesses: case of Querétaro, Mexico* (Bachelor's thesis). University of Twente. Retrieved from:http://essay.utwente.nl/70221/1/Kalinina_BA_BMS.pdf

Kanyenze, Kondo, & Martens. (2006). The search for sustainable human development in Southern Africa. Alternatives to neo-liberalism in Southern Africa (ANSA).

Kanyenze. (2011). Beyond the Enclave. Towards a Pro-Poor and Inclusive Development Strategy for Zimbabwe. Weaver Press.

Kariwo, M. T. (2007). Widening access in higher education in Zimbabwe. *The Journal of Educational Research, 20*(3), 23–50.

Karseth, B., & Nerland, M. (2007). Building professionalism in a knowledge society: Examining discourses of knowledge in four professional associations†. *Journal of Education and Work, 20*(4), 335–355. doi:10.1080/13639080701650172

Karthick, M., & Prakash, N. (2013). *Cycling to school: increasing secondary school enrollment for girls in India*. NBER Working Paper #19305.

Katz, R. L., Koutroumpis, P., & Callorda, F. (2013). The Latin American path towards digitization. *Info, 15*(3), 6–24. doi:10.1108/14636691311327098

Kazianga, H., Levy, D., Linden, L. L., & Sloan, M. (2013). The effects of "girl-friendly" schools: Evidence from the BRIGHT school construction program in Burkina Faso. *American Economic Journal. Applied Economics, 5*(3), 41–62. doi:10.1257/app.5.3.41

Kennedy. (2006). *Written Constitutions and the Common Law Tradition*. 20th Sultan Azlan Shah Law Lecture, Kuala Lumpur, Malaysia.

Khare, M. (2015). India's Emergence as a Regional Education Hub. *International Higher Education, 83*, 26-28. https://ejournals.bc.edu/ojs/index.php/ihe/article/download/9088/8195

Kim, W., & Ham, S. (2007). The impact of information technology implementation on service quality in the hotel industry. *Information Technology in Hospitality, 4*(4), 143–151. doi:10.3727/154595306779868430

Klecun-Dabrowska, E., & Cornford, T. (2000, January 1). Telehealth acquires meanings: information and communication technologies within health policy. In *Information Systems Journal*. Blackwell Publishing. Retrieved from http://eprints.lse.ac.uk/7366/

Klironomos, I., Antona, M., Basdekis, I., & Stephanidis, C. (2006). White Paper: Promoting Design for All and e-Accessibility in Europe. *Universal Access in the Information Society, 5*(1), 105–119. doi:10.100710209-006-0021-4

Knol, J. A. (2013). *Decision Enhancement for Sourcing and Sharing in the Dutch Government* (PhD Thesis). University of Groningen, The Netherlands.

Kolfschoten, G., Lukosch, S., & Seck, M. (2011). Simulating Collaboration Processes to Understand and Predict Group Performance. *Proceedings of the 44th Hawaii International Conference on Systems Sciences*. 10.1109/HICSS.2011.376

Konate, J., Sahraoni, A., & Kolfschoten, G. L. (2014). *Collaboration requirements elicitation: A process-centered approach.* http://linkspringer.com/article/10.1007

Kruja, A. (2012). The Impact of Tourism Sector Development in the Albanian Economy. *Economia. Seria Management,* 204-218.

Kruja, A. (2013). Entrepreneurship and knowledge-based economies. *Revista Românească pentru Educaţie Multidimensională, 5*(1), 7-17.

Kruja, A. D., & Berberi, E. (2020). Tourism and Handicraft Industry: Opportunities and Challenges of Operating in the Albanian Market. In I. Chirino-Klevans (Ed.), Cases on Global Leadership in the Contemporary Economy (pp. 119-136). IGI Global.

Kruja, A. D., & Hysi, K. (2020). Influence of Practice Management Software on Dental Services: A Case Study Approach. In B. Nogalski, A. A. Szpitter, A. Jabłoński, & M. Jabłoński (Eds.), Networked Business Models in the Circular Economy (pp. 241-267). IGI Global. doi:10.4018/978-1-5225-7850-5.ch011

Kruja, A. D. (2020). Enterprise investments, innovation and performance: Evidence from Albania. *International Journal of Innovation in the Digital Economy, 11*(1), 68–80. doi:10.4018/IJIDE.2020010105

Kruja, A. D., Hysa, X., Duman, T., & Tafaj, A. (2019). Adoption of Software as a Service (Saas) in Small and Medium-Sized Hotels in Tirana. *Enlightening Tourism, 9*(2), 137–167. doi:10.33776/et.v9i2.3625

Kuo, C. Y., & Low, L. (2011). Information Economy and Changing Occupational Structure in Singapore. *The Information Society, 17*(4), 281–293. doi:10.1080/019722401753330878

Kurebwa, J. (2000). *The Politics of Multilateral Economic Sanctions on Rhodesia (Zimbabwe) during the Unilateral Declaration of Independence Period, 1965 to 1979* (Unpublished PhD thesis). University of Zimbabwe.

Lam, C., & Law, R. (2019). Readiness of upscale and luxury-branded hotels for digital transformation. *International Journal of Hospitality Management, 79*(May), 60–69. doi:10.1016/j.ijhm.2018.12.015

Lasker, R. D., Weiss, E. S., & Miller, R. (2001). *Partnership Synergy: A practical framework for studying and strengthening the collaborative advantage.* http://www.jstor.org/stable/3350547

Law, R., Buhalis, D., & Cobanoglu, C. (2014). Progress on information and communication technologies in hospitality and tourism. *International Journal of Contemporary Hospitality Management, 26*(5), 727–750. doi:10.1108/IJCHM-08-2013-0367

Law, R., & Hsu, C. H. (2006). Importance of hotel website dimensions and attributes: Perceptions of online browsers and online purchasers. *Journal of Hospitality & Tourism Research (Washington, D.C.), 30*(3), 295–312. doi:10.1177/1096348006287161

Law, R., & Jogaratnam, G. (2005). A study of hotel information technology applications. *International Journal of Contemporary Hospitality Management*, *17*(2), 170–180. doi:10.1108/09596110510582369

Lazzarato, M. (2003). Trabalho e capital na produção dos conhecimentos: uma leitura através da obra de Gabriel Tarde. In *Capitalismo cognitivo, trabalho, redes e inovação. Tradução: Eliana Aguiar*. DP&A.

Lee, G., & Xia, W. (2006). Organizational size and IT innovation adoption: A meta-analysis. *Information & Management*, *43*(8), 957–985. doi:10.1016/j.im.2006.09.003

Lee, S., Marcu, M., & Lee, S. (2011). An empirical analysis of fixed and mobile broadband diffusion. *Information Economics and Policy*, *23*(3–4), 227–233. doi:10.1016/j.infoecopol.2011.05.001

Levi, M., & Stoker, L. (2000, June). Political Trust and Trustworthiness. *Annual Review of Political Science*, *3*(1), 475–507.

Lewin, K., & Caillods, F. (2001). *Financing Secondary Education in Developing Countries: Strategies for Sustainable Growth*. UNESCO, International Institute for Educational Planning. doi:10.1007/BF03220050

Lewrick, M., Omar, M., Raeside, R., & Saier, K. (2010). Education for entrepreneurship and innovation: `Management capabilities for sustainable growth and success. *World Journal of Entrepreneurship, Management and Sustainable Development*, *6*(1/2), 1–18. doi:10.1108/20425961201000001

Leydesdorff, L., & Deakin, M. (2011). The Triple-Helix Model of Smart Cities: A Neo-Evolutionary Perspective. *Journal of Urban Technology*, *18*(2), 53–63. doi:10.1080/10630732.2011.601111

Lim, J., Richardson, V., & Roberts, T. (2004). Information technology investment and firm performance: A meta-analysis. *Proceedings of the 37th Hawaii International Conference on Systems Sciences*.

Lindberg, M., Danilda, I., & Torstensson, B.-M. (2011). Women Resource Centres—A Creative Knowledge Environment of Quadruple Helix. *Journal of the Knowledge Economy*, *3*(1), 36–52. doi:10.100713132-011-0053-8

Lloyd, S., Kinti, I., Simpson, A., & Hayward, G. (2005). Managing collaborative expertise: Issues and Challenges. In *Proceedings of OKLC 2005*. MA Hhtp. orgns.man.ac.uk/projects/include/experiment

London, P. T. I. (2019). *Indian universities move up in global ranking; 25 institutions in top 200*. Retrieved from https://www.thehindubusinessline.com/news/education/indian-universities-move-up-in-global-ranking-25-institutions-in-top-200/article26000998.ece

Lytras, A. F. M., & Ordóñez de Pablos, P. (2011). Software Technologies in Knowledge Society. *J.UCS*. Retrieved from https://digibuo.uniovi.es/dspace/handle/10651/23937

Maathai. (2009). *The Challenge for Africa. Arrow* Books.

Maertens, A. (2013). Social Norms and Aspirations: Age of Marriage and Education in Rural India. *World Development, 47*, 1-15. doi:10.1016/j.worlddev.2013.01.027

Majumder, R. (2007). *Emergence of Knowledge Society: The Indian Scenario.* MPRA Paper. Retrieved from https://ideas.repec.org/p/pra/mprapa/12808.html

Mamlook, R., Aljumah, A., & Farooqui, N. K. (2011). Knowledge on the Move. *Journal of Applied Sciences (Faisalabad), 11*(16), 3062–3069. doi:10.3923/jas.2011.3062.3069

Mansell, R. (1999). Information and communication technologies for development: Assessing the potential and the risks. *Telecommunications Policy, 23*(1), 35–50. doi:10.1016/S0308-5961(98)00074-3

Maravanyika, O. E. (1990). *Implementing educational policies in Zimbabwe.* World Bank discussion paper no. 91. Africa Technical Department Series. Washington, DC: World Bank.

Mariscal, J. (2005). Digital divide in a developing country. *Telecommunications Policy, 29*(5–6), 409–428. doi:10.1016/j.telpol.2005.03.004

Marongwe, N. (2004). Socio-economic conflicts of the Fast Track Resettlement Programme. In Medicine Masiiwa, Post-independence land reform in Zimbabwe: Controversies and Impact on the Economy. Harare: Friedrich Ebert Stiftung and Institute of Development Studies, University of Zimbabwe.

Mart, C. T. (2011). British colonial education policy in Africa. *Internal Journal of English and Literature, 2*(9), 190-194. Available online http://www.academicjournals.org/ijel

Martin Dutch, D. M. (2001). The Public Library, Social Exclusion and the Information Society in the United Kingdom. *Libri.* Retrieved from http://citeseerx.ist.psu.edu/viewdoc/summary?doi=10.1.1.178.5939

Martin, R., & Milway, J. (2005). *Commercialization and the Canadian Business Environment: A Systems Perspective.* Institute for Competitiveness & Prosperity.

Melian-Gonzales, S., & Bulchand-Gidumal, J. (2016). A model that connects information technology and hotel performance. *Tourism Management, 53*(April), 30–37. doi:10.1016/j.tourman.2015.09.005

Melnikas B. (2010). Sustainable development and creation of the knowledge economy: The new theoretical approach. *Technological and Economic Development of Economy, 16*(3), 516-540. doi:10.3846/tede.2010.32

Melody, W. H. (1996). Toward a framework for designing information society policies. *Telecommunications Policy, 20*(4), 243–259. doi:10.1016/0308-5961(96)00007-9

Melville, N., Kraemer, K., & Gurbaxani, V. (2004). Review: Information technology and organizational performance: An integrative model of IT business value. *Management Information Systems Quarterly, 28*(2), 283–322. doi:10.2307/25148636

Menou, M. J., & Taylor, R. D. (2006). A "Grand Challenge": Measuring Information Societies. *The Information Society, 22*(5), 261–267. doi:10.1080/01972240600903904

Mensal, R., & Tremblay, G. (2013). *Renewing the knowledge society's vision: towards knowledge societies for peace & sustainable development. In WSIS+10 Conference. United Nations Education Scientific and Cultural Organization.* UNESCO.

MHRD, Department of School Education and Literacy. (2016). *Adult Education.* Retrieved from https://mhrd.gov.in/adult-education

Ministry of Ayush. (2017). *About the Ministry.* Retrieved from http://ayush.gov.in/about-us/about-the-ministry

Ministry of Human Resource Development (MHRD). Government of India, Department of School Education & Literacy, Department of Higher Education. (2017). *Annual Report 2016-17.* Retrieved from http://mhrd.gov.in/sites/upload_files/mhrd/files/document-reports/HRD_AR%20 2016-17.pdf

Ministry of Information Technology and Communications, Republic of Rwanda. (2017). *ICT Sector Strategic Plan (2018-2024) "Towards digital enabled economy".* http://www.mitec.gov. rw/fileadmin/Documents/Strategy/ICT_SECTOR_STRATEGIC_PLAN__2018-2024_.pdf

Ministry of Skill Development and Entrepreneurship. (n.d.). *National Skill development Mission.* Retrieved from https://www.msde.gov.in/nationalskillmission.html

Minn, J. (2009). Rule of Law: What Does it Mean? *Journal of International Law, 18*(2), 293–303.

Mirembe, D. P. (2015). *The Threat Nets Approach to Information Systems Security Risk Analysis* (PhD Thesis). University of Groningen.

Misuraca, G. (2012). Envisioning digital Europe 2030: scenarios for ICT in future governance and policy modelling. *European Foresight Platform, 63.*

Misuraca, G., Broster, D., & Centeno, C. (2012). Digital Europe 2030: Designing scenarios for ICT in future governance and policy making. *Government Information Quarterly, 29,* S121–S131. doi:10.1016/j.giq.2011.08.006

Moore, M., & Kearsley, G. (2013). Educação a distância: sistemas de aprendizagem on-line. Tradução: Ez2Translate. 3 ed. São Paulo: Cengage Learning.

Moreto, J. A. (2002). *A Educação continuada do diretor de escola: avaliação da po-lítica implementada pela secretaria municipal da educação de campinas, no período de 1994 a 2000* (Mestrado em Educação). Faculdade de Educação, Universidade Estadual de Campinas, São Paulo.

Morimoto, S. A., & Friedland, L. A. (2010). The Lifeworld of Youth in the Information Society. *Youth & Society, 43*(2), 549–567. doi:10.1177/0044118X10383655

Moro, V. (2007). *Educação continuada: um processo itinerante na construção de si com vistas à transformação da prática docente de professores de educação básica* (Mestrado em Educação). Faculdade de Educação, Pontifícia Universidade Católica do Rio Grande do Sul, Porto Alegre.

Mósesdóttir, L. (2011). Gender (In)equalities in the Knowledge Society. *Gender, Work and Organization, 18*(1), 30–47. doi:10.1111/j.1468-0432.2010.00533.x

Mourdoukoutas, P. (2017). *Modi's India The World's 4th Fastest Growing Economy*. Retrieved from https://www.forbes.com/sites/panosmourdoukoutas/2017/06/22/modis-india-the-worlds-4th-fastest-growing-economy/#664b1d674120

Mouzakitis, S. G. (2010). The role of vocational education and training curricula in economic development. *Procedia: Social and Behavioral Sciences, 2*(2), 3914–3920. doi:10.1016/j.sbspro.2010.03.616

Moyo, D. (2009). *Dead aid: Why aid is not working and how there is a better way for Africa*. Farrar, Straus and Giroux.

Mpofu, B. (2016, Mar. 11). Local Banks' Nostro Accounts Depleted. *Zimbabwe Independent*. Available online: www.theindependent.co.zw

Mugadas, F., Muggadas, R., & Aslam, U. (2016). Exploring the challenges, Trends and Issues for Knowledge Management. A study of Employees in Public Sector Universities, Punjab, Pakistan. *Journal of Information and Knowledge Management Systems, 47*(1), 2017.

Munongerwa, C. (2016). An evaluation of the relevance of the AK model to developing countries such as Zimbabwe. *Afro Asian Journal of Social Sciences, 7*(2), 2229–5313.

Munyati, C. (2016, Apr. 21). Zimbabwe's Liquidity Crisis: The Curse of China's Slowdown and a Strong Dollar. *The Source*. Available online: source.co.zw

Mutula, S. M. (2004). Making Botswana an information society: Current developments. *The Electronic Library, 22*(2), 144–153. doi:10.1108/02640470410533407

Mutula, S. M. (2008). Digital divide and economic development: Case study of sub-Saharan Africa. *The Electronic Library, 26*(4), 468–489. doi:10.1108/02640470810893738

Myers, K. A. (2015). *In the Shadow of Cortés: Conversations Along the Route of Conquest*. University of Arizona Press. Retrieved from: https://books.google.co.in/books?Hl=en&lr=&id=hr9tcgaaqbaj&oi=fnd&pg=PR5&dq=Myers,+K.+A.,+Loaeza,+P.+G.,+%26+Wray,+G.+C.+(2015).+In+the+shadow+of+Cort%C3%a9s:+Conversations+along+the+route+of+conquest.+Tucson:+The+University+of+Arizona+Press.&ots=5lqjg67lse&sig=dwhm-WLEZ3uy5H_jkx0ruq3qjue

Nalanda University. (n.d.). Retrieved from https://www.nalandauniv.edu.in/about-nalanda/history-and-revival/

Nascimento, C. O. C. (2003). *O que querem os professores ante a educação contínua?* (Mestrado em Educação). Faculdade de Educação, Universidade Federal da Bahia, Salvador.

National Institution for Transforming India (NITI Aayog), Government of India. (2011). *Literacy rate- 7+ years (%)*. Retrieved from http://niti.gov.in/content/literacy-rate-7years on 23.8.18.

Nchise, A., Boateng, R., Mbarika, V., Saiba, E., & Johnson, O. (2012). The challenge of taking baby steps—Preliminary insights into telemedicine adoption in Rwanda. *Journal Health Policy and Technology*. Available at: https://www.healthpolicyandtechnology.org/article/S2211-8837(12)00079-2/abstract

Neuenkirch, M., & Neumeier, F. (2014). The Impact of UN and US Economic Sanctions on GDP Growth. *Research Papers in Economics*, *8*(14).

New Vision. (2014). *Support Women's Efforts to attain Financial Independence*. Author.

Nherera, C. (1999). *Capacity building in educational research in Southern Africa. Empirical insights into Qualitative research*. Human Resources Research Centre.

Nissen, A. H., Evald, R. M., & Clark, A. H. (2014). Knowledge Sharing in Heterogeneous Teams through Collaboration and Cooperation; Exemplified through Public-Private Innovation Pattern ships. *Industrial Marketing*, *43*(3), 473–482. doi:10.1016/j.indmarman.2013.12.015

Nonaka, I., Byosiere, P., Borucki, C. C., & Konno, N. (1994). Organizational knowledge creation theory: A first comprehensive test. *International Business Review*, *3*(4), 337–351. doi:10.1016/0969-5931(94)90027-2

Nonaka, I., Reinmoeller, P., & Senoo, D. (1998). The art of knowledge. *European Management Journal*, *16*(6), 673–684. doi:10.1016/S0263-2373(98)00044-9

Nonaka, I., & Takeuchi, H. (1995). *The Knowledge-creating Company. How Japanese Companies Create the Dynamics of Innovation*. Oxford University Press.

Nonaka, I., & Takeuchi, H. (1995). *The Knowledge-creating Company: How Japanese companies create the dynamics of innovation*. Oxford University Press.

Nonaka, I., & von Krogh, G. (2009). Tacit knowledge and knowledge conversion: Controversy and Advancement in Organisational Knowledge Creation Theory. *Organization Science*, *20*(3), 635–652. doi:10.1287/orsc.1080.0412

Noti, E. (2014). *Ndikimi i teknologjise se informacionit ne sipermarrjet turistike ne Shqiperi*. Tirana University.

Ntirenganya, E. (2017). How technology is primed to transform farming in Rwanda. *The New Times*. Accessed on 6th January 2019 from: https://www.newtimes.co.rw/section/read/223291

O'Neill, B. (2012). Trust in the information society. *Computer Law & Security Review*, *28*(5), 551–559. doi:10.1016/j.clsr.2012.07.005

OECD. (2005). *Glossary of Statistical Terms*. Accessed on 2nd May 2018 from: https://stats.oecd.org/glossary/detail.asp?ID=6864

Olaniyan, D. A., & Okemakinde, T. (2008). Human Capital Theory: Implications for Educational Development. *European Journal of Scientific Research*, *24*(2), 157–162.

Oliveira, J. Q. (2011). *Percepções sobre a Educação continuada no formato MBA pelo executivo em sua carreira: um estudo de caso em São Paulo* (Mestrado em Administração). Faculdade de Administração, Pontifícia Universidade Católica de São Paulo, São Paulo.

Oliveira, S. G. D. (2007). *Políticas de formação continuada de professores que atuam no ensino fundamental* (Mestrado em Educação). Faculdade de Ciências Humanas, Letras e Artes. Universidade Tuiuti do Paraná, Curitiba.

Omolewa, M. (2006). Educating the "Native": A Study of the Education Adaptation Strategy in British Colonial Africa, 1910-1936. *Journal of African American History*, *91*(3), 267–287. doi:10.1086/JAAHv91n3p267

Open Universities in India. (2019). Retrieved from https://www.eduvidya.com/Open-Universities-in-India

Pape, R. A. (1997). Why economic sanctions do not work. *International Security*, *22*(2), 90–136. doi:10.1162/isec.22.2.90

Pareek, S. (2014). *The Ancient Indian University Which Is Taking Students Again After 800 Years!* Retrieved from https://www.thebetterindia.com/13918/ancient-nalanda-university-reopens-monday-know-lesser-known-facts-great-university/

Peters, A. M., & Humes, W. (2003). Education in the Knowledge Economy. *Policy Futures in Education*, *1*(1), 1–19. doi:10.2304/pfie.2003.1.1.1

Pfister, T. (2009). *Governing the Knowledge Society: Studying Lisbon as Epistemic Setting.* Retrieved from https://papers.ssrn.com/abstract=1553798

Phillips, P., & Louvieris, P. (2005). Performance Measurement Systems in Tourism, Hospitality, and Leisure Small Medium-Sized Enterprises: A Balanced Scorecard Perspective. *Journal of Travel Research*, *44*(2), 201–211. doi:10.1177/0047287505278992

Phillips, P., & Moutinho, L. (2014). Critical review of strategic planning research in hospitality and tourism. *Annals of Tourism Research*, *48*, 96–120. doi:10.1016/j.annals.2014.05.013

Pohn, C., Rist, S., & Zimmmermann, P. F. (2010, May). Researchers' Roles in Knowledge Co-Production: Experiences from Sustainability Research in Kenya, Switzerland, Bolivia and Nepal. *Science & Public Policy*, *37*(4), 267–281. doi:10.3152/030234210X496628

Powell, W. W., & Snellman, K. (2004). The Knowledge Economy. *Annual Review of Sociology*, *30*(1), 199–220. doi:10.1146/annurev.soc.29.010202.100037

Pranicevic, D. G., Alfirevic, N., & Stemberger, M. I. (2011). Information system maturity and the hospitality enterprise performance. *Economic and Business Review for Central and South-Eastern Europe*, *13*(4), 227.

Preston, P. (1997). *Beyond the "Information Society": selected atoms and bits of a national strategy in Ireland. Dublin.* Retrieved from http://www.tara.tcd.ie/handle/2262/64423

Psacharopoulos, G., & Woodhall, M. (1997). *Education for Development: An Analysis of Investment Choice.* New York Oxford University Press.

Ranganathan, A. (2004). *Using ICT to place IKS at the heart of education for sustainable Development.* https://www.ceeindia.org/esf/download/paper47.pdf

Rani, G. P. (2007). Secondary Education in India: Development and Performance. In *43rd Annual Conference of the Indian Econometric Society (TIES).* Indian Institute of Technology.

Raynolds, L. T., & Bennett, E. A. (Eds.). (2015). *Handbook of Research on Fair Trade.* Edward Elgar Publishing. doi:10.4337/9781783474622

Report of the UN Secretary –General's High –Level Panel on Women's Economic Empowerment. (2016). *Leave no one behind-A call to action for gender equality and women's economic empowerment.* UN.

Ricci, A. (2000). Measuring information society. *Telematics and Informatics, 17*(1–2), 141–167. doi:10.1016/S0736-5853(00)00002-2

Robertson, S. (2003). É o Teu Cérebro que Nós Queremos: A Bala de Prata da Sociedade do Conhecimento. *A Página da Educação, 129*(12).

Robertson, S. (2008). Professoras/es são importantes, não? Posicionando as/os professoras/es e seu trabalho na economia do conhecimento global. *Espaço do Currículo, 1*(1), 34-64.

Rodney, W. (1972). How Europe Underdeveloped Africa. Bogle – L'ouverture Publications.

Rupera, P. (2017). *Ancient Vallabhi University to be revived.* Retrieved from https://timesofindia. indiatimes.com/city/vadodara/ancient-vallabhi-university-to-be-revived/articleshow/60811468. cms

Rwanda Information Society Authority. (2019). https://www.risa.rw/home/

Rwanda: Government Gives a Sneak Peek into Vision 2050 Blueprint. (n.d.). https://allafrica. com/stories/201612190503.html

Sadeghi, A.-R. (2008). *SOFSEM 2008: Theory and Practice of Computer Science* (V. Geffert, J. Karhumäki, A. Bertoni, B. Preneel, P. Návrat, & M. Bieliková, Eds., Vol. 4910). Springer Berlin Heidelberg. doi:10.1007/978-3-540-77566-9

Säfström, C. A. (2005). The European knowledge society and the diminishing state control of education: The case of Sweden. *Journal of Education Policy, 20*(5), 583–593. doi:10.1080/02680930500222386

Sahlberg, P., & Boce, E. (2010). Are teachers teaching for a knowledge society? *Teachers and Teaching: Theory and Practice.* Retrieved from https://www.tandfonline.com/doi/abs/10.1080/13540600903475611

Sakamota, A., & Powers, P.A. (1995). Education and the dual labour market for Japanaese men. *American Sociological Review, 60*(2), 222-246.

Sankaran, S. V. (2012). *From Vedas To Cloud: The Transformation Of Education In India*. Retrieved from https://www.forbes.com/sites/sap/2012/10/09/from-vedas-to-cloud-the-transformation-of-education-in-india/#763c1e4a646f on 22.8.2018

Santos, J. D. (2006). Formação continuada: cartas de alforria & controles reguladores (Doutorado em Educação). Faculdade de Educação, Universidade Federal do Rio Grande do Sul, Porto Alegre.

Saraiva, K., & Veiga-Neto, A. (2009). Modernidade Líquida, capitalismo cognitivo e educação contemporânea. Educação e Realidade, 34(2), 187-201.

Sarikakis, K., & Terzis, G. (2000). Pleonastic exclusion in the European Information Society. *Telematics and Informatics, 17*(1–2), 105–128. doi:10.1016/S0736-5853(99)00029-5

Schaefer Richard, J. (1995). National information infrastructure policy: A theoretical and normative approach. *Internet Research, 5*(2), 4–13. doi:10.1108/10662249510094740

Schmoker, M. (2000). The results we want. *Educational Leadership, 57*(5), 62-65.

Schoof, H., & Watson Brown, A. (1995). Information highways and media policies in the European Union. *Telecommunications Policy, 19*(4), 325–338. doi:10.1016/0308-5961(95)00006-R

Schultz, T. W. (1971). *Investment in Human Capital*. The Free Press.

Schweke, W. (2004). *Smart Money: Education and Economic Development*. Economic Policy Institute.

Selwyn, N., & Facer, K. (2010). *Handbook of Research on Overcoming Digital Divides* (E. Ferro, Y. K. Dwivedi, J. R. Gil-Garcia, & M. D. Williams, Eds.). IGI Global. doi:10.4018/978-1-60566-699-0

Sen, A. (2015). India: The Stormy Revival of an International University. *The New York Review*. Retrieved from https://www.nybooks.com/articles/2015/08/13/india-stormy-revival-nalanda-university/

Sennett, R. (2011). A corrosão do caráter - consequências pessoais do trabalho no novo capitalismo (16ª ed.). Tradução: Marcos Santarrita. Rio de Janeiro: Record.

Serrano, A., & Fialho, C. (2005). *Gestão do conhecimento. O novo paradigma das organizações*. FCA Editora Informática.

Servaes, J., & Heinderyckx, F. (2002). The 'new' ICTs environment in Europe: Closing or widening the gaps? *Telematics and Informatics, 19*(2), 91–115. doi:10.1016/S0736-5853(01)00008-9

Shafique, F., & Mahmood, K. (2008). Indicators of the Emerging Information Society in Pakistan. *Information Development, 24*(1), 66–78. doi:10.1177/0266666907087698

Shah, A., & Patel, R. (2016). *E-Commerce And Rural Handicraft Artisans* (No. 2016-12-07). Retrieved from: http://www.voiceofresearch.org/Doc/Dec-2016/Dec-2016_7.pdf

Sharma, C. N. (2017). *India ranks 5th in global research publication output: report.* Retrieved from https://www.livemint.com/Education/QYkn6doeciNSv2m7CzG7dP/India-ranks-5th-in-global-research-publication-output-repor.html

Sharma, R. S., Samuel, E. M., & Ng, E. W. J. (2009). Beyond the digital divide: Policy analysis for knowledge societies. *Journal of Knowledge Management, 13*(5), 373–386. doi:10.1108/13673270910988178

Shelat, K. & Mbuya, O. (2018). *Building Climate Smart Farmers: Doubling of Income in Arena of climate Change.* Kindle edition.

Shin, D.-H. (2007). A critique of Korean National Information Strategy: Case of national information infrastructures. *Government Information Quarterly, 24*(3), 624–645. doi:10.1016/j.giq.2006.06.011

Simon, H. A. (1960). *The new science of management decisions.* Harper and Row. doi:10.1037/13978-000

Simons, M. (2007). The 'Renaissance of the University' in the European knowledge society: An exploration of principled and governmental approaches. *Studies in Philosophy and Education, 26*(5), 433–447. doi:10.100711217-007-9054-2

Singh, S. (2010). The South African 'Information Society', 1994–2008: Problems with Policy, Legislation, Rhetoric and Implementation. *Journal of Southern African Studies, 36*(1), 209–227. doi:10.1080/03057071003607444

Sinha, E., & Bagarukayo, K. (2019). Online Education in Emerging Knowledge Economies: Exploring factors of motivation, de-motivation and potential facilitators; and studying the effects of demographic variables. *International Journal of Education and Development Using Information and Communication Technology, 15*(2), 5–30.

Sliva, S. M., Greenfield, J. C., Bender, K., & Freednthal, S. (2019). Introduction to Special Section on Public Impact Scholarship in Social Work: A conceptual review and call to action. *Journal of the Society for Social Work and Research, 10*(4), 529–544. doi:10.1086/706112

Sockwell, D. W. (2007). The Solow Growth Model. *The Journal of Economic Education, 38*(4), 483–483. doi:10.3200/JECE.38.4.483

Solt, F. (2014). *The Standardized World Income Inequality Database.* Working paper. SWIID Version 5.0. Downloaded on 7th Nov 2014 from https://myweb.uiowa.edu/fsolt/papers/Solt2015a_pre.pdf

Solt, F. (2015). Economic inequality and non-violent protest. *Social Science Quarterly, 96*(5), 1314–1327. doi:10.1111squ.12198

Som, C., Hilty, L. M., & Köhler, A. R. (2009). The Precautionary Principle as a Framework for a Sustainable Information Society. *Journal of Business Ethics*, *85*(S3), 493–505. doi:10.100710551-009-0214-x

Stewart, T. (2002). A riqueza do conhecimento: o capital intelectual e a nova organização. Tradução: Afonso Celso da Cunha Serra. Rio de Janeiro: Campus.

Strack, H. (1978). *Sanctions: the case of Rhodesia*. Syracuse University Press.

STYLE, University of Brighton. (2018). *Knowledge Society*. STYLE, University of Brighton. Retrieved from: https://www.style-research.eu/resource-centre/glossary/knowledge-society/

Sustainable development Goals. (n.d.). Retrieved from: http://www.undp.org/content/undp/en/home/sustainable-development-goals.html

Tan, C. N. (2016). Enhancing Knowledge Sharing and Research Collaboration among Academics: The Role of Knowledge Management. *Higher Education*, *71*(4), 525–556. doi:10.100710734-015-9922-6

Terepiszczy, S. (2016). The concept of" knowledge society" in the context of information era. *Studia Warmińskie, 53*, 77-84. Retrieved from: https://www.infona.pl/resource/bwmeta1.element. desklight-66c870ff-31db-4717-b833-a37083baef03

Terepyschyi, S. (2016). The concept of "knowledge society" in the context of information era. *Studia Warminskie, 53*.

Thomson Gale. (2008). Knowledge Society. *International Encyclopedia of the Social Sciences*. Retrieved from:https://www.encyclopedia.com/social-sciences/applied-and-social-sciences magazines/knowledge-society

Tilak, J. B. G. (1989). *Education and its Relation to Economic Growth, Poverty and Income Distribution: Past Evidence and Further Analysis*. World Bank Discussion Paper No.3, World Bank, Washington, DC.

Tilak, J. B. G. (2001). *Building Human Capital: What Others Can Learn*. World Bank Institute Working Paper, World Bank, Washington, DC.

Tilak, J. B. G. (2005). *Post-Elementary Education, Poverty and Development in India*. Working Paper Series, No.6, Centre of African Studies, University of Edinburgh, UK.

Towards knowledge-based economies in APEC. (2000). Retrieved from https://www.voced.edu. au/content/ngv%3A15963

Tripathi, M. (2006). Transforming India into a knowledge economy through information communication technologies—Current developments. *The International Information & Library Review*, *38*(3), 139–146. doi:10.1080/10572317.2006.10762715

Tweheyo, R. (2018). *Indigenous Knowledge and Food Security: Enhancing Decisions of Rural Farmers* (PhD Thesis). University of Groningen, The Netherlands.

Tweheyo, R., Lubega, J., & Baguma, R. (2018). A mobile Artefact for collecting and availing indigenous knowledge to farmers for food security enhancement. *6th International Conference on M4D Mobile Communication Technology for Development, Kampala Uganda.*

Uhegbu, A. N. (2001). Deterrents to information service for community development. *Library Review, 50*(5), 237–242. doi:10.1108/00242530110394493

UNESCO (2016). *Global Education Monitoring report. Indigenous knowledge and implications for sustainable development agenda.* UNESCO.

UNESCO. (2012) *Culture and Sustainable Development. The future we want.* www.unesco.org

UNESCO-Korean Republic Funds-in-Trust (KFIT) Project. (2017). *ICT Transforming Education in Africa.* Ministry of Education, Republic of Rwanda. https://unesdoc.unesco.org/images/0026/002614/261449E.pdf

United Nations (UN). (2005). Understanding knowledge societies. Department of Economic & Social Affairs. UN Publishing Section.

United Nations. (n.d.). *Sustainable development Goals-Quality Education.* Retrieved from https://www.un.org/sustainabledevelopment/education/

University Grant Commission Annual Report (UGC). (2016-17). Retrieved from: https://www.ugc.ac.in/pdfnews/9764381_Complete-AR-2016-17-English.pdf

Urch, E. G. (1971). Education and Colonialism in Kenya. *History of Education Quarterly, 11*(3), 249–264. doi:10.2307/367292

US Department of the Treasury. (2013). *Zimbabwe Sanctions Program, Office of Foreign Asset Control.* Available online: www.treasury.gov

Uwamiyara, M., Cremer, S., & Loebbecke, C. (2015). ICT for Economic Development in Rwanda: Fostering E-Commerce Adoption in Tourism SMEs. *Proceedings of SIG GlobDev Eighth Annual Workshop.* Available at: http://www.globdev.org/files/SigGlobDev_2015_paper_3_0.pdf

Van Bergeijk, P. A. G. (1994). *Economic Diplomacy, Trade and Commercial Policy, Positive and Negative sanctions in a new World Order.* Edward Elgar Publishing.

Van de Ven, A. H., & Johnson, P. E. (2006). Knowledge for Science and Practice. *Academy of Management Review, 31*(4), 822–829. doi:10.5465/amr.2006.22527385

Van de Ven, H. A. (2007). *Engaged Scholarship: A guide for Organizational and Social Research.* Oxford University Press.

Vargas, E. J. (2017). La idea de universidad en vilo. Gestión de calidad, capitalismo cognitivo y autonomca. *Revista Colombiana de Educación, 72.*

Venturelli, S. (2002). Inventing e-regulation in the US, EU and East Asia: Conflicting social visions of the Information Society. *Telematics and Informatics, 19*(2), 69–90. doi:10.1016/S0736-5853(01)00007-7

Verdegem, P. (2011a, January 13). Social Media for Digital and Social Inclusion: Challenges for Information Society 2.0 Research & Policies. *TripleC: Communication, Capitalism & Critique. Open Access Journal for a Global Sustainable Information Society*. Retrieved from https://www.triple-c.at/index.php/tripleC/article/view/225

Verdegem, P. (2011b, January 13). Social Media for Digital and Social Inclusion: Challenges for Information Society 2.0 Research & Policies. *TripleC: Communication, Capitalism & Critique. Open Access Journal for a Global Sustainable Information Society*. Retrieved from https://www.triple-c.at/index.php/tripleC/article/view/225

Vittal, N. (2005, Sept. 24). Moral Values Must Prevail. *The Tribune*, p. 15.

Vreede, G. J., Kolfschoten, G. L. & Briggs, R.O. (2006). ThinkLets: A collaboration Engineering Pattern Language. *International Journal of Computer Applications in Technology, 25*(2-3).

Wang, L. F. (1991). Trade sanctions, sector-specific unemployment and income distribution: A dual approach. *South African Journal of Economics, 59*(2), 72-76.

Weerakoon, C., McMurray A. J., Rametse N., & Arenius P. (2020). Knowledge Creation Theory of Entrepreneurial Orientation in Social Enterprises. *Journal of Small Business Management, 58*(4), 834-870. Doi:10.1080/00472778.2019.1672709

Wheeless, L.R., & Grotz, J. (1977). The Measurement of Trust and Its Relationship to Self-Disclosure. *Human Communication Research, 3*(3), 250-257.

Wilcox, K., & Ryder, R. (2002). Standardized Testing and Improving Educational Opportunity in Brazil. *The Educational Forum, 66*(3), 214–219. doi:10.1080/00131720208984831

Winata, L., & Mia, L. (2005). Information technology and the performance effect of managers' participation in budgeting: Evidence from the hotel industry. *International Journal of Hospitality Management, 24*(1), 21–39. doi:10.1016/j.ijhm.2004.04.006

Wong, D. (2010). *Knowledge management catalyst for sustainable development*. Academic Press.

Wood, R. M. (2008). A Hand upon the Throat of the Nation: Economic sanctions and state repression, 1976–2001. *International Studies Quarterly, 52*(3), 489–513. doi:10.1111/j.1468-2478.2008.00512.x

Wooldridge, J. M. (2010). *Econometric Analysis of Cross Section and Panel Data*. MIT press.

World Bank. (1997). *Knowledge and Skills for the Information Age, the first meeting of the Mediterranean Development Forum*. www.worldbank.org/afr/ik/basic.htmfpd/technet/mdf/objective/htm

World Bank. (1998). *Indigenous Knowledge for Development: A Framework for Action*. https://www.worldbank.org/afr/ik/ikrept.pdf

World Bank. (2002). *World Development Indicators*.

World Bank. (2005). Expanding Opportunities and Building Competences of Young People. A New Agenda for Secondary Education. World Bank.

World Bank. (2007). *Zimbabwe Manpower Development and Training Project, Staff Appraisal report number 7005-Zim*. Population and Human Resources Department.

World Bank. (2009). *Albania: Building Competitiveness in Albania*. Europe and Central Asia Region: World Bank. Retrieved from World Bank: http://siteresources.worldbank.org/EXTAR2009/Resources/6223977-1252950831873/AR09_Complete.pdf

World Bank. (2017). *Ease of doing business index (1=most business-friendly regulations)*. Accessed on 1st November 2019 rom: https://data.worldbank.org/indicator/IC.BUS.EASE.XQ

World development Report. (2018). *Learning to realize Education's Promise*. Retrieved from: https://www.worldbank.org/en/publication/wdr2018

World Economic Forum. (2019). https://www.weforum.org/agenda/2017/02/rwandas-digital-ambassadors-are-boosting-computer-literacy/

World Survey on the Role of Women in Development. (2014). *Gender Equality and Sustainable Development states*. Author.

Worsley, P. (1970). *Introducing Sociology. Hamondsworth* Penguin.

WTTC. (2018). *Travel & Tourism Economic Impact 2018*. World Travel & Tourism Council.

Wu, D. (2009). *Measuring performance in small and medium enterprises in the information and communication technology industries*. RMIT University.

Young, M. (2010). Alternative Educational Futures for a Knowledge Society. *European Educational Research Journal, 9*(1), 1–12. doi:10.2304/eerj.2010.9.1.1

Zabala, A., & Arnau, L. (2010). *Como aprender e ensinar competências*. Artmed.

Zayas, E. L. (2012). A elaboração de programas inovadores de educação permanente. In *O Paradigma da Educação continuada. Tradução: Alexandre Salvaterra*. Penso.

Zembere, M. (2018). *Democratic citizenship education in Zimbabwe's higher education system and its implications for teaching and learning* (PhD dissertation). Stellensboch University.

Related References

To continue our tradition of advancing media and communications research, we have compiled a list of recommended IGI Global readings. These references will provide additional information and guidance to further enrich your knowledge and assist you with your own research and future publications.

Abashian, N., & Fisher, S. (2018). Intercultural Effectiveness in Libraries: Supporting Success Through Collaboration With Co-Curricular Programs. In B. Blummer, J. Kenton, & M. Wiatrowski (Eds.), *Promoting Ethnic Diversity and Multiculturalism in Higher Education* (pp. 219–236). Hershey, PA: IGI Global. doi:10.4018/978-1-5225-4097-7.ch012

Adebayo, O., Fagbohun, M. O., Esse, U. C., & Nwokeoma, N. M. (2018). Change Management in the Academic Library: Transition From Print to Digital Collections. In R. Bhardwaj (Ed.), *Digitizing the Modern Library and the Transition From Print to Electronic* (pp. 1–28). Hershey, PA: IGI Global. doi:10.4018/978-1-5225-2119-8.ch001

Adegbore, A. M., Quadri, M. O., & Oyewo, O. R. (2018). A Theoretical Approach to the Adoption of Electronic Resource Management Systems (ERMS) in Nigerian University Libraries. In A. Tella & T. Kwanya (Eds.), *Handbook of Research on Managing Intellectual Property in Digital Libraries* (pp. 292–311). Hershey, PA: IGI Global. doi:10.4018/978-1-5225-3093-0.ch015

Adesola, A. P., & Olla, G. O. (2018). Unlocking the Unlimited Potentials of Koha OSS/ILS for Library House-Keeping Functions: A Global View. In M. Khosrow-Pour (Ed.), *Optimizing Contemporary Application and Processes in Open Source Software* (pp. 124–163). Hershey, PA: IGI Global. doi:10.4018/978-1-5225-5314-4.ch006

Adigun, G. O., Sobalaje, A. J., & Salau, S. A. (2018). Social Media and Copyright in Digital Libraries. In A. Tella & T. Kwanya (Eds.), *Handbook of Research on Managing Intellectual Property in Digital Libraries* (pp. 19–36). Hershey, PA: IGI Global. doi:10.4018/978-1-5225-3093-0.ch002

Adomi, E. E., Eriki, J. A., Tiemo, P. A., & Akpojotor, L. O. (2016). Incidents of Cyberbullying Among Library and Information Science (LIS) Students at Delta State University, Abraka, Nigeria. *International Journal of Digital Literacy and Digital Competence*, 7(4), 52–63. doi:10.4018/IJDLDC.2016100104

Afolabi, O. A. (2018). Myths and Challenges of Building an Effective Digital Library in Developing Nations: An African Perspective. In A. Tella & T. Kwanya (Eds.), *Handbook of Research on Managing Intellectual Property in Digital Libraries* (pp. 51–79). Hershey, PA: IGI Global. doi:10.4018/978-1-5225-3093-0.ch004

Agrawal, P. R. (2016). Google Search: Digging into the Culture of Information Retrieval. In E. de Smet & S. Dhamdhere (Eds.), *E-Discovery Tools and Applications in Modern Libraries* (pp. 210–239). Hershey, PA: IGI Global. doi:10.4018/978-1-5225-0474-0.ch012

Ahuja, Y., & Kumar, P. (2017). Web 2.0 Tools and Application: Knowledge Management and Sharing in Libraries. In B. Gunjal (Ed.), *Managing Knowledge and Scholarly Assets in Academic Libraries* (pp. 218–234). Hershey, PA: IGI Global. doi:10.4018/978-1-5225-1741-2.ch010

Ajmi, A. (2018). Developing In-House Digital Tools: Case Studies From the UMKC School of Law Library. In L. Costello & M. Powers (Eds.), *Developing In-House Digital Tools in Library Spaces* (pp. 117–139). Hershey, PA: IGI Global. doi:10.4018/978-1-5225-2676-6.ch006

Akakandelwa, A. (2016). A Glimpse of the Information Seeking Behaviour Literature on the Web: A Bibliometric Approach. In A. Tella (Ed.), *Information Seeking Behavior and Challenges in Digital Libraries* (pp. 127–155). Hershey, PA: IGI Global. doi:10.4018/978-1-5225-0296-8.ch007

Akande, F. T., & Adewojo, A. A. (2016). Information Need and Seeking Behavior of Farmers in Laduba Community of Kwara State, Nigeria. In A. Tella (Ed.), *Information Seeking Behavior and Challenges in Digital Libraries* (pp. 238–271). Hershey, PA: IGI Global. doi:10.4018/978-1-5225-0296-8.ch012

Al-Kharousi, R., Al-Harrasi, N. H., Jabur, N. H., & Bouazza, A. (2018). Soft Systems Methodology (SSM) as an Interdisciplinary Approach: Reflection on the Use of SSM in Adoption of Web 2.0 Applications in Omani Academic Libraries. In M. Al-Suqri, A. Al-Kindi, S. AlKindi, & N. Saleem (Eds.), *Promoting Interdisciplinarity in Knowledge Generation and Problem Solving* (pp. 243–257). Hershey, PA: IGI Global. doi:10.4018/978-1-5225-3878-3.ch016

Alenzuela, R. (2017). Research, Leadership, and Resource-Sharing Initiatives: The Role of Local Library Consortia in Access to Medical Information. In S. Ram (Ed.), *Library and Information Services for Bioinformatics Education and Research* (pp. 199–211). Hershey, PA: IGI Global. doi:10.4018/978-1-5225-1871-6.ch012

Allison, D. (2017). When Sales Talk Meets Reality: Implementing a Self-Checkout Kiosk. In E. Iglesias (Ed.), *Library Technology Funding, Planning, and Deployment* (pp. 36–54). Hershey, PA: IGI Global. doi:10.4018/978-1-5225-1735-1.ch003

Anglim, C. T., & Rusk, F. (2018). Empowering DC's Future Through Information Access. In A. Burtin, J. Fleming, & P. Hampton-Garland (Eds.), *Changing Urban Landscapes Through Public Higher Education* (pp. 57–77). Hershey, PA: IGI Global. doi:10.4018/978-1-5225-3454-9.ch003

Asmi, N. A. (2017). Social Media and Library Services. *International Journal of Library and Information Services*, 6(2), 23–36. doi:10.4018/IJLIS.2017070103

Awoyemi, R. A. (2018). Adoption and Use of Innovative Mobile Technologies in Nigerian Academic Libraries. In J. Keengwe (Ed.), *Handbook of Research on Digital Content, Mobile Learning, and Technology Integration Models in Teacher Education* (pp. 354–389). Hershey, PA: IGI Global. doi:10.4018/978-1-5225-2953-8.ch019

Awoyemi, R. A. (2018). Adoption and Use of Innovative Mobile Technologies in Nigerian Academic Libraries. In J. Keengwe (Ed.), *Handbook of Research on Digital Content, Mobile Learning, and Technology Integration Models in Teacher Education* (pp. 354–389). Hershey, PA: IGI Global. doi:10.4018/978-1-5225-2953-8.ch019

Ayson, M. C. (2016). Maximizing Social Media Tools: Planning and Evaluating Social Media Strategies for Special Libraries. In J. Yap, M. Perez, M. Ayson, & G. Entico (Eds.), *Special Library Administration, Standardization and Technological Integration* (pp. 166–179). Hershey, PA: IGI Global. doi:10.4018/978-1-4666-9542-9.ch007

Babatope, I. S. (2018). Social Media Applications as Effective Service Delivery Tools for Librarians. In M. Khosrow-Pour, D.B.A. (Ed.), Encyclopedia of Information Science and Technology, Fourth Edition (pp. 5252-5261). Hershey, PA: IGI Global. doi:10.4018/978-1-5225-2255-3.ch456

Bakare, A. A. (2018). Digital Libraries and Copyright of Intellectual Property: An Ethical Practice Management. In A. Tella & T. Kwanya (Eds.), *Handbook of Research on Managing Intellectual Property in Digital Libraries* (pp. 377–395). Hershey, PA: IGI Global. doi:10.4018/978-1-5225-3093-0.ch019

Baker, W. (2016). Responding to High-Volume Water Disasters in the Research Library Context. In E. Decker & J. Townes (Eds.), *Handbook of Research on Disaster Management and Contingency Planning in Modern Libraries* (pp. 282–310). Hershey, PA: IGI Global. doi:10.4018/978-1-4666-8624-3.ch013

Baker-Gardner, R., & Smart, C. (2017). Ignorance or Intent?: A Case Study of Plagiarism in Higher Education among LIS Students in the Caribbean. In D. Velliaris (Ed.), *Handbook of Research on Academic Misconduct in Higher Education* (pp. 182–205). Hershey, PA: IGI Global. doi:10.4018/978-1-5225-1610-1.ch008

Baker-Gardner, R., & Stewart, P. (2018). Educating Caribbean Librarians to Provide Library Education in a Dynamic Information Environment. In S. Bhattacharyya & K. Patnaik (Eds.), *Changing the Scope of Library Instruction in the Digital Age* (pp. 187–226). Hershey, PA: IGI Global. doi:10.4018/978-1-5225-2802-9.ch008

Bassuener, L. (2016). Knowledge in the Shrinking Commons: Libraries and Open Access in a Market-Driven World. In E. Railean, G. Walker, A. Elçi, & L. Jackson (Eds.), *Handbook of Research on Applied Learning Theory and Design in Modern Education* (pp. 358–379). Hershey, PA: IGI Global. doi:10.4018/978-1-4666-9634-1.ch017

Baylen, D. M., & Cooper, O. P. (2016). Social Media and Special Collections: Exploring Presence, Prevalence, and Practices in Academic Libraries. In J. Yap, M. Perez, M. Ayson, & G. Entico (Eds.), *Special Library Administration, Standardization and Technological Integration* (pp. 180–201). Hershey, PA: IGI Global. doi:10.4018/978-1-4666-9542-9.ch008

Belden, D., Phillips, M. E., Carlisle, T., & Hartman, C. N. (2016). The Portal to Texas History: Building a Partnership Model for a Statewide Digital Library. In B. Doherty (Ed.), *Space and Organizational Considerations in Academic Library Partnerships and Collaborations* (pp. 182–204). Hershey, PA: IGI Global. doi:10.4018/978-1-5225-0326-2.ch009

Bengtson, J. (2017). Funding a Gamification Machine. In E. Iglesias (Ed.), *Library Technology Funding, Planning, and Deployment* (pp. 99–112). Hershey, PA: IGI Global. doi:10.4018/978-1-5225-1735-1.ch006

Bhebhe, S., & Ngwenya, S. (2016). Adoption and Use of Discovery Tools by Selected Academic Libraries in Zimbabwe. In E. de Smet & S. Dhamdhere (Eds.), *E-Discovery Tools and Applications in Modern Libraries* (pp. 168–180). Hershey, PA: IGI Global. doi:10.4018/978-1-5225-0474-0.ch009

Blummer, B., & Kenton, J. M. (2017). Access and Accessibility of Academic Libraries' Electronic Resources and Services: Identifying Themes in the Literature From 2000 to the Present. In H. Alphin Jr, J. Lavine, & R. Chan (Eds.), *Disability and Equity in Higher Education Accessibility* (pp. 242–267). Hershey, PA: IGI Global. doi:10.4018/978-1-5225-2665-0.ch011

Blummer, B., & Kenton, J. M. (2018). Academic and Research Libraries' Portals: A Literature Review From 2003 to the Present. In R. Bhardwaj (Ed.), *Digitizing the Modern Library and the Transition From Print to Electronic* (pp. 29–63). Hershey, PA: IGI Global. doi:10.4018/978-1-5225-2119-8.ch002

Blummer, B., & Kenton, J. M. (2018). International Students and Academic Libraries: Identifying Themes in the Literature From 2001 to the Present. In B. Blummer, J. Kenton, & M. Wiatrowski (Eds.), *Promoting Ethnic Diversity and Multiculturalism in Higher Education* (pp. 237–263). Hershey, PA: IGI Global. doi:10.4018/978-1-5225-4097-7.ch013

Bodolay, R., Frye, S., Kruse, C., & Luke, D. (2016). Moving from Co-Location to Cooperation to Collaboration: Redefining a Library's Role within the University. In B. Doherty (Ed.), *Space and Organizational Considerations in Academic Library Partnerships and Collaborations* (pp. 230–254). Hershey, PA: IGI Global. doi:10.4018/978-1-5225-0326-2.ch011

Boom, D. (2017). The Embedded Librarian: Do More With less. In B. Gunjal (Ed.), *Managing Knowledge and Scholarly Assets in Academic Libraries* (pp. 76–97). Hershey, PA: IGI Global. doi:10.4018/978-1-5225-1741-2.ch004

Bosire-Ogechi, E. (2018). Social Media, Social Networking, Copyright, and Digital Libraries. In A. Tella & T. Kwanya (Eds.), *Handbook of Research on Managing Intellectual Property in Digital Libraries* (pp. 37–50). Hershey, PA: IGI Global. doi:10.4018/978-1-5225-3093-0.ch003

Bradley-Sanders, C., & Rudshteyn, A. (2018). MyLibrary at Brooklyn College: Developing a Suite of Digital Tools. In L. Costello & M. Powers (Eds.), *Developing In-House Digital Tools in Library Spaces* (pp. 140–167). Hershey, PA: IGI Global. doi:10.4018/978-1-5225-2676-6.ch007

Brisk, A. T., Pittman, K., & Rosendahl, M. (2016). Collaborating Off Campus: Creating Communities of Practice with New Partners. In B. Doherty (Ed.), *Technology-Centered Academic Library Partnerships and Collaborations* (pp. 245–274). Hershey, PA: IGI Global. doi:10.4018/978-1-5225-0323-1.ch009

Brown, V. (2018). Technology Access Gap for Postsecondary Education: A Statewide Case Study. In M. Yildiz, S. Funk, & B. De Abreu (Eds.), *Promoting Global Competencies Through Media Literacy* (pp. 20–40). Hershey, PA: IGI Global. doi:10.4018/978-1-5225-3082-4.ch002

Carroll, V. (2016). Conservation Since 2000. In E. Decker & J. Townes (Eds.), *Handbook of Research on Disaster Management and Contingency Planning in Modern Libraries* (pp. 467–493). Hershey, PA: IGI Global. doi:10.4018/978-1-4666-8624-3.ch020

Chaiyasoonthorn, W., & Suksa-ngiam, W. (2018). Users' Acceptance of Online Literature Databases in a Thai University: A Test of UTAUT2. *International Journal of Information Systems in the Service Sector*, *10*(1), 54–70. doi:10.4018/IJISSS.2018010104

Chandler, D. R. (2016). Prepared for Anything and Everything: Libraries, Archives, and Unexpected Small Scale Disasters. In E. Decker & J. Townes (Eds.), *Handbook of Research on Disaster Management and Contingency Planning in Modern Libraries* (pp. 240–256). Hershey, PA: IGI Global. doi:10.4018/978-1-4666-8624-3.ch011

Chaudron, G. (2016). After the Flood: Lessons Learned from Small-Scale Disasters. In E. Decker & J. Townes (Eds.), *Handbook of Research on Disaster Management and Contingency Planning in Modern Libraries* (pp. 389–411). Hershey, PA: IGI Global. doi:10.4018/978-1-4666-8624-3.ch017

Chaudron, G. (2016). Managing the Commonplace: Small Water Emergencies in Libraries. *International Journal of Risk and Contingency Management*, *5*(1), 42–61. doi:10.4018/IJRCM.2016010104

Chaudron, G. (2018). Burst Pipes and Leaky Roofs: Small Emergencies Are a Challenge for Libraries. In K. Strang, M. Korstanje, & N. Vajjhala (Eds.), *Research, Practices, and Innovations in Global Risk and Contingency Management* (pp. 211–231). Hershey, PA: IGI Global. doi:10.4018/978-1-5225-4754-9.ch012

Chemulwo, M. J. (2018). Managing Intellectual Property in Digital Libraries and Copyright Challenges. In A. Tella & T. Kwanya (Eds.), *Handbook of Research on Managing Intellectual Property in Digital Libraries* (pp. 165–183). Hershey, PA: IGI Global. doi:10.4018/978-1-5225-3093-0.ch009

Chen, J., Lan, X., Huang, Q., Dong, J., & Chen, C. (2017). Scholarly Learning Commons. In L. Ruan, Q. Zhu, & Y. Ye (Eds.), *Academic Library Development and Administration in China* (pp. 90–109). Hershey, PA: IGI Global. doi:10.4018/978-1-5225-0550-1.ch006

Chigwada, J. P. (2018). Adoption of Open Source Software in Libraries in Developing Countries. *International Journal of Library and Information Services*, 7(1), 15–29. doi:10.4018/IJLIS.2018010102

Chisita, C. T., & Chinyemba, F. (2017). Utilising ICTs for Resource Sharing Initiatives in Academic Institutions in Zimbabwe: Towards a New Trajectory. In B. Gunjal (Ed.), *Managing Knowledge and Scholarly Assets in Academic Libraries* (pp. 174–187). Hershey, PA: IGI Global. doi:10.4018/978-1-5225-1741-2.ch008

Colmenero-Ruiz, M. (2016). Discussion on Digital Inclusion Good Practices at Europe's Libraries. In B. Passarelli, J. Straubhaar, & A. Cuevas-Cerveró (Eds.), *Handbook of Research on Comparative Approaches to the Digital Age Revolution in Europe and the Americas* (pp. 352–369). Hershey, PA: IGI Global. doi:10.4018/978-1-4666-8740-0.ch021

Costello, B. (2016). Academic Libraries in Partnership with the Government Publishing Office: A Changing Paradigm. In B. Doherty (Ed.), *Space and Organizational Considerations in Academic Library Partnerships and Collaborations* (pp. 87–110). Hershey, PA: IGI Global. doi:10.4018/978-1-5225-0326-2.ch005

Costello, L., & Fazal, S. (2018). Developing Unique Study Room Reservation Systems: Examples From Teachers College and Stony Brook University. In L. Costello & M. Powers (Eds.), *Developing In-House Digital Tools in Library Spaces* (pp. 168–176). Hershey, PA: IGI Global. doi:10.4018/978-1-5225-2676-6.ch008

Cowick, C., & Cowick, J. (2016). Planning for a Disaster: Effective Emergency Management in the 21st Century. In E. Decker & J. Townes (Eds.), *Handbook of Research on Disaster Management and Contingency Planning in Modern Libraries* (pp. 49–69). Hershey, PA: IGI Global. doi:10.4018/978-1-4666-8624-3.ch003

Cui, Y. (2017). Research Data Management: Models, Challenges, and Actions. In L. Ruan, Q. Zhu, & Y. Ye (Eds.), *Academic Library Development and Administration in China* (pp. 184–195). Hershey, PA: IGI Global. doi:10.4018/978-1-5225-0550-1.ch011

Das, T. (2016). Academic Library Collaborations to Strengthen Open Government Data and Expand Librarianship. In B. Doherty (Ed.), *Technology-Centered Academic Library Partnerships and Collaborations* (pp. 167–193). Hershey, PA: IGI Global. doi:10.4018/978-1-5225-0323-1.ch006 de Smet, E. (2016). E-Discovery with the ABCD Information Management System. In E. de Smet & S. Dhamdhere (Eds.), *E-Discovery Tools and Applications in Modern Libraries* (pp. 332–357). Hershey, PA: IGI Global. doi:10.4018/978-1-5225-0474-0.ch017

Decker, E. N., & Odom, R. Y. (2016). Publish or Perish: Librarians Collaborating to Support Junior Faculty to Publish within the Academic Environment. In B. Doherty (Ed.), *Space and Organizational Considerations in Academic Library Partnerships and Collaborations* (pp. 298–316). Hershey, PA: IGI Global. doi:10.4018/978-1-5225-0326-2.ch014

Desilets, M. R., DeJonghe, J., & Filkins, M. (2016). Better Together: The Successful Public/Academic Joint Use Library. In B. Doherty (Ed.), *Space and Organizational Considerations in Academic Library Partnerships and Collaborations* (pp. 1–21). Hershey, PA: IGI Global. doi:10.4018/978-1-5225-0326-2.ch001

Dhamdhere, S. N., De Smet, E., & Lihitkar, R. (2017). Web-Based Bibliographic Services Offered by Top World and Indian University Libraries: A Comparative Study. *International Journal of Library and Information Services*, 6(1), 53–72. doi:10.4018/IJLIS.2017010104

Dhamdhere, S. N., & Lihitkar, R. (2016). Commercial and Open Access Integrated Information Search Tools in Indian Libraries. In E. de Smet & S. Dhamdhere (Eds.), *E-Discovery Tools and Applications in Modern Libraries* (pp. 41–55). Hershey, PA: IGI Global. doi:10.4018/978-1-5225-0474-0.ch002

Dixon, J., & Abashian, N. (2016). Beyond the Collection: Emergency Planning for Public and Staff Safety. In E. Decker & J. Townes (Eds.), *Handbook of Research on Disaster Management and Contingency Planning in Modern Libraries* (pp. 120–140). Hershey, PA: IGI Global. doi:10.4018/978-1-4666-8624-3.ch006

Doherty, B. (2016). Marriage after Divorce: The Challenges and Opportunities of a Shared Library after Institutions Separate. In B. Doherty (Ed.), *Space and Organizational Considerations in Academic Library Partnerships and Collaborations* (pp. 22–44). Hershey, PA: IGI Global. doi:10.4018/978-1-5225-0326-2.ch002

Dongardive, P. (2016). Digital Libraries as Information Superhighway. In A. Tella (Ed.), *Information Seeking Behavior and Challenges in Digital Libraries* (pp. 304–315). Hershey, PA: IGI Global. doi:10.4018/978-1-5225-0296-8.ch015

Dougan, K. (2016). Music Information Seeking Opportunities and Behavior Then and Now. In P. Kostagiolas, K. Martzoukou, & C. Lavranos (Eds.), *Trends in Music Information Seeking, Behavior, and Retrieval for Creativity* (pp. 42–57). Hershey, PA: IGI Global. doi:10.4018/978-1-5225-0270-8.ch003

Eiriemiokhale, K. A. (2018). Copyright Issues in a Digital Library Environment. In A. Tella & T. Kwanya (Eds.), *Handbook of Research on Managing Intellectual Property in Digital Libraries* (pp. 142–164). Hershey, PA: IGI Global. doi:10.4018/978-1-5225-3093-0.ch008

El Mimouni, H., Anderson, J., Tempelman-Kluit, N. F., & Dolan-Mescal, A. (2018). UX Work in Libraries: How (and Why) to Do It. In L. Costello & M. Powers (Eds.), *Developing In-House Digital Tools in Library Spaces* (pp. 1–36). Hershey, PA: IGI Global. doi:10.4018/978-1-5225-2676-6.ch001

Emiri, O. T. (2017). Digital Literacy Skills Among Librarians in University Libraries In the 21st Century in Edo And Delta States, Nigeria. *International Journal of Library and Information Services*, 6(1), 37–52. doi:10.4018/IJLIS.2017010103

Entico, G. J. (2016). Knowledge Management and the Medical Health Librarians: A Perception Study. In J. Yap, M. Perez, M. Ayson, & G. Entico (Eds.), *Special Library Administration, Standardization and Technological Integration* (pp. 52–77). Hershey, PA: IGI Global. doi:10.4018/978-1-4666-9542-9.ch003

Esposito, T. (2018). Exploring Opportunities in Health Science Information Instructional Outreach: A Case Study Highlighting One Academic Library's Experience. In S. Bhattacharyya & K. Patnaik (Eds.), *Changing the Scope of Library Instruction in the Digital Age* (pp. 118–135). Hershey, PA: IGI Global. doi:10.4018/978-1-5225-2802-9.ch005

Esse, U. C., & Ohaegbulam, H. (2016). Library and Information Services for Open and Distance Learning: Assessing the Role of Mobile Technologies and Distance Learning in Higher Education. In G. Eby, T. Yuzer, & S. Atay (Eds.), *Developing Successful Strategies for Global Policies and Cyber Transparency in E-Learning* (pp. 29–45). Hershey, PA: IGI Global. doi:10.4018/978-1-4666-8844-5.ch003

Fagbohun, M. O., Nwokocha, N. M., Itsekor, V., & Adebayo, O. (2016). Responsive Library Website Design and Adoption of Federated Search Tools for Library Services in Developing Countries. In E. de Smet & S. Dhamdhere (Eds.), *E-Discovery Tools and Applications in Modern Libraries* (pp. 76–108). Hershey, PA: IGI Global. doi:10.4018/978-1-5225-0474-0.ch005

Fagbola, O. O. (2016). Indexing and Abstracting as Tools for Information Retrieval in Digital Libraries: A Review of Literature. In A. Tella (Ed.), *Information Seeking Behavior and Challenges in Digital Libraries* (pp. 156–178). Hershey, PA: IGI Global. doi:10.4018/978-1-5225-0296-8.ch008

Fan, Y., Zhang, X., & Li, G. (2017). Research Initiatives and Projects in Academic Libraries. In L. Ruan, Q. Zhu, & Y. Ye (Eds.), *Academic Library Development and Administration in China* (pp. 230–252). Hershey, PA: IGI Global. doi:10.4018/978-1-5225-0550-1.ch014

Farmer, L. S. (2017). ICT Literacy Integration: Issues and Sample Efforts. In J. Keengwe & P. Bull (Eds.), *Handbook of Research on Transformative Digital Content and Learning Technologies* (pp. 59–80). Hershey, PA: IGI Global. doi:10.4018/978-1-5225-2000-9.ch004

Farmer, L. S. (2017). Data Analytics for Strategic Management: Getting the Right Data. In V. Wang (Ed.), *Encyclopedia of Strategic Leadership and Management* (pp. 810–822). Hershey, PA: IGI Global. doi:10.4018/978-1-5225-1049-9.ch056

Farmer, L. S. (2017). Managing Portable Technologies for Special Education. In V. Wang (Ed.), *Encyclopedia of Strategic Leadership and Management* (pp. 977–987). Hershey, PA: IGI Global. doi:10.4018/978-1-5225-1049-9.ch068

Fujishima, D., & Kamada, T. (2017). Collective Relocation for Associative Distributed Collections of Objects. *International Journal of Software Innovation, 5*(2), 55–69. doi:10.4018/IJSI.2017040104

Gaetz, I. (2016). Processes, Opportunities, and Challenges Creating and Managing a Scholarly Open Access Journal: An Investigation of "Collaborative Librarianship". In B. Doherty (Ed.), *Space and Organizational Considerations in Academic Library Partnerships and Collaborations* (pp. 205–229). Hershey, PA: IGI Global. doi:10.4018/978-1-5225-0326-2.ch010

Galloup, A. (2016). One Plan, Four Libraries: A Case Study in Disaster Planning for a Four-Campus Academic Institution. In E. Decker & J. Townes (Eds.), *Handbook of Research on Disaster Management and Contingency Planning in Modern Libraries* (pp. 166–183). Hershey, PA: IGI Global. doi:10.4018/978-1-4666-8624-3.ch008

Gamtso, C. W., Vogt, R. B., Donahue, A., Donovan, K., & Jefferson, J. (2016). Librarian and Peer Research Mentor Partnerships that Promote Student Success. In B. Doherty (Ed.), *Space and Organizational Considerations in Academic Library Partnerships and Collaborations* (pp. 255–279). Hershey, PA: IGI Global. doi:10.4018/978-1-5225-0326-2.ch012

Ghani, S. R. (2017). Ontology: Advancing Flawless Library Services. In T. Ashraf & N. Kumar (Eds.), *Interdisciplinary Digital Preservation Tools and Technologies* (pp. 79–102). Hershey, PA: IGI Global. doi:10.4018/978-1-5225-1653-8.ch005

Gibbons, P. (2016). Disaster Management and Exhibition Loans: Contingency Planning for Items on Display. In E. Decker & J. Townes (Eds.), *Handbook of Research on Disaster Management and Contingency Planning in Modern Libraries* (pp. 141–165). Hershey, PA: IGI Global. doi:10.4018/978-1-4666-8624-3.ch007

Gibbons, P. (2016). Assessing Risk and Safeguarding Rare Library Materials During Exhibition Loans. *International Journal of Risk and Contingency Management*, 5(1), 15–25. doi:10.4018/IJRCM.2016010102

Gibson, R. (2016). Wearable Technologies in Academic Information Search. In J. Holland (Ed.), *Wearable Technology and Mobile Innovations for Next-Generation Education* (pp. 122–146). Hershey, PA: IGI Global. doi:10.4018/978-1-5225-0069-8.ch007

Goldman, B. (2016). Two Fires and a Flood: Lasting Impact on a Public Library, Its Staff, and Community. In E. Decker & J. Townes (Eds.), *Handbook of Research on Disaster Management and Contingency Planning in Modern Libraries* (pp. 560–581). Hershey, PA: IGI Global. doi:10.4018/978-1-4666-8624-3.ch024

Goovaerts, M., Nieuwenhuysen, P., & Dhamdhere, S. N. (2016). VLIR-UOS Workshop 'E-Info Discovery and Management for Institutes in the South': Presentations and Conclusions, Antwerp, 8-19 December, 2014. In E. de Smet, & S. Dhamdhere (Eds.), E-Discovery Tools and Applications in Modern Libraries (pp. 1-40). Hershey, PA: IGI Global. doi:10.4018/978-1-5225-0474-0.ch001

Gu, J. (2017). Library Buildings on New Campuses. In L. Ruan, Q. Zhu, & Y. Ye (Eds.), *Academic Library Development and Administration in China* (pp. 110–124). Hershey, PA: IGI Global. doi:10.4018/978-1-5225-0550-1.ch007

Guan, Z., & Wang, J. (2017). The China Academic Social Sciences and Humanities Library (CASHL). In L. Ruan, Q. Zhu, & Y. Ye (Eds.), *Academic Library Development and Administration in China* (pp. 31–54). Hershey, PA: IGI Global. doi:10.4018/978-1-5225-0550-1.ch003

Gul, S., & Shueb, S. (2018). Confronting/Managing the Crisis of Indian Libraries: E-Consortia Initiatives in India - A Way Forward. In R. Bhardwaj (Ed.), *Digitizing the Modern Library and the Transition From Print to Electronic* (pp. 129–163). Hershey, PA: IGI Global. doi:10.4018/978-1-5225-2119-8.ch006

Gunjal, B. (2017). Managing Knowledge and Scholarly Assets in Academic Libraries: Issues and Challenges. In B. Gunjal (Ed.), *Managing Knowledge and Scholarly Assets in Academic Libraries* (pp. 270–279). Hershey, PA: IGI Global. doi:10.4018/978-1-5225-1741-2.ch013

Guo, J., Zhang, H., & Zong, Y. (2017). Leadership Development and Career Planning. In L. Ruan, Q. Zhu, & Y. Ye (Eds.), *Academic Library Development and Administration in China* (pp. 264–279). Hershey, PA: IGI Global. doi:10.4018/978-1-5225-0550-1.ch016

Hallis, R. (2018). Leveraging Library Instruction in a Digital Age. In S. Bhattacharyya & K. Patnaik (Eds.), *Changing the Scope of Library Instruction in the Digital Age* (pp. 1–23). Hershey, PA: IGI Global. doi:10.4018/978-1-5225-2802-9.ch001

Hamilton, R., & Brown, D. (2016). Disaster Management and Continuity Planning in Libraries: Changes since the Year 2000. In E. Decker & J. Townes (Eds.), *Handbook of Research on Disaster Management and Contingency Planning in Modern Libraries* (pp. 1–24). Hershey, PA: IGI Global. doi:10.4018/978-1-4666-8624-3.ch001

Hamilton, R., & Brown, D. (2016). Disaster Management and Continuity Planning in Libraries: Literature Review. *International Journal of Risk and Contingency Management*, 5(1), 26–41. doi:10.4018/IJRCM.2016010103

Hartsock, R., & Alemneh, D. G. (2018). Electronic Theses and Dissertations (ETDs). In M. Khosrow-Pour, D.B.A. (Ed.), Encyclopedia of Information Science and Technology, Fourth Edition (pp. 6748-6755). Hershey, PA: IGI Global. doi:10.4018/978-1-5225-2255-3.ch584

Haugh, D. (2018). Mobile Applications for Libraries. In L. Costello & M. Powers (Eds.), *Developing In-House Digital Tools in Library Spaces* (pp. 76–90). Hershey, PA: IGI Global. doi:10.4018/978-1-5225-2676-6.ch004

Hill, V. (2017). Digital Citizens as Writers: New Literacies and New Responsibilities. In E. Monske & K. Blair (Eds.), *Handbook of Research on Writing and Composing in the Age of MOOCs* (pp. 56–74). Hershey, PA: IGI Global. doi:10.4018/978-1-5225-1718-4.ch004

Horne-Popp, L. M., Tessone, E. B., & Welker, J. (2018). If You Build It, They Will Come: Creating a Library Statistics Dashboard for Decision-Making. In L. Costello & M. Powers (Eds.), *Developing In-House Digital Tools in Library Spaces* (pp. 177–203). Hershey, PA: IGI Global. doi:10.4018/978-1-5225-2676-6.ch009

Huang, C., & Xue, H. F. (2017). The China Academic Digital Associative Library (CADAL). In L. Ruan, Q. Zhu, & Y. Ye (Eds.), *Academic Library Development and Administration in China* (pp. 20–30). Hershey, PA: IGI Global. doi:10.4018/978-1-5225-0550-1.ch002

Hunsaker, A. J., Majewski, N., & Rocke, L. E. (2018). Pulling Content out the Back Door: Creating an Interactive Digital Collections Experience. In L. Costello & M. Powers (Eds.), *Developing In-House Digital Tools in Library Spaces* (pp. 205–226). Hershey, PA: IGI Global. doi:10.4018/978-1-5225-2676-6.ch010

Ibrahim, H., Mustapa, R., Edzan, N., & Yahya, W. A. (2016). Profiling Prominent Malaysians in Bernama Library and Infolink Service. In J. Yap, M. Perez, M. Ayson, & G. Entico (Eds.), *Special Library Administration, Standardization and Technological Integration* (pp. 315–336). Hershey, PA: IGI Global. doi:10.4018/978-1-4666-9542-9.ch014

Idiegbeyan-Ose, J., Ifijeh, G., Iwu-James, J., & Ilogho, J. (2016). Management of Institutional Repositories (IR) in Developing Countries. In E. de Smet & S. Dhamdhere (Eds.), *E-Discovery Tools and Applications in Modern Libraries* (pp. 306–331). Hershey, PA: IGI Global. doi:10.4018/978-1-5225-0474-0.ch016

Idiegbeyan-ose, J., Nkiko, C., Idahosa, M., & Nwokocha, N. (2016). Digital Divide: Issues and Strategies for Intervention in Nigerian Libraries. *Journal of Cases on Information Technology*, *18*(3), 29–39. doi:10.4018/JCIT.2016070103

Ifijeh, G., Adebayo, O., Izuagbe, R., & Olawoyin, O. (2018). Institutional Repositories and Libraries in Nigeria: Interrogating the Nexus. *Journal of Cases on Information Technology*, *20*(2), 16–29. doi:10.4018/JCIT.2018040102

Ifijeh, G., Idiegbeyan-ose, J., Segun-Adeniran, C., & Ilogho, J. (2016). Disaster Management in Digital Libraries: Issues and Strategies in Developing Countries. *International Journal of Risk and Contingency Management*, *5*(1), 1–14. doi:10.4018/IJRCM.2016010101

Iglesias, E. (2017). Insourcing and Outsourcing of Library Technology. In E. Iglesias (Ed.), *Library Technology Funding, Planning, and Deployment* (pp. 113–123). Hershey, PA: IGI Global. doi:10.4018/978-1-5225-1735-1.ch007

Ikolo, V. E. (2018). Transformational Leadership for Academic Libraries in Nigeria. In M. Khosrow-Pour, D.B.A. (Ed.), Encyclopedia of Information Science and Technology, Fourth Edition (pp. 5726-5735). Hershey, PA: IGI Global. doi:10.4018/978-1-5225-2255-3.ch497

Jaafar, T. M. (2016). Law Library Consortium in Metro Manila: A Proposed Model and the Management of Law Libraries. In J. Yap, M. Perez, M. Ayson, & G. Entico (Eds.), *Special Library Administration, Standardization and Technological Integration* (pp. 134–164). Hershey, PA: IGI Global. doi:10.4018/978-1-4666-9542-9.ch006

Joe, J. A. (2018). Changing Expectations of Academic Libraries. In M. Khosrow-Pour, D.B.A. (Ed.), Encyclopedia of Information Science and Technology, Fourth Edition (pp. 5204-5212). Hershey, PA: IGI Global. doi:10.4018/978-1-5225-2255-3.ch452

Johnson, H., & Simms, S. (2016). Concept, Conversion, Cultivation, and Consequence: The Four Cs of Successful Collaboration. In B. Doherty (Ed.), *Space and Organizational Considerations in Academic Library Partnerships and Collaborations* (pp. 280–297). Hershey, PA: IGI Global. doi:10.4018/978-1-5225-0326-2.ch013

Jones, A. (2016). Shortcomings and Successes: A Small-Scale Disaster Case Study. In E. Decker & J. Townes (Eds.), *Handbook of Research on Disaster Management and Contingency Planning in Modern Libraries* (pp. 412–435). Hershey, PA: IGI Global. doi:10.4018/978-1-4666-8624-3.ch018

Juliana, I., Izuagbe, R., Itsekor, V., Fagbohun, M. O., Asaolu, A., & Nwokeoma, M. N. (2018). The Role of the School Library in Empowering Visually Impaired Children With Lifelong Information Literacy Skills. In P. Epler (Ed.), *Instructional Strategies in General Education and Putting the Individuals With Disabilities Act (IDEA) Into Practice* (pp. 245–271). Hershey, PA: IGI Global. doi:10.4018/978-1-5225-3111-1.ch009

Kalusopa, T. (2018). Preservation and Access to Digital Materials: Strategic Policy Options for Africa. In P. Ngulube (Ed.), *Handbook of Research on Heritage Management and Preservation* (pp. 150–174). Hershey, PA: IGI Global. doi:10.4018/978-1-5225-3137-1.ch008

Kamau, G. W. (2018). Copyright Challenges in Digital Libraries in Kenya From the Lens of a Librarian. In A. Tella & T. Kwanya (Eds.), *Handbook of Research on Managing Intellectual Property in Digital Libraries* (pp. 312–336). Hershey, PA: IGI Global. doi:10.4018/978-1-5225-3093-0.ch016

Karbach, L. (2016). Public Libraries: Analysis of Services for Immigrant Populations and Suggestions to Improve Outreach. In K. González & R. Frumkin (Eds.), *Handbook of Research on Effective Communication in Culturally Diverse Classrooms* (pp. 153–182). Hershey, PA: IGI Global. doi:10.4018/978-1-4666-9953-3.ch008

Karmakar, R. (2018). Development and Management of Digital Libraries in the Regime of IPR Paradigm. *International Journal of Library and Information Services*, 7(1), 44–57. doi:10.4018/IJLIS.2018010104

Kasemsap, K. (2016). Mastering Digital Libraries in the Digital Age. In E. de Smet & S. Dhamdhere (Eds.), *E-Discovery Tools and Applications in Modern Libraries* (pp. 275–305). Hershey, PA: IGI Global. doi:10.4018/978-1-5225-0474-0.ch015

Kasemsap, K. (2017). Mastering Knowledge Management in Academic Libraries. In B. Gunjal (Ed.), *Managing Knowledge and Scholarly Assets in Academic Libraries* (pp. 27–55). Hershey, PA: IGI Global. doi:10.4018/978-1-5225-1741-2.ch002

Kehinde, A. (2018). Digital Libraries and the Role of Digital Librarians. In A. Tella & T. Kwanya (Eds.), *Handbook of Research on Managing Intellectual Property in Digital Libraries* (pp. 98–119). Hershey, PA: IGI Global. doi:10.4018/978-1-5225-3093-0.ch006

Kenausis, V., & Herman, D. (2017). Don't Make Us Use the "Get Along Shirt": Communication and Consensus Building in an RFP Process. In E. Iglesias (Ed.), *Library Technology Funding, Planning, and Deployment* (pp. 1–22). Hershey, PA: IGI Global. doi:10.4018/978-1-5225-1735-1.ch001

Kohl, L. E., Lombardi, P., & Moroney, M. (2017). Moving from Local to Global via the Integrated Library System: Cost-Savings, ILS Management, Teams, and End-Users. In E. Iglesias (Ed.), *Library Technology Funding, Planning, and Deployment* (pp. 23–35). Hershey, PA: IGI Global. doi:10.4018/978-1-5225-1735-1.ch002

Kowalsky, M. (2016). Analysis of Initial Involvement of Librarians in the Online Virtual World of Second Life. In B. Baggio (Ed.), *Analyzing Digital Discourse and Human Behavior in Modern Virtual Environments* (pp. 126–148). Hershey, PA: IGI Global. doi:10.4018/978-1-4666-9899-4.ch007

Kumar, K. (2018). Library in Your Pocket Delivery of Instruction Service Through Library Mobile Apps: A World in Your Pocket. In S. Bhattacharyya & K. Patnaik (Eds.), *Changing the Scope of Library Instruction in the Digital Age* (pp. 228–249). Hershey, PA: IGI Global. doi:10.4018/978-1-5225-2802-9.ch009

Kwanya, T. (2016). Information Seeking Behaviour in Digital Library Contexts. In A. Tella (Ed.), *Information Seeking Behavior and Challenges in Digital Libraries* (pp. 1–25). Hershey, PA: IGI Global. doi:10.4018/978-1-5225-0296-8.ch001

Kwanya, T. (2018). Social Bookmarking in Digital Libraries: Intellectual Property Rights Implications. In A. Tella & T. Kwanya (Eds.), *Handbook of Research on Managing Intellectual Property in Digital Libraries* (pp. 1–18). Hershey, PA: IGI Global. doi:10.4018/978-1-5225-3093-0.ch001

LaMoreaux, N. E. (2016). Collaborating to Create a Fashionable Event: A Guide for Creating a Library-Sponsored Conference. In B. Doherty (Ed.), *Space and Organizational Considerations in Academic Library Partnerships and Collaborations* (pp. 317–334). Hershey, PA: IGI Global. doi:10.4018/978-1-5225-0326-2.ch015

Lewis, J. K. (2018). Change Leadership Styles and Behaviors in Academic Libraries. In M. Khosrow-Pour, D.B.A. (Ed.), Encyclopedia of Information Science and Technology, Fourth Edition (pp. 5194-5203). Hershey, PA: IGI Global. doi:10.4018/978-1-5225-2255-3.ch451

Lillard, L. L. (2018). Is Interdisciplinary Collaboration in Academia an Elusive Dream?: Can the Institutional Barriers Be Broken Down? A Review of the Literature and the Case of Library Science. In M. Al-Suqri, A. Al-Kindi, S. AlKindi, & N. Saleem (Eds.), *Promoting Interdisciplinarity in Knowledge Generation and Problem Solving* (pp. 139–147). Hershey, PA: IGI Global. doi:10.4018/978-1-5225-3878-3.ch010

Lock, M. B., Fansler, C., & Webb, M. (2016). (R)Evolutionary Emergency Planning: Adding Resilience through Continuous Review. *International Journal of Risk and Contingency Management*, *5*(2), 47–65. doi:10.4018/IJRCM.2016040103

Long, X., & Yao, B. (2017). The Construction and Development of the Academic Digital Library of Chinese Ancient Collections. In L. Ruan, Q. Zhu, & Y. Ye (Eds.), *Academic Library Development and Administration in China* (pp. 126–135). Hershey, PA: IGI Global. doi:10.4018/978-1-5225-0550-1.ch008

Lowe, M., & Reno, L. M. (2018). Academic Librarianship and Burnout. In *Examining the Emotional Dimensions of Academic Librarianship: Emerging Research and Opportunities* (pp. 72–89). Hershey, PA: IGI Global. doi:10.4018/978-1-5225-3761-8.ch005

Lowe, M., & Reno, L. M. (2018). Emotional Dimensions of Academic Librarianship. In *Examining the Emotional Dimensions of Academic Librarianship: Emerging Research and Opportunities* (pp. 54–71). Hershey, PA: IGI Global. doi:10.4018/978-1-5225-3761-8.ch004

Lowe, M., & Reno, L. M. (2018). Why Isn't This Being Studied? In *Examining the Emotional Dimensions of Academic Librarianship: Emerging Research and Opportunities* (pp. 90–108). Hershey, PA: IGI Global. doi:10.4018/978-1-5225-3761-8.ch006

Lowe, M., & Reno, L. M. (2018). Research Agenda: Research Ideas and Recommendations. In *Examining the Emotional Dimensions of Academic Librarianship: Emerging Research and Opportunities* (pp. 109–125). Hershey, PA: IGI Global. doi:10.4018/978-1-5225-3761-8.ch007

Related References

Luyombya, D., Kiyingi, G. W., & Naluwooza, M. (2018). The Nature and Utilisation of Archival Records Deposited in Makerere University Library, Uganda. In P. Ngulube (Ed.), *Handbook of Research on Heritage Management and Preservation* (pp. 96–113). Hershey, PA: IGI Global. doi:10.4018/978-1-5225-3137-1.ch005

Mabe, M., & Ashley, E. A. (2017). The Natural Role of the Public Library. In *The Developing Role of Public Libraries in Emergency Management: Emerging Research and Opportunities* (pp. 25–43). Hershey, PA: IGI Global. doi:10.4018/978-1-5225-2196-9.ch003

Mabe, M., & Ashley, E. A. (2017). I'm Trained, Now What? In *The Developing Role of Public Libraries in Emergency Management: Emerging Research and Opportunities* (pp. 87–95). Hershey, PA: IGI Global. doi:10.4018/978-1-5225-2196-9.ch007

Mabe, M., & Ashley, E. A. (2017). Emergency Preparation for the Library and Librarian. In *The Developing Role of Public Libraries in Emergency Management: Emerging Research and Opportunities* (pp. 61–78). Hershey, PA: IGI Global. doi:10.4018/978-1-5225-2196-9.ch005

Mabe, M., & Ashley, E. A. (2017). The CCPL Model. In *The Developing Role of Public Libraries in Emergency Management: Emerging Research and Opportunities* (pp. 15–24). Hershey, PA: IGI Global. doi:10.4018/978-1-5225-2196-9.ch002

Mabe, M., & Ashley, E. A. (2017). The Local Command Structure and How the Library Fits. In *In The Developing Role of Public Libraries in Emergency Management: Emerging Research and Opportunities* (pp. 44–60). Hershey, PA: IGI Global. doi:10.4018/978-1-5225-2196-9.ch004

Mabe, M. R. (2016). Libraries to the Rescue. *International Journal of Risk and Contingency Management, 5*(1), 62–81. doi:10.4018/IJRCM.2016010105

Mabe, M. R. (2016). The Library as Lifeboat. In E. Decker & J. Townes (Eds.), *Handbook of Research on Disaster Management and Contingency Planning in Modern Libraries* (pp. 494–515). Hershey, PA: IGI Global. doi:10.4018/978-1-4666-8624-3.ch021

Manzoor, A. (2018). Social Media: A Librarian's Tool for Instant and Direct Interaction With Library Users. In R. Bhardwaj (Ed.), *Digitizing the Modern Library and the Transition From Print to Electronic* (pp. 112–128). Hershey, PA: IGI Global. doi:10.4018/978-1-5225-2119-8.ch005

Maringanti, H. (2018). A Decision Making Paradigm for Software Development in Libraries. In L. Costello & M. Powers (Eds.), *Developing In-House Digital Tools in Library Spaces* (pp. 59–75). Hershey, PA: IGI Global. doi:10.4018/978-1-5225-2676-6.ch003

Markman, K. M., Ferrarini, M., & Deschenes, A. H. (2018). User Testing and Iterative Design in the Academic Library: A Case Study. In R. Roscoe, S. Craig, & I. Douglas (Eds.), *End-User Considerations in Educational Technology Design* (pp. 160–183). Hershey, PA: IGI Global. doi:10.4018/978-1-5225-2639-1.ch008

Marks, A. B., & Owen, E. (2016). It Is Everywhere: Handling a Mold Outbreak in a Library's High-Density Storage Collection. In E. Decker & J. Townes (Eds.), *Handbook of Research on Disaster Management and Contingency Planning in Modern Libraries* (pp. 311–339). Hershey, PA: IGI Global. doi:10.4018/978-1-4666-8624-3.ch014

Mavodza, J. (2016). Relationship between Knowledge Management and Academic Integrity in a Middle Eastern University. In A. Goel & P. Singhal (Eds.), *Product Innovation through Knowledge Management and Social Media Strategies* (pp. 241–264). Hershey, PA: IGI Global. doi:10.4018/978-1-4666-9607-5.ch011

Maynor, A. (2016). Response to the Unthinkable: Collecting and Archiving Condolence and Temporary Memorial Materials following Public Tragedies. In E. Decker & J. Townes (Eds.), *Handbook of Research on Disaster Management and Contingency Planning in Modern Libraries* (pp. 582–624). Hershey, PA: IGI Global. doi:10.4018/978-1-4666-8624-3.ch025

McFall, L. M., Simons, J. T., Lord, G., MacDonald, P. J., Nieves, A. D., & Young, S. (2016). Collaborations in Liberal Arts Colleges in Support of Digital Humanities. In B. Doherty (Ed.), *Technology-Centered Academic Library Partnerships and Collaborations* (pp. 31–60). Hershey, PA: IGI Global. doi:10.4018/978-1-5225-0323-1.ch002

Na, L. (2017). Library and Information Science Education and Graduate Programs in Academic Libraries. In L. Ruan, Q. Zhu, & Y. Ye (Eds.), *Academic Library Development and Administration in China* (pp. 218–229). Hershey, PA: IGI Global. doi:10.4018/978-1-5225-0550-1.ch013

Nagarkar, S. P. (2017). Biomedical Librarianship in the Post-Genomic Era. In S. Ram (Ed.), *Library and Information Services for Bioinformatics Education and Research* (pp. 1–17). Hershey, PA: IGI Global. doi:10.4018/978-1-5225-1871-6.ch001

Natarajan, M. (2016). Exploring the E-Discovery Tools on the Use of Library Collections by Users. In E. de Smet & S. Dhamdhere (Eds.), *E-Discovery Tools and Applications in Modern Libraries* (pp. 122–137). Hershey, PA: IGI Global. doi:10.4018/978-1-5225-0474-0.ch007

Natarajan, M. (2017). Exploring Knowledge Sharing over Social Media. In R. Chugh (Ed.), *Harnessing Social Media as a Knowledge Management Tool* (pp. 55–73). Hershey, PA: IGI Global. doi:10.4018/978-1-5225-0495-5.ch003

Nazir, T. (2017). Preservation Initiatives in E-Environment to Protect Information Assets. In T. Ashraf & N. Kumar (Eds.), *Interdisciplinary Digital Preservation Tools and Technologies* (pp. 193–208). Hershey, PA: IGI Global. doi:10.4018/978-1-5225-1653-8.ch010

Ngulube, P. (2017). Embedding Indigenous Knowledge in Library and Information Science Education in Anglophone Eastern and Southern Africa. In P. Ngulube (Ed.), *Handbook of Research on Social, Cultural, and Educational Considerations of Indigenous Knowledge in Developing Countries* (pp. 92–115). Hershey, PA: IGI Global. doi:10.4018/978-1-5225-0838-0.ch006

Nicolajsen, H. W., Sørensen, F., & Scupola, A. (2016). The Potential of Workshops vs Blogs for User Involvement in Service Innovation. *International Journal of E-Services and Mobile Applications*, 8(4), 1–19. doi:10.4018/IJESMA.2016100101

Nicolajsen, H. W., Sorensen, F., & Scupola, A. (2018). User Involvement in Service Innovation Processes. In M. Khosrow-Pour (Ed.), *Optimizing Current Practices in E-Services and Mobile Applications* (pp. 42–61). Hershey, PA: IGI Global. doi:10.4018/978-1-5225-5026-6.ch003

Nixon, M. L. (2016). Safety Doesn't Happen by Accident: Disaster Planning at the University of Pittsburgh. In E. Decker & J. Townes (Eds.), *Handbook of Research on Disaster Management and Contingency Planning in Modern Libraries* (pp. 184–206). Hershey, PA: IGI Global. doi:10.4018/978-1-4666-8624-3.ch009

Nwabueze, A. U., & Ibeh, B. O. (2016). Extent of ICT Literacy Possessed by Librarians in Federal University Libraries in South East Nigeria. *International Journal of Digital Literacy and Digital Competence*, 7(3), 13–22. doi:10.4018/IJDLDC.2016070102

O'Grady, A. R. (2016). The Boston Library Consortium and RapidR: Partnering to Develop an Unmediated Book Sharing Module. In B. Doherty (Ed.), *Technology-Centered Academic Library Partnerships and Collaborations* (pp. 194–219). Hershey, PA: IGI Global. doi:10.4018/978-1-5225-0323-1.ch007

Ochonogor, W. C., & Okite-Amughoro, F. A. (2018). Building an Effective Digital Library in a University Teaching Hospital (UTH) in Nigeria. In A. Tella & T. Kwanya (Eds.), *Handbook of Research on Managing Intellectual Property in Digital Libraries* (pp. 184–204). Hershey, PA: IGI Global. doi:10.4018/978-1-5225-3093-0.ch010

Oladapo, Y. O. (2018). Open Access to Knowledge and Challenges in Digital Libraries. In A. Tella & T. Kwanya (Eds.), *Handbook of Research on Managing Intellectual Property in Digital Libraries* (pp. 260–291). Hershey, PA: IGI Global. doi:10.4018/978-1-5225-3093-0.ch014

Oladokun, O., & Zulu, S. F. (2017). Document Description and Coding as Key Elements in Knowledge, Records, and Information Management. In P. Jain & N. Mnjama (Eds.), *Managing Knowledge Resources and Records in Modern Organizations* (pp. 179–197). Hershey, PA: IGI Global. doi:10.4018/978-1-5225-1965-2.ch011

Olin, J. R. (2016). Libraries and Digital Media. In B. Guzzetti & M. Lesley (Eds.), *Handbook of Research on the Societal Impact of Digital Media* (pp. 163–177). Hershey, PA: IGI Global. doi:10.4018/978-1-4666-8310-5.ch007

Oluwaseun, A. A. (2016). Barriers to Information Seeking in the Digital Libraries. In A. Tella (Ed.), *Information Seeking Behavior and Challenges in Digital Libraries* (pp. 291–303). Hershey, PA: IGI Global. doi:10.4018/978-1-5225-0296-8.ch014

Omeluzor, S. U., Abayomi, I., & Gbemi-Ogunleye, P. (2018). Contemporary Media for Library Users' Instruction in Academic Libraries in South-West Nigeria: Contemporary Library Instruction in the Digital Age. In S. Bhattacharyya & K. Patnaik (Eds.), *Changing the Scope of Library Instruction in the Digital Age* (pp. 162–185). Hershey, PA: IGI Global. doi:10.4018/978-1-5225-2802-9.ch007

Ondari-Okemwa, E. (2016). Information-Seeking Behaviour of Users in the Digital Libraries' Environment in Sub-Saharan Africa. In A. Tella (Ed.), *Information Seeking Behavior and Challenges in Digital Libraries* (pp. 26–56). Hershey, PA: IGI Global. doi:10.4018/978-1-5225-0296-8.ch002

Oshilalu, A. H., & Ogochukwu, E. T. (2017). Modeling a Software for Library and Information Centers. *International Journal of Library and Information Services*, 6(2), 1–10. doi:10.4018/IJLIS.2017070101

Osterman, A. C., O'Gara, G., & Armstrong, A. M. (2016). The Evolution of Collaborative Collection Development within a Library Consortium: Data Analysis Applied in a Cultural Context. In B. Doherty (Ed.), *Space and Organizational Considerations in Academic Library Partnerships and Collaborations* (pp. 157–181). Hershey, PA: IGI Global. doi:10.4018/978-1-5225-0326-2.ch008

Oswal, S. K. (2017). Institutional, Legal, and Attitudinal Barriers to the Accessibility of University Digital Libraries: Implications for Retention of Disabled Students. In H. Alphin Jr, J. Lavine, & R. Chan (Eds.), *Disability and Equity in Higher Education Accessibility* (pp. 223–241). Hershey, PA: IGI Global. doi:10.4018/978-1-5225-2665-0.ch010

Otike, J. (2016). Legal Considerations of Providing Information in Support of Distance Learning by Digital Libraries in Universities in Kenya. In A. Tella (Ed.), *Information Seeking Behavior and Challenges in Digital Libraries* (pp. 57–69). Hershey, PA: IGI Global. doi:10.4018/978-1-5225-0296-8.ch003

Oukrich, J., & Bouikhalene, B. (2017). A Survey of Users' Satisfaction in the University Library by Using a Pareto Analysis and the Automatic Classification Methods. *International Journal of Library and Information Services*, 6(1), 17–36. doi:10.4018/IJLIS.2017010102

Özel, N. (2018). Developing Visual Literacy Skills Through Library Instructions. In V. Osinska & G. Osinski (Eds.), *Information Visualization Techniques in the Social Sciences and Humanities* (pp. 32–48). Hershey, PA: IGI Global. doi:10.4018/978-1-5225-4990-1.ch003

Patel, D., & Thakur, D. (2017). Managing Open Access (OA) Scholarly Information Resources in a University. In A. Munigal (Ed.), *Scholarly Communication and the Publish or Perish Pressures of Academia* (pp. 224–255). Hershey, PA: IGI Global. doi:10.4018/978-1-5225-1697-2.ch011

Patnaik, K. R. (2018). Crafting a Framework for Copyright Literacy and Licensed Content: A Case Study at an Advanced Management Education and Research Library. In S. Bhattacharyya & K. Patnaik (Eds.), *Changing the Scope of Library Instruction in the Digital Age* (pp. 136–160). Hershey, PA: IGI Global. doi:10.4018/978-1-5225-2802-9.ch006

Paynter, K. (2017). Elementary Library Media Specialists' Roles in the Implementation of the Common Core State Standards. In M. Grassetti & S. Brookby (Eds.), *Advancing Next-Generation Teacher Education through Digital Tools and Applications* (pp. 262–283). Hershey, PA: IGI Global. doi:10.4018/978-1-5225-0965-3.ch014

Perez, M. J. (2016). Local Studies Centers in the Philippines: An Introductory Text. In J. Yap, M. Perez, M. Ayson, & G. Entico (Eds.), *Special Library Administration, Standardization and Technological Integration* (pp. 249–266). Hershey, PA: IGI Global. doi:10.4018/978-1-4666-9542-9.ch011

Perry, S. C., & Waggoner, J. (2018). Processes for User-Centered Design and Development: The Omeka Curator Dashboard Project. In L. Costello & M. Powers (Eds.), *Developing In-House Digital Tools in Library Spaces* (pp. 37–58). Hershey, PA: IGI Global. doi:10.4018/978-1-5225-2676-6.ch002

Phuritsabam, B., & Devi, A. B. (2017). Information Seeking Behavior of Medical Scientists at Jawaharlal Nehru Institute of Medical Science: A Study. In S. Ram (Ed.), *Library and Information Services for Bioinformatics Education and Research* (pp. 177–187). Hershey, PA: IGI Global. doi:10.4018/978-1-5225-1871-6.ch010

Pina, P. (2016). Copyright Issues in the Context of the Digital Library. In A. Tella (Ed.), *Information Seeking Behavior and Challenges in Digital Libraries* (pp. 70–83). Hershey, PA: IGI Global. doi:10.4018/978-1-5225-0296-8.ch004

Pionke, J. (2016). Disaster is in the Eye of the Beholder. In E. Decker & J. Townes (Eds.), *Handbook of Research on Disaster Management and Contingency Planning in Modern Libraries* (pp. 516–533). Hershey, PA: IGI Global. doi:10.4018/978-1-4666-8624-3.ch022

Quadri, R. F., & Sodiq, O. A. (2018). Managing Intellectual Property in Digital Libraries: The Roles of Digital Librarians. In A. Tella & T. Kwanya (Eds.), *Handbook of Research on Managing Intellectual Property in Digital Libraries* (pp. 337–355). Hershey, PA: IGI Global. doi:10.4018/978-1-5225-3093-0.ch017

Ram, S. (2017). Library Services for Bioinformatics: Establishing Synergy Data Information and Knowledge. In S. Ram (Ed.), *Library and Information Services for Bioinformatics Education and Research* (pp. 18–33). Hershey, PA: IGI Global. doi:10.4018/978-1-5225-1871-6.ch002

Rao, M. (2017). Use of Institutional Repository for Information Dissemination and Knowledge Management. In B. Gunjal (Ed.), *Managing Knowledge and Scholarly Assets in Academic Libraries* (pp. 156–173). Hershey, PA: IGI Global. doi:10.4018/978-1-5225-1741-2.ch007

Rao, Y., & Zhang, Y. (2017). The Construction and Development of Academic Library Digital Special Subject Databases. In L. Ruan, Q. Zhu, & Y. Ye (Eds.), *Academic Library Development and Administration in China* (pp. 163–183). Hershey, PA: IGI Global. doi:10.4018/978-1-5225-0550-1.ch010

Razip, S. N., Kadir, S. F., Saim, S. N., Dolhan, F. N., Jarmil, N., Salleh, N. H., & Rajin, G. (2017). Predicting Users' Intention towards Using Library Self-Issue and Return Systems. In N. Suki (Ed.), *Handbook of Research on Leveraging Consumer Psychology for Effective Customer Engagement* (pp. 102–115). Hershey, PA: IGI Global. doi:10.4018/978-1-5225-0746-8.ch007

Ress, A. D., McLaughlin, J. A., & Bertuca, C. (2016). Online Video Tutorials and Interlibrary Resource Sharing: A Model for Understanding the Role of Internet Video in Library Science and Education. In B. Doherty (Ed.), *Technology-Centered Academic Library Partnerships and Collaborations* (pp. 61–88). Hershey, PA: IGI Global. doi:10.4018/978-1-5225-0323-1.ch003

Rothwell, S. L. (2018). Librarians and Instructional Design Challenges: Concepts, Examples, and a Flexible Design Framework. In S. Bhattacharyya & K. Patnaik (Eds.), *Changing the Scope of Library Instruction in the Digital Age* (pp. 24–59). Hershey, PA: IGI Global. doi:10.4018/978-1-5225-2802-9.ch002

Roy, L., & Frydman, A. (2018). Community Outreach. In M. Khosrow-Pour, D.B.A. (Ed.), Encyclopedia of Information Science and Technology, Fourth Edition (pp. 6685-6694). Hershey, PA: IGI Global. doi:10.4018/978-1-5225-2255-3.ch579

Rutto, D., & Yudah, O. (2018). E-Books in University Libraries in Kenya: Trends, Usage, and Intellectual Property Issues. In A. Tella & T. Kwanya (Eds.), *Handbook of Research on Managing Intellectual Property in Digital Libraries* (pp. 120–141). Hershey, PA: IGI Global. doi:10.4018/978-1-5225-3093-0.ch007

Ryan, S. M., & Grubbs, W. T. (2016). Curricular Collaborations: Using Emerging Technologies to Foster Innovative Partnerships. In B. Doherty (Ed.), *Technology-Centered Academic Library Partnerships and Collaborations* (pp. 89–125). Hershey, PA: IGI Global. doi:10.4018/978-1-5225-0323-1.ch004

Sabharwal, A. (2017). The Transformative Role of Institutional Repositories in Academic Knowledge Management. In B. Gunjal (Ed.), *Managing Knowledge and Scholarly Assets in Academic Libraries* (pp. 127–155). Hershey, PA: IGI Global. doi:10.4018/978-1-5225-1741-2.ch006

Sadiku, S. A., Kpakiko, M. M., & Tsafe, A. G. (2018). Institutional Digital Repository and the Challenges of Global Visibility in Nigeria. In A. Tella & T. Kwanya (Eds.), *Handbook of Research on Managing Intellectual Property in Digital Libraries* (pp. 356–376). Hershey, PA: IGI Global. doi:10.4018/978-1-5225-3093-0.ch018

Sahu, M. K. (2018). Web-Scale Discovery Service in Academic Library Environment: A Birds Eye View. *International Journal of Library and Information Services*, *7*(1), 1–14. doi:10.4018/IJLIS.2018010101

Salim, F., Saigar, B., Armoham, P. K., Gobalakrishnan, S., Jap, M. Y., & Lim, N. A. (2017). Students' Information-Seeking Intention in Academic Digital Libraries. In N. Suki (Ed.), *Handbook of Research on Leveraging Consumer Psychology for Effective Customer Engagement* (pp. 259–273). Hershey, PA: IGI Global. doi:10.4018/978-1-5225-0746-8.ch017

San Kong, E. W., Chiu, D. K., & Ho, K. K. (2016). Applications of Social Media in Academic Library Services: A Case of the Hong Kong Polytechnic University Library. *International Journal of Systems and Service-Oriented Engineering, 6*(2), 53–65. doi:10.4018/IJSSOE.2016040103

Saroja, G. (2017). Changing Face of Scholarly Communication and Its Impact on Library and Information Centres. In A. Munigal (Ed.), *Scholarly Communication and the Publish or Perish Pressures of Academia* (pp. 100–117). Hershey, PA: IGI Global. doi:10.4018/978-1-5225-1697-2.ch006

Sawant, S. (2016). Collaborative Online Learning Tools and Types: Few Perspectives of Its Use in Academic Library. In H. Rahman (Ed.), *Human Development and Interaction in the Age of Ubiquitous Technology* (pp. 94–119). Hershey, PA: IGI Global. doi:10.4018/978-1-5225-0556-3.ch005

Sawsaa, A. F., & Lu, J. (2017). Research Background on Ontology. In J. Lu & Q. Xu (Eds.), *Ontologies and Big Data Considerations for Effective Intelligence* (pp. 443–509). Hershey, PA: IGI Global. doi:10.4018/978-1-5225-2058-0.ch011

Schuster, D. W. (2017). Selection Process for Free Open Source Software. In E. Iglesias (Ed.), *Library Technology Funding, Planning, and Deployment* (pp. 55–71). Hershey, PA: IGI Global. doi:10.4018/978-1-5225-1735-1.ch004

Segaetsho, T. (2018). Environmental Consideration in the Preservation of Paper Materials in Heritage Institutions in the East and Southern African Region. In P. Ngulube (Ed.), *Handbook of Research on Heritage Management and Preservation* (pp. 183–212). Hershey, PA: IGI Global. doi:10.4018/978-1-5225-3137-1.ch010

Shakhsi, L. (2017). Cataloging Images in Library, Archive, and Museum. In T. Ashraf & N. Kumar (Eds.), *Interdisciplinary Digital Preservation Tools and Technologies* (pp. 119–141). Hershey, PA: IGI Global. doi:10.4018/978-1-5225-1653-8.ch007

Sharma, C. (2017). Digital Initiatives of the Indian Council of World Affairs' Library. In T. Ashraf & N. Kumar (Eds.), *Interdisciplinary Digital Preservation Tools and Technologies* (pp. 231–241). Hershey, PA: IGI Global. doi:10.4018/978-1-5225-1653-8.ch012

Shaw, M. D. (2016). Navigating Campus Disasters from Within the Library: Lessons and Implications from Gulf Coast Institutions. In E. Decker & J. Townes (Eds.), *Handbook of Research on Disaster Management and Contingency Planning in Modern Libraries* (pp. 340–365). Hershey, PA: IGI Global. doi:10.4018/978-1-4666-8624-3.ch015

Shawish, A., & Salama, M. (2016). Cloud-Based Digital Library Era. In J. Yap, M. Perez, M. Ayson, & G. Entico (Eds.), *Special Library Administration, Standardization and Technological Integration* (pp. 226–247). Hershey, PA: IGI Global. doi:10.4018/978-1-4666-9542-9.ch010

Siddaiah, D. K. (2018). Commonwealth Professional Fellowship: A Gateway for the Strategic Development of Libraries in India. In R. Bhardwaj (Ed.), *Digitizing the Modern Library and the Transition From Print to Electronic* (pp. 270–286). Hershey, PA: IGI Global. doi:10.4018/978-1-5225-2119-8.ch012

Silvana de Rosa, A. (2018). Mission, Tools, and Ongoing Developments in the So.Re. Com. "A.S. de Rosa" @-library. In M. Khosrow-Pour, D.B.A. (Ed.), Encyclopedia of Information Science and Technology, Fourth Edition (pp. 5237-5251). Hershey, PA: IGI Global. doi:10.4018/978-1-5225-2255-3.ch455

Silverman, R., Nakashima, T., Hunt, J. M., & Tuia, J. (2016). A Stitch in Time: Disaster Mitigation Strategies for Cultural Heritage Collections. In E. Decker & J. Townes (Eds.), *Handbook of Research on Disaster Management and Contingency Planning in Modern Libraries* (pp. 208–239). Hershey, PA: IGI Global. doi:10.4018/978-1-4666-8624-3.ch010

Smart, C. (2016). The Public Library's Role in Enabling E-Government: A View of Two Countries in the English-Speaking Caribbean. *International Journal of Public Administration in the Digital Age*, *3*(3), 18–32. doi:10.4018/IJPADA.2016070102

Smolenski, N., Kostic, M., & Sofronijevic, A. M. (2018). Intrapreneurship and Enterprise 2.0 as Grounds for Developing In-House Digital Tools for Handling METS/ALTO Files at the University Library Belgrade. In L. Costello & M. Powers (Eds.), *Developing In-House Digital Tools in Library Spaces* (pp. 92–116). Hershey, PA: IGI Global. doi:10.4018/978-1-5225-2676-6.ch005

Sochay, L., & Junus, R. (2017). From Summon to SearchPlus: The RFP Process for a Discovery Tool at the MSU Libraries. In E. Iglesias (Ed.), *Library Technology Funding, Planning, and Deployment* (pp. 72–98). Hershey, PA: IGI Global. doi:10.4018/978-1-5225-1735-1.ch005

Sonawane, C. S. (2018). Library Catalogue in the Internet Age. In R. Bhardwaj (Ed.), *Digitizing the Modern Library and the Transition From Print to Electronic* (pp. 204–223). Hershey, PA: IGI Global. doi:10.4018/978-1-5225-2119-8.ch009

Sonawane, M. (2016). Creating an Agile Library. In E. de Smet & S. Dhamdhere (Eds.), *E-Discovery Tools and Applications in Modern Libraries* (pp. 109–121). Hershey, PA: IGI Global. doi:10.4018/978-1-5225-0474-0.ch006

Staley, C., Kenyon, R. S., & Marcovitz, D. M. (2018). Embedded Services: Going Beyond the Field of Dreams Model for Online Programs. In D. Polly, M. Putman, T. Petty, & A. Good (Eds.), *Innovative Practices in Teacher Preparation and Graduate-Level Teacher Education Programs* (pp. 368–381). Hershey, PA: IGI Global. doi:10.4018/978-1-5225-3068-8.ch020

Stavridi, S. V., & Hamada, D. R. (2016). Children and Youth Librarians: Competencies Required in Technology-Based Environment. In J. Yap, M. Perez, M. Ayson, & G. Entico (Eds.), *Special Library Administration, Standardization and Technological Integration* (pp. 25–50). Hershey, PA: IGI Global. doi:10.4018/978-1-4666-9542-9. ch002

Stewart, M. C., Atilano, M., & Arnold, C. L. (2017). Improving Customer Relations with Social Listening: A Case Study of an American Academic Library. *International Journal of Customer Relationship Marketing and Management*, 8(1), 49–63. doi:10.4018/IJCRMM.2017010104

Sukula, S. K., & Bhardwaj, R. K. (2018). An Extensive Discussion on Transition of Libraries: The Panoramic View of Library Resources, Services, and Evolved Librarianship. In R. Bhardwaj (Ed.), *Digitizing the Modern Library and the Transition From Print to Electronic* (pp. 255–269). Hershey, PA: IGI Global. doi:10.4018/978-1-5225-2119-8.ch011

Taylor, L. N., Alteri, S. A., Minson, V. I., Walker, B., Hawley, E. H., Dinsmore, C. S., & Jefferson, R. J. (2016). Library Collaborative Networks Forging Scholarly Cyberinfrastructure and Radical Collaboration. In B. Doherty (Ed.), *Technology-Centered Academic Library Partnerships and Collaborations* (pp. 1–30). Hershey, PA: IGI Global. doi:10.4018/978-1-5225-0323-1.ch001

Tella, A., & Babatunde, B. J. (2017). Determinants of Continuance Intention of Facebook Usage Among Library and Information Science Female Undergraduates in Selected Nigerian Universities. *International Journal of E-Adoption*, 9(2), 59–76. doi:10.4018/IJEA.2017070104

Tella, A., Okojie, V., & Olaniyi, O. T. (2018). Social Bookmarking Tools and Digital Libraries. In A. Tella & T. Kwanya (Eds.), *Handbook of Research on Managing Intellectual Property in Digital Libraries* (pp. 396–409). Hershey, PA: IGI Global. doi:10.4018/978-1-5225-3093-0.ch020

Tella, A., Oyeniran, S., & Ojo, O. J. (2016). Digital Libraries and Copyright Issues. In A. Tella (Ed.), *Information Seeking Behavior and Challenges in Digital Libraries* (pp. 108–126). Hershey, PA: IGI Global. doi:10.4018/978-1-5225-0296-8.ch006

Thull, J. J. (2018). Librarians and the Evolving Research Needs of Distance Students. In I. Oncioiu (Ed.), *Ethics and Decision-Making for Sustainable Business Practices* (pp. 203–216). Hershey, PA: IGI Global. doi:10.4018/978-1-5225-3773-1.ch012

Titilope, A. O. (2017). Ethical Issues in Library and Information Science Profession in Nigeria: An Appraisal. *International Journal of Library and Information Services*, 6(2), 11–22. doi:10.4018/IJLIS.2017070102

Tutu, J. M. (2018). Intellectual Property Challenges in Digital Library Environments. In A. Tella & T. Kwanya (Eds.), *Handbook of Research on Managing Intellectual Property in Digital Libraries* (pp. 225–240). Hershey, PA: IGI Global. doi:10.4018/978-1-5225-3093-0.ch012

Upev, M. T., Beetseh, K., & Idachaba, J. A. (2016). Usability of Digital Resources: A Study of Francis Sulemanu Idachaba Library University of Agriculture Makurdi. In A. Tella (Ed.), *Information Seeking Behavior and Challenges in Digital Libraries* (pp. 224–237). Hershey, PA: IGI Global. doi:10.4018/978-1-5225-0296-8.ch011

Verplaetse, A., Mascareñas, P., & O'Neill, K. (2016). Zen and the Art of Disaster Planning: Collaboration Challenges in Library Disaster Plan Design and Execution. In E. Decker & J. Townes (Eds.), *Handbook of Research on Disaster Management and Contingency Planning in Modern Libraries* (pp. 96–119). Hershey, PA: IGI Global. doi:10.4018/978-1-4666-8624-3.ch005

Walker, B., & Pursley, T. (2016). A Statewide Collaborative Storage and Print Repository Model: The Florida Academic Repository (FLARE). In B. Doherty (Ed.), *Space and Organizational Considerations in Academic Library Partnerships and Collaborations* (pp. 111–129). Hershey, PA: IGI Global. doi:10.4018/978-1-5225-0326-2.ch006

Wallace, D., & Hemment, M. (2018). Enabling Scholarship in the Digital Age: A Case for Libraries Creating Value at HBS. In S. Bhattacharyya & K. Patnaik (Eds.), *Changing the Scope of Library Instruction in the Digital Age* (pp. 86–117). Hershey, PA: IGI Global. doi:10.4018/978-1-5225-2802-9.ch004

Wani, Z. A., Zainab, T., & Hussain, S. (2018). Web 2.0 From Evolution to Revolutionary Impact in Library and Information Centers. In M. Khosrow-Pour, D.B.A. (Ed.), Encyclopedia of Information Science and Technology, Fourth Edition (pp. 5262-5271). Hershey, PA: IGI Global. doi:10.4018/978-1-5225-2255-3.ch457

Waring, S. M. (2016). Teaching with Primary Sources: Moving from Professional Development to a Model of Professional Learning. In T. Petty, A. Good, & S. Putman (Eds.), *Handbook of Research on Professional Development for Quality Teaching and Learning* (pp. 295–306). Hershey, PA: IGI Global. doi:10.4018/978-1-5225-0204-3.ch014

Weiss, A. P. (2018). Massive Digital Libraries (MDLs). In M. Khosrow-Pour, D.B.A. (Ed.), Encyclopedia of Information Science and Technology, Fourth Edition (pp. 5226-5236). Hershey, PA: IGI Global. doi:10.4018/978-1-5225-2255-3.ch454

Wentao, C., Jinyu, Z., & Zhonggen, Y. (2016). Learning Outcomes and Affective Factors of Blended Learning of English for Library Science. *International Journal of Information and Communication Technology Education, 12*(3), 13–25. doi:10.4018/IJICTE.2016070102

White, G. W. (2016). The Library as a Center for Innovation: A Collaboration at the University of Maryland. In B. Doherty (Ed.), *Space and Organizational Considerations in Academic Library Partnerships and Collaborations* (pp. 68–86). Hershey, PA: IGI Global. doi:10.4018/978-1-5225-0326-2.ch004

Wu, S. K., Bess, M., & Price, B. R. (2018). Digitizing Library Outreach: Leveraging Bluetooth Beacons and Mobile Applications to Expand Library Outreach. In R. Bhardwaj (Ed.), *Digitizing the Modern Library and the Transition From Print to Electronic* (pp. 193–203). Hershey, PA: IGI Global. doi:10.4018/978-1-5225-2119-8.ch008

Wulff, E. (2018). Evaluation of Digital Collections and Political Visibility of the Library. In R. Bhardwaj (Ed.), *Digitizing the Modern Library and the Transition From Print to Electronic* (pp. 64–89). Hershey, PA: IGI Global. doi:10.4018/978-1-5225-2119-8.ch003

Xiao, L., & Liu, Y. (2017). Development of Innovative User Services. In L. Ruan, Q. Zhu, & Y. Ye (Eds.), *Academic Library Development and Administration in China* (pp. 56–73). Hershey, PA: IGI Global. doi:10.4018/978-1-5225-0550-1.ch004

Xin, X., & Wu, X. (2017). The Practice of Outreach Services in Chinese Special Libraries. In L. Ruan, Q. Zhu, & Y. Ye (Eds.), *Academic Library Development and Administration in China* (pp. 74–89). Hershey, PA: IGI Global. doi:10.4018/978-1-5225-0550-1.ch005

Yao, X., Zhu, Q., & Liu, J. (2017). The China Academic Library and Information System (CALIS). In L. Ruan, Q. Zhu, & Y. Ye (Eds.), *Academic Library Development and Administration in China* (pp. 1–19). Hershey, PA: IGI Global. doi:10.4018/978-1-5225-0550-1.ch001

Yap, J. M. (2016). Social Media Literacy of Agricultural Librarians in the Philippines. In J. Yap, M. Perez, M. Ayson, & G. Entico (Eds.), *Special Library Administration, Standardization and Technological Integration* (pp. 202–224). Hershey, PA: IGI Global. doi:10.4018/978-1-4666-9542-9.ch009

Yasue, A. (2016). Preservation Management in Company Libraries. In J. Yap, M. Perez, M. Ayson, & G. Entico (Eds.), *Special Library Administration, Standardization and Technological Integration* (pp. 305–314). Hershey, PA: IGI Global. doi:10.4018/978-1-4666-9542-9.ch013

Yin, Q., Yingying, W., Yan, Z., & Xiaojia, M. (2017). Resource Sharing and Mutually Beneficial Cooperation: A Look at the New United Model in Public and College Libraries. In L. Ruan, Q. Zhu, & Y. Ye (Eds.), *Academic Library Development and Administration in China* (pp. 334–352). Hershey, PA: IGI Global. doi:10.4018/978-1-5225-0550-1.ch019

Yuhua, F. (2018). Computer Information Library Clusters. In M. Khosrow-Pour, D.B.A. (Ed.), Encyclopedia of Information Science and Technology, Fourth Edition (pp. 4399-4403). Hershey, PA: IGI Global. doi:10.4018/978-1-5225-2255-3.ch382

Yusuf, F., Owolabi, S., Aregbesola, A., Oguntayo, S., Okocha, F., & Eyiolorunse, T. (2016). Demographics, Socio-Economic and Cognitive Skills as Barriers to Information Seeking in a Digital Library Environment. In A. Tella (Ed.), *Information Seeking Behavior and Challenges in Digital Libraries* (pp. 179–202). Hershey, PA: IGI Global. doi:10.4018/978-1-5225-0296-8.ch009

Yusuf, F., & Owolabi, S. E. (2018). Open Access to Knowledge and Challenges in Digital Libraries: Nigeria's Peculiarity. In A. Tella & T. Kwanya (Eds.), *Handbook of Research on Managing Intellectual Property in Digital Libraries* (pp. 241–259). Hershey, PA: IGI Global. doi:10.4018/978-1-5225-3093-0.ch013

Yuvaraj, M. (2016). Impact of Discovery Layers on Accessing E-Resources in Academic Libraries: A Case Study of Central University of Bihar. In E. de Smet & S. Dhamdhere (Eds.), *E-Discovery Tools and Applications in Modern Libraries* (pp. 181–200). Hershey, PA: IGI Global. doi:10.4018/978-1-5225-0474-0.ch010

Zaremohzzabieh, Z., Ahrari, S., Abu Samah, B., & Bolong, J. (2016). Researching Information Seeking in Digital Libraries through Information-Seeking Models. In A. Tella (Ed.), *Information Seeking Behavior and Challenges in Digital Libraries* (pp. 84–107). Hershey, PA: IGI Global. doi:10.4018/978-1-5225-0296-8.ch005

Zhu, S., & Shi, W. (2017). A Bibliometric Analysis of Research and Services in Chinese Academic Libraries. In L. Ruan, Q. Zhu, & Y. Ye (Eds.), *Academic Library Development and Administration in China* (pp. 253–262). Hershey, PA: IGI Global. doi:10.4018/978-1-5225-0550-1.ch015

Zimeras, S., Kostagiolas, P., & Lavranos, C. (2016). Dealing with the Uncertainty of Satisfaction Surveys in Organizations That Employ Interactive Multimedia: An Analysis of False Answers Statistical Models through a Digital Music Library Case Study. In I. Deliyannis, P. Kostagiolas, & C. Banou (Eds.), *Experimental Multimedia Systems for Interactivity and Strategic Innovation* (pp. 160–175). Hershey, PA: IGI Global. doi:10.4018/978-1-4666-8659-5.ch008

About the Contributors

Nuno Vasco Lopes is a researcher at the United Nations University Operating Unit on Policy-Driven Electronic Governance (UNU-EGOV) and a professor on a part-time basis at the University of Minho. Currently, he holds two Postdoctoral positions. One on Computer Science at the University of Coimbra and other on Electronic Governance at the United Nations University. Since 1998 he has been teaching several courses in the areas of computer science and mathematics in different public, private, national and international universities. During his working life, he has been involved in several national, European and international projects, such as Electronic Governance for Context-Specific Public Service Delivery, Knowledge Society Policy Handbook, Policy Monitoring on Digital Technology for Inclusive Education, Intelligent Computing for Internet and Services, Internet of Things for Disabled People, Smart Defence and Smart Cities for Sustainable Development. He also delivers on a regular basis professional courses, seminars, and workshops on ICT, e-learning, computer networks, cybersecurity, smart cities, amongst others. [Biography pulled from the Profile]

* * *

Innocent Chirisa: DPhil, MSc, BSc Hons. Rural & Urban Planning, (University of Zimbabwe), DipLMISR (IHS, Erasmus University), MZIRUP (Zimbabwe), Full Professor teaching Urban and Environmental Planning courses in the Department of Rural & Urban Planning, University of Zimbabwe. Currently is serving as the Deputy Dean of the Faculty of Social Studies, University of Zimbabwe. Also he is currently serving as the Acting Chairman of the Department of Rural & Urban Planning, University of Zimbabwe Prof Chirisa was recently appointed as a Research Fellow, Department of Urban and Regional Planning, University of Free State, Bloemfontein, South Africa for the period 2016 to 2020.

Daiana Dai has a doctorate in progress in Information Science by the Fernando Pessoa University (Porto – Portugal), Master in Education by ULBRA (2013), Specialist in Educational Management by PUC-RS (2011) and Pedagogy with Qualification in Early Childhood Education, Early Education, Education and Matters Higher Education Pedagogics by ULBRA (2009). Experience in Distance Education, Early Childhood Education, Educational / Vocational Guidance and Pedagogical Counseling. Working as teacher in Distance Education in the courses of Pedagogy, Letters and Social Sciences of ULBRA and Manager of production of EAD content in Grupo A Educação - SAGAH.

Alba Kruja is lecturer at Epoka University in Albania, Department of Business Administration. She holds an MBA degree from Nebraska University, Lincoln, USA and a PhD degree in Entrepreneurship. She teaches courses of Entrepreneurship and Management Science on Bachelor, Master and PhD level. At Epoka University she holds also the administrative duties as Academic Coordinator of Business Informatics Program, board member of Permanent Commission on Quality Assurance and board member of Yunus Center for Social Business and Sustainability. Dr. Kruja has been a visiting professor at various other universities and is involved in many EU and regional projects. She is engaged in other contractual positions as Expert for national and international organizations such as European Commission; UK Tech Hub; EU for Innovation; Public Accreditation Agency for Higher Education, Republic of Albania. Dr. Kruja is the author of many research articles and book chapters. Her main research focus is on Entrepreneurship, Innovation and Small Business Management.

Abraham Rajab Matamanda holds a BSc Degree in Rural and Urban Planning and MSc in Social Ecology from the University of Zimbabwe. Currently, he is a PhD candidate in the Department of Urban and Regional Planning at the University of the Free State, South Africa. His study focuses on Applied Systems Analysis in planning with reference to urban dilemmas and emerging human settlements forms nexus. Abraham has published more than 10 articles and book chapters in national and international peer-reviewed journals that include Springer and two book chapters in Urbanisation and Its Impact on Socio-Economic Growth in Developing Regions. His research areas are urban sustainability, environmental planning and management, rural development and the planning of cities and towns.

Gift Mhlanga holds a BSc Hons in Economics from the University of Zimbabwe. Currently he is a Post-Graduate pursuing MSc, Economics, University of Zimbabwe. He is as a Graduate Teaching Assistant in the same department. His research interests are in development economics.

Roselin Ncube is a lecturer of Gender and Development at the Women's University in Africa (WUA). Her areas of research interest are gender, female entrepreneurship, and social innovation.

Lerida Shkrepa was born in Sarande, Albania in 15th of June 1994. In 2012 graduated from high school and successfully completed bachelor of Business Informatics in June 2017 at Epoka University. Currently studying masters of science of Business Informatics at University of Mannheim, Germany.

Ekta Sinha is working with Saraf College, University of Mumbai at present. She is associated with the Dept. of Management studies. Her area of interests are: Organizational behavior- Human Resources, Entrepreneurship, Education and ICT, Emotional Intelligence, Organizational communication and Gender studies.

Robert Tweheyo is a lecturer in the Department of sociology and Social Administration at Kyambogo University, Uganda. He holds a PhD in Social interventions focusing on indigenous knowledge and food security from the University of Groningen, The Netherlands. He is the founding head of the department of Sociology and Social Administration, at Kyambogo University. He has taught several course units in the department including Social Planning, Social Policy analysis, Theory and management of Organizations, Rural growth and Development among others. Robert enjoys engaged scholarship research approach that brings in various stakeholders in generating knowledge for solving society problems. His research interests are in areas of food security and community development. During the course of his PhD, he developed intervention schemata for aiding community development workers to enhance rural communities' decisions on food security. He has attended international conferences presented papers and in Germany, Netherlands and Uganda.

Showkat Ahmad Wani is the Research Fellow in Department of Library and Information Science, University of Kashmir-(190006) and currently working on UGC approved Mega Research Project (MRP) - "towards designing an information portal for arts and crafts in J&K state". He did his master's degree in Library & Information Science from the same Department and University. He had also qualified the J&KSET-exam (Eligibility for Assistant Professor Post). Besides, he had also done master's degree in History from IGNOU-Delhi, Bachelor of Education degree (B.ED) from University of Kashmir and One-year diploma in Computer Operator and Programming Assistant (C.O.P.A) from Govt. ITI GANDERBAL, Directorate of Technical Education J&K. He has authored the number of journal publications & book chapters in reputed journals and books published by renowned publishers (e.g. Emerald, IGI-Global etc.). Author has also attended several national & international conferences, seminars and workshops on different themes.

Index

A

Africa 2, 56, 60, 63-66, 68, 70, 73, 75, 83, 114, 140, 149, 156, 180, 183, 189-193, 195, 198, 201-203

Artisans and Craftsmen 158-159, 163-166, 168-171, 178

C

capabilities 11, 13, 20, 65-66, 78, 81, 85-86, 99, 166, 185, 223

Census 87, 90, 101, 120

cognitive capitalism 123, 131-134

Collaborative Decision-Making 13-15, 20

commitment 28, 141, 181, 184, 204

community workers 181, 190, 204

Connubio for Transformation 181, 204

continuing education 101, 122-128, 132, 134

D

development 1-2, 4-8, 11-12, 15-20, 22-23, 28, 31, 38, 43, 46, 48, 50, 52, 55-57, 60-61, 63-72, 74-76, 78-83, 85-87, 89, 93-100, 103-106, 108-111, 113, 115-119, 121, 123, 128, 130-131, 133, 139-140, 142-145, 148, 151-154, 156, 158-166, 168-173, 175-176, 178-180, 182-183, 186, 191, 193-195, 197, 199, 201-204, 206-209, 219, 222-223

Digital India 102-103, 105

dimensions 20-21, 24, 26, 48, 52, 55, 207, 223

E

economic sanctions 181, 183, 185, 187-191, 193-196, 198-199, 201-204

Endogenous Arrangements 181, 204

Engaged scholarship 1, 3, 6, 8-12, 14, 16-17, 19-20

entrepreneurship 36, 38, 40-41, 56, 74-75, 87, 94, 106, 112, 117, 120, 222-223

F

facilitate 11, 72, 85, 103, 105, 114, 120, 192, 219

Family-Centric Roles 86, 120

Financial Discipline 181, 198, 204

framework 3, 7, 17, 19, 21, 24, 38, 43, 48, 52, 55, 60, 62, 64-65, 67-70, 81, 86, 90, 121, 182, 197-198, 212-213

G

globalization 9, 30, 34-35, 43, 56, 97, 105, 108, 113, 122-123, 125-129, 132-134, 182, 198

governance 3, 24, 26-30, 48, 60, 67, 72, 111, 141-142, 154, 184, 192, 194

H

hospitality businesses 206, 210

hotel performance 208-210, 212-213, 216-218, 223-225

human capital 85, 87, 94, 102, 112, 118, 120, 127, 182, 186, 203

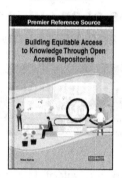

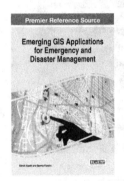

www.igi-global.com

Publisher of Peer-Reviewed, Timely, and Innovative Academic Research Since 1988

IGI Global's Transformative Open Access (OA) Model:
How to Turn Your University Library's Database Acquisitions Into a Source of OA Funding

Well in advance of Plan S, IGI Global unveiled their OA Fee Waiver (Read & Publish) Initiative. Under this initiative, librarians who invest in IGI Global's InfoSci-Books and/or InfoSci-Journals databases will be able to subsidize their patrons' OA article processing charges (APCs) when their work is submitted and accepted (after the peer review process) into an IGI Global journal.

How Does it Work?

Step 1: **Library Invests in the InfoSci-Databases:** A library perpetually purchases or subscribes to the InfoSci-Books, InfoSci-Journals, or discipline/subject databases.

Step 2: **IGI Global Matches the Library Investment with OA Subsidies Fund:** IGI Global provides a fund to go towards subsidizing the OA APCs for the library's patrons.

Step 3: **Patron of the Library is Accepted into IGI Global Journal (After Peer Review):** When a patron's paper is accepted into an IGI Global journal, they option to have their paper published under a traditional publishing model or as OA.

Step 4: **IGI Global Will Deduct APC Cost from OA Subsidies Fund:** If the author decides to publish under OA, the OA APC fee will be deducted from the OA subsidies fund.

Step 5: **Author's Work Becomes Freely Available:** The patron's work will be freely available under CC BY copyright license, enabling them to share it freely with the academic community.

Note: This fund will be offered on an annual basis and will renew as the subscription is renewed for each year thereafter. IGI Global will manage the fund and award the APC waivers unless the librarian has a preference as to how the funds should be managed.

Hear From the Experts on This Initiative:

"I'm very happy to have been able to make one of my recent research contributions *freely available* along with having access to the *valuable resources* found within IGI Global's InfoSci-Journals database."

— **Prof. Stuart Palmer,** Deakin University, Australia

"Receiving the support from IGI Global's OA Fee Waiver Initiative *encourages me to continue my research work without any hesitation.*"

— **Prof. Wenlong Liu,** College of Economics and Management at Nanjing University of Aeronautics & Astronautics, China

For More Information, Scan the QR Code or Contact:
IGI Global's Digital Resources Team at eresources@igi-global.com.

Printed in the United States
By Bookmasters